CONVEYANCING

GREENS CONCISE SCOTS LAW

CONVEYANCING

By
George L. Gretton, B.A., LL.B., W.S., N.P.,
Reader in Private Law, University of Edinburgh

and

Kenneth G. C. Reid, M.A., LL.B., Solicitor,
Senior Lecturer in Private Law, University of Edinburgh

W. GREEN/Sweet & Maxwell
EDINBURGH
1993

First published 1993
Reprinted 1994

ISBN 0 414 01054 X

A catalogue record for this book
is available from the British Library.

Typeset by Wyvern Typesetting, Bristol.
Printed in Great Britain by
M. & A. Thomson Litho Ltd.

For
A.A.G. and G.C.R.

FOREWORD

This book seeks to be of use both to practitioners and to students preparing for the examination in the Diploma in Legal Practice. Some of the material which will be of use to the latter will, of course, be familiar to the former. The book deals mainly with domestic, or residential, conveyancing, and thus certain special topics, such as commercial leases, are not covered. Being a text on conveyancing, there is little coverage of land law as such. In order to keep the book within a reasonable compass, we have, with some reluctance, included almost no styles.

The law is stated as at April 30, 1993.

CONTENTS

Page

Foreword vii
Table of Cases ix
Table of Statutes xxii
Abbreviations xxiii

1. The Conveyancing Transaction 1
2. Missives I: Making the Contract 26
3. Missives II: Content 47
4. Missives III: Breach of Contract 74
5. Good and Marketable Title 91
6. Examination of Sasine Titles 105
7. Searches and Letters of Obligation 126
8. Matrimonial Homes 146
9. Dispositions 162
10. Real Burdens and Servitudes 198
11. The Mortgage Market and the Mortgage Package 218
12. Heritable Securities 246
13. Preparing the Security Documentation 277
14. Assignations 289
15. Execution of Deeds 297
16. Stamp Duty 311
17. Sasine Registration 322
18. Other Registers 329
19. Post-Settlement Claims 334
20. Registration of Title 349
21. Feudal Conveyancing 363
22. Deeds by Uninfeft Parties 371
23. Trusts and Executries 383
24. Destinations 402
25. Partnerships 416
26. Companies 426
27. Insolvency 430
28. Miscellaneous Cases 436

Index 447

TABLE OF CASES

ABBEY NATIONAL BUILDING SOCIETY *v.* Barclays Bank plc, 1990 S.C.L.R. 639 276
Aberdeen Varieties Ltd. *v.* James F. Donald (Aberdeen Cinemas) Ltd., 1939 S.C. 788; 1940 S.C.(H.L.) 52 .... 207, 210, 214
Advocate (Lord) *v.* Bank of India, 1991 S.C.L.R. 320 276
Aitken *v.* Hyslop, 1977 S.L.T. (Notes) 50 45
Alba Homes Ltd. *v.* Duell, 1993 S.L.T. (Sh et.) 49 204
Alvis *v.* Harrison, 1991 S.L.T. 64 214
American Express Europe Ltd. *v.* Royal Bank of Scotland (No. 2), 1989 S.L.T. 650 299
Anderson *v.* Dickie, 1915 S.C.(H.L.) 79 .... 202, 216
—— *v.* Lambie, 1954 S.C.(H.L.) 43 119
—— *v.* Valentine, 1957 S.L.T. 57 212
Angus *v.* Bryden, 1992 S.L.T. 884 .... 34, 42, 49
Anstruther's Trs. *v.* Burgh of Pittenween, 1943 S.L.T. 160 211
Armia *v.* Daejan Developments Ltd., 1978 S.C. 152; 1979 S.C.(H.L.) 56 .... 46, 53, 93, 95, 120
Armour & Mycroft, *Petrs.*, 1983 S.L.T. 453 435
Associated Relays *v.* Turnbeam, 1988 S.C.L.R. 220 272
Atlas Insurance Co. *v.* Dollar Land Holdings plc, 1992 G.W.D. 32–1902 ... 46
Auld *v.* Hay (1880) 7 R. 663 112
Ayr, Magistrates of *v.* Dobbie (1898) 25 R. 1184 176
Ayton *v.* Romanes (1895) 3 S.L.T. 303 293

BALFOUR *v.* Kinsey, 1987 S.L.T. 144 .... 121, 198, 208
Bank of Scotland *v.* Graham's Tr., 1991 S.L.T. 879; aff'd. 1993 S.L.T. 252 195
Barclay's Bank *v.* McGreish, 1983 S.L.T. 344 415
Barratt Scotland Ltd. *v.* Keith, 1993 G.W.D. 3–205; 1992 G.W.D. 4–208 .. 49, 145
Ben Challum Ltd. *v.* Buchanan, 1955 S.C. 348 215
Bisset *v.* Walker, 26 Nov. 1799, Fac. Coll. 408
Blair *v.* North British and Mercantile Insurance Co. (1889) 16 R. 325 307
Boag, *Petr.*, 1967 S.L.T. 275 82
Boland (T.) & Co. *v.* Dundas's Trs., 1975 S.L.T. (Notes) 80 38
Bourton *v.* Claydon, 1990 S.L.T. (Sh.Ct.) 7 341
Bowie *v.* Semple's Exrs., 1978 S.L.T. (Sh.Ct.) 9 85
Brock *v.* Brock, 1908 S.C. 964 298
Brookfield Developments Ltd. *v.* Keeper of the Registers of Scotland, 1989 S.L.T. (Lands Tr.) 105 .... 214, 359
Brown *v.* Cheyne (1833) 12 S. 176 .... 99, 107
—— *v.* Crum-Ewing's Trs., 1918 1 S.L.T. 340 211
—— *v.* Gamsu, 1992 G.W.D. 40–2429 87
Brown's Tr. *v.* Brown, 1943 S.C. 488 409
Brownlee *v.* Robb, 1907 S.C. 1302 290
Bruce *v.* Stewart (1900) 2 F. 948 .... 97, 100

Buchanan *v.* Marr (1883) 10 R. 936 .... 211, 212

CALDER *v.* Police Commissioners of North Berwick (1899) 1 F. 491 210
Caledonian Property Group Ltd. *v.* Queensferry Property Group Ltd., 1992 S.L.T. 738 81
Cameron *v.* Williamson (1895) 22 R. 293 .... 102, 259
Campbell *v.* Dunn (1825) 1 W. & S. 690; (1828) 6 S. 679 210
—— *v.* McCutcheon, 1963 S.C. 505 .... 50, 78, 365
Cargill *v.* Craigie (1822) 1 Shaw App. 134 103
Carswell *v.* Goldie, 1967 S.L.T. 339 211
Carter *v.* McIntosh (1862) 24 D. 925 290
Cattanach's Tr. *v.* Jamieson (1884) 11 R. 972 173
Chapman's Trs. *v.* Anglo-Scottish Group Services Ltd., 1980 S.L.T. (Sh.Ct.) 27 .... 69, 81
Christie *v.* Cameron (1898) 25 R. 824 348
Church of Scotland General Trs. *v.* Phin, 1987 S.C.L.R. 240 211
Clark *v.* Glasgow Assurance Co. (1854) 1 Macq. 668 211
Clayton's Case (sub nom. Devaynes *v.* Noble) (1816) 1 Merivale 529 434
Cobham *v.* Minter, 1986 S.L.T. 336 348
Cochrane *v.* Ewart (1861) 23 D. (H.L.) 3; 4 Macq. 117 .... 57, 208
Cochrane *v.* Paterson (1882) 9 R. 634 .... 211, 212
Colgan *v.* Mooney, 1992 G.W.D. 34–2009 85
Colquhoun's C.B. *v.* Glen's Tr., 1920 S.C. 737 212
Co-operative Wholesale Society *v.* Usher's Brewery, 1975 S.L.T. (Lands Tr.) 9 210
Cooper's Exr. *v.* City of Edinburgh District Council, 1991 S.L.T. 518; 1991 S.C.L.R. 664 443
Cooper's Exrs. *v.* Stark's Trs. (1898) 25 R. 1160 .... 112, 182
Corbett *v.* Robertson (1872) 10 M. 329 .... 73, 200
Cowan *v.* Magistrates of Edinburgh (1887) 14 R. 682 212

DALRYMPLE *v.* Herdman (1878) 5 R. 847 216
Davidson *v.* Tilburg Ltd., 1991 G.W.D. 18–1109 .... 78, 87
Devaynes *v.* Noble (sub nom. Clayton's Case) (1816) 1 Merivale 529 434
Devonshire (Duke of) *v.* Fletcher (1874) 1 R. 1056 .... 97, 99, 100
Dewar & Finlay *v.* Blackwood, 1968 S.L.T. 196 39
Dick *v.* Clydesdale Bank, 1991 S.L.T. 678 272
Draper *v.* Thomson, 1954 S.C. 136 299
Dryburgh *v.* Gordon (1896) 24 R. 1 .... 101, 102
Dunlop *v.* Crawford (1849) 11 D. 1062 99
Dunlop (A.) & Sons' J.F. *v.* Armstrong, 1993 G.W.D. 2–127 275

EDINBURGH DISTRICT COUNCIL, CITY OF *v.* Gardner, 1990 S.L.T. 600 ... 59, 440
Edinburgh, Magistrates of *v.* Begg (1882) 11 R. 352 210
Edmonds *v.* Magistrates of Aberdeen (1855) 18 D. 47; (1858) 3 Macq. 116 185
Ellis & Sons Second Amalgamated Properties Ltd., *v.* Pringle, 1974 S.C. 200 39
Elwood *v.* Ravenseft Properties Ltd., 1991 S.L.T. 44 .... 45, 46
Emslie *v.* James Thomson & Sons, unreported 143
Errol *v.* Walker, 1966 S.C. 93 .... 33, 34

FETHERSTON *v.* McDonald, 1988 S.L.T. (Sh.Ct.) 39 339
Fielding *v.* Newell, 1987 S.L.T. 530 80
Findlater *v.* Mann, 1990 S.L.T. 465 32
Finlayson *v.* McRobb, 1987 S.L.T. (Sh.Ct.) 150 .... 83, 85, 339

Fleming *v.* Ure (1896) 4 S.L.T. 26 212
Ford Sellar Morris Properties plc *v.* E. W. Hutchison Ltd., 1990 S.L.T. 500.. 37, 38
Fortune Engineering Ltd. *v.* Precision Components (Scotland) Ltd., 1993 G.W.D. 1–49 36
Frame *v.* Cameron (1864) 3 M. 290 211
Fyfe *v.* Fyfe, 1987 S.L.T. (Sh.Ct.) 38 .... 158, 159

G. A. Estates Ltd. *v.* Caviapen Trustees Ltd., 1991 G.W.D. 32–1933; 1993 G.W.D. 24–1482 44
Gammell's Trs. *v.* The Land Commission, 1970 S.L.T. 254 212
Gardner *v.* City of Edinburgh District Council, 1991 S.L.T. 1149 58
Gibson *v.* Hunter Home Designs Ltd., 1976 S.C. 23 89
Gillon's Tr. *v.* Gillon (1890) 17 R. 435 412
Gordon *v.* Grant (1850) 13 D. 1 182
Gordon District Council *v.* Wimpey Homes Holdings Ltd., 1989 S.L.T. 141; 1988 S.L.T. 481 .... 44, 51, 52
Gordon - Rodgers *v.* Thomson's Exr., 1986 S.L.T. 618 409
Gow's Trs. *v.* Mealls (1875) 2 R. 729 208
Graham *v.* Graham (1898) 5 S.L.T. 319 259
—— *v.* Shiels (1901) 8 S.L.T. 368 211
Grahame *v.* Ewen's Trs. (1824) 2 S. 612 412
Grant *v.* Keir (1694) Mor. 16913 298
—— *v.* Peter G. Gauld & Co., 1985 S.C. 251 48
—— *v.* Ullah, 1987 S.L.T. 639 .... 76, 80–82
Grieves *v.* Abercromby, 1989 S.C.L.R. 11 .... 339, 342

Hadley *v.* Baxendale (1854) 9 Ex. 341 81
Halifax Building Society *v.* Gupta, 1993 G.W.D. 14–948 270
—— *v.* Smith, 1985 S.L.T. (Sh.Ct.) 25 275
Hardwick *v.* Gebbie, 1991 S.L.T. 258 .... 85, 342
Harland Engineering Co. *v.* Stark's Trs., 1914 2 S.L.T. 292; 1913 2 S.L.T. 448 396
Hay *v.* Jamieson (1672) Mor. 1009 118
Hay's Tr. *v.* Hay's Trs., 1951 S.C. 329 .... 406, 409
Heron *v.* Thomson, 1989 G.W.D. 11–469 27
Hislop *v.* MacRitchie's Trs. (1881) 8 R. (H.L.) 95 203
Hoey *v.* Butler, 1975 S.C. 87 .... 82, 84, 342
Hopkinson *v.* Williams, 1993 G.W.D. 14–945 .... 80, 81
Houldsworth *v.* Gordon Cumming, 1910 S.C. (H.L.) 49 49
Hughes and Hamilton *v.* Gordon, 15 June 1815, Fac. Coll. 334
Hunter *v.* Boog (1834) 13 S. 205 163
—— *v.* J. & E. Shepherd, 1992 S.L.T. 1095 15
Hynd's Tr. *v.* Hynd's Trs., 1955 S.C. (H.L.) 1 306
Hyslop *v.* Shaw (1863) 1 M. 535 191

Imry Property Holdings Ltd. *v.* Glasgow Y.M.C.A., 1979 S.L.T. 261 ... 39, 46
Inglis *v.* Lownie, 1990 S.L.T. (Sh.Ct.) 60 45
Iona Hotels Ltd. *v.* Craig, 1990 S.C.L.R. 614 138

Jack's Exrs. *v.* Falkirk District Council, 1992 S.L.T. 5 444
Jamieson *v.* Stewart, 1989 S.L.T. (Sh.Ct.) 13 .... 84, 339, 342, 343
—— *v.* Welsh (1900) 3 F. 176 .... 183, 342
Jayner Ltd. *v.* Allander Holdings Ltd., 1990 G.W.D. 30–1717 46
Johnston *v.* MacRitchie (1893) 20 R. 539 212

—— *v.* The Walker Trustees (1897) 24 R. 1061 216
Johnstone's Exrs. *v.* Harris, 1977 S.C. 365 80
Jolly's Exr. *v.* Stonehaven, 1958 S.C. 635 206
Jones *v.* Heenan, 1988 S.L.T. (Sh.Ct.) 53 .... 341, 343

KEITH *v.* Texaco Ltd., 1977 S.L.T. (Lands Tr.) 16 204
Ker *v.* Gibson (1693) Mor. 16805 299
Kildrummy (Jersey) Ltd. *v.* Inland Revenue, 1992 S.L.T. 787 115
King *v.* Brodt, 1993 G.W.D. 13–886 208
—— *v.* Gebbie, 1993 S.L.T. 512 .... 84, 342
Korner *v.* Shennan, 1950 S.C. 285 335

LAMB'S TRS. *v.* Reid (1883) 11 R. 76 99
Laurie *v.* Ogilvy, 6 Feb. 1810, Fac. Coll. 290
Law *v.* Thomson, 1978 S.C. 343 33
Lawson *v.* Hay, 1989 G.W.D. 24–1049 212
—— *v.* Wilkie (1897) 24 R. 649 203
Leeds Permanent Building Society *v.* Aitken Malone & Mackay, 1987 S.L.T. 338 138
Lees *v.* North East Fife District Council, 1987 S.L.T. 769 210
Libertas - Kommerz GmbH *v.* Johnson, 1977 S.C. 191 290
Liebermann *v.* G. W. Tait & Co., 1987 S.L.T. 585 145
Littlejohn *v.* MacKay, 1974 S.L.T. (Sh.Ct.) 82 .... 27, 302
Lloyds Bank *v.* Bauld, 1976 S.L.T. (Notes) 53 77
Longmuir *v.* Longmuir, 1985 S.L.T. (Sh.Ct.) 33 158
Lothian & Border Farmers Ltd. *v.* McCutcheon, 1952 S.L.T. 450 .... 189, 347
Lothian Regional Council *v.* Rennie, 1991 S.L.T. 465; 1991 S.C.L.R. 709 .. 211
Lousada & Co. Ltd. *v.* J. E. Lesser (Properties) Ltd., 1990 S.L.T. 823 46
Louttit's Trs. *v.* Highland Railway Co. (1892) 19 R. 791 84
Love - Lee *v.* Cameron, 1991 S.C.L.R. 61 115
Low *v.* Scottish Amicable Building Society, 1940 S.L.T. 295 212

MAC ELECTRICAL AND HEATING ENGINEERS LTD. *v.* Calscot Electrical (Distributors) Ltd., 1990 G.W.D. 16–694 195
McConnell *v.* Chassels (1903) 10 S.L.T. 790 92
Macdonald *v.* Hall (1893) 20 R. (H.L.) 88 412
—— *v.* Keeper of the Registers, 1914 S.C. 854 .... 180, 327
—— *v.* Newall (1898) 1 F. 68 46
McIntosh *v.* Mitchell Thomson (1900) 8 S.L.T. 48 192
Mackay *v.* Campbell, 1966 S.C. 237 82
McKendrick *v.* Wilson, 1970 S.L.T. (Sh.Ct.) 39 183
McKillop *v.* Mutual Securities Ltd., 1945 S.C. 166 .... 84, 342
McLean *v.* Kennaway (1904) 11 S.L.T. 719 206
—— *v.* Marwhirn Developments Ltd., 1976 S.L.T. (Notes) 47 207
MacLeod's Exr. *v.* Barr's Trs., 1989 S.L.T. 392 51
McMillan *v.* Caldwell, 1991 S.L.T. 325 32
Mactaggart (J. A.) & Co. *v.* Harrower (1906) 8 F. 1101 203
Magistrates of Ayr *v.* Dobbie. *See* Ayr, Magistrates of *v.* Dobbie. 176
Magistrates of Edinburgh *v.* Begg. *See* Edinburgh, Magistrates of *v.* Begg. .. 210
Mannofield Residents Property Co. Ltd. *v.* Thomson, 1983 S.L.T. (Sh.Ct.) 71 213
Marshall *v.* Callander & Trossachs Hydropathic Hospital Ltd. (1895) 22 R. 954 191
—— *v.* Marshall's Exr., 1987 S.L.T. 49 410

Martin *v*. Bell-Ingram, 1986 S.L.T. 575 15
Martone *v*. Zani, 1992 G.W.D. 32–1903 49
Massy Scott's Trs. (1872) 11 M. 173 409
Matheson *v*. Tinney, 1989 S.L.T. 535 210
Meehan *v*. Silver, 1972 S.L.T. (Sh.Ct.) 70 69
Melrose *v*. Davidson and Robertson, 1992 S.L.T. 395 15
Middleton *v*. Leslie (1894) 21 R. 781 212
Miller *v*. Carmichael (1888) 15 R. 991 212
Moir's Trs. *v*. McEwan (1880) 7 R. 1141 .... 210, 212
Morris *v*. Ritchie, 1991 G.W.D. 12–712; 1992 G.W.D. 33–1905 .... 73, 79, 93, 200
Morrison *v*. McLay (1874) 1 R. 1117 212
Mounsey *v*. Maxwell (1808) Hume 237 .... 167, 168
Mowbray *v*. Mathieson, 1989 G.W.D. 6–267 46
Mulhern *v*. Mulhern, 1987 S.L.T. (Sh.Ct.) 62; 1987 S.C.L.R. 252 34
Munro *v*. Munro, 1972 S.L.T. (Sh.Ct.) 6 407
Murray *v*. Cherry, 1980 S.L.T. (Sh.Ct.) 131 45
—— *v*. Medley, 1973 S.L.T. (Sh.Ct.) 75 208
Murray's Tr. *v*. Wood (1887) 14 R. 856 .... 173, 180
—— *v*. Trs. for St. Margaret's Convent (1906) 8 F. 1109; 1907 S.C.(H.L.) 8 212

National Commercial Bank *v*. Millar's Tr., 1964 S.L.T. (Notes) 57 296
Neilson *v*. Barratt, 1987 G.W.D. 13–467 41
Newcastle Building Society *v*. White, 1987 S.L.T. (Sh.Ct.) 81 .... 102, 103, 137, 273, 276
Norcross *v*. Kirkcaldy District Council, 1993 G.W.D. 3–146 59

Oliver *v*. Gaughan, 1990 G.W.D. 22–1247 .... 34, 195
Orr *v*. Mitchell (1893) 20 R. (H.L.) 27 195

Packman (George) & Sons *v*. Dunbar's Trs., 1977 S.L.T. 140 77
Palmer *v*. Beck, 1993 S.L.T. 485 .... 35, 346
Park *v*. Morrison Developments Ltd., 1993 G.W.D. 8–571 .... 38, 44
Parker *v*. O'Brien, 1992 S.L.T. (Sh.Ct.) 31 .... 339, 343
Paul *v*. Boyd's Trs. (1835) 13 S. 818 185
Pegg *v*. City of Glasgow District Council, 1988 S.L.T. (Sh.Ct.) 49 .... 59, 190
Perrett's Trs. *v*. Perrett, 1909 S.C. 522 409
Phillips *v*. Lavery, 1962 S.L.T. (Sh.Ct.) 57 210
Porch *v*. Macleod, 1992 S.L.T. 661 .... 74, 338–341
Porter *v*. Campbell's Trs., 1923 S.C.(H.L.) 94 .... 212, 213
Precision Relays Ltd. *v*. Beaton, 1980 S.C. 220 366
Prestwick Cinema Co. Ltd. *v*. Gardiner, 1951 S.C. 98 87
Purves *v*. City of Edinburgh District Council, 1987 S.C.L.R. 381; 1987 S.L.T. 366 .... 59, 440

Renouf's Trs. *v*. Haining, 1919 S.C. 497 407
Rhodes *v*. Peterson, 1971 S.C. 56 299
Robbie *v*. Graham & Sibbald, 1989 S.L.T. 870 15
Robertson *v*. Hay-Boyd, 1928 S.C.(H.L.) 8 409
Rodger (Builders) Ltd. *v*. Fawdry, 1950 S.C. 451, 483 .... 73, 76, 77
Ross *v*. Cuthbertson (1854) 16 D. 732 211
Royal Bank *v*. Christie (1841) 2 Rob. 118 434
Royal Bank of Scotland *v*. Johnston, 1987 G.W.D. 1–5 272

Runciman *v.* Borders Regional Council, 1988 S.L.T. 135 54
Rutterford *v.* Allied Breweries, 1990 S.L.T. 249 .... 32, 34

SAUNDERS *v.* Edwards [1987] 2 All E.R. 651 314
Scott *v.* J. B. Livingstone & Nicol, 1990 S.L.T. 305 27
Scottish Flavour Ltd. *v.* Watson, 1982 S.L.T. 78 190
Scottish Temperance Life Assurance Co. *v.* Law Union & Rock Insurance Co., 1917 S.C. 175 202
Shand *v.* Brand (1907) 14 S.L.T. 704 211
Shand's Trs. *v.* Shand's Trs., 1966 S.C. 178 409
Sibbald's Heir *v.* Harris, 1947 S.C. 601 .... 97, 118
Simsons *v.* Simsons (1893) 10 R. 1247 298
Singh *v.* Cross Entertainments Ltd., 1990 S.L.T. 77 89
Skipton Building Society *v.* Wain, 1986 S.L.T. 96 272
Sloans Dairies Ltd. *v.* Glasgow Corporation, 1977 S.C. 223 60
Smith *v.* MacIntosh, 1989 S.L.T. 148 .... 409, 412
—— *v.* Paterson, unreported, O.H., Feb. 18, 1986 .... 35, 49
—— *v.* Soeder (1895) 23 R. 60 92
Spook Erection (Northern) Ltd. *v.* Kaye, 1990 S.L.T. 676 34
Steel *v.* Bradley (Scotland) Homes Ltd., 1974 S.L.T. 133 42
Steele *v.* Caldwell, 1979 S.L.T. 228 412
Stewart's Exrs. *v.* Stewart, 1993 S.L.T. 440 33
Stirling's Trs., 1977 S.L.T. 229 410
Stirling Stuart *v.* Stirling Crawfurd's Trs. (1885) 12 R. 610 299
Stone *v.* MacDonald, 1979 S.C. 363 36
Stuart *v.* Lort-Phillips, 1977 S.C. 244 189
Sutherland *v.* Garrity, 1941 S.C. 196 98
Suttie *v.* Baird, 1992 S.L.T. 133 112

TAILORS OF ABERDEEN *v.* Coutts (1834) 13 S. 226; 1837 2 Sh. & Macl. 609; (1840) 1 Rob. 296 .... 199, 204, 210
Tainsh *v.* McLaughlin, 1990 S.L.T. (Sh.Ct.) 102 .... 84, 85
Tarditi *v.* Drummond, 1989 S.L.T. 554 37
Taylor *v.* McLeod, 1990 S.L.T. 194 .... 84, 337, 340–343
Taylor's Exrs. *v.* Brunton, 1939 S.C. 444 409
Tennant *v.* Napier (1888) 15 R. 671 210
Thom *v.* Chalmers (1886) 13 R. 1026 212
Thompson *v.* Clarkson's Trs. (1892) 20 R. 59 298
Thomson *v.* Vernon, 1983 S.L.T. (Sh.Ct.) 17 87
Thomson (George) Services Ltd. *v.* Moore, 1992 S.C.L.R. 295 34
Tiffney *v.* Bachurzewski, 1985 S.L.T. 165; 1988 G.W.D. 37–1530 ..... 81–83, 87
Toynar Ltd. *v.* R. & A. Properties (Fife) Ltd., 1989 G.W.D. 2–82 78
Trade Development Bank *v.* Warriner & Mason (Scotland) Ltd., 1980 S.C. 74 .... 142, 252, 285
Turner *v.* Macmillan-Douglas, 1989 S.L.T. 293 45

UDT, NOTERS, 1978 S.L.T. (Notes) 56 270
UDT *v.* Site Preparations Ltd., 1978 S.L.T. (Sh.Ct.) 14, 21 270
Umar *v.* Murtaza, 1983 S.L.T. (Sh.Ct.) 79 .... 34, 93, 96
Union Bank *v.* National Bank (1886) 14 R. (H.L.) 1 261
University of Edinburgh, Court of the *v.* City of Edinburgh District Council, 1987 S.L.T. (Sh.Ct.) 103 .... 59, 440
Urquhart *v.* Halden (1835) 13 S. 844 92

VARNEY (SCOTLAND) LTD. *v.* Burgh of Lanark, 1974 S.C. 245 57
Viewpoint Housing Association *v.* Lothian Regional Council, 1991 G.W.D. 39–2408 55
Voeten *v.* Campbell Brook & Myles, 1987 G.W.D. 26–1009 80

WALKER *v.* Whitwell, 1916 S.C.(H.L.) 75 .... 298, 303
Walker (Peter) & Son (Edinburgh) Ltd. *v.* Church of Scotland General Trs., 1967 S.L.T. 297 211
Walker's Trs. *v.* Haldane (1902) 4 F. 594 211
Wallace *v.* University of St. Andrews (1904) 6 F. 1093 115
Watson *v.* Swift's J. F., 1986 S.L.T. 217 346
Watson (David) Property Management *v.* Woolwich Equitable Building Society, 1992 S.L.T. 430 .... 190, 210, 217, 271
Wells *v.* New House Purchasers Ltd., 1964 S.L.T. (Sh.Ct.) 2 210
Welsh *v.* Russell (1894) 21 R. 769 .... 85, 346
White & Carter (Councils) Ltd. *v.* McGregor, 1962 S.C.(H.L.) 1 76
Whyte *v.* Lee (1879) 6 R. 699 92
Winston *v.* Patrick, 1981 S.L.T. 41 .... 26, 31, 336, 337, 339, 341–343
Wood *v.* Edwards, 1988 S.L.T. (Sh.Ct.) 17 .... 41, 339
Wyllie (John H.) *v.* Ryan Industrial Fuels Ltd., 1989 S.L.T. 302 44

ZEBMOON LTD. *v.* Akinbrook Investment Developments Ltd., 1988 S.L.T. 146 .... 37, 39
Zemhunt (Holdings) Ltd. *v.* Control Securities Ltd., 1992 S.L.T. 151 .. 73, 76, 82
Zetland (Earl of) *v.* Hislop (1882) 9 R. (H.L.) 40 214

TABLE OF STATUTES

1449 Leases Act (c. 18) 353
1540 Subscription of Deeds Act (c. 37) 297
1579 Subscription of Deeds Act (c. 18) 297
1617 Prescription Act (c. 12) 110
1617 Registration Act (c. 16) 131, 323
1672 Lyon King of Arms Act (c. 47) 299
1681 Subscription of Deeds Act (c. 5) 297, 298, 301, 308, 309
1696 Deeds Act (c. 15) 297, 298
1698 Registration Act (c. 4) 329
1747 Tenures Abolition Act (20 Geo. 2, c. 50) 363
s.10 210
1845 Lands Clauses Consolidation (Scotland) Act (8 & 9 Vict. c. 19) ....
s.80 153
1857 Registration of Leases (Scotland) Act (20 & 21 Vict. c. 26) 284
s.1 321
1858 Titles to Land (Scotland) Act (21 & 22 Vict. c. 76) 369
s.1 371
1862 Land Registry Act (25 & 26 Vict. c. 53) 350
1862 Transmission of Moveable Property (Scotland) Act (25 & 26 Vict. c. 85) ....
s.1 290
1867 Policies of Assurance Act (30 & 31 Vict. c. 144)
s.5 292
1868 Registration of Writs (Scotland) Act 329
1868 Land Registers (Scotland) Act (31 & 32 Vict. c. 64) 323, 324
1868 Land Registers (Scotland) Act—*cont.*
s.12 .... 326, 330
s.15 325
s.141 325
s.142 326
1868 Titles to Land Consolidation (Scotland) Act (31 & 32 Vict. c. 101)
s.5 188
s.8 .... 185–187, 345
s.10 184
s.15 371
s.17 372
ss.19 & 20 384
s.25 374
s.26 397
s.117 260
s.155 .... 133, 140
s.157 139
s.159 140
Sched. B 185, 188
1874 Conveyancing (Scotland) Act (37 & 38 Vict. c. 94) 371
s.4 189
(2) 191
s.6 367
s.22 210
s.25 363
s.27 171
s.28 190
s.32 .... 111, 184, 205–207, 209, 436
s.38 .... 297, 298, 301
s.39 .... 194, 302–304, 310
s.45 .... 397, 424
s.46 384
s.47 252
s.61 .... 111, 179
Sched. C 367
Sched. H 184, 209
1877 Writs Execution (Scotland) Act (40 & 41 Vict. c. 40) ....
s.5 330

1882 Bills of Exchange Act (45 & 46 Vict. c. 61)
s.29 291
s.38(2) 291
1889 Commissioners for Oaths Act (c. 10) ....
s.1 151
1890 Partnership Act (53 & 54 Vict. c. 39) ....
s.33 422
1891 Stamp Act (54 & 55 Vict. c. 39) 311
s.1 311
s.5 .... 170, 314
s.12(5) 320
s.14(1), (4) 319
s.15(1), (2) (*c*) 319
s.17 319
s.54 311
s.58(4) 315
s.72 318
s.73 316
s.75 317
s.122(1) 311
Sched. 1 .... 311, 316–318
1894 Heritable Securities (Scotland) Act (57 & 58 Vict. c. 44) 268
s.5 270
1898 Finance Act (61 & 62 Vict. c. 10) ....
s.6 311
1900 Executors (Scotland) Act (63 & 64 Vict. c. 55)
s.6 .... 391, 392, 423
s.7 391
1907 Sheriff Courts (Scotland) Act (7 Edw. 7, c. 51).
s.5A 82
1913 Bankruptcy (Scotland) Act (3 & 4 Geo. 5, c. 20)
s.100 379
1921 Trusts (Scotland) Act (11 & 12 Geo. 5, c. 58) ....
s.2 387
s.3 .... 395, 396
s.4 .... 393, 398
s.5 398
s.7 396
s.19 .... 396, 420
s.20 .... 396, 420
s.21 .... 395, 420
s.22 .... 391, 423
1921 Trusts (Scotland) Act—*cont.*
s.23 422
s.24 .... 391, 423
Sched. A 396
Sched. B 395, 420
1924 Conveyancing (Scotland) Act (14 & 15 Geo. 5, c. 27) 376–378
s.2(6) 306, 326
(7) 326
s.3 .... 169, 375
s.4 372
s.5 374
s.8 .... 179, 184
s.9 184
(1) 209, 251
(3), (4) 209
s.10(1), (3) 325
s.11 367
s.15 252
s.18 306
s.38 272
s.41 .... 154, 273, 274
s.44 132
(4) 138
s.46(1) 117
Sched. A 375
Sched. B 209, 372
Form 1 373
Sched. D 179, 184
Note 3 181
Sched. F 325
Note 1 326
Sched. G 367
Sched. I 306
1926 Burgh Registers (Scotland) Act (16 & 17 Geo. 5, c. 50) 324
1931 Finance Act (21 & 22 Geo. 5, c. 28) ....
s.28 321
s.35(*x*) 321
1938 Conveyancing Amendment (Scotland) Act (1 & 2 Geo. 6, c. 24) ....
s.1 374
s.8 210
s.9 210
1958 Finance Act (6 & 7 Eliz. 2, c. 56) ....
s.34(4) 313
1959 Building (Scotland) Act (7 & 8 Eliz. 2, c. 24). 58,

1959 Building (Scotland) Act—*cont.* 62, 68
s.4 67
s.6(1) 63, 64
s.10 64
s.11 67
s.13 60
s.29(9) 63
1961 Trusts (Scotland) Act (9 & 10 Eliz. 2, c. 57) ....
s.1 398
s.2 .... 167, 387, 393, 397, 398, 419
s.21 420
1963 Stock Transfer Act (c. 18) 289
1963 Finance Act (c. 25) ....
s.35(1) 312
1964 Succession (Scotland) Act (c. 41) 383–385, 389, 400
s.15 388
(2) 380, 404
s.17 .... 386, 394
s.18(2) 408
s.20 .... 387, 396
proviso 395
s.30 410
Sched. 1 388
1968 Sewerage (Scotland) Act (c. 47) ....
s.1 57
(3) 57
1969 Housing (Scotland) Act (c. 34) ....
s.24 61
1970 Conveyancing and Feudal Reform (Scotland) Act (c. 35) 222, 246, 258, 260, 268, 294, 331
s.1 368
(3) 216
(4) 216, 369
s.3 124
s.9 248
(2) 256, 285
(3) 256
(8) (*b*) 256, 285
s.10 .... 248, 249, 251
s.11 251
s.12 .... 251, 376
s.13 .... 240, 261
s.14 255
s.15 257
s.16 .... 252, 254
1970 Conveyancing and Feudal Reform (Scotland) Act—*cont.*
(4) 254
s.17 257
s.18 .... 259, 286
s.19 .... 263, 268
s.20 269
s.21 269
s.22 269
s.23(3) 274
s.24 .... 268–271, 274
s.25 .... 267, 272
s.26 276
(1) 102
s.27 .... 264, 275, 276
s.28 274
s.32 .... 209, 251, 273
s.40 .... 247, 248
s.41 122
s.44 .... 194, 298
s.45 .... 328, 330
s.53(1) 249
Sched. 2 248
Note 1 250
Note 5 262
Sched. 3 251
Standard Condition 5 262
6 .... 23, 280, 285
9 269
12 277
Sched. 4, Form F 257
1970 Building (Scotland) Act (c.38) 63, 67
1971 Administration of Estates Act (c. 25) ....
s.3 374
1971 Redemption of Standard Securities (Scotland) Act (c. 45) 287
s.1 223
1972 Town and Country Planning (Scotland) Act (c. 52) ....
s.31 333
s.50 62
s.84(3) 62
Sched. 12, para. 6 333
1973 Prescription and Limitation (Scotland) Act (c. 52) ....
s.1 .... 110, 111, 361
(1) 110, 111, 114
(1) (*a*), (*b*) 113
(1) (*b*), (i) 112

1973 Prescription and Limitation (Scotland) Act—*cont.*
(1A) 112
(2) 110
(4) 113
s.3 .... 110, 209
s.5(1) 111
s.6 125
s.7 215
s.8 215
s.14 113
s.15(1) 110
Sched. 1, para. 2 (*e*) 145
para. 2 (1) 302
para. 4 (6) 302
1973 Local Government (Scotland) Act (c. 65) ....
s.194 309
s.222 .... 374, 378
1974 Land Tenure Reform (Scotland) Act (c. 38) 122, 365
s.1 369
s.2 210
s.4 123
(3) 124
s.5 123
(3) 124
(5), (6) 123
(7) 123, 124
(8) 123
Pt. II 284
1974 Consumer Credit Act (c. 39) 226, 260, 268, 269, 287
1974 Solicitors Act (c. 47) ....
s.81 151
1979 Land Registration (Scotland) Act (c. 33) 160, 273, 326, 350
s.2 .... 321, 351
s.3 (1) 352
(1) (*a*) 214, 352, 360
(3) 353
(5) 187
(6) 360, 378, 386
s.4 (1) 362
s.5 (3) 353
s.6 (1) (*a*) 359
(2) 214
(4) 215, 353
(5) 352
s.9 .... 98, 354
s.12 354
1979 Land Registration (Scotland) Act—*cont.*
(2) 354
(3) 354
(3) (*g*) 214
(3) (*h*) 160
s.15 (1) 209, 360
(2) 184, 360
(3) 169, 360, 378
s.16 .... 126, 164, 185, 187, 348, 365
(1) 186
(1) (*a*) (i) 106
(2) 365
(3) 192
(3) (*b*) 365
s.17 .... 198, 201, 206, 436
s.18 .... 215, 369
s.19 193
s.28 .... 215, 321, 353
1979 Estate Agents Act (c. 38) ... 1
1979 Sale of Goods Act (c. 54)
s.11 (5) 84
s.17 .... 50, 314
(1) 70
s.18, r. 1 70
s.20 70
s.53 84
1980 Water (Scotland) Act (c. 45) ....
s.6 57
1980 Solicitors (Scotland) Act (c. 46) ....
s.32 1
1980 Tenants' Rights Etc. (Scotland) Act (c. 52).. 443
1981 Matrimonial Homes (Family Protection) (Scotland) Act (c. 59) 26, 72, 96, 106, 108, 137, 146, 254, 274, 353, 356, 361
s.1 .... 153, 155, 159
(5) 150
(6) 151
s.4 (1) 147
s.6 .... 151, 153, 156, 159
(1) 148, 432
(2) 155, 156
(2) (*b*) 159
(3) (*a*) (i) 1657
(3) (*b*) 157
(3) (*e*) 153, 155
s.7 158
s.8 .... 151, 153, 156

1981 Matrimonial Homes (Family Protection) (Scotland) Act—*cont.*
(2A) 155
s.12 154
s.18 .... 148, 156
s.19 155
s.20 154
s.22 147
1982 Civic Government (Scotland) Act (c. 45) 58
s.87 .... 61, 190
1984 Finance Act (c. 43) ....
s.109 (1) 312
s.111 317
s.112 (1) 315
1984 Roads (Scotland) Act (c. 54)
s.13 56
s.16 55
s.17 56
s.115 56
s.151 (1) 55
1985 Companies Act (c. 6) ....
s.35 426
s.35A 426
(1), (2) (*b*) 427
s.35B 426
s.36 (3) 307
s.36A 309
s.36B 307, 309
(3), (4) 307, 308
(8) (*a*) 308
s.288 143
s.395 *et seq.* 141, 427, 428
s.410 *et seq.* 141, 427
s.410 .... 428, 434
(2), (5) 332
s.420 .... 332, 428
s.463 142
s.464 (1) 429
s.652 .... 142, 332, 428
1985 Family Law (Scotland) Act (c. 37) ....
s.8 72
s.14 73
s.18 117
1985 Finance Act (c. 54) ....
s.82 318
1985 Bankruptcy (Scotland) Act (c. 66) 379
s.1 134
s.1A 332
s.6 424
s.14 .... 133, 138, 140, 431
1985 Bankruptcy (Scotland) Act—*cont.*
s.15 (5) 140
s.17 (8) 140
s.31 .... 378, 425
(2) 138, 432
s.33 423
s.40 .... 149, 432
Sched. 5 .... 138, 432
para. 2 .... 133, 140
1985 Law Reform (Miscellaneous Provisions) (Scotland) Act (c. 73) 149, 152, 157
s.8 .... 34, 45, 140, 195
(1) (*b*) 194
(2) 195
s.9 .... 45, 195
s.10 35
s.17 82
Sched. 2, para. 4 140
1986 Gas Act (c. 44) 58
1986 Insolvency Act (c. 45) 138
s.11 435
s.15 435
s.21 (2) 435
s.53 142
(1), (6) 434
s.61 435
s.84 433
s.109 433
s.127 270
s.130 433
s.245 .... 434, 435
(2) 434
s.388 431
1986 Building Societies Act (c. 53) 238
s.97 222
1986 Financial Services Act (c. 60) 220, 234
1987 Register of Sasines (Scotland) Act (c. 23) 323, 327
1987 Housing (Scotland) Act (c. 26) 21, 58, 219, 266, 443
s.72 444
s.73 444
s.85 (1) 60
s.86 (1) 60
s.88 60
ss.89–92 61
s.108 61
s.114 61

1987 Housing (Scotland) Act—*cont.*
s.115 61
s.216 219
Pt. XIV 443
1987 Abolition of Domestic Rates Etc. (Scotland) Act (c. 47) ....
s.5 439
1988 Income and Corporation Taxes Act (c. 1) ....
ss.353–379 282
s.365 242
s.656 242
Pt. XIV, Chap. III 236
1989 Electricity Act (c. 29) 58
1989 Companies Act (c. 40) 141, 332
s.95 434
s.108 426
s.112 426
s.207 289
1990 Law Reform (Miscellaneous Provisions) (Scotland) Act (c. 40) 1, 149, 155
s.71 304
s.72 (1) 307
Sched. 8, para. 31 155
para. 34 72
1990 Environmental Protection Act (c. 43) ....
s.143 333
1991 Property Misdescriptions Act (c. 29) 5, 35
1991 Coal Mining Subsidence Act (c. 45) 51
1991 Age of Legal Capacity (Scotland) Act (c. 50)
s.1 166
(1) (*b*) 297
(3) (*e*) 166
s.2 166
s.3 .... 117, 166
s.9 297
1992 Stamp Duty (Temporary Provisions) Act (c. 2). 312
1992 Local Government Finance Act (c. 14) 10
s.75 190
1993 Bankruptcy (Scotland) Act (c. 6) 138, 332, 432

ABBREVIATIONS

Halliday: J. M. Halliday, *Conveyancing Law and Practice* (4 vols., 1985, 1986, 1987 and 1990).

Gordon: W. M. Gordon, *Scottish Land Law* (1989).

ROTPB: *Registration of Title Practice Book* (HMSO, looseleaf).

1868 Act: Titles to Land Consolidation (Scotland) Act 1868 (c. 101).

1874 Act: Conveyancing (Scotland) Act 1874 (c. 94).

1921 Act: Trusts (Scotland) Act 1921 (c. 58).

1924 Act: Conveyancing (Scotland) Act 1924 (c. 27).

1964 Act: Succession (Scotland) Act 1964 (c. 41).

1970 Act: Conveyancing and Feudal Reform (Scotland) Act 1970 (c. 35).

1973 Act: Prescription and Limitation (Scotland) Act 1973 (c. 52).

1974 Act: Land Tenure Reform (Scotland) Act 1974 (c. 38).

1979 Act: Land Registration (Scotland) Act 1979 (c. 33).

Chapter 1

THE CONVEYANCING TRANSACTION

Introduction

In a typical conveyancing transaction each client is simultaneously a purchaser (of the new house) and a seller (of the old one), and also a borrower (in respect of the mortgage on the new house). The conveyancer thus has to handle all three aspects at the same time. It is like learning to drive a car: to change gear one must manipulate the accelerator, the clutch and the gearstick. It is tricky at first but gets easier with practice. The object of this chapter is twofold. In the first place it seeks to give an overview of the whole process of buying and selling a house, with details to follow in later chapters. In the second place it covers various matters, especially relations with the client, which are not fully covered later.

Who can do conveyancing?

Whereas estate agency work can be done by anyone,[1] conveyancing has hitherto been restricted to solicitors and advocates,[2] though in practice advocates do not do it. More precisely, the rule is that only a solicitor or advocate can do conveyancing for reward. Anyone can do conveyancing on an unpaid basis. So do-it-yourself conveyancing is possible, though it is rarer in practice in Scotland than in England. In 1990 the law was modified[3] to allow conveyancing to be done by a new breed called the licensed conveyancer. It had been expected that the first licensed conveyancers would start practice in 1996, but the scheme has now been put on ice.[4] A similar development in England some years ago has had only lim-

[1] Subject to the Estate Agents Act 1979.

[2] Solicitors (Scotland) Act 1980, s. 32.

[3] Law Reform (Miscellaneous Provisions) (Scotland) Act 1990.

[4] See a note on the suspension of the Conveyancing and Executry Services Board at 1992 S.L.T. (News) 283.

ited impact. However, in England institutions such as banks and building societies can now do conveyancing, thus offering a one-stop service which is attractive to some clients.[5] The Government wished in 1990 to introduce this so-called corporate conveyancing into Scotland as well but failed to get the legislation through Parliament.

Contract and conveyance

The sale of property has two main stages: contract and conveyance. The contract usually takes the form of missives: a missive of offer, generally followed by further missives adjusting terms, and finalized by a missive of acceptance. A contract for the sale of land is an *obligatio literis* and so must be in formal writing, and this is generally done by adopting the letters as holograph. The missives can be direct between the parties, but normally are between their solicitors on their behalves. By the missives the seller binds himself to convey and the buyer binds himself to pay. The contract is then performed by conveyance and by payment, which normally happen simultaneously at a meeting between the two solicitors, this being called settlement. When the last missive is sent, the missives are said to be concluded.[6] The whole process typically takes about 10 days to a fortnight but can be faster or slower. The period from conclusion of missives to settlement will be stipulated in the missives themselves, but is typically between one and two months. After settlement, the conveyance, which will normally be a disposition, is then registered by the buyer, either in the General Register of Sasines or in the Land Register.[7] It is at the moment of registration that legal ownership passes to the buyer.

Coordinating the purchase and the sale

People need a roof over their heads. So a person does not wish to sell until he has another house to go to. But equally he does not want to buy another house until he has sold the old one because

[5] In practice the institutions contract-out the work to law firms rather than doing it in-house.

[6] Until then the missives are said to be "open." Open missives are not binding.

[7] Depending mainly on which of the 33 registration areas the property is situated in.

if he were to do that he would be faced by financing the loans on two houses, which may be ruinously expensive. This is one of the features of buying and selling houses which is distinctive from other transactions.

In Scotland this problem is handled in a way very different from in England. Indeed, Scottish conveyancing is very different from English conveyancing. In England the usual practice is to have a gentleman's agreement to sell (called a sale subject to contract), which lasts for a considerable period, often running to several months. This is mainly to enable the buyer to sell his existing property. That sale will also be subject to contract for the same reason. Hence what the English call a chain develops. This may include 10 or 20 or more persons. Each will know only two others—the prospective buyer and prospective seller. During this period either side can walk away from the agreement. (If the seller does so in order to accept a higher offer, this is called gazumping.) Finally something happens to switch the system on, for example at one end of the chain there appears someone who can make a cash purchase. Then the contract is made ("exchanging contracts"), and the transaction is finally settled ("completed") one month later. By contrast, in Scotland there is only a brief period, while the missives are open, when the parties are not bound. The global effect is that domestic house purchases and sales move more quickly in Scotland than in England.

What happens in Scotland varies to some extent from case to case. But if the housing market is good, a person will usually buy first and then sell. He looks for a new house and then bids for it. Missives are concluded. He then puts his old house on the market, and a purchaser is quickly found. He will typically have to pay for the new house rather sooner than he is paid for his old house. This gap is covered by bridging, which means taking a short-term loan from a bank. Thus, for a period the client is indeed financing two houses, but the period is very short. However, in a bad market it is risky to buy first because the old house may stick on the market, which would mean open-ended bridging, at high cost. So in a bad market the usual practice is to sell first and then buy. The client puts his old house on the market first. When he finds a buyer he then bids for a new house. Because the market is bad there will, he hopes, be plenty of houses to bid for. Temporary bridging may again be necessary. In both cases careful consideration needs to be given to the entry date stated in the missives. The client must not be left without a roof (unless he is prepared to go into temporary rented accommodation), but on the other hand, if the entry on the purchase is long before the entry on the sale, there will be high bridging charges. Coordinating all this is not so difficult as it sounds. Of course these points have to be discussed with the client.

The mortgage

The buyer will normally need a loan, usually from a bank or building society, and this will be secured over the property by a standard security (*i.e.* what in England is called a mortgage), which will become a real right upon its registration. The property being sold will also usually have a standard security over it and the debt secured will be paid off out of the proceeds of sale, with the lender granting a discharge which will then be registered.

Fixed price and upset sales

A property may be offered at a fixed price, or by the upset system.[8] In the first, the seller is announcing that he will accept the first offer at that price, though he is not legally bound to do so. Fixed price sales are unusual, though they become more common in property slumps. However, newly built houses are always sold at a fixed price. In the upset system, the property is advertised at offers over a stated figure. The upset is lower (10 per cent. or more) than the estimated value. Interested parties are then invited to bid, and the seller normally accepts the highest offer. One problem with this system is that all bidders incur survey charges. Some clients spend a lot of money on surveys for unsuccessful bids, and this can cause bitter complaints about this system. It has often been suggested that the seller should obtain a survey and make this available to anyone interested, but this suggestion has not yet been adopted in practice. If the sale is by the upset method, and more than one potential buyer is interested, it is usual to set a closing date. This means that the interested parties are told that all offers must be received by a certain time, when they will be opened by the seller.

[8] Or by roup (auction), though this is uncommon. Occasionally a seller will find a buyer privately, without ever actually marketing the property.

Initiating the sale

The estate agency side of a sale is the advising on a sale price, advertising the property, and generally trying to find a buyer. Most law firms offer this service, except in the Glasgow area, and many have special estate agency departments.[9] Of course, even outside the Glasgow area it may be that the client goes to a non-solicitor estate agent, in which case the first a solicitor learns of the sale is when the estate agent sends him an offer with instructions to accept. This book does not seek to cover the estate agency aspects.[10]

As soon as the selling solicitor is instructed, he needs to do two things. The first is to obtain the title deeds. If there is a mortgage, which is usually the case, the deeds will normally be held by the lender. A letter needs to be sent asking to borrow the deeds. The other letter which must be sent out at once is the request for the property inquiry certificates. These are issued by the local authority and cover such matters as planning, roads, statutory repairs notices and so on.[11] Both the deeds and the certificates should be at hand before conclusion of missives. Usually they can be obtained within a couple of weeks. If the selling solicitor is also acting as estate agent, there will be plenty of time to obtain them. But if the seller is using a non-solicitor estate agent, there is a problem, because the agent will not have done anything about them, so that one may be confronted by an offer to purchase without having the opportunity to inspect the titles or the property certificates. In that case there are various possibilities, but commonly missives are concluded with clauses enabling the purchaser to withdraw if the certificates and titles, when available, reveal anything unsatisfactory to the purchaser. If the sale will switch the property from the Sasine Register to the Land Register one should also send off to Register House a Form 10 (application for a preregistration report on title[12]

[9] In the Edinburgh area about 80 per cent. of sales are done through law firms as opposed to non-solicitor estate agents.

[10] One new development in estate agency to be noted is the Property Misdescriptions Act 1991.

[11] The cost of these varies according to the local authority in question. £60 is currently a typical figure.

[12] However there is a tendency to dispense with the Form 10 until shortly before settlement.

and, in appropriate cases, a Form P16 (comparison of the title boundary with the Ordnance map)).

If the selling solicitor is acting as estate agent, then he or someone else from his firm, will visit the property. In that case, an eye must be kept open for problems. Some examples are: (1) The property has a shared private access road. There may be problems about servitudes and maintenance. The titles should be checked for this. (2) The property's boundaries are unclear on the ground. Again, check against the titles. (3) The house has major recent alterations. Check that both planning permission and building consent have been obtained. (4) The property is tenanted. Will a purchaser be able to obtain vacant possession?

Solicitor as agent

Solicitors are often called law agents and this brings out the fact that the solicitor is an agent and his client is the principal. Though this may seem obvious, it can be too easy to forget in practice. One aspect is that agency is a contract requiring the principal to instruct the agent to act. The solicitor must check that he has been duly instructed. For instance, if Mrs Baxter calls in to say that her aged mother, Mrs Mathers, wants to sell her house, it is vital to have direct contact with the mother to confirm the instructions.[13] Again, if Mr Macdonald says that he and his wife wish to buy a house, it is vital to confirm this direct with Mrs Macdonald. Again, if a problem crops up in the course of a transaction, it is for the client to decide what to do. For instance, the purchasing agent on examining the title finds that there is a defect. It is for the client to decide whether to refuse to settle, not for his solicitor, though the latter's advice is obviously important.[14] A law agent simply does what the client tells him, provided only that this is legal and ethical. Of course, the client does not want to be bothered by technical details. There is no point in asking the client whether the search should be for 20 or for 40 years. The client expects his solicitor to handle

[13] "Solicitors must accept instructions only from clients or recognised agents authorised to give instructions on behalf of clients; for example persons authorised by power of attorney or another lawyer" (Law Society of Scotland Code of Conduct). Mrs Baxter is neither of these.

[14] If the client is obtaining a mortgage, the lender would also have to approve the decision.

such points, referring to him only for policy issues. But deciding what needs to be referred to the client and what does not can be difficult, and solicitors have often got into trouble by deciding something themselves which should have been referred. If in doubt, it is necessary to refer to the client. The client must always be kept informed, for instance by copying the missives to him, so that if anything worries him he can make his views known.

Communications with the selling client

Nowadays, solicitors are more conscious than they used to be of the need to keep in touch with the client and to keep him informed. The days are gone when a client simply put a matter in the hands of his solicitor and left it at that. The client has a right to know and a right to be consulted and, moreover, there is always the danger of the client complaining to the Law Society or even suing for negligence if he is not kept informed. So the client must be written to regularly telling him what is happening. For instance, each missive should be copied to him. In addition, whenever a client gives an instruction orally or by telephone, one should the same day send out a letter to him confirming what he has said. That outgoing copy letter in the file can be vital evidence at a later stage if things go wrong. What needs to be discussed with the selling client at the outset will vary from case to case but the following are likely candidates.

(1) Whether there have been any alterations in the property within the past, say, 10 years which would require planning or building consent.

(2) Whether the property has wet or dry rot or woodworm, whether any eradication work has been done for these recently, whether the central heating is in working order, and any other similar matters which are likely to be raised in an offer to purchase.

(3) Whether any statutory repairs notice has been received.

(4) Whether the client has received any "neighbour notification" for any planning applications for nearby property.

(5) Whether the client has received any court writs. The classic example would be an inhibition, which would prevent any sale, but there are other possibilities such as a sequestration or an action by a neighbour about, for instance, a boundary dispute.

(6) What debts are secured over the property, since all secured debts will have to be paid off at sale. Typically there will be a bank

or building society mortgage and the client should know roughly what is due. The lender normally sends an annual statement. The exact amount can be found out from the lender in due course. The great danger is that there is also a second security which the client has granted. He may not reveal this unless asked.

(7) What the sale will cost the client. Many firms have quotation forms which detail the various costs. There will be the conveyancing fee, and outlays such as the search fee, the fee for the property inquiry certificates, and the fee for recording the discharge of the existing standard security. If the selling solicitor is also acting as estate agent, there will be a sale fee, and outlays connected with the marketing of the property, such as newspaper advertising charges. Value Added Tax will be chargeable on top, except on outlays.

(8) What moveables are included in the sale, e.g. carpets, etc.

(9) The solicitor should also outline to the client the conveyancing procedures including the likely timetable.

On receipt of the successful offer

If there is more than one offer, the selling solicitor will discuss with the client which to accept. He then sends a copy of that offer to the client by first-class post, asking him to get in touch on receipt. He then goes over the whole offer clause by clause, explaining the meaning of each, and discussing points which may arise. Typical clauses which may require discussion are those concerning the physical condition of the property and the existence of planning and building consents for any alterations that have taken place. Discussing the offer can be a lengthy process—perhaps a 30 minute phone conversation. After this the solicitor sends off the qualified acceptance, copying this to the client.

After concluding missives

Once the missives are concluded the seller's agent sends to the buyer's agent various items, notably (1) the title deeds, (2) the property inquiry certificates, (3) a draft of the discharge of the existing standard security, if any, (4) a draft memorandum for continuation of search,[15] and (5) a draft of the letter of oblig-

[15] *i.e.* the draft instructions to a firm of searchers to search the Sasine Register and the personal register and, in appropriate cases, the Companies Register.

ation[16] to be granted. These last three are generally called "the usual seller's drafts." There may be other items as well as these five (for instance planning and building consents for recent building work). It is not now general practice to send a draft of the Matrimonial Homes Act affidavit (if one is needed) since these are such standard-form documents. If the sale will switch the property from the Sasine Register to the Land Register, there should be sent, instead of the draft memorandum, (1) the replies received from Register House to the Form 10 and, if applicable, the Form P16 and (2) a draft Form 11. If the property has already been registered in the Land Register, the land certificate will be sent instead of the title deeds, and instead of the memorandum a draft Form 12 will be sent.

The purchaser's agent may come back with queries about the title or other matters. With luck the seller's agent's answers will satisfy him. He will also send to the seller's solicitor a draft disposition, which the latter approves, with any suggested changes, and sends back. (The traditional practice is that a conveyancing deed is drafted by the grantee's solicitor, and then revised by the grantor's solicitor. But there are some exceptions, notably feu dispositions and leases, which are usually drafted by the grantor's solicitor.)

The purchaser's agent will also have revised the draft memorandum for continuation of the search, and the selling solicitor then sends this off to a firm of searchers. They will send an interim report on the search shortly before settlement, which the buyer's agent will of course need to see. The final search does not become available until some months after settlement. In Land Register cases the role of the search is taken by Forms 10, 11, 12 and 13. Again a report will be available before settlement.

After a while the selling agent receives the engrossment (*i.e.* a fair copy on deed paper) of the disposition from the purchaser's agent. The selling agent has his client execute it, also completing the "signing schedule." which gives details of the date and place of signing and the names and addresses of the witnesses. This schedule is for the benefit of the purchaser's agent, who will use it after settlement to complete the testing clause. The selling solicitor

[16] This is delivered at settlement to the buyer's agent, and in it the seller's agent guarantees that the final searches will not contain any unknown entries. The letter may also cover other matters, such as delivery of a recorded discharge of the old standard security.

now sits back in his chair doing the crossword, until the settlement date arrives.

Settlement

Settlement normally takes place at the office of the seller's solicitor.[17] In a typical case the seller's agent hands over:

(1) the executed disposition, with the signing schedule;
(2) the title deeds, or land certificate;
(3) the executed letter of obligation, with the draft for comparison;
(4) the interim report (or Land Register equivalent);
(5) the executed discharge of the existing standard security;
(6) the Matrimonial Homes Act affidavit (or other document), if required;
(7) the keys, unless this is being dealt with separately by the clients themselves; and
(8) any other necessary documents, such as feuduty redemption receipt, property inquiry certificates, building warrants, etc.

In return, the selling solicitor receives the cheque, ensuring that it is signed and for the right amount. Traditionally, a "state for settlement" was prepared, an account between the parties, giving the price with any additions and subtractions,[18] thus producing a final figure which should appear on the cheque. Nowadays, however, states for settlement are often not used. The cheque will be from the purchaser's solicitor[19] rather than the purchaser himself. (There would be no guarantee that a personal cheque from the purchaser would be honoured.) The selling agent then banks the

[17] If the agents are in different towns, postal settlement is generally the practice. The covering letters will state that the contents are to be held as undelivered, and then mutual delivery is agreed by telephone, confirmed by letter. There is, however, some current controversy about the status of a cheque in this type of case: see 1992 J.L.S. 323 and 342.

[18] With the introduction of the Council Tax (Local Government Finance Act 1992) there may have to be an apportionment of the tax between seller and purchaser, as used to happen for domestic rates. But the conveyancing consequences of the new tax are not yet clear at the time of writing.

[19] Cheques are generally used in domestic conveyancing, and bank transfers in commercial conveyancing. Whether a seller could demand legal tender is an interesting, but perhaps academic, question.

cheque, pays the old lender the amount outstanding on the outgoing mortgage, puts through a fee note and sends an account to the client.[20] When the final search comes in some months later, it should be forwarded to the purchaser's agent. The same applies to the discharge of the old standard security, which normally comes back from the registers to the seller's agent in the first instance. Assuming, as is generally the case, that the letter of obligation will have been satisfied by delivery of the final search and the recorded discharge, the selling solicitor will ask for it to be returned, marked as implemented. In a Land Register case there will be no search, and the land certificate will be sent by the Keeper to the purchaser's agent, who at that point should return the letter of obligation marked as implemented. At this stage it should be possible to close the sale file.

Discharging the old mortgage

At the same time as carrying out the conveyancing for the sale itself, the selling solicitor will be arranging for the discharge of any standard security over the property. He writes to the lender asking for a redemption statement, *i.e.* a letter which says exactly how much will be outstanding at settlement. The draft discharge of security, once approved by the purchaser's agent, is immediately engrossed and sent to the lender for execution and return. This should be in advance of settlement, so the deed of discharge is held as undelivered, for the loan at this stage has not yet been paid off. At settlement the usual practice is to hand over the executed discharge to the purchaser's agent who will then arrange for its registration. The amount outstanding will be repaid (by the seller's agent out of funds in his hands) on the day of the settlement of the sale. If the existing mortgage is an endowment mortgage, the seller's solicitor will also have to arrange for the retrocession of the life policy. Again the lender will execute this in advance, and after settlement the seller's solicitor intimates the retrocession of the policy to the life assurance company. The life policy has nothing to do with the title to the house, so the purchaser's agent is not interested in its retrocession and there will be no communication about this between the solicitors.

[20] The balance is applied as instructed by the client. Very often it will be applied to finance a new house.

Insurance

After settlement the seller's house insurance policy should be cancelled. The purchaser's solicitor needs to ensure that there is insurance cover from the moment when risk passes, which in current practice is normally at settlement. If there is to be a mortgage, the lender will normally effect cover. Otherwise the purchaser's solicitor must do this, unless the client is doing so himself. Temporary cover can be obtained immediately by a simple phone call to an insurance broker, who will then post out a proposal form for the client to complete.

Taking instructions in a purchase

Most buyers are also sellers, and vice versa, but for convenience of exposition the two sides are treated separately here. In office practice some solicitors use a single file for both the purchase and the sale, while others use separate files. Sometimes the purchasing client may contact his solicitor only when he is ready to bid for a house. If, however, he makes contact sooner, his solicitor has the chance to discuss with him the sort of property he wants, current market prices for that sort of property, his finances, the sale of his present house, if any, the type of mortgage he needs, and so on. It is not usual to charge for such advice, but as well as being useful to the client it also helps the solicitor to keep close contact with him, which is a key element in retaining client loyalty. One thing that should be explained at the first meeting is the general outline of a purchase transaction, including the likely timetable.

Finances of buying

Some clients have the finances of buying and selling at their fingertips, and hardly need advice, while others are vague, and some are unrealistic. The solicitor is under a professional duty to make reasonably sure (1) that his client will be able to come up with the purchase price at settlement date and (2) that he will be able to keep up with the monthly mortgage payments thereafter. The first of these is particularly important when the client is a new one or one about whom the solicitor knows little. If the client says that he is going to pay part of the price from certificates of deposit issued by Dresdner Bank held for him at the Milan branch of the First National Bank of Texas, denominated in euroyen, and the balance from selling zero-coupon 1997–1999 secured bearer dollar bonds issued by the Citroen (Brazil) Corporation, which are traded exclusively on the Frankfurt Stock Exchange, is he taking you for a ride? In Scotland (unlike England) it is not normal practice for the seller to demand a deposit.[21] The main reason for this is that it is assumed that a solicitor acting for a buyer will have done at least a preliminary check on his client's finances. In the typical case the finances are simple. The purchaser will have the proceeds of the sale of his old house (which are known or can be estimated) less the outstanding loan (which can be checked), less costs (which can be estimated), plus the loan which will be obtained for the new house (which can be estimated). If the price is to come from other sources, the question is whether the client can be trusted. If so, the solicitor must insist that cleared funds be in the firm's hands by a stated date in good time for settlement. If the solicitor does not believe the client, he should decline to act for him. Of course, the danger that a purchaser will fail to come up with the price can never be wholly eliminated. But a solicitor is under a professional responsibility to make reasonably sure that he will be able to do so before he submits any offer on his behalf.

An important element of course is the new mortgage. It may be that the client has already arranged this, either directly or through someone else such as an estate agent. If not, the solicitor must do this himself. He must find out how much the client will be able to borrow, which can vary considerably from one lender to another. Mortgage packages also vary in numerous other respects. Moreover, the packages on offer are constantly changing. The client will expect his solicitor to be on top of the mortgage market and be able to give the best advice.

Making the offer

The first thing to do is to "note interest" to the seller's agent. This is done simply by a phone call. The effect is that the seller will not sell without first giving to the person who has noted interest a

[21] In domestic conveyancing. In commercial conveyancing a deposit of, say, 10 per cent. on conclusion of missives is common.

chance to bid. The next step is to arrange for the mortgage lender to instruct a valuation survey. The amount borrowable cannot be known until this report is available. With luck the lender will be able to telephone the outcome of the report on the next day, and a written copy will usually follow. The client will of course have to pay for this survey. This valuation is made for the lender, not for the purchaser, and moreover is not a detailed survey, and may well not find out about less obvious defects such as dry rot in ceiling joists. These points must be explained to the client, and the solicitor should discuss with him whether he wishes to have his own survey done, and if so, how thorough a survey.[22] Where a purchaser suffers loss as a result of a negligent survey report, the question of the liability of the surveyor is a complex one, which cannot be discussed here.[23]

The purchasing solicitor will need to discuss with his client what figure to offer. The solicitor's own knowledge of the market will help here (and the client may to some extent be relying on that knowledge), and it is wise to check the computer record of recent sales in the area kept at the local Solicitors' Property Centre. Another obvious factor is the valuation put on the property by the survey.

There will very likely be other points to be discussed such as what moveables (if any) in the property are to be included in the purchase. The purchasing solicitor should have in front of him, when preparing the offer, the schedule of particulars issued by the seller. Other points are discussed later in this chapter and elsewhere in this book.

At some stage the client will have to submit the application form for the new mortgage. The solicitor should check that this is done. In modern practice this is usually done after a successful offer has been made. In theory this exposes the client to the risk that the lender might not agree to lend, but in practice the mortgage will have been informally agreed with the lender before submission of the offer, and the lender will not back off unless the application form discloses something unexpected.

[22] Of course this will increase the cost to the client, especially if he bids unsuccessfully for several properties, incurring two surveys fees on each bid.

[23] See *Martin* v. *Bell-Ingram*, 1986 S.L.T. 575; *Robbie* v. *Graham & Sibbald*, 1989 S.L.T. 870; *Melrose* v. *Davidson & Robertson*, 1993 S.L.T. 611 ; *Hunter* v. *J. & E. Shepherd*, 1992 S.L.T 1095.

After concluding missives to buy

After the conclusion of missives, the seller's agent will send the title deeds and seller's drafts to the purchaser's agent, as outlined above. The latter then examines the title, and checks, as far possible, other matters, such as statutory notices and planning and building consents, and raises any queries with the seller's agent. The purchasing agent then drafts the disposition and sends it to the seller's agent for revision. At the same time the purchasing agent revises and returns the seller's drafts, and returns the title deeds. As settlement approaches, the purchaser's solicitor must make sure that he will have sufficient funds on the day, to cover not only the price but other items such as stamp duty. This may involve arranging a bridging loan for the client until the proceeds of the sale of his old house are available. Settlement itself has already been outlined above. At the settlement meeting the purchaser's agent should check that the terms of the letter of obligation conform to the draft, and that all the relevant deeds have been properly executed. In return he hands over the cheque.[24]

One essential thing at settlement is to obtain the keys from the seller's agent, unless delivery of the keys is being arranged direct between the clients. The novice conveyancer, trying desperately to keep on top of the legal procedures, can forget that for the purchaser the main point of the whole business is to get the keys. If the purchaser is standing outside the house with a laden removal truck plus hungry family at 6 p.m. on Friday with no keys, with the seller uncontactable and his own solicitor's switchboard shut till 9 a.m. on Monday, he will have some choice remarks to make when he phones his solicitor from the hotel where he has spent the weekend.

After settlement the purchasing solicitor adds the testing clause to the disposition, and signs the warrant of registration.[25] He then at once sends the disposition to the Inland Revenue for payment

[24] Though obvious, it cannot be overstressed that the purchasing agent should not pay except in exchange for the disposition, a clear interim report and so on. Cases are too frequent where, after prepayment, the seller becomes insolvent, and title can never be obtained. See *Mason* v. *A. & R. Robertson & Black*, 1993 S.L.T. 773.

[25] No warrant of registration is used if the title is to be registered in the Land Register.

of stamp duty, and on its return at once sends it to the Sasine Register for recording, together with the discharge of the old standard security (which will normally have been delivered at settlement), and the new standard security being granted by the buyer to his lender. If this sale will switch the title from the Sasine Register to the Land Register, one sends the deeds to the Land Register instead, together with a Form 1 (application for first registration), Form 2 (registration of a dealing, in this case the new standard security), and Form 4 (inventory of writs). If the property has already been registered in the Land Register, one uses a Form 2 instead of a Form 1. The terms of the Form 1 or 2 will have been adjusted with the selling agents in advance. The Keeper will not normally insist on a Form 2 for the discharge of the existing standard security.

The new mortgage

In domestic conveyancing the usual system is for the purchaser's agent to act for the lender as well, since this speeds things up and is also cheaper for the client.[26] In that case, it must not be overlooked that the solicitor has in law two clients, the borrower/buyer and the lender. Once the mortgage has been agreed, the lender will send to the solicitor a formal letter of instruction, and this will typically include standard form documents which are to be used. The standard security is drafted and engrossed, and sent for signature to the client (*i.e.* the borrower) in advance of settlement. If a life policy is to be assigned in security, an assignation must be prepared and executed in advance of settlement. It may be that a new life policy is being taken out for this purpose, and if so one may have to liaise with the life assurance company to ensure that it is issued in time. Shortly before settlement is due one "requisitions the loan cheque" from the lender. After settlement the security must be registered in the Sasine Register or Land Register at once, for until registration the lender is unsecured. If a life policy has been assigned to the lender, this must be formally intimated to the life office.

[26] The borrower must pay the lender's legal fees, but these will be lower where the same agent acts for both borrower and lender than they would be if separate agents were to act. In commercial loans it is usual to have separate agents.

Closing the file

The purchaser's solicitor then puts through a fee note and sends an account to his client. Some months later he will receive the deeds back from the Sasine Register,[27] and he then forwards them to the lender for safekeeping. Soon after this the seller's agent will send him the final search. After checking it to see that it is clear, he forwards it to the lender, and returns the seller's agent's letter of obligation marked as implemented. He can then close the file. In a Land Register case what will be received from Register House is not the deeds but a land certificate, plus a charge certificate for the standard security. It is important to check these carefully. In particular it is important to read the land certificate from cover to cover, checking, among other things, that the plan is accurate, that the client is correctly named, that the seller's security does not appear in the charges section, that the real burdens and servitudes are as expected, that there is the appropriate clause about matrimonial occupancy rights, and, perhaps most important of all, that there is no exclusion of indemnity. The certificates are then sent to the lender.

What does the buyer expect of his solicitor?

In the distant past, solicitors were hired by clients to get a good title for them. That remains an important task. However, the modern client expects far more. One of the problems of modern conveyancing practice is that no one is very sure what the solicitor is expected to do, apart from the conveyancing work itself. There is too often a mismatch of expectations between client and solicitor. Later, when something goes wrong, the client blames the solicitor. Nowadays, negligence claims are becoming commoner. They can be hard to settle (whether "amicably" or otherwise) simply because there are uncertainties as to what a "reasonably competent" solicitor is expected to do. One of the worst problem areas concerns the physical condition of the new house.

It must be explained to the client that a seller of heritage (unlike a seller of goods) does not normally warrant the condition of the

[27] The discharge of the old security will normally come from the seller's agent to whom Register House will have returned it.

property.[28] He warrants the title only. If the house collapses the day after entry, the seller has at common law no liability. He warranted the title, and the purchaser's title to the shattered bricks and splintered beams is indeed perfectly good. It must be explained that buying a second-hand house is like buying anything second-hand. There is always a risk. Even the best surveyor may overlook some defect, such as deeply-hidden wood rot. It must be explained that the lender's survey report may be superficial, and that it may be advisable for the client to have his own survey. One will explain what clauses will be put in the offer, and explain their limitations. For instance the offer will probably not cover plumbing, and the rot clause will only ask the seller to warrant that there is no rot "so far as he is aware," which is obviously very different from an absolute guarantee. The client must be asked whether he wishes to have additional provisions, but it should also be explained that a seller will very likely reject any unusual terms in the missives. One should also explain that even if the seller can be made liable in law, in practice he may be unsueable. Often missives provide that any defects which the seller is liable for must be notified to the seller within, say, seven days of entry, and obviously the buying client must be alerted to such deadlines. If the client is concerned about, say, the plumbing, he may be best advised to arrange for a plumber to visit the property before settlement, or before conclusion of missives. But of course this will cost money. As a checklist, the following are common physical problems: timber (wet rot, dry rot and woodworm), subsidence, roofing, electrics (wiring and appliances), gas (piping and appliances), central heating, drains, plumbing, and damp (rising, penetrating and condensing).

Another problem which can arise is that while a solicitor acting in a purchase will check the planning situation for the property itself, he will not usually do so for adjacent properties. What happens next can easily be imagined. The client moves in and one month later finds that the charming field next door, over which he has views to the sea and the hills, is being converted into an all-year, open-air, 60 metre-high pop concert venue. The client, whose musical tastes go no later than Brahms, and who has three children

[28] This is the conventional view. For discussion, see R. Black at 1982 J.R. 31; J.M. Halliday at 1983 J.R. 1; D.J. Cusine at 1983 J.L.S. 228, and K.G.C. Reid in an essay in D.J. Cusine (ed.), *A Scots Conveyancing Miscellany: Essays in Honour of Professor J.M. Halliday* (W. Green, 1987).

under five, is unhappy. Why wasn't he told? His solicitor didn't tell him because he didn't know, and he didn't know because he didn't ask the local council.[29] Why not, the client asks? His wife has had a nervous breakdown and his house is unsellable. Here there has been a mismatch of expectations. Clarity at the outset is the aim.

As mentioned earlier, a major problem in modern practice is that many houses[30] have been altered at some stage without building consent. (Many such alterations, however, though technically in breach of building regulations, are trivial.) Missives almost always have a clause requiring the seller to warrant that there have been no such alterations within the past, say, 10 years. But there is the usual problem that sueing a seller is unsatisfactory at best and that at worst the seller may be unsueable.[31] Clients seldom understand the position, and will invariably assume that the "lawyer" will "see to" all "legal questions." If it turns out later that the local council require demolition of that ground-floor extension, the client will blame his solicitor. The latter must explain the problem of unauthorised alterations in outline, and explain that he himself cannot check whether the house conforms to building regulations. The survey report will help, but even a surveyor may miss things. The client, who will have visited the property, and who, if his bid is successful, will very likely visit it again before settlement, should be asked whether he has seen any such potential problems. Classic examples are ground-floor extensions, removal of internal walls, and extensions at attic level.

Another point which needs to be explained is that in a typical conveyancing transaction the purchaser's agent will not visit the property. He is too busy and the fee chargeable does not cover the time spent on a site visit, which in most cases would be pointless anyway. But occasionally this can cause problems. The unauthorised new garage, the problem of access rights, the boundary dispute, which cause such trouble later, might all have been spotted in time if the buyer's agent had visited the property. But most firms

[29] Modern missives often ask the seller to disclose any "neighbour notifications" received for planning applications. But the seller may fail so to disclose.

[30] No one knows how many. Estimates vary from 20 per cent to over 50 per cent.

[31] He may be bankrupt, or have disappeared, or enforcement of the missives may have become time-barred.

will only make a site visit if the client will pay for it. However, if at any stage it becomes clear that a site visit is advisable, then obviously it must be made.

Another point concerns the real burdens. It is important to find out what the client plans to do with the property. The burdens may for instance forbid any commercial use. If the client wishes to convert the property into a hotel, he will need to know this before he is committed to the purchase. So he must be asked. And as soon as the burdens writs have been seen, the client must be informed of their provisions.[32]

Finally, when acting for a buyer, as for a seller, keep in regular communication with the client, which includes following up telephone conversations with a confirming letter. If something goes wrong later, the solicitor will be blamed.[33]

Fees, outlays and getting paid

The solicitor needs to be paid two things: his fees and the outlays. The latter are moneys paid out for the benefit of the client, such as advertising charges, search fees, recording dues, stamp duty and so on. Some firms will require the client to pay disbursements as they are made or in advance, thus giving the client credit only for the fees. On being presented with the final account, clients often look only at the bottom line, and exclaim in horror at how much it is all costing. The distinction between fees and outlays should therefore be explained. There was once a Law Society scale of fees for conveyancing, but this disappeared in 1984, since when charging has been unregulated. The old scale kept fees high, so the effect of deregulation has been that fee levels have fallen.[34] Some people will shop around seeking quotations from different firms. "Feeing up" a transaction is thus no longer the fairly mechanical

[32] Even such an apparently minor condition as on the keeping of cats can cause major problems: see *e.g.*, 1992 J.L.S. 118.

[33] The question of the relation of solicitor to client in conveyancing transactions has attracted little literature, but is enormously important. In practice, if something goes wrong it is just as likely to be misunderstanding with the client and consequent blame (and a possible negligence action) as a traditional conveyancing problem.

[34] To the point where some firms are now wondering whether conveyancing is still profitable. For discussion of the profitability of conveyancing see B.D. Allingham, "Conveyancing—the Profit Motive," 1992 J.L.S. 439.

process it once was. The factors involved include the time involved, the value of the property, the responsibility factor,[35] and so on.[36]

Sometimes at the end of the transaction the solicitor will be holding funds for his client, and so the payment of the fee is relatively painless, being simply a deduction. The client is sent two bits of paper, namely the fee note and an account showing all the receipts and disbursements and the fee. At the start of the transaction the firm's cash room will have opened an internal account for the client, and an eye should be kept on this. It is of course the basis for preparing the final account. There is nothing worse than having to contact clients six months after the transaction to say that one forgot to charge them for the recording dues and please could they send a cheque.

Non-standard transactions

By definition, non-standard transactions defy classification. There is the cash buyer, who does not need a mortgage. There is the first-time buyer, who will not have an old house to sell at the same time. There is the last-time seller, such as a widow who is selling her house and will move in with her son and family. Here of course there is only a sale and not a purchase. There is the purchase by a tenant of his own house from his landlord. A variant of this is the council house purchase, where the tenant is purchasing at a discount under the right-to-buy legislation.[37] There is the mortgage sale, where an owner has defaulted on his mortgage and the sale is by the lender. There is the executry sale, where the sale is by the executor of the deceased owner. There is the insolvency sale, where the owner has become insolvent and the property is being sold by the trustee in sequestration or liquidator or whatever. And there is the new house, where the client is buying from a builder. Some of these are mentioned again later, but a detailed account of non-standard transactions is outwith the scope of this book.

[35] Most firms charge more for an expensive house even if the work involved is no greater, because the financial consequences of a mistake are greater.

[36] See 1984 J.L.S. 433 for the Law Society's guidelines.

[37] Currently contained in the Housing (Scotland) Act 1987.

Negligence

Negligence actions against solicitors are commoner today than they used to be. This is almost certainly not because standards have declined, but rather because clients expect more. We do not intend to say much about this unhappy subject here. But it should be noted that a conveyancer is not liable merely because something goes wrong and a client loses money. Nor is he liable merely because the loss has been caused by his mistake. Liability requires all the following: (1) A mistake which (2) causes loss to the client and (3) which is one which would not have been made by an ordinarily competent conveyancer. The law does not expect perfection, but only an ordinary level of competence. Of course this is a somewhat vague standard, and if a negligence action goes all the way to proof an expert is called to court to give his opinion as to whether the defender met that standard. It must be borne in mind that what was acceptable conveyancing practice at one period may not be at a later period. For instance, a conveyancer acting for a seller who fails to include in the missives a clause requiring interest on the price in the event of late settlement would probably be liable in negligence to his client if the client suffered loss thereby. For such clauses are standard good practice. But 30 years ago such clauses were uncommon, and so a conveyancer could not then have been held liable. In other words, changing practice itself changes the level of ordinary competence. One moral of this is that the conveyancer must keep abreast of new developments, whether new legislation, new case law or simply new standard practices. A conveyancer must therefore, if only for his own protection, keep an eye on current legal journals.[38]

Although the law does not expect perfection, but only a standard of ordinary competence, the conveyancer often has to act under pressure. In a negligence action, counsel for the pursuer may ask the solicitor why he drafted some clause as he did. With the 20/20 vision of hindsight it may seem indefensible, and in law it may

[38] The "Caveat" column in the *Journal of the Law Society of Scotland* (J.L.S.) gives cases where liability has arisen against solicitors. According to the column at 1992 J.L.S. 156, 47 per cent of claims arise in respect of conveyancing. The column is useful reading for any conveyancer, as are, unfortunately, the reports of the discipline tribunal.

indeed be indefensible. What the solicitor knows, and what other conveyancers know, but what the counsel and the judge and the (former) client will never know, is the pressure of practice, when a clause must be drafted immediately, the drafting being interrupted several times by the ringing of the telephone and the consumption of aspirins, all in pursuit of a fee which, though no client ever believes it, may not do much more than cover overheads. At times like this the solicitor rues the day when he filled in "law" on his UCCA form.

Law firms, of course, are required to insure against negligence, though, as is usual with insurance policies, there is an excess provision, meaning that smaller claims are not covered.

Finally, there is an old business adage that you can never win a dispute with a customer. If you lose, you lose, while if you win, you lose. A disgruntled client will tell all his friends and relations, which means negative advertising, especially if the dispute finds its way into the local newspaper. In most cases it is in a firm's long-term interests to reach an amicable settlement with an aggrieved client, and to do so as quickly as possible.

Fraud

Beware of fraud. A client may be misrepresenting his financial circumstances to the lender. Or he may be claiming that he will be living in the property but in fact intends to let it out. That would contravene Standard Condition 6 of the 1970 Act and is likely also to be a tax fraud in that the client may intend to claim tax relief on the footing that the property will be his main residence. Or, quite separate from mortgage fraud, the purchase may be money laundering, *i.e.* transferring into property the profits of criminal activities. The solicitor must have a suspicious mind. He must never, at a later date, have to confess to having been naive. The identity of a new client must always be checked. It is possible that future legislation to combat money laundering may affect conveyancing practice.

THE COURSE OF A TYPICAL CONVEYANCING TRANSACTION (SASINE)

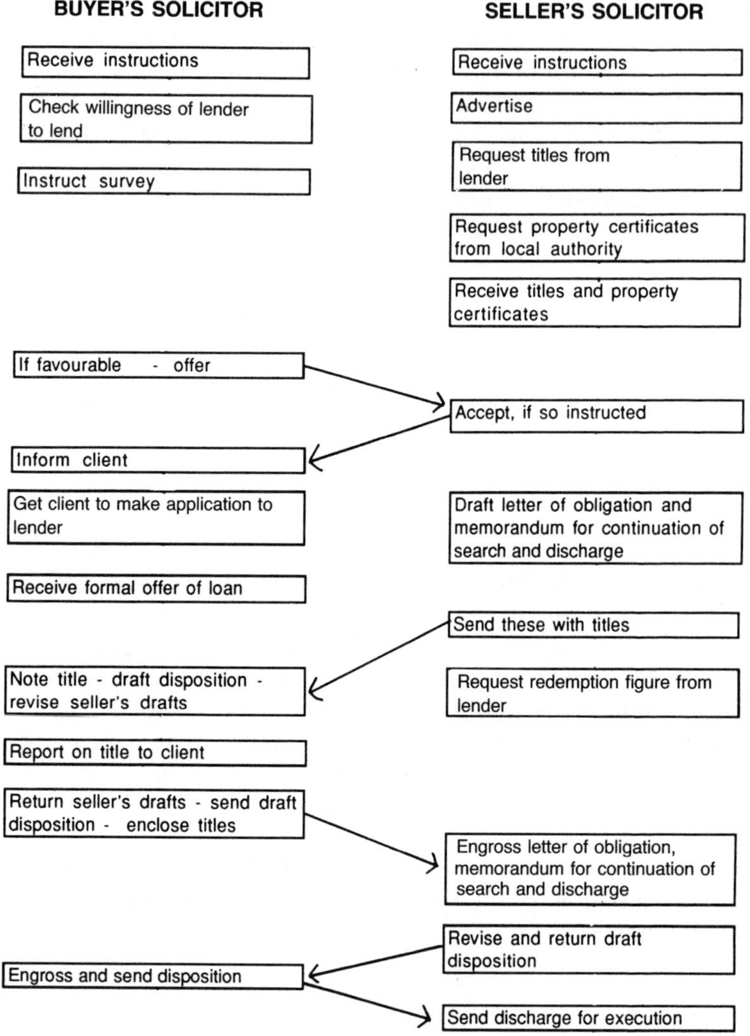
BUYER'S SOLICITOR
SELLER'S SOLICITOR
Receive instructions
Receive instructions
Check willingness of lender to lend
Advertise
Instruct survey
Request titles from lender
Request property certificates from local authority
Receive titles and property certificates
If favourable - offer
Accept, if so instructed
Inform client
Get client to make application to lender
Draft letter of obligation and memorandum for continuation of search and discharge
Receive formal offer of loan
Send these with titles
Note title - draft disposition - revise seller's drafts
Request redemption figure from lender
Report on title to client
Return seller's drafts - send draft disposition - enclose titles
Engross letter of obligation, memorandum for continuation of search and discharge
Revise and return draft disposition
Engross and send disposition
Send discharge for execution

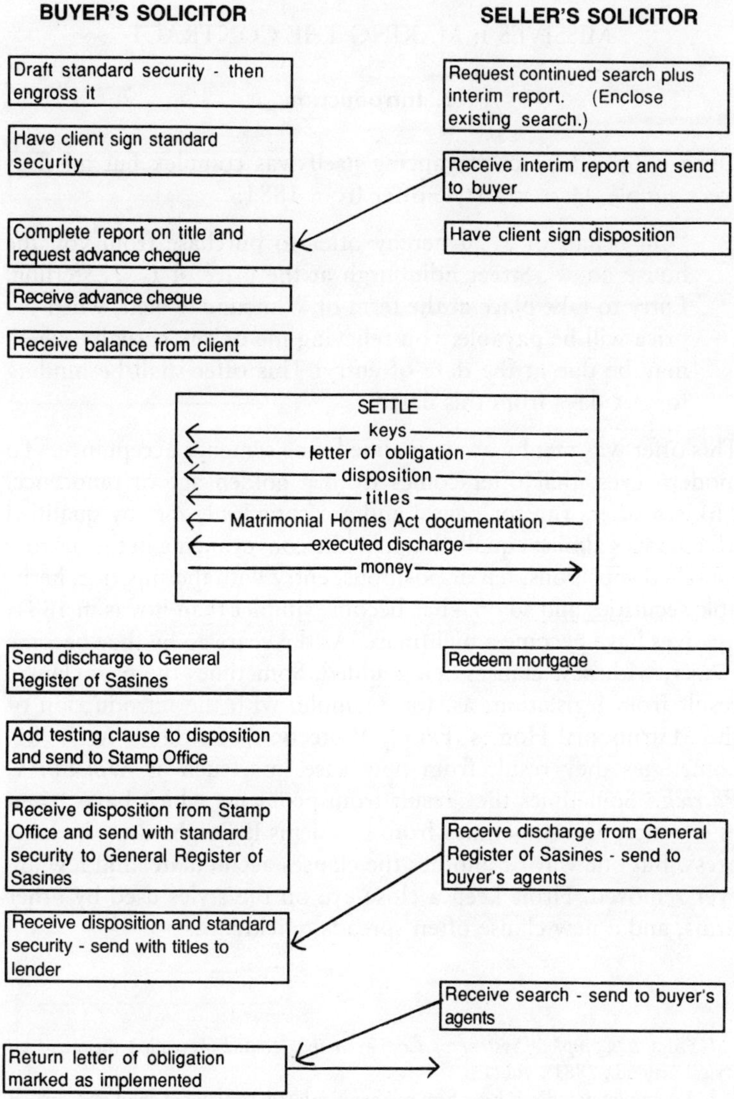

BUYER'S SOLICITOR	SELLER'S SOLICITOR
Draft standard security - then engross it	Request continued search plus interim report. (Enclose existing search.)
Have client sign standard security	Receive interim report and send to buyer
Complete report on title and request advance cheque	Have client sign disposition
Receive advance cheque	
Receive balance from client	

SETTLE

- ← keys
- ← letter of obligation
- ← disposition
- ← titles
- ← Matrimonial Homes Act documentation
- ← executed discharge
- money →

BUYER'S SOLICITOR	SELLER'S SOLICITOR
Send discharge to General Register of Sasines	Redeem mortgage
Add testing clause to disposition and send to Stamp Office	
Receive disposition from Stamp Office and send with standard security to General Register of Sasines	Receive discharge from General Register of Sasines - send to buyer's agents
Receive disposition and standard security - send with titles to lender	
	Receive search - send to buyer's agents
Return letter of obligation marked as implemented	

Chapter 2

MISSIVES I: MAKING THE CONTRACT

1. Introduction

Once upon a time conveyancing itself was complex but missives were simple. Here is a style offer from 1881:

> "On behalf of . . . I hereby offer to purchase from you the house no . . . Street Edinburgh at the price of £ . . . sterling. Entry to take place at the term of Whitsunday next, when the price will be payable, you relieving me of any casualty which may be due at the date of entry. This offer shall be binding for . . . days from this date."

This offer was met by an unqualified, one sentence acceptance.[1] To modern eyes, that offer comes from a golden age of innocence. Modern offers run for pages[2] and are commonly met by qualified acceptances almost equally long. While conveyancing in the narrow sense—dispositions, feu dispositions, entry with the superior, heritable securities and so on—has become simpler than it was in 1881, missives have become a nightmare. As the years go by they become longer, with new clauses being added. Sometimes the new clauses result from legislation, as, for example, with the introduction of the Matrimonial Homes (Family Protection) (Scotland) Act 1981. Sometimes they result from new case law, such as *Winston* v. *Patrick*.[3] Sometimes they result from problems which have arisen in practice, and sometimes from problems highlighted in the legal press. But one way or another the clauses accumulate, and few are ever removed. Firms keep a close eye on the styles used by other firms, and a new clause often spreads quickly.

[1] From *A Complete System of Conveyancing* (commonly called the *Juridical Styles*) (5th ed., 1881), vol. 1.

[2] A common practice is for a firm to have a printed schedule of conditions which is attached to an offer, and to which the offer refers.

[3] 1981 S.L.T. 41.

2. Formation

Throughout the transaction the solicitor acts as agent for his client. So the solicitor must make sure that he has authority to act. (If the client is a stranger who has just walked in the door it may be prudent to get this in writing). If a solicitor purports to conclude missives on behalf of a client and it turns out that no proper agency had been constituted, there is no contract—but the solicitor is personally liable in delict to the other would-be party to the contract for breach of an implied warranty that he had authority to act.[4] Once appointed, the solicitor has implied authority to conclude the contract (in consultation with the client) and to carry out the usual steps in a conveyancing transaction, *e.g.* the instruction of searches.[5]

Formal writing

The letters making up missives of sale must be in formal writing, and in practice are adopted as holograph in the firm name by a partner[6] of the firm.

Bargaining

The proper way of expressing interest in buying a house is to "note interest" with the solicitor (or estate agent) representing the seller. This is done simply by a phone call. On the purchaser's side noting interest is an indication (while committing him to nothing) that he will have the property surveyed and then put in an offer.[7] On the seller's side it is an undertaking (probably not legally enforceable) that the property will not be sold without first giving the person noting interest a chance to make an offer.

In a buoyant housing market a seller will hope to collect a number of noted interests. But once interest has been noted for the

[4] *Scott* v. *J.B. Livingstone & Nicol*, 1990 S.L.T. 305.

[5] *Heron* v. *Thomson*, 1989 G.W.D. 11–469.

[6] *Littlejohn* v. *Mackay*, 1974 S.L.T. (Sh. Ct.) 82, though see also Cusine and Pearson at 1991 J.L.S. 73.

[7] In theory, missives could equally well be initiated by an offer to sell made by the seller. Occasionally this is seen. But in the normal case the missives begin by an offer to buy.

first time there is immediate pressure to set a closing date: potential buyers will be looking at other houses as well and they will not want to hang around indefinitely waiting for this one. Normally a closing date follows within a week to 10 days. It is usually at noon, and often on a Friday. The closing date is the date by which all offers must be submitted. The offerers are offering blind. They will have a valuation figure provided by their surveyor. They may also know, through the local Solicitors' Property Centre computer, the recent selling prices of comparable property. And they may know how many other people are bidding against them. If advising an offeror, the trick is to offer enough to get the property but not so much that he pays more than absolutely necessary. But in practice there is a lot of luck involved and it is difficult to fix on the right figure. The client may be up against another offeror who has just lost seven houses in a row, and is willing to offer an absurd figure to secure this one. If the market is weak there may be no noted interests at all. In that case offers can sometimes be enticed by making the house available at a fixed price: in principle the first person to submit an offer at that price is then the person to whom the property will be sold, although it does not always work out like that, partly because two offers may be submitted at about the same time.

The seller's solicitor must go over the offers carefully, both on his own and with the client. If there is more than one offer a decision must be made as to which one to accept (usually the highest, but where there is not much between the first two offers there may be other reasons, *e.g.* better date of entry or personal reasons, for preferring the second highest.) Once a decision has been made in principle to accept a particular offer, the various offerors should be informed as soon as possible (usually by phone). Occasionally at this stage an unsuccessful offeror may increase his offer, but the Law Society considers that the decision made at the time of the closing date should be regarded as final and that no negotiations should be entered into with an unsuccessful offeror (unless of course the successful offeror has withdrawn). If the client insists on entering into such negotiations, the proper practice is to decline to act further for him.[8]

[8] See Law Society of Scotland Practice Guideline 1991 No. 1 (Status of Closing Dates).

It is seldom possible to meet the offer with a *de plano* (*i.e.* unqualified) acceptance. Indeed, so rare have *de plano* acceptances become[9] that the receipt of one may induce panic in the recipient, on the basis that a seller who is so keen to have the contract concluded must have something terrible to hide. Why must the purchaser's offer be qualified? One reason is to redress the balance of the contract so that it does not operate unfairly as against the seller. (Indeed the temptation is to load it down the other way.) Another is that the property may not satisfy all the conditions laid down in the offer. In order to judge this the seller's solicitor must consult properly with his client and also have at least a nodding acquaintance with the title. (The seller's agent should have the title deeds and the property inquiry certificates to hand before any offer is received, although for one reason or another it is not always possible to manage this.) If the selling firm acted for their client at the time of the original purchase it should have notes on title on file. A third reason for a qualified acceptance is that it may be necessary to alter, say, the date of entry, or the list of extras to be included in the price, etc. Where possible, qualifications like this should be agreed with the other side by telephone at the time when they are told that the offer is to be accepted. Not only does this cut down on work later but there is always the chance that in the immediate euphoria of success the purchaser will be more accommodating than on the morning after.

The drafting of a qualified acceptance is difficult and should be done with care. As every offer is different, so is every qualified acceptance. There is no style to follow. Though there is pressure of time, it is vital to get the acceptance right: the client will be bound and errors can be costly. It should be borne in mind that certain obligations, most notably the obligation to provide a good and marketable title, are implied by law, so that in cases such as this it is not enough to delete the obligation as stated in the offer: the common law obligation is only excluded if the qualified acceptance expressly states that the client will not, for instance, guarantee the absence of unduly onerous burdens.

Missives nowadays may take a long time to conclude. Gone are

[9] Where the offeror has used the Law Society's recommended form of offer (see below) an unqualified acceptance may be possible, at least in theory. But at the time of writing this style is not in widespread use.

the days of short offer met by short acceptance. To some extent the balance of work in a conveyancing transaction has swung from examination of title to conclusion of missives. After the seventh missive[10] has passed from one party to the other, examination of title may seem like light recreation. Is all this frantic negotiation really worth the effort?[11] In many cases the answer is no. Much of the work may really be self-induced. The purchaser produces an offer, long and lethal, bristling with Exocet missiles and (more dangerous) concealed land mines. The seller replies in kind: the purchaser's armoury is ruthlessly dismantled and replaced by the seller's own weaponry. And so it goes on. Qualified acceptance is met by a further qualified acceptance as each side tries to wear the other down. Sometimes it becomes unpleasant. Much may be threatened in the names of one's client, including the ultimate threat, withdrawal. Meanwhile of course the clients are blithely unaware of the war raging around them: the buyer believes from day 1 that he has bought the house and the seller believes that he has sold it. Usually neither has the slightest intention of withdrawing. And of course they are right. It is rare for a party to withdraw just because his solicitor cannot negotiate precisely the contract he would like and few solicitors would dare suggest such a thing.[12]

Of course, in some cases there are real issues between the parties, so that time spent in negotiation is time well spent. But this is more likely to occur in commercial conveyancing than in domestic conveyancing. In domestic conveyancing there is something a little absurd about treating a transaction as a rerun of the battle of Waterloo. (There may of course be psychological benefits for the participants, but that is another matter.) On a practical level there is no point in loading the offer (or qualified acceptance) with oppressive conditions if these are promptly removed by the solicitor acting for the other side. The path of wisdom is that a firm's style offer should be such that the firm would, if acting for a seller, be

[10] By no means all missives follow the course here described. Missives are still sometimes concluded within a week, relations between the agents may be cordial, and the terms of missive letters reasonable. But not always.

[11] Again, if the Law Society's style offer achieves popularity, things may change.

[12] Of course, parties do sometimes withdraw for other reasons, *e.g.* because they have changed their minds or because they are offered more money by someone else.

prepared to accept *de plano*.[13] But in practice some firms cannot resist the temptation of trying to slip something past the other side. Sometimes indeed this happens. But unless one is transacting with Rip van Winkle, W.S., the final contract is likely to be much the same no matter how long is spent on negotiations. Meanwhile, as the days lengthen into weeks without the contract being concluded, the client is being exposed to the risk that the other party may (for some quite unconnected reason) decide to withdraw. The solicitor involved will then have great difficulty in justifying his tactics to his own client.

Law Society Standard Clauses

In an attempt to deal with some of the problems just described the Law Society produced in September 1991 a set of standard clauses for domestic conveyancing which it hoped that solicitors would use as the basis for offers to purchase. The clauses were registered in the form of a Deed of Declaration in the Books of Council and Session, so that they could be incorporated into offers by reference. The style did not prove popular[14] and in April 1992 a revised version was published and registered.[15]

So far, however, the standard clauses have had an unenthusiastic reception. Most solicitors like to make their own contracts for their own clients and do not like being told what to do by the Law Society. There was also concern that there had been no consultation. Inevitably, too, the clauses have been criticised on points of detail (though not always fairly). At the time of writing the revised version seems unlikely to prove any more popular. It suffers from some of the defects of the first version, and among other points does not seem to cope with the new developments in the *Winston* v. *Patrick* saga.[16] The use of the standard clauses cannot be recom-

[13] See an article by one of the authors at 1989 J.L.S. 19.

[14] Partly because the first of the three parts was declared unalterable. This was an unenforceable but irksome attempt to limit freedom of contract, particularly as many of the clauses might easily need variation in particular cases. The restriction has been removed from the revised version. See a letter from P. Mann at 1991 J.L.S. 380 for a characteristic response from the profession.

[15] The first version was registered on August 9, 1991 and the second on April 3, 1992. For discussion see M.J.R. Smith at 1993 J.L.S. 60.

[16] See chap. 19.

mended with confidence. One basic problem with any standard form offer is that it tends to get out of date quickly.[17]

Offer and acceptance

Unlike many contracts, missives fit neatly into the textbook category of offer and acceptance. Once an offer has been made, it remains available for acceptance for a "reasonable time." The same is true of qualified acceptances (which in law are considered as new offers). In practice the initial offer invariably contains an express, and short, time limit by which acceptance must be made. In practice, though, time limits often matter little, because most offers are met by qualified acceptances, and a qualified acceptance is regarded as an entirely new offer, which therefore need not adhere to the time limit in the previous missive. It is only where a missive constitutes a final acceptance that it has to meet the time limit in the previous missive. In practice, however, each missive usually has a clause expressly deleting the time limit stated in the previous missive.

A party making an offer is always free to withdraw it, even within the "reasonable time" for acceptance. The withdrawal need not be in formal writing and indeed may be oral,[18] though of course from a practical point of view a formal written withdrawal is preferable.

On receipt of an offer two choices are in theory open: to accept or to reject. In practice a successful offer is usually met by a qualified acceptance, and a qualified acceptance is deemed to be both (1) a rejection and (2) a new offer.[19] It is easy to overlook (1). Once a qualified acceptance is sent the original offer is rejected once and for all and cannot be revived by withdrawing the qualified acceptance.[20] The only effect of withdrawing a qualified acceptance is that there is now no live offer available for the other party to

[17] In principle a standard form offer has a certain value. It should speed up missives and reduce disputes. But in practice there are grave problems. One possible compromise solution would be to have just some standardised clauses.

[18] *McMillan* v. *Caldwell*, 1991 S.L.T. 325.

[19] Thus, in theory a qualified acceptance by a seller is a rejection of an offer to buy and at the same time an offer to sell.

[20] *Rutterford* v. *Allied Breweries*, 1990 S.L.T. 249, and *cf. Findlater* v. *Mann*, 1990 S.L.T. 465.

accept. The earlier offer does not revive. Care should be taken with the use of qualified acceptances, particularly at a late stage in the negotiations where the qualification may concern a trivial point. For as soon as a qualified acceptance is sent the ball is back in the other party's court and the chance to bring about a concluded contract is lost, until the ball is returned. It may not be returned.

Sometimes fax is used as a means of transmitting an offer or a qualified acceptance. While a document arriving on a fax machine is just a photocopy of the original and so fails to comply with the rules of execution of deeds, the facts (1) that there is a properly executed original in existence and (2) that the terms of that original have been communicated to the other party, may make the sending of the original unnecessary. If that is correct, then a contract could be concluded entirely by fax, even although each party kept their own originals. But this, of course, is speculation. To be on the safe side, the originals should always be sent, even if a fax has gone first.

Personal bar

Contracts for the sale of heritage must be constituted in formal writing. But where formal writing has not been used a contract may still be set up by *rei interventus* (actings by the person seeking to uphold the contract) or homologation (actings by the person seeking to deny the contract which contradict his denial). This is a familiar area of contract law, but conveyancers need to bear in mind the celebrated case of *Errol* v. *Walker*.[21] In that case the potential purchaser of a house made a formal offer, which was never accepted. Substantial actings followed on the part of the purchaser, on the basis of which the court held there to be a contract. The novelty of *Errol* was that it allowed the use of *rei interventus* not merely to cure the absence of form (*i.e.* of an acceptance not being in formal writing) but to cure the absence of *consensus in idem* (*i.e.* of there being no acceptance at all). The decision has had a mixed reception. It has been held not to apply to homologation[22] and while it has been followed in one case invol-

[21] 1966 S.C. 93.

[22] *Law* v. *Thomson*, 1978 S.C. 343. See also *Stewart's Exrs.* v. *Stewart*, 1993 S.L.T. 440 rev. 1993 G.W.D. 22–1387.

ving *rei interventus* where the facts were very close,[23] in a later case[24] the court felt able to distinguish it on the basis that the alleged contract was entirely oral whereas in *Errol* there had at least been a written offer. The moral of *Errol* v. *Walker* is that if the parties effectively behave as if there were a binding contract, then one side may not be allowed to wriggle out on the ground that there are no formally concluded missives. Of course, the actings of the parties must be sufficient. Thus in one case[25] the purchaser had done no more than draft a disposition and prepare a few other forms and this was held not to amount to *rei interventus*.

Defects of consent

Like any contract, missives may be affected by defects of consent such as essential error or undue influence. This subject, which belongs to the general law of contract, will not be dealt with here, except for a few words about error. In the typical case, error is both unilateral and also uninduced and so gives rise to no remedy. A standard example is where the buyer thinks that he is getting a larger piece of land than turns out to be the case.[26] Unilateral error may, however, be relevant where the error was known to, and taken advantage of by, the other party to the contract.[27] Where the missives mis-describe the property, or mis-state some other matter, so that the missives fail to represent the *common* intention of the parties, rectification may be available under section 8 of the Law Reform (Miscellaneous Provisions) (Scotland) Act 1985.[27a] In practice, parties may be in dispute as to whether the error is unilateral (for which there is, in general, no remedy) or whether the error is in expression, mis-stating a prior common intention (for which rectification is competent). Unilateral error will found reduction

[23] *Umar* v. *Murtaza*, 1983 S.L.T. (Sh. Ct.) 79.

[24] *Mulhern* v. *Mulhern*, 1987 S.L.T. (Sh. Ct.) 62; 1987 S.C.L.R. 252.

[25] *Rutterford* v. *Allied Breweries*, 1990 S.L.T. 249.

[26] As in *Oliver* v. *Gaughan*, 1990 G.W.D. 22–1247.

[27] Compare *Spook Erection (Northern) Ltd.* v. *Kaye*, 1990 S.L.T. 676 with *Angus* v. *Bryden*, 1992 S.L.T. 884. See further J.M. Thomson at 1992 S.L.T. (News) 215.

[27a] *Angus* v. *Bryden*, 1992 S.L.T. 884; *George Thomson Services Ltd.* v. *Moore*, 1992 S.C.L.R. 295. Rectification is discussed further in chap. 9. Prior to missives, parties are still at the stage of negotiation so that it will be difficult to prove a common intention.

where it has been *induced* by the other party to the contract; and damages are also due if the misrepresentation was either fraudulent or negligent.[28] If there is misrepresentation in a conveyancing transaction, it is almost always by the seller. The problem may be caused by a loquacious or agitated client, prone to exaggeration, under the strain of showing potential buyers round the house. The printed sale particulars may also contain misrepresentations, but the effect of these is negatived[29] by the more or less standard disclaimer that their accuracy is not guaranteed. (Some contracts avoid this disclaimer by express incorporation of the sale particulars.) Typical misrepresentations by the seller are that the roof is in good condition ("never a day's worry in 20 years"), that the central heating system was recently overhauled, or that the next-door neighbours are aged and as quiet as mice. In *Smith* v. *Paterson*[30] reduction was granted where the seller had, by deliberately careless words, misrepresented the extent of the front garden. But, as *Smith* itself shows, it is often very difficult to prove oral representations.

Misrepresentations by purchasers are almost unknown. A theoretical example might be misrepresentation as to creditworthiness, but if a buyer proves uncreditworthy he will hardly be worth suing for misrepresentation. In domestic conveyancing a seller normally assumes the creditworthiness of the buyer. (In commercial transactions evidence of creditworthiness is often required before the seller will conclude missives.)

Promises and options

It is competent to have a promise for the sale or gift of land, but the promise must be in formal writing. Of course, such promises are rare in practice. More important is the option. In an option, the owner undertakes to sell land on certain terms at a certain price, but the other party is not bound to buy. He may buy or not as he sees fit. The option will be open for a stated period, such as a year, and if the option holder chooses not to exercise his option

[28] Law Reform (Miscellaneous Provisions) (Scotland) Act 1985, s. 10. See *e.g.*, *Palmer* v. *Beck*, 1993 S.L.T. 485.

[29] From the angle of private law. False sales particulars may, however, amount to an offence: Property Misdescriptions Act 1991.

[30] Unreported, Outer House, February 18, 1986.

in that time, the option lapses.[30a] Options are occasionally granted gratuitously but more commonly for consideration, *i.e.* a person buys an option to buy. If he exercises the option the price for the land will be in addition to this. If he chooses not to exercise the option he then writes off the price he paid for it. In commercial conveyancing options are not uncommon,[31] but in domestic conveyancing they are unusual. One example is where missives are concluded for the sale of plot A with an option to purchase plot B. An option must be exercised in the form and within the timescale laid down in the initial grant of the option. But unless the grant specifies otherwise, an option need not be exercised in formal writing or indeed in any writing at all, though the original option itself must have been in formal writing.[32]

3. Suspensive Conditions

A suspensive condition,[33] at least in the normal usage of the term, is a condition in a contract which is suspensive of performance. In other words there is a concluded contract between the parties; each is bound to the other; but neither can be made to perform unless or until the condition is purified, so that if the condition is not purified within the timelimit set for that purpose both parties are freed from its terms. While the suspensive condition remains unpurified, the contract is in suspense. Its activation depends on the purification of the condition. No obligation arises under the suspensive condition itself. Indeed, typically its purification is out of the control of both parties. If the condition is not met no damages are due. The contract simply falls away.

Suspensive conditions are quite common, chiefly in commercial conveyancing. Thus, a contract may be made conditional on the granting of planning permission or on the transfer of a liquor

[30a] There may sometimes be disputes as to whether the timelimit has been complied with: see *Fortune Engineering Ltd.* v. *Precision Components (Scotland) Ltd.*, 1993 G.W.D. 1–49.

[31] They can provide commercial flexibility and can save capital gains tax. See Halliday, para. 15–135.

[32] *Stone* v. *MacDonald*, 1979 S.C. 363.

[33] For a general discussion see J.M. Thomson "Suspensive and Resolutive Conditions in the Scots Law of Contract" in A.J. Gamble (ed.), *Obligations in Context: Essays in Honour of Professor D.M. Walker* (W. Green, 1990).

licence. The reason for the use of suspensive (as opposed to ordinary) conditions is that the property is generally worthless to the purchaser if the condition is not met.

Identifying suspensive conditions

It is not always easy to say whether a particular contractual term is an ordinary condition or a suspensive condition.[34] Of course, a well-drafted term should leave no doubt on the matter, but not all terms are well-drafted. The standard way of introducing a suspensive condition is with the words "this contract is conditional on" or "this contract is subject to" (*e.g.* the obtaining of planning permission). Clauses which begin this way are usually suspensive. But less will do. In *Zebmoon Limited* v. *Akinbrook Investment Developments Limited*[35] a clause which began with the words "it is an essential condition of this offer" was held to be suspensive even though these words are often found introducing non-suspensive conditions as well.

Sometimes conditions are apparently suspensive but are coupled with an express right to rescind for the purchaser if the condition is not purified. This is a natural attempt by the draftsman to protect his client. If the condition is truly suspensive such a provision is unnecessary. (For if there is no purification the contract is automatically null). Indeed, such a provision may encourage the court to interpret the clause as an ordinary (non-suspensive) condition.[36] A possible alternative interpretation of such a clause is as a suspensive condition but with a right in the purchaser to waive purification. (For if he has an express right to rescind he also appears to have an implied right not to rescind).

In England the standard expression in contracts for the sale of land, "subject to contract," is treated as suspensive of performance until purification by the formal exchange of contracts shortly

[34] Or a resolutive condition. In this latter case the formula is generally that if a certain condition is not met, either party may resile without liability to either side. For an example see *Ford Sellar Morris Properties plc* v. *E.W. Hutchison Ltd.*, 1990 S.L.T. 500.

[35] 1988 S.L.T. 146.

[36] See *Tarditi* v. *Drummond*, 1989 S.L.T. 554 at 557–558. But no objection was raised on this account in *Zebmoon Ltd.* v. *Akinbrook Investment Developments Ltd.*, 1988 S.L.T. 146.

before completion.[37] Until then either party is free to withdraw, which they not infrequently do. This formula is not used in Scotland.[38] Since suspensive conditions of any sort are uncommon in domestic conveyancing, last-minute withdrawals are correspondingly rare. Once missives are concluded both parties are bound to perform.

Timelimit for purification of suspensive conditions

From the seller's point of view it is essential that a timelimit for purification be stipulated. Otherwise he may be left in the situation where he does not know whether the sale will proceed (and does not know when he will know) but yet cannot lawfully withdraw and remarket the property. If no date for purification is given the rules appear to be the following: (1) Where missives have a date of entry which is fixed independently of the suspensive condition,[39] the condition must be fulfilled by that date; (2) Otherwise, the condition must be fulfilled within a reasonable time.[40] Time is of the essence here,[41] so that if the condition is not purified within the prescribed timelimit the contract is immediately at an end.

Can the buyer waive a suspensive condition?

If a suspensive condition is not purified, the purchaser will usually wish to withdraw from the purchase and, generally speaking, the effect of non-purification is for the contract to fall. Sometimes, though, the purchaser may wish to proceed after all, and the question then arises as to whether he is entitled to waive the suspensive condition. It seems that such waiver is allowed in two circum-

[37] The English term for settlement.

[38] Halliday, at para. 15–03, takes the view that if it were used it would not be suspensive.

[39] As opposed, for example, to a clause which provided that the date of entry would be one week after the grant of a liquor licence. Such clauses tying entry to purification are common.

[40] See *T. Boland & Co.* v. *Dundas's Trs.*, 1975 S.L.T. (Notes) 80, *per* Lord Keith.

[41] See the *Boland* case, above. See also *Ford Sellar Morris Properties plc* v. *E.W. Hutchison Ltd.*, 1990 S.L.T. 500. In other contractual terms time is not normally of the essence. For a case in which the seller argued, unsuccessfully, that the purchaser was personally barred from founding on the expiry of the timelimit, see *Park* v. *Morrison Developments Ltd.* 1993 G.W.D. 8–571.

stances only. The first is where an express right of waiver is reserved. The second is where the condition was inserted solely in the purchaser's interest *and* it is severable from the rest of the contract. The second set of circumstances is not easily established. In only one reported case has the purchaser succeeded on this ground,[42] and that decision has been questioned in subsequent cases.[43] In these later cases the purchaser has failed either because the seller also had an express right to resile in the event of non-purification (which negatived the idea of the condition being for the sole benefit of the purchaser) or because the date of entry was tied to the date of purification (which prevented it from being severable). These were perhaps fairly straightforward cases. In *Imry Property Holdings Limited* v. *Glasgow Y.M.C.A.*,[44] Lord Dunpark said that the mere fact there was nothing in the missives to show that the seller had an interest was not enough, and that the missives must give positive evidence that the suspensive condition was conceived in favour of the purchaser only. But the later cases suggest that the rule may be less strict than this.

This rule restricting waiver applies to suspensive conditions only. A party is always free to waive the performance of ordinary contractual obligations incumbent on the other party to the contract. For instance, the fact that the seller cannot produce a flawless title does not prevent the purchaser from proceeding with the contract if he wishes to do so.

4. Drafting

> "The moment a new term was invented by any body, and known, the ordinary list became enriched by it; in so much, indeed, that in many charters we find repetitions of the same thing, under different words; which proves that conveyancers were more attentive to the practice of each other, than to the sense of what they themselves were doing."

Thus Walter Ross writing about the *tenendas* clause in a feu char-

[42] *Dewar & Finlay* v. *Blackwood*, 1968 S.L.T. 196.

[43] *Ellis & Sons Second Amalgamated Properties Ltd.*, 1974 S.C. 200; *Imry Property Holdings Ltd.* v. *Glasgow Y.M.C.A.*, 1979 S.L.T. 261; *Zebmoon Ltd.* v. *Akinbrook Investment Developments Ltd.*, 1988 S.L.T. 146.

[44] 1979 S.L.T. 261.

ter.[45] Little, it seems, has changed. Except for those firms which use the Law Society Standard Clauses,[46] each firm maintains its own *pro forma* offer, either on the word processor or in the form of a preprinted schedule.[47] But the offer is constantly revised and updated to take account of the practice of other firms. If firm A, being a large and well-known firm, think fit to insert a new clause in their offer, it will not be long before it appears in the offers of innumerable other firms. There are obvious advantages in this method of proceeding. But there are also disadvantages. One is that offers become ever longer as new clauses are invented and then copied. Offers have probably doubled in length in the last 15 years. Another disadvantage is that the imported clause may sit uneasily in the home style, and the problem is compounded where, as is often the case, clauses are imported from a number of different sources. It sometimes happens that "revising" the firm's offer means merely adding to it, without removing any existing clause or adapting old and new clauses to make them fully consistent. This can make offers difficult to understand. It can also lead to unexplained inconsistencies of language which might be treated as significant by a court when no significance was actually intended.

In domestic conveyancing many firms use the same *pro forma* offer for quite different types of property—for Victorian flats, modern villas, urban and rural properties, houses subject to registration of title as well as for houses held on a Sasine title, and so on. Hence, for any given property the offer will probably contain several redundant clauses. Offer a field for sale, and one may get an offer asking the seller to warrant the condition of the central heating and to guarantee that there is a right to the *solum*. This practice is often criticised, no doubt rightly, but convenience speaks louder than criticism.

Drafting missives is a difficult and skilled business. There are very few sets of missives which are beyond criticism. In the end, drafting can only be learned by practice, but here are a few suggestions of a general nature.

[45] Walter Ross, *Lectures on the History and Practice of the Law of Scotland relative to Conveyancing and Legal Diligence* (commonly called *Ross's Lectures*), (1792), p. 165 of the 1822 edition.

[46] At the time of writing, not many.

[47] A word-processed offer is better for client relations. The client likes to see an offer which has been carefully tailored to his own case.

(1) It is worth defining the principal terms, *e.g.* seller, buyer and subjects. The buyer should not be referred to as "the buyer" on one page and "our client" on the next.

(2) Introductory formulae such as "it is understood that" or "it is a condition of the contract that" should generally be avoided. Not only are they inelegant, but they may also affect the enforceability of the provision. Of the first of these, it has been said[48]:

> "The use of the introductory phrase 'It is understood' in these missives suggests to my mind that cl. 7 is intended, not to create an obligation on one party, the defenders, which they have to implement, but to express the understanding of both parties as to a state of facts existing as at the time when they [the missives] were concluded. If their understanding turned out to be wrong then either party, or at least the pursuers, would be entitled to resile from the bargain."

If this is correct,[49] then the phrase "it is understood" prevents the imposition of a direct obligation on the party at whom it is directed (usually the seller). In effect it deprives the purchaser of the two remedies of implement and damages, leaving him only with the possibility of rescission. It acts rather like a suspensive condition, at least so far as remedies are concerned, but in circumstances where that is probably not what the buyer wants.

The other phrase ("it is a condition of the contract that") suggests, especially where used only for one or two clauses, that the clause has a special status, perhaps even that it is suspensive of performance. Once again, this is not usually what the purchaser wants.

(3) Where the seller is to warrant something (*e.g.* that the central heating system is in good working order or that there are no unusual or unduly onerous real burdens) the applicable date for the warranty should normally be the date of entry and not the date of conclusion of missives. Otherwise the warranty may be regarded as superseded when the disposition is delivered at settlement.[49a]

(4) Most positive obligations in missives (*i.e.* obligations to do

[48] *Wood* v. *Edwards*, 1988 S.L.T. (Sh. Ct.) 17, *per* Sheriff R.J.D. Scott at 21.

[49] Which is perhaps arguable: see *Neilson* v. *Barratt*, 1987 G.W.D. 13–467.

[49a] See chap. 19.

something) are on the seller. Indeed, in domestic conveyancing often the only obligation on the purchaser is to pay the price. But whichever party is subject to obligations it is important to stipulate the date by which the obligation in question must be performed. (Otherwise the rule is probably that the obligation need not be performed until a "reasonable time" has elapsed, whatever that means.) Normally obligations need to be performed by the date of entry. But there is a potential ambiguity here. If the transaction actually settles on the contractual date of entry, well and good. But sometimes transactions do not settle then, in which case there are two dates of entry, *i.e.* the contractual date and the date on which entry was actually taken.[50] It is wise to anticipate this difficulty by providing in missives for *two* defined dates, namely the "date of entry" and the "date of settlement," the latter being the date on which entry is actually taken. For each obligation it should be made clear which of the two dates is the relevant one. Time is presumed not to be of the essence in a contract of sale, by which is meant that failure to perform by the stipulated date, though it may be a breach of contract, is not in itself material breach entitling the other party to rescind.

(5) Before an offer or a qualified acceptance is sent, it should be checked carefully for errors, bearing in mind that there is usually no remedy for a unilateral error. An offer to purchase which states the price at £150,000, being a typing error for £105,000, is binding.[51]

(6) As far as possible it should be ensured that each clause deals with just one item. If the item is complex, split it into sub-clauses. It makes the offer far easier to understand. Moreover, when the other side prepare the qualified acceptance, they can deal with the whole of a clause or sub-clause, and are not forced to say something like: "With reference to your fourth schedule clause, the words from 'and if' to 'penalty' are deleted and the following words are substituted." That is messy and, with drafting being done at high speed, can cause errors.[52]

[50] See discussion by the authors at 1988 J.L.S. 431 and 1989 J.L.S. 175.

[51] See *Steel* v. *Bradley (Scotland) Homes Ltd.*, 1974 S.L.T. 133. However, the doctrine of "unfair advantage" may apply. See *Angus* v. *Bryden*, above.

[52] Some agents deliberately insert a "nasty" in a clause dealing with some other (innocuous) matter. This is unethical, and in the long term disadvantageous, since it will give the firm a bad reputation in the profession.

Preparing the qualified acceptance

The offer must be gone through carefully with the client. Are the facts as stated correct? Is the client really willing to throw in the stair carpet and the tumble dryer? Is the date of entry suitable or should the purchaser be pushed on this?

The number of qualifications should not be excessive, lest this delays conclusion of missives unnecessarily. The seller's solicitor should have ordered up the titles and the property inquiry certificates before putting the property on the market and so should be in a position to deal intelligently with the contents of the offer. Thus, if he knows from the property inquiry certificates that, for example, the roads *ex adverso* the subjects have been taken over by the local authority, there is no point in qualifying the relevant clause in the purchaser's offer.

Sometimes the selling solicitor may not have the necessary information to deal with a particular clause in an offer, or may have the information but be uncertain whether it meets the terms of the buyer's clause. The second case often arises with the "no unusual or unduly onerous burdens" clause. Typically the seller's agent has the titles in front of him, and so knows what the burdens are, but may be uncertain whether they can be regarded as usual and not unduly onerous. In this situation it is acceptable to meet the purchaser's clause with the over-used "the buyer shall satisfy himself" provision, provided that the titles are sent so that the purchaser's agent can do just that. If the titles are not yet to hand, it is common to provide that they will be sent when available, with a timelimit of, for example, five working days after receipt for the other agent to satisfy himself.[53] In the absence of such a timelimit there is the danger (at least on one view of the law) that the pur-

[53] However, disputes often arise as to how this period is to be calculated. (See the entry on "Time" in *The Laws of Scotland: Stair Memorial Encyclopaedia,* vol. 23.) The law is probably as follows: Suppose the documents are sent by Rutland Exchange on Friday, April 10. They will be received on Monday, April 13. This is Day 0. Tuesday, April 14 is Day 1. Friday, April 17 is Day 4. Saturday, April 18 is probably not a "working day" in modern practice. So Day 5 will be Monday, April 20. If the buyer's agent wishes to resile, he thus has until close of business on that day to do so. "Five" days have thus become 10 days. The resiling letter must, it is thought, be actually received by the seller's agent by close of business on April 20: it is probably not sufficient to put it into the Monday night post. Scottish

chaser could pronounce on the morning of settlement that he was not satisfied and did not wish to proceed with the purchase.

Wherever possible the offer should be amended by outright deletion (*e.g.* "Clause 6 of your Schedule is deleted" or "The second sentence of clause 3 of your letter is deleted"). This is better than pretending to leave the buyer's clause intact while adding Gothic qualifications which contradict it, resulting in a legal dog's-breakfast. If the offer incorporates a schedule of conditions, it should be made clear whether the clause being qualified is a clause of the letter or a clause of the schedule.

5. Interpretation

In missives both parties have usually been professionally advised and in interpretation of the contract no favour is shown to either side.[53a]

There is probably an implied term in missives that parties will act reasonably. So in *Gordon District Council* v. *Wimpey Homes Holdings Limited*,[54] where missives were subject to a suspensive condition that planning permission would be granted "to the satisfaction of the purchaser" and the permission ultimately granted was fenced in with conditions, Lord Clyde rejected the purchaser's argument that what was to his "satisfaction" was a matter for him alone and not subject to challenge, and took the view that "each party must have intended that the other would act reasonably."[55] Presumably it would be open to the parties to contract so as to exclude this "reasonable" criterion. It may be added that one party to a contract (usually the seller) may be taken as bound to use all reasonable endeavours to bring a particular event about. The

bank holidays are presumably not "working days" though in practice law offices sometimes open on some bank holidays. Many areas also have non-statutory local holidays when local law offices are usually shut. Again, these are probably not "working days" where the holiday is in the area of the buyer's law office. Hence "five" will sometimes work out as being more than even 10 days.

[53a] Thus there is no scope for the *contra proferentem* rule. See *G.A. Estates Ltd.* v. *Caviapen Trs. Ltd.*, 1992 G.W.D. 31–1846 and *Park* v. *Morrison Developments Ltd.*, 1993 G.W.D. 8–571.

[54] 1989 S.L.T. 141.

[55] *Ibid.* p. 142. In the event the court in fact held that the purchaser had acted reasonably. See also *John H. Wyllie* v. *Ryan Industrial Fuels Ltd.*, 1989 S.L.T. 302, and *Rockcliffe Estates plc* v. *Co-operative Wholesale Society Ltd.*, 1993 G.W.D. 21–1302.

meaning of this phrase is discussed in *Elwood* v. *Ravenseft Properties Limited*.[56]

As a general rule, extrinsic evidence ("prior communings") cannot be used to alter or contradict the terms of missives.[57] So in *Murray* v. *Cherry*[58] the seller argued, in vain, that by prior informal agreement, not subsequently reflected in the missives, part of the garden was to be excluded from the sale. But while prior communings are excluded it may be that subsequent communings are not. In *Turner* v. *Macmillan-Douglas*[59] missives were interpreted by reference to subsequent correspondence between the parties' solicitors. If this decision is correct,[60] care must be taken not to offer hostages to fortune in the course of correspondence. Subsequent correspondence may also be regarded as evidence of variation or waiver.

Extrinsic evidence, while it cannot alter missives, may be used to explain an existing contractual term where that term requires explanation. Thus it is competent, indeed necessary, to use extrinsic evidence in order to link the verbal description of the subjects of sale to the actual subjects on the ground.

6. Variation and Waiver

The terms of missives can be varied but this requires the consent of both parties expressed in formal writing (or expressed informally but followed by *rei interventus* or homologation). In the absence of actings, oral variation is ineffectual.[61]

Missives commonly contain a clause on the following lines: "Entry and physical possession will be given on February 14, 1993 or on such other date as may be mutually agreed." Do these last words authorise an informal (*e.g.* oral) fixing of a fresh date of entry? It is far from invariable practice to fix a revised date of entry

[56] 1991 S.L.T. 44.

[57] Subject however to s. 8 and 9 of the Law Reform (Miscellaneous Provisions) (Scotland) Act 1985. Moreover, prior communings may be founded on not to contradict the missives, but to resolve ambiguities therein.

[58] 1980 S.L.T. (Sh. Ct.) 131.

[59] 1989 S.L.T. 293.

[60] See W.W. McBryde, *The Law of Contract* in Scotland (W. Green, 1987), para. 19–13; *Hall* v. *McWilliam*, 1993 G.W.D. 23–1457.

[61] *Aitken* v. *Hyslop*. 1977 S.L.T. (Notes) 50; *Inglis* v. *Lownie*, 1990 S.L.T. (Sh. Ct.) 60.

by formally executed letter. In fact, conflicting views have been expressed on this question.[62] The safe course is that if the date of entry is changed by mutual agreement, there should be two letters, both adopted as holograph, one setting forth the new date and the other, from the other side, confirming it.

Similar in effect to variation is waiver.[63] Apart from the special case of suspensive conditions, it is always open to a party unilaterally to waive one or more of his rights under the contract. Waiver may be express, or be implied by actings, and in practice the latter is more common. But arguments based on implied waiver often fail. In order to succeed it is necessary to show, first, that one party to the contract has acted in such a way as to indicate clearly that he will not found on a particular contractual right, and secondly that the other party has acted in reliance[64] on the alleged waiver.

The commonest case in which implied waiver is pled is where, the seller having failed to perform in some material respect,[65] the purchaser delays in rescinding the contract. The argument then arises that the buyer has implicitly waived his right to rescind. Mere delay by itself (unless very lengthy) is no bar to rescission. After all, the reason for delay is usually that the purchaser hopes that performance will ultimately be forthcoming. Nor is taking entry to the property a bar to rescission, although rescission may then be prevented on the different ground that *restitutio in integrum* is not possible.[66] Nor does it make any difference that the contract itself contains a fixed date after which rescission is expressly permitted and the date is allowed to pass.[67] An example of waiver is *Macdonald* v. *Newall*[68] where the buyer, having examined title and taken no objection to it (except on another unrelated point), took entry and did not then raise her objection until some further months had passed.[69]

[62] Contrast *Imry Property Holdings Ltd.* v. *Glasgow Y.M.C.A.*, 1979 S.L.T. 262 with *Jayner Ltd.* v. *Allander Holdings Ltd.*, 1990 G.W.D. 30–1717.

[63] On which see McBryde, *Contract*, p. 541 *et seq.*

[64] Not necessarily prejudicial reliance.

[65] Typically in failing to produce a good and marketable title.

[66] See *Armia* v. *Daejan Developments Ltd.*, 1979 S.C. (H.L.) 56.

[67] *Lousada & Co. Ltd.* v. *J.E. Lesser (Properties) Ltd.*, 1990 S.L.T. 823; *Elwood* v. *Ravenseft Properties Ltd.*, 1991 S.L.T. 44; *Atlas Assurance Co.* v. *Dollar Land Holdings plc*, 1992 G.W.D. 32–1902.

[68] (1898) 1 F. 68.

[69] See also *Mowbray* v. *Mathieson*, 1989 G.W.D. 6–267.

CHAPTER 3

MISSIVES II: CONTENT

1. Essential Terms

A contract for the sale of land requires, as a minimum, express agreement as to the "three Ps"—the parties to the transaction, the property being sold, and the price. Without such agreement there is no contract. At one time express agreement as to date of entry was also thought to be essential but it now seems that an appropriate date of entry will, if necessary, be read into the contract. Not much needs to be said here about identifying the parties. An offer may not identify the seller, but just says "your client," but in that case the qualified acceptance should identify the seller.

Subjects of sale

The parties must agree on the subjects being sold. Therefore the missives must contain an adequate description. But only rarely is a full conveyancing description given in missives. For houses the postal address is usually sufficient, but for undeveloped plots of ground or for commercial developments more is usually necessary, and, indeed, in commercial conveyancing the offer usually has a detailed plan attached to it, which will have been made available to bidders by the seller. If the purchase is a first break-off—*i.e.* if the property has not previously existed as a separate unit—a full description is required, preferably incorporating a plan. The property to be conveyed in the eventual disposition will be the property agreed in the missives, so it is important that the missives clearly set forth the intentions of both parties.

It is no objection to a description that it needs to be supplemented by extrinsic evidence. Thus, in the event of a dispute, it is competent to bring evidence as to what subjects are known, for example, by the name "number 4 High Street." But the extrinsic evidence cannot be made to do the work of the written description, and if the description itself is hopelessly vague there is no place for extrinsic evidence. *Grant* v. *Peter G. Gauld & Co.*[1] provides a cautionary tale here. The missives in that case began with the words:

> "We hereby offer to purchase from you the ground presently being quarried by our client and the surroundings thereto extending to twelve acres . . . and that on the following terms and conditions, namely: 1. The actual boundaries will be agreed between you and our client."

Since clause 1 amounted to a direct admission that no agreement as to subjects had been reached it was held that there was no contract between the parties. But the court indicated that even without clause 1 the result might have been the same on the basis that the expression "the surroundings thereto extending to twelve acres" was too vague to allow extrinsic evidence. In practice, disputes about the definition of the subjects are fairly uncommon. But where a dispute does arise extrinsic evidence will determine which party is right. Roughly speaking, extrinsic evidence can be of two kinds, namely "objective" and "subjective." Objective evidence answers the question, what are the subjects which are known as "number 4 High Street?" The kind of evidence which is relevant here are the boundaries as stated in the seller's title, physical features such as hedges or fences, and the position as understood by neighbours. Subjective evidence answers the question, what are the subjects which were agreed between the parties in the course of negotiations? Often nothing was clearly agreed between the parties. But sometimes negotiations are conducted by reference to a plan or a site visit.

Often there is only objective evidence, or if subjective evidence exists it is consistent with the objective evidence. But if the two are not the same a choice has to be made, and while each case will of course turn on its own facts, a major consideration seems to be whether the seller is selling all or only part of what he owns.[2] In the former case, the subjects will usually be construed as those described in his title (*i.e.* objective evidence). Even if the seller in fact indicated a larger area to the purchaser (*i.e.* subjective

[1] 1985 S.C. 251.

[2] In a sense, of course, this line of approach may beg the question, for the seller's position may precisely be that he was not selling all he owned.

evidence) the case will be analysed as (1) a contract for the smaller area as per the titles but (2) one which is voidable at the instance of the purchaser for misrepresentation.[3] Conversely, where the seller is selling part only of what he owns there is less scope for objective evidence, and subjective evidence will often be conclusive.[4]

Since sellers are more likely to overstate than understate the extent of the property, subjective evidence usually favours the purchaser. One method commonly used to ensure that full weight is given to evidence of this kind is to incorporate it expressly into missives, typically by adding to the brief description of the property the words "all as advertised by you and as seen by the purchaser."

Where parties are in dispute as to the subjects, one of them must be in error and the task of the court is to find out which one. Thus, the seller thinks he sold plot A while the buyer thinks he bought plot B (which includes but extends beyond plot A). One of them must be wrong and, since the error will have been unilateral it gives rise to no remedy against the other party (except where it has been induced). But occasionally it is impossible to reach a concluded view as to who is right. The evidence is consistent with plot A or with plot B—or very likely with plot C as well—and in that case there is mutual error and so no contract at all, because there is no *consensus*.

Parts and pertinents

Offers usually stipulate for parts and pertinents, although these are of course implied.[5] In practice, the only parts and pertinents which need cause concern at the missives stage are (1) fixtures and (2) minerals.

First, fixtures. If the contract is silent, a purchaser is entitled to fixtures (since they are part of the land) but not fittings (since they are moveable[6]). But often certain fittings, *e.g.* curtains and carpets,

[3] *Smith* v. *Paterson*, unreported, Outer House, February 18, 1986. In this case reduction was granted where the seller had, by deliberately careless words, misrepresented the extent of the garden.

[4] *Houldsworth* v. *Gordon Cumming*, 1910 S.C. (H.L.) 49 (especially *per* Lord Shaw); *Angus* v. *Bryden*, 1992 S.L.T. 884; *Barratt Scotland Ltd.* v. *Keith*, 1992 G.W.D. 4–208, affirmed on a different point, 1993 G.W.D. 3–205; *Martone* v. *Zani*, 1992 G.W.D. 32–1903.

[5] See chap. 9.

[6] "Fittings" and "fixtures" are terms of art, the former meaning things connected

are included in the sale. And it is not always clear whether certain other items are fixtures or fittings. The only way to avoid disputes later is to give a full list in the offer of the fittings, etc., which the purchaser expects to receive. Obviously the purchaser's agent must ask his client about this. The seller's schedule of particulars will usually form the basis of this list of extras. Because the borderline between fittings and fixtures can be arguable, it is common to list items which are probably fixtures anyway, such as built-in wardrobes and kitchen units. The sale of moveables is governed by the Sale of Goods Act 1979 and accordingly ownership passes in accordance with section 17 of that Act and not by virtue of the disposition.

Secondly, minerals.[7] Unlike legal separate tenements such as salmon fishings, minerals are included in the subjects of sale unless expressly excluded.[8] So an offer for "4 High Street" includes the minerals unless otherwise stated. If it then turns out that the seller has no title to the minerals (and often they were long ago reserved by the superior), he is in breach of contract and the purchaser can rescind.[9] At one time this rule could be used by a purchaser as a handy method of escaping from a contract where it was unsatisfactory for other reasons, but nowadays it is normal for the offer to provide that the minerals are included in the sale only in so far as the seller has right to them, so that if the seller does own the minerals, they will pass to the purchaser, but if he does not own them, the purchaser cannot complain. This is a rare example of a clause which, although appearing in the purchaser's offer, is solely for the seller's benefit. But the seller's agent must check the point. There is at least one firm which does not include the clause in its offers, leaving it to the seller to make the necessary qualification.[10] If the seller's agent overlooks the point, and if the seller has no

with the subjects which have not acceded, and are therefore moveable, such as carpets, the latter meaning things which have acceded and become part of the heritage, and are therefore heritable, such as doors. The expression which is sometimes encountered, "heritable fittings," is thus unsatisfactory.

[7] For minerals see Gordon, chap. 6.

[8] This is because they are "conventional" separate tenements. See the *Stair Memorial Encyclopaedia*, vol. 18, para. 209.

[9] *Campbell* v. *McCutcheon*, 1963 S.C. 505.

[10] It may be questioned whether, in the light of modern circumstances, this practice is entirely ethical.

right to the minerals, this gives the purchaser the right to rescind if, for whatever reason, he does not wish to proceed.

The purchaser of a house is seldom interested in the mineral rights. But there is a danger that the minerals may be worked in the future—or, more usually nowadays, that they have been worked in the past—and while the withdrawal of support causing subsidence is a delict of strict liability, clauses of reservation of minerals sometimes vary the common law by excluding liability for subsidence. Hence it is wise for an offer to stipulate that any third party's right to the minerals must be subject to satisfactory compensation provisions and must not include any right to enter upon or change the level of the surface.[11] In the case of subsidence caused by coal-mining, there is a statutory compensation scheme.[12]

Price

The contract must state the price, or alternatively some method of calculating it which does not depend on future agreement being reached by the parties. For a case in which there was no agreed price and hence no contract see *MacLeod's Executor* v. *Barr's Trustees*.[13]

Date of entry

It was finally settled in *Gordon District Council* v. *Wimpey Homes Holdings Limited*[14] that it is not fatal for their validity if missives fail to state an entry date. But a practical problem remains, because if there is no date of entry, the parties' obligations will never become due and missives can never be enforced. This problem has yet to be faced up to directly by the courts. But it appears that the law is more accurately stated as being, not that a date of entry is

[11] Some such clause is probably implied into missives at common law in any case. For more details on the whole subject, see Dr Robert Rennie *Non-oil Related Minerals and Reservation Clauses* (P.Q.L.E. April 1988); *Stair Memorial Encyclopaedia*, vol. 18, paras. 252 *et seq*. As to the marketability of a title which is not protected by a right to compensation, see D.J. Cusine (ed.), *The Conveyancing Opinions of J.M. Halliday* (W. Green, 1992), pp. 437–439.

[12] Coal Mining Subsidence Act 1991.

[13] 1989 S.L.T. 392.

[14] 1988 S.L.T. 481.

not required, but that an express date of entry is not required. So if no express date is given the court will assume that the parties, being agreed on so much else, must be agreed that the obligations will at some stage become prestable, and an appropriate date will be read into the contract. In *Gordon* it was suggested that, where the contract depends on a suspensive condition being purified, the date of entry should be the date of purification. Otherwise, presumably, entry will be at a reasonable time after conclusion of missives, what is "reasonable" depending on the facts and circumstances of the case. It is in practice almost unknown for missives to omit a date of entry.

2. Good and Marketable Title

It is provided in missives (and if it were not so provided, it would anyway be implied) that the seller must exhibit or deliver a good and marketable title to the subjects sold. The meaning of this important provision is considered in Chapter 5.

3. Burdens

In a typical case the offer will stipulate that the property is subject to no "unusual or unduly onerous burdens."[15] The seller will usually respond to this in one of three ways. First, he may simply accept it. Secondly, if he (or rather his agent) has the deeds he may send copies of the burdens writs and ask the purchaser to satisfy himself. That will mean that the clause about the burdens will actually be deleted from the missives. Thirdly, if he does not yet have the deeds, he may say that the burdens writs will be forwarded within a certain period and that the purchaser shall have, say, five working days thereafter to satisfy himself. In the latter two cases, the purchaser effectively has a let out from the contract in that he can declare himself unsatisfied, provided he does so timeously. It is important for the purchaser's solicitor to find out what his client plans to use the property for. In practice, real burdens often forbid commercial use. If the purchaser's solicitor assumes that his client intends to use the property as a dwelling-house, and accepts the burdens accordingly, he may find himself being sued for negligence.

[15] For the meaning of this, see chap. 5.

If the client has some particular use in mind, the offer should stipulate that there are no burdens which would prevent that use of the subjects.[16]

4. Property Inquiry Certificates

The solicitor buying a house for a client is concerned with a number of matters which come under the control of local authorities. The main ones are planning law, building control law, the provision of certain services, and statutory notices requiring the building to be repaired or, worse, demolished.

Does the local authority provide all the normal services, *e.g.* roads and sewage, or are they a private responsibility, in which case the maintenance costs will have to be met by the purchaser? The agent must find out the position and advise the client accordingly, and the normal practice is to specify in the offer that these services are available so that, if they are not, it is for the seller to say so. In towns and cities all services are usually, although not invariably, provided by the local authority. If the house the client is buying turns out to be the exception, the position must be carefully explained to the client, who might then wish to withdraw from the purchase.

Much information can be obtained from the local authority, and this is done by the seller asking the council for property inquiry certificates. On payment of a fee local authorities will issue standard form certificates giving certain information in relation to the property. These can take several weeks to arrive, so the seller's agent should order them as soon as he is instructed in the sale. Without these certificates the seller's agents will not be able to respond properly to the clauses in the offer dealing with such matters, and indeed offers usually require the seller to produce evidence on such matters, which effectively means production of the certificates. In an emergency some councils will give information over the phone, but of course this may not always be accurate. It is vital to write to the correct council.[17] The appropriate fee must be sent

[16] As in *Armia* v. *Daejan Developments Ltd.*, 1978 S.C. 152; 1979 S.C. (H.L.) 56.

[17] J.H. Sinclair, *Handbook of Conveyancing Practice in Scotland* (2nd ed., Butterworth, 1990), p. 290 contains a useful map. The local authorities, in conjunction

at the same time as the application: no fee, no certificates. Obviously it is important, in the letter to the council, to identify the property adequately. A postal address is generally sufficient, especially in towns, but sometimes more precision is needed, especially in rural areas or for urban development sites. In some cases a plan should be sent.

The purchaser's agent must obviously check the certificates carefully.[18] Property inquiry certificates are seldom wrong, but if they are, and if loss arises as a result, the council may be liable in damages.[19] Usually the certificates are clear, *i.e.* they disclose nothing adverse to the property. This, however, is a matter for two cheers rather than three, for their scope is limited. For property inquiry certificates will not normally show whether there have been any breaches of planning or building law. Nor does it follow from the absence of statutory notices in the certificates that the house is actually in a good state of repair. The technical services departments of district councils do not maintain a large and vigilant band of inspectors who ceaselessly patrol the streets looking for cracks in stonework. Further, at least with some councils, property certificates do not disclose statutory notices of more than a certain age even if the notice has not been obtempered. These, then, are the limitations, but property certificates are nonetheless enormously useful.

Roads

The purchaser will be concerned about the road outside his new house in two respects. He wishes to be sure that he has a right of access, and he will not wish to have to maintain the road at his own expense. If the road is a publicly maintained road it will also be a public right of way. But the converse does not always hold good, in that some public rights of way are private as far as upkeep is concerned. Private rights of way, *i.e.* servitude roads, are of course privately maintained. The property inquiry certificates will

with the Law Society, issue an annual *Directory of Information for Property Certificates* which sets forth the division of responsibilities between councils, gives addresses, the current fee charged, and so forth.

[18] For a cautionary tale see 1992 J.L.S. 408.

[19] *Runciman* v. *Borders Regional Council*, 1988 S.L.T. 135.

show whether the road is publicly maintained, which it usually is. If it is not publicly maintained, the client will be liable for upkeep, and moreover it will be necessary to inquire whether there is a right of access, either public or private (by servitude).

Roads can be divided into those in which there is a public right of way, and those where no such right exists. Use of the latter is based on ownership of the road itself, or on the existence of a servitude over it. Roads are sometimes called "public" or "private" according to this classification. However the public/private distinction is also applied in a different way, according to whether the roadway is maintained at public or private expense. Private roads (in the sense of no public right of way) are naturally maintained at private expense. But public roads (*i.e.* public right of way) are sometimes maintained at public expense and sometimes at private expense, and the expressions "public road" and "private road" are often used in this latter sense. It is this latter usage which is employed in the Roads (Scotland) Act 1984, which is the main Act.[20] It is the "roads authority" which is responsible for the upkeep of roads which are public in the latter sense. The roads authority is the local authority for most roads, and the Secretary of State for "trunk" roads.

Where a road is constructed by a roads authority, the land on which the road is built will first have been acquired by the authority either by agreement or by compulsory purchase. Such roads are public from their birth. But many roads are built by private builders in the course of developing a housing estate. These begin life as private roads, but the idea is that, by the time the development is completed, the roads authority will have taken them over. By section 16 of the Roads (Scotland) 1984, a roads authority must "take over" a road[21] provided it is built to a sufficient standard. It used to be a worry, in buying a new house, that the builder might become insolvent before completing the development, so that the bill for making up the road would have to be picked up by the houseowners. To meet this risk builders commonly obtained a com-

[20] Section 151(1) defines "road." On this see *Viewpoint Housing Association* v. *Lothian Regional Council*, 1991 G.W.D. 39–2408.

[21] *i.e.* assume responsibility for upkeep. A road which has been taken over is thus a public road in the second sense. The statute is not clearly drafted, but the idea is that if a road is taken over, it thereby becomes public in both senses.

mercial guarantee (called a road bond) to cover the costs of completing the roads. Nowadays the problem has been more or less solved by section 17 of the 1984 Act and regulations made thereunder[22] which provide that no building work can begin until the developer grants a road bond in favour of the local authority.[23] There are potential liabilities if the road outside (*ex adverso*) the newly purchased house has not been taken over by the council. For if the road is public in the sense of being subject to a public right of way, which it usually will be, the council can require the purchaser, as a "frontager," to maintain both the road and the pavement.[24] And even if there is no public right of way the road will require a certain amount of upkeep if it is to remain passable.

Who owns the *solum* beneath the road? There are three main possibilities. (1) It may belong to the roads authority. This will usually be the case with trunk roads and other major roads. (2) It may belong to the frontagers, in sections. When houses are built—or plots sold for building—the boundaries between individual properties are often the centre line of the road. And this ownership is not affected by the road subsequently being taken over by the local authority for maintenance. (3) It may belong to the original developer or his successors (who may also be the superior of the houses), simply because on conveying the houses he never parted with ownership of the *solum* of the road. Often it can be difficult to find out who owns the *solum*. Ownership is seldom of much practical significance except when a road is "stopped up" by the roads authority so that the former road becomes available for other purposes. By section 115 of the 1984 Act, ownership of a stopped-up road vests in the frontagers "subject to the prior claim of any person by reason of title."[25]

[22] Security for Private Road Works (Scotland) Regulations 1985 (S.I. 1985 No. 2080).

[23] But some developers flout the law and fail to obtain a road bond. Unfortunately, it is precisely this type of cowboy that is most likely to become insolvent, at which point the absence of a road bond becomes a disaster. So an offer for a house being built should still stipulate that a road bond exists and must be exhibited.

[24] Roads (Scotland) Act 1984, s.13.

[25] Presumably this is to cover the case where ownership is vested in another party such as the original developer or his successors—case 3 in the text.

Sewage

The purchaser will normally expect public sewage provision and indeed public water, electricity and gas. In towns this may usually be taken for granted (except for gas), but in the countryside there may be no public supply and each public utility has its own rules about entitlement. Where public provision is made, the rule is usually that the local authority (or other utility) will bring the resource in question up to the property but the cost of making and maintaining connections remains with the owner.

Sewage is governed by the Sewerage (Scotland) Act 1968. By section 1 of the Act the local authority must construct adequate sewers. Note that if impatient developers construct the sewers themselves, they cannot recover the cost in recompense.[26] The obligation to construct adequate sewers is qualified (section 1(3)) by the proviso that nothing need be done "which is not practicable at a reasonable cost." So in many rural areas there is no public system, and the outflow drains into a septic tank. If the tank is located in a neighbouring property, which it sometimes is, a servitude of drainage is necessary.[27]

Water

Water supply is the responsibility of the local authority, and is governed by the Water (Scotland) Act 1980, section 6 of which imposes a general duty (but subject to a reasonable cost proviso) to supply wholesome water for domestic purposes. As with sewage, in some rural areas there will be no public supply, with the owner taking water from a well or from a burn. If the private water supply comes from an adjacent property, it should be established by the appropriate servitudes.[28]

[26] *Varney (Scotland) Ltd.* v. *Burgh of Lanark*, 1974 S.C. 245.

[27] The relevant servitude appears to be "sinks," which is the servitude right to discharge foul water into a neighbouring property. See, *e.g.*, *Cochrane* v. *Ewart* (1861) 4 Macq. 117.

[28] Of *aquaehaustus*—the right to water from a source in another property, and of *aquaeductus*, also called watergang—the right to pipe water across or underneath another's land.

Electricity and gas

Electricity and gas are not a matter for local authorities, and so will not be covered by the property inquiry certificates. In practice, the purchasing client will generally know whether or not there are mains gas and electricity. Gas is supplied by British Gas and regulated by the Gas Act 1986. Electricity is supplied by Scottish Power or Scottish Hydro Electric and is regulated by the Electricity Act 1989. British Gas is under a statutory duty to supply any premises within a specified (short) distance from a pre-existing mains. But there is a great deal of discretion about the establishment of new mains, and in areas outwith the main towns and cities it will often be found that there is no public gas supply. Electricity companies have a general duty to supply electricity but once again subject to a reasonableness test.[29]

Statutory notices

Local authorities have wide-ranging statutory powers to require the repair or demolition of buildings.[30] There are a number of different statutory provisions, but most work in much the same way. First the council is alerted to a defective building either by its own inspectors or, very often in the case of tenement property, by a telephone call from a proprietor who cannot persuade the other owners to carry out repairs. The council then serves on the proprietor or proprietors of the building a formal statutory notice which requires specified works to be carried out within a specified (and usually short) time. The notice must specify adequately the work to be carried out.[31] In the case of tenements some councils serve a

[29] See, further, the *Stair Memorial Encyclopaedia*, vol. 9, pp. 354–402 and 472–497.

[30] Chiefly under the Building (Scotland) Act 1959, the Housing (Scotland) Act 1987, and the Civic Government (Scotland) Act 1982. See C. Himsworth, *Public Sector Housing Law in Scotland*, (3rd ed., W. Green, 1989) for a useful summary.

[31] In practice, the specification is sometimes vague. It is, however, unusual for the notice to be challenged. For an example of a successful challenge see *Gardner* v. *City of Edinburgh District Council*, 1991 S.L.T. 1149.

notice on all the proprietors in the building even for repairs which concern only one or more individual flats.[32]

There is a right of appeal against the notice, usually to the sheriff, but the right must be exercised with the statutory time limit which, typically, is 21 days.[32a] Once a notice is served the proprietors must carry out the work. If they fail to do so the council may and often does instruct contractors to do the necessary work,[33] recovering the cost from the proprietors. The amount then due to the council can be secured by a charging order (a statutory heritable security) on the building. It is always more expensive in the end if the council has to carry out the work but, particularly in a tenement, the proprietors may be unable to reach agreement on carrying out the work themselves.

If the property is subject to a statutory notice, the purchaser's agent must find out more details. If the notice has been complied with, well and good. If the notice is about to be complied with, that is also acceptable provided that there is clear agreement that the seller is to pay the costs.[34] The main problem which arises is where the notice has not been complied with and the council has, or is about to, carry out the work itself. Thereafter the council is entitled to recover the cost from the new owner,[35] and there seems to be no satisfactory right of relief under the general law.[35a] Therefore, if the agreement is that the seller is to be liable, this should be stated expressly in the missives.

Offers vary considerably as to how they handle the possibility of statutory notices. A common approach is for the seller to be asked to warrant that there are no such notices at the time of missives, and that any notices issued between missives and entry shall be the seller's responsibility. If there is an existing notice the

[32] They are entitled to do this: *University of Edinburgh* v. *City of Edinburgh District Council*, 1987 S.L.T. (Sh. Ct.) 103; *City of Edinburgh District Council* v. *Gardner*, 1990 S.L.T. 600. See, further, K.G.C. Reid at 1990 J.L.S. 368.

[32a] On rights of appeal, see *Norcross* v. *Kirkcaldy District Council*, 1993 G.W.D. 3–146.

[33] *Crawford* v. *City of Edinburgh District Council*, 1993 G.W.D. 21–1270. In practice, however, councils often delay taking this step for long periods.

[34] As with all missive clauses there is the danger of eventual supersession. The liability of the seller should thus not normally be limited by the standard two-year period.

[35] *Purves* v. *City of Edinburgh District Council*, 1987 S.L.T. 366; *Pegg* v. *City of Glasgow District Council*, 1988 S.L.T. (Sh. Ct.) 49.

[35a] See the discussion of the obligation of relief clause in chap. 9.

seller's agent will so state in the qualified acceptance, and this may then lead to an agreement that the seller will be responsible for the costs. Further provision is sometimes made that in the latter event there shall be a retention from the purchase price of enough money to cover the costs, this sum to be put on deposit receipt in the joint names of the agents.[36] A simpler solution is simply to agree to reduce the purchase price by the amount of the estimated costs, which will then be the responsibility of the purchaser.[37]

The main statutory notices are, in order of seriousness[38]:

(a) Dangerous buildings

If a building is actually dangerous, whether to its occupants or to the public at large, the council can serve a notice under section 13 of the Building (Scotland) Act 1959 (commonly called "a section 13 notice") requiring the owner either to demolish the building or to secure and repair it. The work required by a section 13 notice must be begun within seven days and completed within the period specified in the notice.

(b) Buildings not of tolerable standard

"Tolerable standard" is concerned less with structural stability than with the provision of basic facilities, and is defined in section 86(1) of the Housing (Scotland) Act 1987. Where a house falls below the tolerable standard the council has a choice of courses of action.[39] (1) It may serve an improvement order requiring the owner to bring the house up to tolerable standard within 180 days.[40] (2)

[36] This is to cover the danger that the seller might later prove unsueable. The retention is often augmented by, *e.g.* 25 per cent to cover cost overruns. When the work is finished and paid for the proceeds of the deposit receipt are then paid to the seller. If, however, the work is not done the purchaser will wish to obtain the contents of the deposit receipt and this can cause technical difficulties.

[37] Logically, the purchase price offered should already have taken account of the state of the building. A building in poor repair will attract lower bids than a building in good repair. In practice, however, purchasers usually take into account only imminent repair bills in making their bids.

[38] For background see Chris Himsworth, *Public Sector Housing Law in Scotland* (3rd ed., W. Green, 1989).

[39] s. 85(1).

[40] s. 88.

It may serve a demolition order.[41] (3) Where a demolition order would be appropriate but for the fact that the house forms part of a larger building in which the other houses are satisfactory it may serve a closing order which prevents the house being used for human habitation.[42] Closing and demolition orders can be revoked or suspended, at the council's discretion, where either the house is brought up to the tolerable standard or where the owner plausibly undertakes to do so. Where a number of houses in the same area are substandard the council can declare a Housing Action Area, which gives it additional powers, including the power of compulsory purchase, and which removes the need for individual statutory notices.[43]

(c) Buildings in disrepair

This is the commonest in modern practice, especially in tenement property. There are two alternative statutory provisions, section 87 of the Civic Government (Scotland) Act 1982 and section 108 of the Housing (Scotland) Act 1987.[44] Some councils tend to use the 1982 Act and others the 1987 Act.

5. Planning Permission

Planning law is a large subject in its own right[45] and the treatment here is necessarily brief. Planning permission is required for any significant building work and for certain changes of use. The concerns of the purchaser's agent are:

(1) *Whether planning permission has been obtained for the present buildings, and for their present use.* Property inquiry certificates will very probably not disclose the answers to these questions, except in the unusual situation of an enforcement notice having been served. So it is important to find out whether there has been

[41] s. 115.

[42] s. 114.

[43] ss. 89–92.

[44] Replacing, with some changes, s.24 of the Housing (Scotland) Act 1969. In practice s. 108 notices are thus sometimes still called "s.24 notices."

[45] See E. Young and J. Rowan-Robinson, *Scottish Planning Law and Procedure* (Hodge, 1985). See also the journal *Scottish Planning Law and Practice.*

any significant and recent building works and, if so, whether permission was obtained. The seller should know.

(2) *Whether any conditions are attached to the grant of planning permission, and if so, whether they are being observed.* In commercial developments there may also be section 50 agreements.[46]

(3) *Whether the building is listed, or in a conservation area.*[47] The property certificates usually reveal this. One of the many consequences of being in a conservation area is that demolition requires permission. Outwith such areas an owner is generally free to demolish without permission, except where the property is listed, or is an ancient monument.

(4) *Whether the subjects are affected, directly or indirectly, by planning applications for neighbouring property.* For instance the next-door neighbour may have applied for, or even obtained, planning permission to build 10 flats in his garden, overlooking the house being purchased. The property inquiry certificates will not normally disclose this. If the purchaser wishes this checked, it will have to be done as an extra request to the council. Apart from that, the missives will normally require the seller to warrant that he has received no notification of any planning application for neighbouring subjects. The local authority's right to object to breaches of planning permission generally prescribes after four years,[48] but there are exceptions.

6. Building Control

Building control[49] is concerned with the nuts and bolts (so to speak) of building and not with aesthetics. The governing legislation is the Building (Scotland) Act 1959 as amended (principally by the Build-

[46] Town and Country Planning (Scotland) Act 1972, s. 50. See J. Rowan-Robinson and E. Young, *Planning by Agreement in Scotland* (W. Green, 1989).

[47] These are very common. Thus, at the time of writing there are 30 such areas in the City of Edinburgh District alone, with a further six areas being considered for designation.

[48] Town and Country Planning (Scotland) Act 1972, s.84(3).

[49] Very little has been written on this important subject. But see Johnstone at 1989 J.L.S. 206, and Sutherland "Surveyor's View of Building Warrants and Planning Permission," General Conveyancing P.Q.L.E., November 1989. See also the papers from the P.Q.L.E. seminars on Unauthorised Alterations (June and November, 1991).

ing (Scotland) Act 1970) together with delegated legislation made under that Act.

When is a building warrant required?

Section 6(1) of the 1959 Act provides that: "No person shall . . . in any place conduct any operations for the construction or demolition of a building of a class to which the building standards regulations apply . . . unless there has been obtained from the buildings authority a warrant."

The buildings authority is the local authority. "Construction" includes altering, erecting, extending and fitting.[50] The current Building Standards (Scotland) Regulations, passed in 1990[51] and in force from April 1, 1991, run to many hundreds of pages and are incomprehensible except to experts, and they apply not just to the initial construction of buildings but to a whole host of fairly minor operations, for example, altering windows.[52] By section 6(1) of the Act a building warrant must be obtained whenever the regulations apply. In practice, warrants are almost always obtained for major works, *e.g.* the construction of a new house or major alterations to an existing house. But until recently they have not usually been obtained for minor alterations. One reason for this is ignorance: most people do not know that a warrant is needed. Tradesmen may know, but may not tell their customer. A second reason is that, even where people are aware in general terms about building warrants they may be uncertain as to precisely what does and what does not require a warrant. And no wonder. The rules are technical and obscure. They are also confusing: thus double glazing requires a warrant where the *type* of window is being altered but not otherwise. In a welcome attempt to meet this difficulty, some councils now issue explanatory leaflets. Thirdly, councils in practice seldom enforce the law in relation to minor alterations. And finally, and partly because of the infrequency of the applications, no special administrative procedure exists for where the work is minor, so that the applicant who wishes to move a sink a few feet must submit the same forms and detailed drawings as the applicant who

[50] Building (Scotland) Act 1959, s.29(9).
[51] S.I. 1990 No. 2179.
[52] Even where no warrant is needed, alterations must still conform to regulations.

wishes to build an entire house.[53] In practice, it is difficult to get a warrant without professional help in preparing the application, preferably from an architect. This is expensive, so that for minor works the expense of the application may exceed the cost of the work itself.

Completion certificates

The building warrant must be obtained before work is started, and it will not be granted unless the proposed work appears to conform to the building standards regulations. On completion, the work is inspected by a building inspector and if it appears to conform to the original warrant and to the building regulations a completion certificate is granted in the statutory form. The certificate is qualified by the words "so far as they are able to ascertain after taking all reasonable steps" and should not be regarded as a guarantee that all is well. There will be much that the inspector has been unable to see and this is so even where, as with the construction of a new house, several visits are made during the course of building.

Consequences of failure to obtain a warrant or certificate

There are two possible consequences of failing to comply with the above rules. First, it is an offence to carry out the work in the first place without a warrant,[54] and it is also an offence to occupy or use the building without a completion certificate. Secondly, the local authority can serve a notice under section 10 of the 1959 Act requiring either that the new work be demolished or that it be brought up to current building regulations standard. In practice, the local authority may never take any enforcement action, but this does not mean that there will be no problem, partly because the unauthorised work may be unsound and eventually have to be repaired, altered or even demolished even without any official action, and partly because when the owner comes to sell he may find that prospective purchasers object to the lack of building consent.

[53] See the Building (Procedure) (Scotland) Regulations 1981 (S.I. 1981 No. 1499).

[54] Building (Scotland) Act 1959, s. 6(1). However, prosecutions seem to be almost unknown in practice.

Will purchasers find out the truth?

For a long time now, missives have contained a clause to the effect that building consents have been obtained where required. But while solicitors acting for purchasers checked building consents for major works, they did not usually bother about minor works. But practice began to change about the middle of the 1980s. The main reason for this was a change in the attitude of surveyors. As a result of negligence claims, surveyors have become more defensive. As well as inserting exclusion of liability clauses in their reports, they now tend to mention items which once might not have been thought worth commenting on, including evidence of recent works which might have required building consent.

The typical pattern is as follows. A client wishes buy a house. The intended lender instructs a valuation survey, which discloses that alterations have been made and that building consents should be verified. The buyer's solicitor writes to the seller's solicitor. The seller's solicitor writes to his client. His client says he has never heard of building warrants and completion certificates. In other words the property suffers from the problem of unauthorised alterations.[55] (If the alterations also required planning consent, that also may turn out to be absent.) The matter must be put right, partly because the lender will so insist,[56] and also for the other reasons mentioned earlier. Unauthorised alterations are common. No one knows what proportion of the housing stock is affected in this way, but almost certainly 25 per cent is and possibly over 50 per cent. The reason that no one knows is that minor alterations are often effectively invisible: how can one tell that the windows are not the original ones? The purchaser's surveyor will not pick this up and so the purchaser himself and his solicitor will be happily unaware. Indeed, in practice, if there is some unauthorised alteration, and the survey does not disclose it, it is very unlikely ever to

[55] The problem is sometimes that there was no warrant (in which case there will, of course, be no completion certificate). Sometimes there was a warrant but no certificate. This latter case is still serious because there is no evidence that the work actually done was in conformity with the warrant.

[56] If the amount to be lent is much less than the value of the property, the lender is really at no risk, but nevertheless such is the modern practice.

come to light at all.[57] It will be seen that the existence of unauthorised alterations normally comes to light at survey stage, which will be before conclusion of missives. Hence the problem can be dealt with in the missives themselves. Occasionally it comes to light after missives, and sometimes even after settlement.

If the problem comes to light after missives, then the question of whether the purchaser has any remedy obviously depends on what the missives say. Usually there will have been a clause whereby the seller warrants that there are no unauthorised alterations. In that case, if settlement has yet to take place, the purchaser can refuse to settle until the matter is put right. If settlement has already taken place, the seller can normally be made liable for the costs of putting the matter right, though here there is always the danger that the missives may have been superseded.

Sometimes a seller will take a hard line, saying that the property is being sold on an as-is basis, and that the purchaser must take it or leave it. In other words he will refuse to accept any missive clause imposing any liability on him. Whether the purchaser is willing to accept this is up to him, though if he is granting a standard security the lender may determine the decision. In practice, if the alterations are minor or old, or where it is clear that the works did in fact meet building standards even though no consents were actually obtained, it may make sense to accept the situation.

What can be done?

Assuming that the problem has come to light before settlement, and assuming that the missives are in standard form, what can be done by the seller? There are three possible solutions which the seller can adopt to deal with the absence of building warrants and/or completion certificates:

(1) Obtain retrospective consents from the council.[58] Some people make a living out of obtaining these – their advertisements appear in the *Journal of the Law Society of Scotland* every month. The whole process is likely to take months rather than weeks and

[57] It can happen that someone buys a house, and no unauthorised alterations are apparent. Later when he sells, the new buyer's surveyor notices that there have been such alterations. The loss will then usually fall on the first buyer, unless he can prove negligence against his surveyor or his solicitors.

[58] Not all councils are happy to do this.

will cost money. The costs will not be too high unless the council insists on remedial work being done before consents are issued. One of the difficulties is that the work may have complied with earlier versions of the building standards regulations but not with the current version.

(2) Obtain a "letter of comfort" from the council, *i.e.* a letter stating that enforcement proceedings will not be taken. This is the cheapest solution, although it may still be necessary to employ an architect to make representations to the council. But not all councils are willing to issue such letters – although the numbers have increased thanks to persuasion by the Law Society.[59] A purchaser is not, however, bound to accept such a letter but can insist that the full terms of the missives be honoured.

(3) Apply for a relaxation of the building regulations in relation to the alterations in question.[60] This is only likely to be an attractive solution where expensive remedial work would otherwise be required to comply with the regulations.

How far back need one go?

The agent for the purchaser will need to see both building warrant and completion certificate for all works which require them. But for how long? For works in the last 10 years? Or 20 years? Or 50 years? Or 100 years? This question is not easily answered for, unlike planning permission, there is no four-year, non-enforcement rule. Some help may be had from long negative prescription: it is arguable that the obligation to obtain a building warrant or completion certificate prescribes after 20 years. But even if the prescription argument is correct, it may not be a complete solution. For occupying or using the property without a completion certificate is a criminal offence which is, it seems, committed afresh every day, and so the criminal aspect would presumably not be subject to prescription. Moreover, section 11 of the 1959 Act gives the council the power to require buildings *at any time* to conform to current

[59] Which has been very concerned about the whole issue. It has been liaising with the local authorities and there is the possibility of legislation to improve matters.

[60] Building (Scotland) Act 1959, s. 4 as amended by the Building (Scotland) Act 1970; Building Standards (Relaxation by Local Authorities) (Scotland) Regulations 1985 (S.I. 1985 No. 1272).

building regulations where this is necessary for "health, safety and convenience."

There are practical difficulties about going back too far. Although councils maintain registers of building warrants and completion certificates, these generally do not go back beyond local government reorganisation in 1975.[61] So if building consent was granted in, say, 1973, but the documents have been lost by the owner, it may be effectively impossible to prove the true situation.

Since there is no clear legal cut-off period, there is no logically defensible place to stop, so that in the purchase of a flat in Edinburgh's New Town one might in theory need to see the original Dean of Guild consents for its construction in 1788 plus consents for all subsequent alterations.[62] But this of course would be absurd. Missives in practice vary considerably on this point. Some have no cut-off period. Some cover the period back to 1959. Others have a 20-year cut-off and others a 10-year period.[63] Others again cover the period in which the building has been in the ownership of the present seller. The agent for the seller should certainly resist an unlimited period, and our own view is that a 10-year period is reasonable. As the law stands there is no correct solution. There is also the obvious practical difficulty of showing that an alteration (for which no documentation exists) was indeed done outwith the defined period.

7. Risk

Risk concerns liability for accidental damage to the subjects of sale in the interval between conclusion of the contract (for precontractual damage see below) and the transfer of ownership.[64] By "accidental" damage is meant damage which is not the fault of either party to the contract. For heritable property the common law rule[65]

[61] Such records generally still exist but are often effectively unsearchable.

[62] For although the current law is regulated by the Building (Scotland) Act 1959, as amended, the need for building consent has existed for hundreds of years. Before 1975 consents were given (in burghs) by the Dean of Guild Court. Such consent originally bore the curious name of the "jedge and warrant of the Dean of Guild."

[63] This is done in the Law Society's standard form of offer.

[64] For an interesting study see A.D.M. Forte, "Must a Purchaser Buy Charred Remains?" (1984) 19 Irish Jurist 1.

[65] *Sloans Dairies Ltd.* v. *Glasgow Corporation*, 1977 S.C. 223.

is that risk passes from the seller to the buyer when the contract of sale is concluded, except where there is a suspensive condition, when, it seems, risk does not pass until its purification. But this rule may be altered by agreement, and this almost always happens in practice, so that risk does not usually pass until the date of settlement. The Scottish Law Commission has recommended that the law be brought into line with practice so that risk passes at settlement unless otherwise agreed.[66] There are thus two possibilities, namely that the risk remains with seller until settlement, and that it passes to the purchaser on conclusion of the contract.

If risk remains with seller

Current practice is almost always that risk stays with the seller. What happens then if the house is accidentally damaged after the conclusion of missives but before settlement? The purchaser could probably rescind if the damage is major, though the law is not quite clear, so that it is common for the point to be covered specifically in the missives. Alternatively he could enforce the contract by insisting that the seller repair the damage (the expense of which will typically be paid by the seller's insurance company). Note that this second remedy will disappear if the recent Law Commission recommendation is adopted to the effect that substantial damage to the property should be regarded as frustrating the contract.

If risk passes to the buyer

Occasionally, the common law position is not altered and risk passes to the buyer as soon as the contract is concluded. This means that he might have to buy charred remains. The fact that risk has passed does not relieve the seller from a duty to take reasonable care of the property. For risk concerns accidental destruction only: if the seller is at fault, he must pay.[67–68]

[66] *Report on the Passing of Risk in Contracts for the Sale of Heritable Property* (Scot. Law Com. No. 127, 1990).

[67–68] This rule was applied in *Meehan* v. *Silver*, 1972 S.L.T. (Sh. Ct.) 70 even though settlement had been delayed and the damage happened after the contractual date of entry. But a different view was expressed, without reference to *Meehan*, in *Chapman's Trs.* v. *Anglo-Scottish Group Services Ltd.*, 1980 S.L.T. (Sh. Ct.) 27 at 28.

Insurance

As soon as risk passes, the buyer should have insurance cover. If he is obtaining a loan, the lender will normally arrange cover. Otherwise, the purchaser's solicitor must do this. Temporary cover can be obtained by phoning an insurance broker, and thereafter the client will have to complete a proposal form.

Moveables

A typical house purchase will include some moveables, such as carpets, and here the legal presumption as to risk is different, risk not passing until the passing of ownership: Sale of Goods Act 1979, section 20. There may be difficulty in establishing when ownership of the moveables passes.[69] But section 20 of the 1979 Act can be contracted out of, and missive clauses which provide that risk passes at settlement are often so worded as to cover moveables.

Precontractual damage

Damage prior to conclusion of the contract is not governed by risk. But such damage occurs more often than might be thought. Thus, suppose that after viewing a house a client makes an offer for it. The offer is accepted in principle but it takes three weeks for missives to be concluded, during which time the house is damaged by fire. What then is the position? The answer seems to be that, unless the contract provides otherwise, the purchaser has no remedy and must accept the house in its damaged state. For until the contract is concluded, the seller has no duty of care to the buyer; and the purchaser's error as to the physical state of the house is unilateral and uninduced. Missives sometimes have a clause stipulating that the subjects must be in substantially the same state at settlement as at conclusion of missives,[69a] but this will be of no help, since the damage was already in place at conclusion of missives. One way

[69] On one view, if the missives make no special provision as to passing of the ownership of the moveables, ownership will pass at missives: Sale of Goods Act 1979, s. 18, r.1. As against this, it could be argued that ownership passes at settlement since this must be presumed to be the intention of the parties: s.17(1).

[69a] *Hall* v. *McWilliam*, 1993 G.W.D. 23–1457.

of dealing with the danger is to use such a clause but making the date of the original offer the reference date for the condition of the property.

8. Warranties of Quality

The seller warrants the title but he does not usually warrant the physical state of the subjects of sale.[70] The rule here is *caveat emptor*: it is for the buyer to have the property surveyed. While the parties are free to insert into the missives warranties as to physical quality, this was seldom done until the late 1970s, since when the practice has steadily increased. The items typically covered are the central heating, dry and wet rot, and woodworm. Sometimes there are other items such as gas and wiring and damp.[71] The seller is sometimes asked to give an absolute guarantee (which he should generally resist) and sometimes a guarantee that these items are satisfactory as far as he is aware. This latter formula is generally regarded as reasonable. Often there will be a further provision, typically inserted in the qualified acceptance, that the buyer must notify any defects within, say, seven days after entry, failing which he will be deemed to have waived his rights. A common problem with these clauses is that the seller may have lived happily with his central heating for years, regarding it as being in reasonably good working order, while the purchaser sees all sorts of defects. Hence disputes.

There is no perfect way of drafting such clauses. What is vital is that both clients be aware of the position. Thus, if the missives are silent as to the plumbing, the purchaser must know this, so that if he finds the plumbing to be defective, he cannot complain. In general, a buyer of a second-hand house is in the same position as the purchaser of anything else second-hand, such as a car. There is always the risk of defects. To the extent that a purchaser wishes to take no risks, he must have surveys done. If he is worried about, say, the plumbing, he may need to have a plumber visit the property before missives are concluded.

[70] See chap. 1.

[71] Damp may be rising damp (from the ground), or penetrating damp (rain or snow meltwater coming through the roof, walls, *etc.*) or condensing damp (water vapour bedewing surfaces on a serious scale).

9. Rot

An offer will typically require the seller to warrant that as far as he knows there is no timber rot, and that if rot eradication has been carried out there is a valid guarantee which will be transferred to the buyer.[72] The latter part of such a clause seems rather pointless since such guarantees are in practice never assigned, either because they are non-assignable or because they enure to the benefit of future owners without need of assignation. Moreover, such a clause is odd in as much as a seller who never obtained a guarantee is in a better position, in this respect, than one who did. It also seems unreasonable for the seller to warrant the guarantee to be completely valid, and in addition it is unclear what his liability would be if the guarantee were defective.

10. Matrimonial Homes Act

The provisions in missives about occupancy rights under the Matrimonial Homes (Family Protection) (Scotland) Act 1981 are considered separately in Chapter 8.

11. Property Transfer Orders

Section 8 of the Family Law (Scotland) Act 1985[73] empowers the court in divorce actions to make an order for the transfer of property from one party to the marriage to the other. "Property" includes heritable property. The risk for a purchaser of a matrimonial home is that the court might have made such an order. Does this matter? The answer is that it depends. For a property transfer order is not in itself a conveyance but merely a direction that one spouse transfer the house to the other spouse. It confers on the transferee spouse a personal right akin to a right under missives. Both the purchaser and the transferee spouse are entitled to a disposition. Whoever registers one first will become owner. But if that person is in bad faith *and* if his personal right is the later of the

[72] See, *e.g.*, clause C6 of the Law Society's standard style.

[73] As amended by Sched. 8, para. 34 to the Law Reform (Miscellaneous Provisions) (Scotland) Act 1990.

two, his title is voidable at the instance of the other.[74] There is little to worry about here in practice. Sales in defiance of a property transfer order are as rare as other fraudulent double sales. No special provision is required in missives – it is covered by the good and marketable title obligation – though in practice it is quite common to put in a special clause.[75] The Act also empowers the court to make "incidental orders" in relation to matrimonial property, but from the list of these given in section 14 it is difficult to see how they could affect a purchaser.

12. Payment of Deposit

Payment of a deposit at conclusion of missives is not usually required, except in commercial conveyancing. If it is required, and the sale aborts due to the fault of the purchaser, it probably cannot be recovered, unless the missives otherwise provide.[76]

13. Content of Disposition

In general, a seller is only bound to grant, and a purchaser is only bound to accept, a disposition drawn up in the "usual" form.[77] Therefore, if either party wishes the disposition to contain something extra, this must be stipulated for expressly in missives. It is for this reason that express provision is always made for the inclusion of a non-supersession clause.

[74] This is the "off-side goals rule" as to which see *Rodger (Builders) Ltd.* v. *Fawdry*, 1950 S.C. 451 and *Stair Memorial Encyclopaedia*, vol. 18, paras. 695 *et seq*. On the whole question see D.J. Cusine at 1990 J.L.S. 52.

[75] See, *e.g.* the Law Society standard style clause A1.

[76] See *Zemhunt (Holdings) Ltd.* v. *Control Securities Ltd.*, 1992 S.L.T. 151.

[77] See *Corbett* v. *Robertson* (1872) 10 M. 329. The point seems to have been overlooked in *Morris* v. *Ritchie*, 1991 G.W.D. 12–712.

Chapter 4

MISSIVES III: BREACH OF CONTRACT

Introduction

This chapter deals with breach of contract prior to settlement. What happens if, after settlement, a remedy is sought for breach of contract, is considered elsewhere.[1]

The terms of missives of sale can be divided into two types, namely, warranties and positive obligations. In a warranty, the seller guarantees that certain facts are true. But there is no accompanying obligation to make them true. A typical example would be: "The central heating system shall be in good working order as at the date of entry." In a positive obligation (*i.e.* an obligation *ad factum praestandum*) the party undertakes to do something positive, such as to pay the purchase price or to deliver a clear search. Sometimes it is possible to rewrite warranties as positive obligations, *e.g.*, "The seller will ensure that the central heating system is in good working order as at the date of entry." In general, this is advantageous to the purchaser because positive obligations are usually easier to enforce. Sometimes too the two types are combined in a single clause. Thus, in *Porch* v. *Macleod*[2] there was the following clause: "All necessary consents . . . have been obtained and complied with for any work undertaken on the subjects or for any use thereof and satisfactory evidence to substantiate this will be exhibited to us before and delivered at the date of entry."

In domestic conveyancing, payment of the price is often the only obligation on the purchaser, the remaining obligations being the responsibility of the seller. But, so far as breach is concerned, the same general principles apply regardless of where the obligation lies.[3]

[1] Chap. 19.

[2] 1992 S.L.T. 661.

[3] This applies to ordinary contractual terms and not to suspensive conditions. The latter, unlike the former, do not normally impose obligations.

Missives are of course binding in the period up to settlement. But after settlement missives are enforceable only to the extent that they have been kept alive. This is dealt with elsewhere, as is the post-settlement right of a purchaser against a seller under the law of warrandice.[4]

This chapter is divided into four parts. The first two parts consider the two methods of responding to breach of contract, namely (1) pulling out and (2) keeping going but claiming damages. The third part considers the particular problems which arise where the breach leads to a delay in settlement. The last part deals with settlement by special agreement, varying the terms of the missives.

1. Pulling Out

Sometimes the client changes his mind about the sale, even after missives are concluded, and wishes to pull out, in which case his agent may find himself casting around for excuses for rescission. But usually a client will not wish to withdraw from a contract unless the breach by the other party is very serious, such as the persistent failure of a purchaser to come up with the money or failure of a seller to produce an acceptable title. Most clients will thus not wish to exercise a right to rescind the moment it emerges, but will hope that the deal can be put back together. A purchaser may be willing to disregard altogether some defect (*e.g.* in title) and will rely on his solicitor to evaluate its seriousness. Note, however, that if a secured lender is involved in the purchase, the decision to disregard defects must be cleared with the lender as well as with the purchaser.

Pulling out can happen in more than one way. The basic classification is repudiation (by the guilty party) and rescission (by the innocent one.)[5] Sometimes the missives may expressly provide for withdrawal under certain defined circumstances. It is unclear what name should be given to that.

[4] See chap. 19.

[5] See McBryde, *Contract*, chap. 14 for analysis.

Repudiation

One party may repudiate the contract, *i.e.* declare that he does not intend to perform. Unless the repudiation is justified,[6] it gives the other party an option: to accept the repudiation, which will end the contract and normally give rise to a claim for damages, or to reject the repudiation and insist on performance.[7] *Grant* v. *Ullah*[8] is a simple and standard example of repudiation by a buyer who was unable to come up with the money. The innocent party should indicate which option he wishes to adopt. (In most cases he will accept the repudiation.) If he fails to indicate his attitude, problems can arise as to whether he has implicitly accepted or rejected the repudiation.

Rescission: positive obligations

Unless the defaulting party repudiates the contract, the mere fact that he has failed to perform a positive obligation timeously does not of itself entitle the other party to bring the contract to an end. For, except in the two special cases noted below, time is not of the essence in a contract of sale and the defaulting party must be given a reasonable time to perform the obligation which he has undertaken (and hitherto failed) to perform. Only after the expiry of a "reasonable time" does the breach become material, permitting rescission.[9]

The normal method of dealing with default is to employ the ultimatum procedure laid down in *Rodger (Builders) Limited* v. *Fawdry*.[10] The chronology of this procedure is as follows.

[6] In which case it would not normally be called "repudiation."

[7] Compare *White & Carter (Councils) Ltd.* v. *McGregor*, 1962 S.C. (H.L.) 1.

[8] 1987 S.L.T. 639.

[9] In practice, conveyancers often use the term "resile" rather than "rescind." However, some contract lawyers argue that one "resiles" when one withdraws from an agreement which is not yet legally binding, and that the term "rescind" should be used where one party withdraws from a binding contract because of breach by the other party. This view has now received support in *Zemhunt (Holdings) Ltd.* v. *Control Securities plc*, 1992 S.L.T. 151. There are other possibilities as well, such as withdrawing on the basis of an express contractual right to do so in certain circumstances, or, again, withdrawing on the ground that the contract was voidable. For all such possibilities conveyancers tend to use the word "resile."

[10] 1950 S.C. 483.

(1) The date for performance of obligation passes without performance being tendered. (2) The defaulting party is then given a "reasonable time" to perform. (3) After expiry of the "reasonable time" the aggrieved party serves an ultimatum with a short expiry date. (4) If performance is still not tendered the aggrieved party may rescind. (For damages claims see below).

It has been suggested that stage (3) is not necessary provided sufficient time elapses at stage (2),[11] but in practice it is always wise to send an ultimatum. The ultimatum cannot be sent until a "reasonable time" has expired.[12] How long is "reasonable" will depend on the facts and circumstances of the individual case. In one case[13] the following time-scale was approved by the court for failure to pay the price: contractual date of entry (at which price due), December 15; ultimatum sent January 13; expiry of ultimatum on January 31. But a longer period may be necessary for other types of failure or where, as in the *Rodger (Builders)* case, ultimate performance is likely. So where a seller has applied for, say, confirmation as executor or for a local authority completion certificate, "reasonable time" probably means the time that it usually takes to obtain a document of the kind in question. There may, of course, be difficult cases and it is always open to a party to seek a declarator,[14] that he has validly rescinded the contract.

Exceptions

In practice, not being able to rescind immediately on default can be unsatisfactory. There may be good reason to believe that the other party will never perform. But unless he absolutely refuses performance (thus repudiating the contract) he must be given the benefit of the doubt, possibly for a number of months. Meanwhile, the innocent client is in a difficult situation. Sellers will be itching to re-sell to someone more reliable, and before the housing market collapses. Meanwhile, they are often paying bridging finance on another house. Buyers have the difficult decision as to whether to

[11] See *George Packman & Sons* v. *Dunbar's Trs.*, 1977 S.L.T. 140 *per* Lord Stott.

[12] Or so at least it seems. The point, however, is arguable. It is difficult to see why an ultimatum, giving a fair time for performance, should not be sent immediately on the default. Certainly this is sometimes done in practice.

[13] *Lloyds Bank* v. *Bauld*, 1976 S.L.T. (Notes) 53.

[14] As in *Lloyds Bank* v. *Bauld*, above.

take entry. On the one hand they may have nowhere else to live; but on the other hand if they do take entry and if the seller ultimately cannot perform they will have to move out again. There is a way out of these difficulties, and that is to stipulate in missives that time is of the essence of the contract. The practice is that this is nowadays almost always done in respect of payment of the price but is less common in respect of the obligations on the seller, *e.g.* the obligation to produce a good and marketable title. So far as payment of the price is concerned, the clause providing for time to be of the essence will normally make its appearance in the seller's qualified acceptance. An alternative way of doing this is to provide that if the price is not timeously paid, the seller may rescind. But care must be taken in the wording. In one case[15] sellers found themselves having to persuade the court that the phrase, "the sellers have the option immediately thereafter [*i.e.* on non-payment] to resile" meant, not that the option must be *exercised* immediately but merely that it *arose* immediately but could be exercised at any time. Sometimes the missives are so worded that the seller's right to rescind emerges not immediately on default but after a defined period, such as two weeks. Such time-of-the-essence or right-to-resile clauses commonly state that rescission is available only where the fault is exclusively on one side. This is a rule which would almost certainly be implied even though not expressed.[16]

There is one other occasion where immediate rescission is permitted. This is where the seller turns out to have no title whatsoever to the subjects or to part thereof.[17] If the seller cannot produce a title by the date of entry he is not entitled further time to acquire one.[18]

Several restrictions on the right to rescind should be noted. One is that where, as occasionally happens, entry has been taken before settlement, it is probably the law that the buyer can rescind only if *restitutio in integrum* remains possible. *Restitutio* would be

[15] *Toynar Ltd.* v. *R. & A. Properties (Fife) Ltd.*, 1989 G.W.D. 2–82. The sellers were successful.

[16] See *Davidson* v. *Tilburg Ltd.*, 1991 G.W.D. 18–1109. This is the "mutuality principle" of contract law.

[17] See *Campbell* v. *McCutcheon*, 1963 S.C. 505.

[18] The purchaser cannot, it is thought, rescind on the ground that the seller has no title, until settlement is due. A seller might have no title when missives are concluded but still be confident that he can obtain such a title in time for settlement.

barred if the purchaser made alterations to the property to any significant extent. The second is that, if a buyer delays in rescinding the contract, there may be an argument that the right to do so has been impliedly waived. On one view this should be classed as a type of homologation. Closely related to this is the case where the party with the right to rescind allows that other party to change his position in reliance on the contract. Here the right to rescind may be defeated by personal bar, on the basis of *rei interventus*.[19] Such things happen surprisingly often. One party sends out a letter of rescission as a sort of bargaining move and thereafter continues to process the transaction. Everything here depends on the exact facts, but the rescission may be held by the court to have been implicitly waived.

Rescission: warranties

A well-drawn warranty should ideally state the date as at which the particular thing is guaranteed: in missives this is usually either the date of conclusion of missives or the date of entry. Examples of warranties are provisions that there are no outstanding statutory notices, that all necessary consents have been obtained for alterations, and that there are no unusual or unduly onerous burdens. It seems that breach of a warranty, provided it is material, gives entitlement to immediate rescission.[20] For the warranty is either satisfied or it is not, and if it is not the seller is in immediate and conclusive breach. There seems no place here for the ultimatum procedure because, unlike a positive obligation, there is nothing for the seller still to do. If this is correct, then, at least in this respect, a warranty is superior to a positive obligation.[21] In practice, though, warranties often concern relatively minor matters and often the purchaser will not wish to rescind.

Damages

Rescission is often accompanied by a claim for damages. On general principles of contract law the innocent party must minimise

[19] However, some contract lawyers would not categorise this as true *rei interventus*, reserving that term for the original constitution of a contract.

[20] It seems that the point has never been expressly decided. See, however, *Morris* v. *Ritchie*, 1992 G.W.D. 33–1905.

[21] But not in other respects, *e.g.*, in relation to the non-supersession of missives.

his loss, but the duty to minimise does not begin until the contract comes to an end, *e.g.* by formal rescission, which may be some time after the contractual date of entry.[22] Under what heads can damages be recovered? There is surprisingly little case law on this very important subject, and what follows is only an educated guess.

(i) Seller in default

A purchaser who rescinds following the seller's failure to produce a good title, or other material default, will have to begin all over again finding a house. And the expenses incurred on the abortive purchase will have been wasted. The only reported case dealing with damages in this situation is *Fielding* v. *Newell*.[23] Unfortunately, the report is not very full and gives only the heads of damage which were disputed. These were: (1) Legal fees for the unsuccessful contract; (2) Survey fee; (3) Travel and accommodation costs to inspect the property; (4) Cost of telephone calls to solicitor and surveyor. The reason for the dispute was that all these expenses were incurred *prior* to the contract being concluded.[24] No final view was reached by the court, which instead allowed proof before answer.

(ii) Buyer in default

If the purchaser fails to pay, the seller will have to remarket the house. Often he will have bought another house in reliance on the sale and so will be faced with interest payments on two loans. Fortunately there is more authority here.[25–26] The following seem allowable:

(1) The shortfall (if any) on the ultimate resale. Of course in a rising market there may be profit rather than shortfall.

(2) The legal, advertising and other expenses of the abortive sale; but not the expenses of the successful resale: since the seller was always going to sell, it is only fair that he meets one set of expenses himself.[27]

(3) Assuming the house is no longer being used (the seller having

[22] *Johnstone's Exrs.* v. *Harris*, 1977 S.C. 365.

[23] 1987 S.L.T. 530.

[24] See McBryde, *Contract*, p. 477.

[25–26] *Grant* v. *Ullah*, 1987 S.L.T. 639; *Voeten* v. *Campbell Brook & Myles*, 1987 G.W.D. 26–1009; *Hopkinson* v. *Williams*, 1993 G.W.D. 14–945.

[27] *Johnstone's Exrs.* v. *Harris*, 1977 S.C. 365.

moved into his new house), the cost of running the house from the abortive date of entry until entry is taken on the resale. This includes insurance and routine maintenance. In one case the cost of employing a caretaker was not allowed as being too remote.[28]

(4) Under the general law, there is no entitlement to interest on the unpaid price unless entry was taken by the buyer, which is unusual. But missives almost invariably contain an express provision that interest is payable notwithstanding that entry has not been taken, and it was held in *Grant* v. *Ullah* that interest is due under this clause for the period between the contractual date of entry and the date on which formal rescission takes place. Some solicitors' firms go further and put in missives a clause allowing interest right up to the time of resale, but it is possible that this could be attacked as a penalty clause.

(5) It may be that little or nothing can be recovered under (4). Yet the fact that payment was not tendered on the date of entry may place the seller in financial difficulties, and this is especially so where, as often occurs, he has bought a new house in reliance on the sale of the old one. In this situation the seller will be financing two loans: on the one hand he will still be paying the mortgage on the old house, and on the other hand (the sale price not having materialised) he will be paying bridging finance on the full purchase price of the new house. This can be ruinously expensive. And it is no fault of the seller's. Can the seller recover the cost of servicing one of these loans from the purchaser?[29] In *Tiffney* v. *Bachurzewski*[30] a claim in respect of a bridging loan failed because the possibility of the seller having to bridge was said not to be within the reasonable contemplation of the parties at the date of the contract and so not allowable under the second rule in *Hadley* v. *Baxendale*.[31] Not many conveyancers—or indeed housebuyers—would accept that the possibility of bridging is as remote as this and it may be that the decision will not stand the test of time.[32]

[28] *Chapman's Trs.* v. *Anglo Scottish Group Services Ltd.*, 1980 S.L.T. (Sh. Ct.) 27.

[29] He cannot recover both, and it is not wholly clear which is appropriate.

[30] 1985 S.L.T. 165. The sale eventually proceeded to settlement, but the principles are the same. See also *Hopkinson* v. *Williams*, above.

[31] (1854) 9 Ex. 341.

[32] Oddly, the position seems to be different where it is the seller who is in default and the buyer who incurs interest charges. See *Caledonian Property Group Ltd.* v. *Queensferry Property Group Ltd.*, 1992 S.L.T. 738.

The best way to get round *Tiffney* is to ensure that the buyer knows at the time the contract was made that the seller has a mortgage or is otherwise relying on borrowed money. The possibility of interest payments will then be within his "reasonable contemplation."[33] If, as occasionally happens, the purchaser has paid a deposit, the seller may be able to keep it.[34]

2. Keeping Going

Usually the parties will try to keep the contract going. Where they succeed there are two possible outcomes. One is that the defaulting party ultimately performs in full. The other is that he does not. In the second case damages are due for non-performance. In the first case damages may be due for late performance.

Late (but complete) performance

Performance may be satisfactory but late, as where the purchaser pays the price two weeks after the date of entry, or the seller needs an extra month to obtain confirmation or a building warrant. Occasionally, the defaulting party may require the stimulus of an action of implement. But four points should be borne in mind here. First, implement is not available for warranties, for there the seller is under no positive obligation. Secondly, implement will be refused if performance is impossible (*e.g.* a defaulting seller with no title cannot be ordered to acquire one). Thirdly, by virtue of the mutuality principle, implement will not be granted if the pursuer is also in breach of contract. Finally, implement against the purchaser runs into the problem that his chief obligation is to pay money, and decree of specific implement is incompetent to compel the payment of money.[35] Where the problem is that the seller refuses to sign the disposition, the court can order its execution by the Deputy Principal Clerk of Session.[36]

[33] See *Grant* v. *Ullah*, 1987 S.L.T. 639, and the *Stair Memorial Encyclopaedia*, vol. 12, para. 1009 *et seq.*

[34] See *Zemhunt (Holdings) Ltd.* v. *Control Securities plc*, 1992 S.L.T. 151.

[35] An action for payment could be raised. But the crave or conclusion has to be conditioned on the pursuer himself tendering performance.

[36] See *Mackay* v. *Campbell*, 1966 S.C. 237; *Boag, Petr.*, 1967 S.L.T. 275; *Hoey* v. *Butler*, 1975 S.C. 87. See also the Sheriff Courts (Scotland) Act 1907, s. 5A as

Late performance may produce consequential loss for the innocent party and in that case damages are usually due.[37] The possible heads of damage are the same as those which arise on rescission. The classic case where damages are claimed is where, as in *Tiffney* v. *Bachurzewski*,[38] payment is made late and the seller has to fund loans over two houses.

Incomplete performance

If there is incomplete performance in domestic conveyancing it is normally by the seller. The typical situation is that the central heating system does not work properly or that there is some minor blemish in the title. In this situation the purchaser will usually wish to proceed with the sale but also to claim damages. But at this point he runs into the difficulty of the rule against the *actio quanti minoris*.

In Roman law, if a seller tendered defective performance, the purchaser could insist on a suitable reduction of the price, or, if the price was already paid, could insist on a return of part of the price by way of compensation. This was called the *actio quanti minoris*. Our common law did not adopt this remedy, except in certain situations.[39] At common law, a disgruntled purchaser had to choose between accepting the thing sold at the agreed price, or rejecting it and claiming damages. He could not have it both ways, *i.e.* both to accept and to claim damages. However, it was always open to the parties to agree that the purchaser should have this option. These rules of the common law of sale continue to apply to heritable property.

In many cases rescission is not what the purchaser wishes. Hence the modern practice[40–41] is that a clause granting the purchaser the

inserted by s. 17 of the Law Reform (Miscellaneous Provisions) (Scotland) Act 1985.

[37] Notwithstanding the statement to the contrary by Lord Hunter in *Tiffney* v. *Bachurzewski*, 1985 S.L.T. 165.

[38] 1985 S.L.T. 165.

[39] For detailed discussion of this complex subject, and for more extensive citation of authority, see articles by A.L. Stewart, 1966. J.L.S. 124, K.G.C. Reid, 1988 J.L.S. 285, R. Evans-Jones, 1991 J.R. 190, and the same writer at 1992 J.L.S. 274.

[40–41] Especially since *Finlayson* v. *McRobb*, 1987 S.L.T. (Sh. Ct.) 150. Before that decision, conveyancers tended to be unaware of the difficulty.

actio quanti minoris of Roman law is almost invariably included in missives. However, even where an express *actio quanti minoris* clause is not included, the courts have shown a benevolent tendency to treat non-supersession clauses[42] as containing an implied incorporation of the *actio quanti minoris*.[43] As a result, the common law rule against the existence of the *actio quanti minoris* only matters in the enforcement of older contracts containing neither an express *actio quanti minoris* clause nor a non-supersession clause.

Several points about the scope of the rule against the *actio quanti minoris* need to be noted. First, the rule excluding the *actio quanti minoris* applies even where the damages claimed are not strictly *quanti minoris* (*i.e.* the diminution in value of the property as a result of the defect) but are calculated by reference to the cost of putting the defect right. Secondly, the rule does not apply to the sale of corporeal moveables.[44] Thirdly, the rule does not apply to positive obligations (as opposed to warranties). With positive obligations damages are not in reduction of the price for defective property but in compensation for failure by the seller to do something which he was contractually bound to do. Indeed, the form of action is often an action of implement which failing damages.[45] Fourthly, the rule against the *actio quanti minoris* does not apply to obligations collateral to the sale itself.[46] Fifthly, the rule against the *actio quanti minoris* does not apply to defects which are unknown to the purchaser until *restitutio in integrum* is no longer possible,[47] though the precise scope of this exception is not wholly clear.

Some doubt exists as to how quantum of damages should be calculated. Often, damages are based on the cost of putting the

[42] *i.e.* a clause which stipulates that the missives will remain in force notwithstanding delivery of the disposition.

[43] See *Tainsh* v. *McLaughlin*, 1990 S.L.T. (Sh. Ct.) 102, and also (though this goes further than the court's reasoning) *Jamieson* v. *Stewart*, 1989 S.L.T. (Sh. Ct.) 13.

[44] Sale of Goods Act 1979, ss. 11(5) and 53.

[45] See *Hoey* v. *Butler*, 1975 S.C. 87, *Taylor* v. *McLeod*, 1990 S.L.T. 194, and *King* v. *Gebbie*, 1993 S.L.T. 512. A possible alternative view is that positive obligations fall within the collateral exception.

[46] *McKillop* v. *Mutual Securities Ltd.*, 1945 S.C. 166. The meaning of "collateral" is unclear. It seems not to have the same sense as "collateral" in the context of supersession of missives.

[47] *Louttit's Trs.* v. *Highland Railway Co.* (1892) 19 R. 791 at 800.

defect right.[48] There is probably no hard and fast rule.[49] Certainly, where the defect is not one which is remediable and which the buyer proposes to remedy (*e.g.* a minor defect in title) diminution in market value will presumably be the appropriate measure of loss.[50]

3. Delay in Settlement

"Delay in settlement" has two meanings, one wider and the other narrower. In the narrow sense it means the case where settlement does happen, but late. But this can be known only by hindsight, and when settlement fails to take place at the agreed date, the parties may not know whether the settlement is merely delayed or whether it will never take place at all. The term is thus sometimes used in a wider sense to cover any situation where settlement is not made on the due date, whatever may happen thereafter. Here, however, we use the term in the narrower sense.[51]

Mutuality principle

If one party cannot or will not perform his (positive) obligations by the stipulated date, the other party has the option of delaying settlement. The reason for this is the mutuality principle in the law of contract, which is that if one party is in breach, then so long as he remains in breach, he cannot insist that the other party perform.[52] For example in *Bowie* v. *Semple's Executors*[53] the buyer was held entitled not to settle where the seller, an executor, had still not obtained confirmation.

The limits of the mutuality principle are unclear. What are the counter-stipulations for payment of the price? Missives usually pro-

[48] *Tainsh* v. *McLaughlin*, 1990 S.L.T. (Sh. Ct.) 102; *Hardwick* v. *Gebbie*, 1991 S.L.T. 258; *Colgan* v. *Mooney*, 1992 G.W.D. 34–2009.

[49] In *Finlayson* v. *McRobb*, 1987 S.L.T. (Sh. Ct.) 150 only the loss in market value was allowed. But this approach was not followed in *Tainsh* v. *McLaughlin*, 1990 S.L.T. (Sh. Ct.) 102.

[50] As in warrandice cases such as *Welsh* v. *Russell* (1894) 21 R. 769.

[51] On this whole subject see D.J. Cusine and P. Love in D.J. Cusine (ed.), *A Scots Conveyancing Miscellany: Essays in Honour of Professor J.M. Halliday.*

[52] See, *e.g.*, McBryde, *Contract*, para 14–25 *et seq.*

[53] 1978 S.L.T. (Sh. Ct.) 9.

vide that "in exchange for the purchase price . . . the seller will deliver" certain specified items. Clearly a purchaser could delay settlement if any of these were missing. But presumably these are not all the counter-stipulations, for there are a number of other obligations on the seller (such as the obligation to produce building consents) which are not included in the list. Indeed, the phrase quoted is arguably a dangerous one and perhaps missives should be redrafted to exclude it.

As to the limits in the other direction, the seller is taken bound to exhibit a good and marketable title. The question arises as to whether absolutely everything must be exhibited before the purchaser can be forced to pay, even, for instance, the most trivial deed referred to for burdens. The answer appears to be affirmative, so that the seller's agent must take great care to obtain in good time all the deeds that are required by a purchaser.

Interest on the price: the common law

One almost inevitable consequence of delay in settlement is that, regardless of which party caused the delay, the price is withheld by the purchaser. Eventually, of course, (unless the transaction collapses) settlement will occur and the price will then be paid. But a problem may then arise as to interest on the price during the period between the contractual date of entry and the ultimate date of settlement. The common law position is clear. It depends on whether or not entry is taken by the purchaser. If entry is taken interest is due. If entry is not taken, interest is not due. This is because the "fruits" of the price (*i.e.* interest) are treated as the equivalent of the "fruits" of the land (*i.e.* possession). If one party has one, the other party must, in equity, have the other.[54] It should be observed that entitlement to interest is not regarded as damages and is not tied to any loss that may or may not have been sustained.

In practice, the rule is less fair than it sounds, especially where the delay is caused by the purchaser. For unless the purchaser takes entry (and often he will not) there is no entitlement to interest. (Interest is not due merely *ex mora.*) It is true that the seller has the benefit of possession, but usually he has bought another house and it is a benefit he could do without. In practice, the house often lies empty.

[54] See Erskine III, iii, 79.

Can the seller do anything to improve his position? Halliday[55] suggests that interest will run if the seller vacates the premises and makes a formal offer of entry to the purchaser, but this does not find support in the case law.[56] Another possibility is to raise an action for payment, in which case interest will run from the date of citation.[57] As well as claiming interest the innocent party may also have a claim in damages.[58]

Where interest does run, no one seems to know what the appropriate rate is.[59] The only rule which is reasonably certain is that if the purchaser takes entry on the basis of putting the purchase price on deposit receipt (this only happens where it is the seller who is in default), the interest due is the interest actually obtained.[60]

Interest on the price: contractual provision

Because the common law can be unfair to the innocent seller, it is now almost universal to have a clause in missives providing that if the purchaser fails to pay at the due date, the price payable shall be augmented by interest on it at a defined rate, typically stated as being four per cent above the current base rate of one of the major Scottish banks. It is normal to add the words "notwithstanding consignation" in order to prevent the argument that interest should be payable at the rate actually earned.[61] It is also usual to state that interest will be due even though the purchaser does not take entry, so as clearly to exclude the common law rule. The clause often provides that the seller is entitled to interest only where he is able to settle and the purchaser is not, though in fact this qualification is implied by law.[62]

[55] At para. 23–56.

[56] See, in particular, *Thomson* v. *Vernon*, 1983 S.L.T. (Sh. Ct.) 17.

[57] See *Tiffney* v. *Bachurzewski*, 1985 S.L.T. 165 at 168 and 1988 G.W.D. 37–1530. However, compare *Thomson* v. *Vernon*, 1983 S.L.T. (Sh. Ct.) 17.

[58] *Brown* v. *Gamsu*, 1992 G.W.D. 40–2429. For damages generally, see above.

[59] See the essay by Cusine and Love cited above.

[60] *Prestwick Cinema Co. Ltd.* v. *Gardiner*, 1951 S.C. 98.

[61] As has been said, this is the common law rule following consignation: see *Prestwick Cinema Co. Ltd.* v. *Gardiner*, above. The point of course is that the seller wishes an interest rate higher than that obtainable at current deposit receipt rates.

[62] *Davidson* v. *Tilburg Ltd.*, 1991 G.W.D. 18–1109. Once again, this is the mutuality principle.

4. Settlement by Special Arrangement

Although the party not in breach cannot be forced to settle (because of the mutuality principle), he may often wish to do so. In that case there may be settlement by special agreement. The form that the agreement takes depends on which party is in default.

If the purchaser is in default (*i.e.* the price is not paid), it is most unlikely that settlement will proceed. This is because, so long as he is protected by an interest clause, the seller has nothing to gain by permitting entry and indeed has something to lose, because the purchaser may never come up with the money and, once in the house, may be difficult to dislodge. The purchaser, by contrast, may be keen to take entry: after all, interest is running on the price and he has nothing to show for it. And he may have nowhere else to live. What this means in practice is obtaining bridging finance (so that the price can be paid in full) until permanent finance is available. Typically, the purchaser is waiting for a building society loan to come through or for the sale of his existing house.

If the seller is in default this is usually because he has failed to come up with all the required titles or other documentation by the contractual date of settlement. Invariably, the seller will be keen to settle, because, being himself in default, he cannot claim interest on the price, and will lose heavily if settlement is delayed. The purchaser may be less keen. His attitude will depend partly on the seriousness of the default and partly on whether he has sold his own house. A purchaser who has sold will have nowhere to live and so will be keen to settle; a purchaser who has not sold may welcome an excuse to delay settlement.

A purchaser is not, of course, bound to settle where the seller is in default; but if he agrees to settle, the agreement usually takes one of the following forms (sometimes in combination).

(1) If the default is minor, settlement often takes place on the basis of a letter of obligation granted by the seller's agents and undertaking to deliver the missing document. Payment is then made in full, except that there is sometimes a small retention (*e.g.* £1000) if the thing missing involves the expenditure of money. Note, however, that the seller's agent may be unwilling to grant a letter of obligation in such terms. Indeed, most firms will refuse to do so unless they are quite certain that the document is one that can

be obtained.[63] This is a matter for negotiation, and a buyer may sometimes be willing to do without a letter of obligation. (After all, the seller is in any case already bound to perform in terms of the missives.)

(2) If the default is more serious, the purchaser may not be willing to hand over the money. Indeed, it may be impossible for him to do so, at least without bridging, because the lender may not be willing to release the loan cheque until the default is put right. The purchaser's solicitor, who is also acting for the lender, must not let his sympathy for the purchaser interfere with his professional duty to the lender. As a general rule, a purchaser should never hand over the price if a valid disposition cannot be produced in exchange. The main, but not only, danger here is of the risk of supervening insolvency.[64] And even for less serious defaults the purchaser may not be willing to pay the seller. But it may be possible for settlement to take place without the seller actually being paid. What happens is that the purchase price is placed ("consigned") on deposit receipt with a bank in the joint names of the solicitors for the seller and the purchaser. Consignation creates a trust, in which the solicitors are trustees. The purposes of the trust are to pay the money either to the seller (if the default is made good) or to the purchaser (if it is not).[65] In either case the interest goes to the seller (unless otherwise agreed), on the basis that the purchaser has had the benefit of possession. The money cannot be released from deposit receipt without the signatures of both firms, and in practice this puts the purchaser in a strong position, for he has what he wants, namely possession, and there is no reason why he should agree to release the money until the seller has fulfilled his obligations in full.

(3) A third method of settlement sometimes found is where the purchaser takes entry on the basis of a deposit, which is either paid over to the seller or put on joint deposit receipt. This will be attractive to a purchaser where the building society cheque has been withheld so that he could not pay the full amount without bridging.

[63] Thus, if what is needed is a confirmation of the seller as executor, there is unlikely to be a problem. But if what is needed is a retrospective building warrant and completion certificate, the law firm cannot be sure that this can be obtained.

[64] See the classic case of *Gibson* v. *Hunter Home Designs Ltd.*, 1976 S.C. 23.

[65] See *Singh* v. *Cross Entertainments Ltd.*, 1990 S.L.T. 77.

Obviously, it is less attractive to the seller. Whether the seller is also due interest on the unpaid balance is a matter for negotiation. If nothing is said interest is due because the purchaser has possession.

Chapter 5

GOOD AND MARKETABLE TITLE

1. Introduction

In a contract for the sale of land the seller gives an absolute guarantee of title. This is implied by law, but in practice an express clause is always included in the missives in the form of an obligation to deliver or exhibit a good and marketable title. The obligation falls into two parts. First, the seller must demonstrate that his title is good and marketable to the reasonable satisfaction of the buyer. Secondly, he must produce clear searches in the property and personal registers, and, if applicable, the Companies Register. Both parts of this obligation are considered in detail below.[1] Both require to be fulfilled. If, as can occasionally happen, the title is good but the search is not clear then the seller is in breach.

2. The essence of good and marketable title

The idea of a good title involves four aspects. First, the purchaser is to be made owner, and his ownership must not be open to reduction by a third party. Secondly, the property must not be burdened by any undischarged heritable security. Thirdly, there must be no unusual conditions of title. Fourthly, the purchaser must acquire the right to vacant possession, which in effect means that the subjects are not leased. These will be looked at in turn.

Purchaser to be made owner

The seller undertakes that he is, or will be at settlement, in a position to confer ownership on the purchaser,[2] *i.e.* that the purchaser's title will not be void. He further undertakes that the purchaser's

[1] The mechanics of searches are considered in chap. 7.

[2] Either because the seller is owner, or, though not the owner, has power of sale (*e.g.* a sale by a heritable creditor after default).

title will not be voidable, *i.e.* will be invulnerable to reduction by a third party. In the case of land to be registered in the Land Register this effectively means that there will be no exclusion of indemnity on the land certificate to be issued to the purchaser by the Keeper.

The seller must offer a title to the whole of the subjects described in the missives. But while on general principles of landownership that necessarily includes a title to the minerals, this is usually negatived by a clause to the effect that the minerals are included only in so far as the seller has right thereto.[3]

No heritable securities

The seller undertakes that the title is not affected by any heritable securities, or if there are any, that they will be discharged at or before settlement.

No unusual conditions of title

Almost every property is subject to real conditions[4] of one kind or another. Thus, there may be real burdens regulating use and apportioning maintenance costs. There may be obligations arising out of common interest. There may be servitudes. A purchaser (or at least his solicitor) knows about these things. They are expected. In themselves they give no ground for complaint: a title subject to real conditions is in most cases still a good title.[5] This is common sense, for otherwise, as Lord Young observed[6]:

> "[I]t would generally be impossible to make an effective sale of a house in town without a very minute and ponderous written contract specifying all restrictions and conditions, however usual, that applied to it. If a man simply buys a house he must be taken to buy it as the seller has it, on a good title, of course, but subject to such restrictions as may exist if of an ordinary character, and such as the buyer may reasonably be supposed to have contemplated as at least not improbable."

[3] See Chap. 3.

[4] Real burdens, servitudes, common interest.

[5] *Urquhart* v. *Halden* (1835) 13 S. 844; *Whyte* v. *Lee* (1879) 6 R. 699; *Smith* v. *Soeder* (1895) 23 R. 60; *McConnell* v. *Chassels* (1903) 10 S.L.T. 790.

[6] *Whyte* v. *Lee* (1879) 6 R. 699 at 701.

As Lord Young indicates, however, not absolutely all real conditions are acceptable. Some title conditions may amount to a breach of the seller's obligations to provide a good title. This is a difficult and uncertain area, both in theory and in practice. It is necessary to distinguish (1) the obligation implied by law; (2) the standard express obligation; and (3) special express obligations.

(1) The implied obligation about title conditions

The obligation implied by law sets three criteria which must be met before a condition of title can be objected to by the purchaser. These are: (1) that the condition must be unknown to the purchaser at the date of conclusion of missives; (2) that it must be unusual or unduly onerous[7]; and (3) that it must materially diminish the value of the property.

In practice the second criterion is the most difficult to apply. A condition is unusual in the sense of criterion (2) if it is unusual in relation to the type and location of the property in question. But *how* unusual does it have to be? The question is important because a wide interpretation would open up an all-too convenient escape route from missives. Unfortunately, the case law is insufficiently developed to provide a clear answer. The leading modern case is *Armia* v. *Daejan Developments Limited*,[8] in which a property in Kirkcaldy High Street bought for redevelopment was found to be subject to a wide servitude right of access affecting the frontage with the street. Although, as will be explained later, the case was actually decided on the basis of a special clause in the missives, the House of Lords indicated that even without such a clause the servitude would have constituted a breach of the seller's obligation to furnish a good title. But it is difficult to generalise from this. Would it have made any difference if the servitude had not prejudiced the redevelopment? Is the position for rural properties different? A servitude of way in itself is presumably not "unusual."[9] Presumably, the test is whether it is "unusual" for a property of a particular type.

As for criterion (3), burdens do commonly diminish the market value of a property. For example, lower flats in a tenement are

[7] "Unusual" and "unduly onerous" probably mean the same in this context. In *Umar* v. *Murtaza*, 1983 S.L.T. (Sh. Ct.) 79 this criterion was overlooked.

[8] 1978 S.C. 152, reversed 1979 S.C. (H.L.) 56.

[9] *Morris* v. *Ritchie*, 1991 G.W.D. 12–712; 1992 G.W.D. 33–1950.

usually burdened with a share in the upkeep of the roof, and this obviously means that their market value is less than it would be otherwise. But a purchaser can object to a burden only if all three criteria are met. A burden of the type mentioned is not unusual, and so the purchaser must accept it, unless the missives otherwise provide. Likewise, a burden on a house forbidding commercial use is common and so cannot be objected to. More problematic is the situation where a burden is common in the particular locality but not elsewhere. Thus, in some urban areas burdens forbidding the sale of alcohol are common. Such a burden is usual for that area, but arguably unusual in the broader context. The law here seems unclear.

(2) The standard express obligation about title conditions

It is normal practice for the obligation about unusual conditions to be made express in the offer. In Sasine transactions the clause typically reads something like this: "There are no unusual, unduly onerous or restrictive conditions of title affecting the subjects." This differs from the implied obligation in failing to make mention of the state of the purchaser's knowledge.[10] But while this opens up the argument that a purchaser could rescind even though he knew of the condition of title before entering missives, it is thought that the argument would not succeed.

In Land Register transactions the clause recommended in the Registration of Title Practice Book (ROTPB) is: "There are no outstanding charges, no unduly onerous burdens, and no unusual or unduly onerous overriding interests which adversely affect the subjects of sale."[11] This is preferable to the clause recommended by the Law Society which contains an unqualified guarantee that there are no overriding interests.

In practice, it is common in missives for the entire clause about burdens to be taken out by the seller in exchange for an opportunity to inspect the titles. Provided that the seller's agent has the titles to hand, this is usually the best practice. It avoids all dispute as to what is or is not unusual or unduly onerous. The purchaser is able to see what he is getting before becoming contractually committed to proceed. In particular, he can verify that the use he proposes to

[10] *i.e.* criterion (1) above.

[11] ROTPB, para. G 3.05.

make of the subjects is not excluded by the terms of the titles. In return the seller has the reassurance of knowing that the purchaser will not resile the day before settlement on some merely technical point about the state of the burdens.

(3) Special express obligations

The standard obligation, whether in its express or its implied form, may not always give the buyer sufficient protection. Consider the following example. Suppose that the purpose behind a particular purchase is to rent the property to students. And suppose further, which is not improbable, that the titles contain a real burden limiting the use of the subjects to occupation by "one family only." The purchaser has a problem. The standard obligation will probably not help him. The restriction is a fairly common one, and so is probably not "unusual." Consequently, the title is probably good and marketable. Unless the discovery is made before the conclusion of missives, the purchaser must proceed. The lesson to be drawn here is, of course, perfectly simple. Where a buyer intends to use the subjects other than simply to live in (or, in commercial properties, to work in), or where his purpose is otherwise esoteric, he should include a special clause in the missives to the effect that the proposed use is not excluded by the terms of the title.

This is what was done in the leading case of *Armia* v. *Daejan Developments Limited*,[12] though ironically litigation nevertheless ensued. The buyer here, intending to redevelop the land, included the following clause in his offer: "There is nothing in the titles of the said subjects which will prevent demolition and redevelopment." It was held by the First Division that this clause replaced the obligation implied by law against unusual burdens, and that since the burden in question (the servitude) could not be said actually to prevent demolition and redevelopment, the purchaser must proceed with the purchase. This was a harsh and, with respect, implausible construction. Fortunately, it did not survive the appeal to the House of Lords, where it was decided that the special clause must be read as adding to and not as replacing the implied obligation. Further, the seller was found to be in breach of the special clause, giving the buyer the right to rescind. The interpretation adopted by the First Division was criticised as placing the buyer at

[12] Above.

a disadvantage in consequence of a clause which had clearly been intended to strengthen his position.[13]

Right to vacant possession

The right to vacant possession in practice means the right to acquire the property free from any leases. The rule for leases appears to be the same as the rule for conditions of title, so that if a reasonable purchaser would have realised that the property was leased, he cannot complain. In practice, however, missives almost always have an express provision on the point. If vacant possession is sought, this will be stated, and if the purchaser is acquiring leased property, typically as an investment, the missives will in practice make this clear and indeed give details of the lease or leases.

Occupancy rights

Though there is no authority, the general view is that if a property is or may be affected by occupancy rights under the Matrimonial Homes (Family Protection) (Scotland) Act 1981, then it is necessary, for the title to be good and marketable, for the seller to produce the affidavits or consents or renunciations contemplated by that Act.[14] This is because the seller must show that the purchaser will have the right to vacant possession.

3. Obligation to Demonstrate a Good Title

It is not sufficient for the seller to have a good title. He must also be in a position to demonstrate that fact to the purchaser. If he cannot do so, then, even if his title is in fact good, he has failed in his obligation and the buyer need not proceed with the purchase.

[13] The view that special clauses generally augment rather than replace the implied obligation has since been given effect to in *Umar* v. *Murtaza* (above).

[14] See generally chap. 8. There can be several practical problems here. One is as follows. A owns a house and dispones it to her daughter B as a gift. B then wishes to sell. B cannot produce an affidavit from A to prove that A is a widow because the Act allows affidavits only for sales and securities and not for other transactions such as gifts. Since nothing can be done, the title is presumably good and marketable even though C bears a theoretical risk that A had a husband with occupancy rights which he now wishes to enforce.

Writs to be produced

What, in evidential terms, must the seller do to satisfy the purchaser? The answer, in the words of Hume,[15] is that he must "furnish him with a sufficient progress of titles to the subject—such a progress (for aught that can be seen) as shall maintain his right against all pretenders." The seller's obligation ends with prima-facie validity (Hume's "for aught that can be seen"). He need not prove that each individual writ is good and unchallengeable. That would be impossible. It is enough to produce writs that *appear* to be valid and it is then for the purchaser, if he can, to show that a particular writ is bad. This rule was settled by the leading case of *Sibbald's Heirs* v. *Harris*.[16] There the purchaser refused to accept a prescriptive progress containing a decree of general service on the basis that such a decree was vulnerable to future reduction, for example by the emergence of a closer heir. But this objection was rejected by the court. A decree of special service was prima-facie valid. It was no more vulnerable to reduction than any other writ. Unless, therefore, the buyer had concrete grounds for fearing reduction—and he had not—the title was one which he was bound to accept.

What writs must the seller actually produce? The answer of course depends upon whether the title is a Sasine title or a Land Register title. In the former case, the seller must produce a good prescriptive progress (including any midcouples), together with a Sasine search. The length of the search will be as agreed in the missives. The obligation implied by law is that it must go back at least to the foundation writ. If, as is usually the case, the foundation writ is less than 40-years-old, there is a view that the implied obligation entitles the purchaser to a search going back 40 years, this being on the basis of traditional conveyancing practice, but the point is unclear. The seller must also produce all writs referred to for burdens and descriptions. But he need not produce writs affecting *other* properties, and the buyer who wants evidence that,

[15] *Lectures*, ii,38.

[16] 1947 S.C. 601. There may, however, be some tension between this decision and *Duke of Devonshire* v. *Fletcher* (1874) 1 R. 1056 and *Bruce* v. *Stewart* (1900) 2 F. 948. However, it is difficult to state a confident view on this question.

for example, roof burdens are fairly allocated in a tenement must probably stipulate for this, as in practice he invariably does. The deeds must actually be produced: it is not sufficient to invite the buyer to inspect them himself on record.[17–18] It is arguable, although undecided, that all deeds within the prescriptive progress must be probative.

In the case of land registered in the Land Register, the seller's obligation is more readily discharged. In most cases the seller will appear as proprietor in the land certificate, and all that is required is that the certificate be updated through Form 12 and 13 reports. If for some reason the seller does not appear as proprietor it is necessary to produce writs (*e.g.*, confirmation as executor) showing why the seller now has title to sell. Where, however, the Keeper has unrestricted powers of rectification,[19] either because indemnity has been excluded or because the buyer does not intend to take possession of the subjects,[20] it will be necessary to go behind the land certificate to the Sasine writs in the same way as if the title had not been registered.

With both registered and unregistered land it is necessary to produce a search in the personal register and, where the seller is a company, in the Companies Register also. In view of the strict rule about clear searches (see below) the seller should take care that the list of persons to be searched against is not longer than is absolutely necessary. Searches are considered further in Chapter 7.

The problem of possession

In Sasine cases title rests on positive prescription.[21] Positive prescription in turn presupposes possession for the requisite period, currently 10 years. Does the seller have to offer to prove this? In practice, the answer is no, the purchaser taking the fact of possession on faith. This is generally safe enough. But take this case: A records in the Sasine Register an *a non domino* disposition in 1982 and in 1993 offers to sell the land to B. A can give a good title if

[17–18] *Sutherland* v. *Garrity*, 1941 S.C. 196.

[19] 1979 Act, s. 9.

[20] The Keeper's view is that "possession" in s. 9 of the 1979 Act includes civil possession. See 1984 J.L.S. 176.

[21] See chap. 6. In registration of title cases, possession is less important.

but only if he has had 10 years of possession. B is clearly taking a real risk if he accepts the fact of possession on faith. But the law is unclear as to whether he is entitled to demand evidence of such possession, and, if so, what evidence is sufficient. Nor is it clear whether evidence of possession can be demanded in other cases.

Disputes as to sufficiency of title

Inevitably, the purchaser and the seller do not always agree as to the sufficiency of the title offered. If so there are various possibilities short of litigation. Thus, the parties may agree to be bound by the opinion of some respected conveyancer. Or the seller may be prepared to give, and the buyer to accept, an indemnity policy. Or again one of the parties may yield. But if both parties remain entrenched in their respective positions, litigation cannot be avoided. It may take a number of forms, for example, an action by the seller to enforce the contract, or an action by the purchaser for declarator of entitlement to rescind, or a special case brought by both parties. But whatever form it takes the seller is in practice at a serious disadvantage. For in order to succeed he must satisfy the court that the title tendered is good beyond "rational doubt"[22]; and that high standard is not attained unless the only step asked of the court is to apply clearly settled law to the facts of the instant case.[23] If the law itself is in doubt the court will not resolve that doubt in an action between purchaser and seller because the "proper contradictors" (*i.e.*, the parties entitled to found on the alleged defect) are absent. Hence, the title will not be forced on a reluctant purchaser unless it is quite clearly a good one. As Lord Deas put it in *Duke of Devonshire* v. *Fletcher*[24]: "No purchaser is obliged to take the risk of law-suits. If, as the sellers say, the adjudications [the defect objected to] are nullities, they are such nullities as I should be sorry to have anything to do with."

It is always open to the seller to avoid the difficulty of no proper contradictors by an action of declarator against the appropriate

[22] *Brown* v. *Cheyne* (1833) 12 S. 176, *per* Lord Meadowbank. See also *Dunlop* v. *Crawford* (1849) 11 D. 1062.

[23] See *Lamb's Trs.* v. *Reid* (1883) 11 R. 76.

[24] (1874) 1 R. 1056. As suggested earlier, it is arguable that in this case the court went too far, imposing too high a standard of proof on the seller.

parties to have the alleged defect found ineffective. Precisely this had been done in the *Duke of Devonshire* case. But it was held that because the action of declarator had been undefended, there was the theoretical danger, however remote, that it might one day be reduced. Hence this case is authority that a title based on a decree in absence is unmarketable,[25] until the possibility of such a reduction has been removed by prescription. There are a number of reasons for doubting the correctness of this view, but the subject is complex and cannot be discussed further here. The practical moral is that if a title does rest on a decree in absence, the seller should ensure that the missives bar the purchaser from objecting to it on this ground.

Title indemnity policies

In practice, disputes are often settled by the seller obtaining, at his expense, a policy of title insurance, though a purchaser cannot be compelled to accept this. If the seller is a major corporation of undoubted standing, such as, for instance, the Bank of Scotland, a policy is arguably pointless. For the seller is usually bound in absolute warrandice in any event, and the chance that the Bank of Scotland would not be able to pay up on a warrandice claim is at least as remote as the chance that Sun Alliance would fail to pay up on a title policy.

Where a policy is obtained, a one-off premium is paid. The premium is calculated according to the value of the property, the risk involved, and so forth. The cover should last until the problem, whatever it may be, will have been removed by prescription. The amount of the cover should not be the present value of the property but its expected maximum value during the cover period. Thus, if a house is bought for £50,000, and seven years later the owner is evicted due to the defect in his title, his loss will probably be more than that sum, because the house will probably be worth more at that stage. There is obviously no way of predicting the future value. But a commonly used formula is to calculate the future value on the assumption of an annual increase of 10 per cent, compound rate.

[25] *Bruce* v. *Stewart* (1900) 2 F. 948 is to the same effect.

4. Obligation to Produce a Clear Search

The obligation to produce a search is part of the obligation to demonstrate a good title. The obligation that the search so produced be clear is, however, a separate and distinct obligation. It is probably implied by law, but in any event it is always expressly stipulated for, both in missives and also in the letter of obligation subsequently granted by the seller's solicitor. The obligation is, of course, closely related to the wider obligation to demonstrate a good title. For usually an unclear search indicates a bad title and the former obligation becomes subsumed in the latter. But it can occasionally happen that a title is good but the search is not clear. For example, a search may disclose a standard security for a fixed sum of £20,000, which has been repaid. Since there is no debt the security is implicitly discharged. So the title is good. But nonetheless the search is not clear for it discloses an apparently undischarged security. It is only in odd cases of this kind that the separate obligation to provide a clear search is of importance.

The question arises as to what a "clear search" means. The answer, according to a famous passage in Burns's *Conveyancing Practice*,[26] is that "[if] deeds or diligences appear on record the search is not clear till they are disposed of, though it is doubtful whether they really affect the purchaser's title, *or even, it may be, though the contrary is true in law*." The final few words of Burns's definition rest on certain remarks in *Dryburgh* v. *Gordon*.[27] In *Dryburgh* the search disclosed two inhibitions predating the sale. Such inhibitions would in the normal course of events strike at the sale, but the seller's agents, whose letter of obligation was the subject of the action, argued that their client's title (a reversionary right under an *ex facie* absolute disposition) was in its nature incapable of being affected by these inhibitions. The Second Division held that the search was not clear. Whatever the merits of the case against the inhibitions, on which the court expressed no decided view, there was an apparent encumbrance on the face of the search which the buyer was entitled to have discharged.

It is suggested that this case is less far-reaching than Burns seems

[26] 4th ed., p. 303.
[27] (1896) 24 R. 1.

to have feared. The point about the inhibitions in *Dryburgh* is that no one could say for certain whether or not they affected the sale, in the absence of litigation involving the inhibitors themselves. The issue was not, or at any rate was not perceived to be, one of settled law.[28] In short, the title was not good and marketable, and the remarks of the court must be read against this background. The rule, therefore, is not, as Burns appears to contemplate, that *any* apparent encumbrance prevents a search from being clear. The facts are subject to the law. And where the encumbrance is one which, as a matter of settled law, could not possibly affect the sale the search is clear.[29] A search is only not clear, therefore, where either the title is actually affected by the encumbrance or where, as in *Dryburgh*, the law, or the application of the law, is in doubt.

This view appears to be confirmed by *Newcastle Building Society* v. *White*,[30] seemingly the only reported case on the point since *Dryburgh*. There, security subjects were sold by a heritable creditor on the default of the debtor. The interim report on the search disclosed an inhibition against the debtor which postdated the granting of the standard security in favour of the creditor. A dispute arose as to whether the search was clear. It was held that it was. In terms of section 26(1) of the 1970 Act the recording of a disposition in such circumstances disburdened the security subjects of all diligences ranking *pari passu* with or postponed to the security. "Accordingly *merely by applying the law* any future purchaser can establish ex facie of the records and without reference to extrinsic material that the inhibition no longer has any relevance to the property."[31]

In evaluating a search, therefore, it is necessary to apply the relevant law to the relevant facts. But while the only limitation as to the law is that it should be certain, there is an important limitation as to the facts to which that law may be applied. Were this not so, the obligation to deliver a clear search would collapse into the more general obligation to demonstrate a good title. The limita-

[28] In fact, the inhibitions probably did strike at the sale: G.L. Gretton, *The Law of Inhibition and Adjudication* (Butterworth, 1987), p. 144

[29] *Cameron* v. *Williamson* (1895) 22 R. 293.

[30] 1987 S.L.T. (Sh. Ct.) 81.

[31] At p. 85. In fact, at common law also the inhibition could not strike at the sale.

tion, in the words already quoted of the Sheriff Principal in *Newcastle Building Society* v. *White*, is that the facts must be "ex facie of the records." "Extrinsic material" is not permitted. The search must be internally clear. This rule, which is now well established, seems first to have been laid down in *Cargill* v. *Craigie*.[32] The search in that case disclosed three inhibitions against the seller. These had in fact been discharged, but the discharges had not been registered. Thus, the title was good, but the buyer was held entitled by the House of Lords (reversing the Court of Session) to have the record cleared.[33]

To establish whether a search is clear it is necessary to look at all the searches and interpret them in the light of common law and statute. Thus, suppose that C is buying from B, who bought from A. C finds that the personal search shows an inhibition against A. But the Sasine search shows that this inhibition was laid on after the disposition by A to B was recorded. Hence the inhibition was too late and the search is clear, because the ineffectiveness of the inhibition as against the sale to B is apparent. Or again, suppose that Y is buying from X, and the personal search shows that X was inhibited six years ago. By statute the inhibition is spent, and so the search is clear.

The rule against extrinsic material must be set in the broader context of the need for such evidence of title as will satisfy a buyer without at the same time placing an unfair burden on the seller. For the most part the rule seems to draw the line in the right place. Thus, it is not unreasonable that a purchaser faced with an apparent standard security or, as in *Cargill* v. *Craigie*, with an apparent inhibition, should be entitled to more than informal evidence that the debt to which they relate has been repaid. If the debt really has been repaid the seller can readily enough obtain and register a discharge. It seems just that he should be made to do so. But the seller's task may not always be so simple. The most irksome case in practice is where a seller is inhibited after conclusion of missives but before registration of the purchaser's disposition. Such an inhibition is ineffectual as far as the sale is concerned because

[32] (1822) 1 Shaw App. 134.

[33] In such cases, where the title is good, but appears from the searches not to be good, the title is sometimes said to be "good" but not "marketable." But this distinction between good and marketable is not universally adopted. The point is purely semantic. It is merely a difference in expressing the law.

it post-dates the missives. The title offered to the purchaser is therefore good. But the search is not clear, for it is only by inspecting an extrinsic document, namely the missives, that the ineffectiveness of the inhibition is revealed.[34]

[34] For possible courses of action see D.J. Cusine (ed.), *The Conveyancing Opinions of J.M. Halliday*, pp. 572–573. See also chap. 7 below.

Chapter 6

EXAMINATION OF SASINE TITLES

Introduction

This chapter considers examination of titles held in the Register of Sasines, including titles which are to be registered in the Land Register for the first time as a result of the current transaction. The examination of Land Register titles is dealt with later, in chapter 20. Every title is different, and this chapter gives only a general indication of the kinds of problems which may arise.[1]

1. Which Deeds?

The purchaser's solicitor receives an unappetising bundle of deeds, many of which may turn out to be irrelevant. Conveyancers traditionally never throw anything away. The size of the bundle depends on the length of time the property has existed as a separate entity. A late eighteenth century villa will have a large number of titles. A recently built house will have very few and it may be necessary to borrow the prior titles (which will deal with the whole development from which the house has been split off) from the builders' solicitors. It is rash to assume that the purchaser's solicitor will necessarily receive all the titles that he needs. What he needs, and what he is therefore entitled to receive,[1a] are the following:

(1) A prescriptive progress of titles, *i.e.* the foundation writ for the purposes of positive prescription, plus all subsequent conveyances.

(2) All security writs and discharges of security writs of the recent past—in practice 40 years is usually regarded as sufficient and people sometimes make do with less.

(3) All writs which impose real burdens and servitudes.

[1] See further Halliday, chap. 21 and J.H. Sinclair, *Handbook of Conveyancing Practice in Scotland* (2nd ed., Butterworth), pp. 57–88.

[1a] As part of the obligation for good and marketable title: see chap. 5.

(4) The principal deed or deeds which describe the property, if not already included under (1) or (3) above. (Usually they are included.)

(5) Miscellaneous other documents, most notably feuduty redemption receipt, and affidavits and other documentation under the 1981 Act.

There will also usually be included the existing searches in the Register of Sasines, the Register of Inhibitions and Adjudications, and, where applicable, the Companies Register. If any of the above are missing the purchaser's solicitor should ask for them. For writs within the prescriptive progress the seller should produce either the original deeds or extract copies (the validity of which is guaranteed by the 1970 Act, section 45). Quick copies (*i.e.* ordinary photocopies) are acceptable for burdens writs. To what extent a seller is bound at common law to deliver the titles (principals or extracts) and to what extent he is bound merely to exhibit them, is not wholly clear. In the absence of special agreement, the matter is now regulated by statute, obliging the seller to deliver all title deeds and searches relating exclusively to the land conveyed.[2]

2. How Exacting Should the Purchaser's Agent Be?

The purchaser's agent must of course examine the title carefully. This is one of the main things he is being paid for. It is obviously much better to discover a title defect before, rather than after, settlement. For one thing, the purchaser can refuse to settle, as opposed to trying later to pursue the seller for damages. For another, the seller's obligations before settlement are more extensive than those after settlement, which are governed by the law of warrandice. In practice, most titles contain something or other which is not quite perfect.[3] How exacting should the purchaser's agent be? Three types of defect may be distinguished. There is the obviously trivial, for instance an alteration of an inessential word in one of the deeds which has not been declared in the testing

[2] Land Registration (Scotland) Act 1979, s. 16(1)(*a*)(i). The word "all" here is odd. Why should some trivial deed, 50 or 150–years-old, perhaps long since lost, have to be delivered?

[3] It is one of the benefits of registration of title that, with the replacement of the title deeds by the title sheet, many such errors simply vanish.

clause. Next there is the obviously fatal defect. For instance, one of the deeds has not been signed, or the seller turns out just to have been sequestrated. Thirdly, there is the intermediate defect. Thus, many defects are sufficient to put the seller in breach of his obligation to produce a good title, without being particularly serious. They are technical defects only. Something has not been done completely correctly. The title may be satisfactory, but it is impossible to be absolutely sure. In other words, there is "rational doubt."[3a] What should be done? Usually there is no real danger of the defect coming home to roost. Even if there is some third party out there who might, in theory, be able to found on the apparent defect, this will almost certainly never happen in practice. The purchaser's solicitor knows that. So does the seller's solicitor. Nonetheless, the purchaser's solicitor will typically object to the title and insist on remedial measures. The main reason for this is that he is worried that when his client comes to resell the property, the solicitor acting for the then purchaser will be less accommodating, with the result that the sale will fall through. If the property is in a county which will shortly become an operational area for registration of title the purchaser's solicitor may also be worried that the Keeper may take a strict line and exclude indemnity from the title (which would itself make the property unmarketable). And in either case—since there has been no judicial eviction—there will then be no remedy against the original seller under the warrandice clause in the disposition. So the purchaser's solicitor will be reluctant to take any risk. In recent years solicitors have shown themselves increasingly nervous in this respect and increasingly disinclined to take any risk at all. No doubt they are quite right, but it does not make for speedy (or harmonious) conveyancing.

Examination of title is a skilled task. Possible defects can arise in many different, and unexpected, ways and it is impossible to examine title properly without a good working knowledge of the whole of conveyancing law. It is important not only to spot defects but to classify them properly. Minor errors should not be confused with more serious ones. The most irritating person to do business with is the smart Alec who reads conveyancing books (such as this one) on the bus on the way to work and who sees it as his duty to give free conveyancing lessons to the solicitor acting for the other

[3a] The phrase of Lord Meadowbank in *Brown* v. *Cheyne* (1833) 12 S. 176.

party. If a defect is trivial, it should be ignored. There is no need to point it out to the other side. That merely wastes time, a point all the more worth remembering in these days when conveyancing fees have become so unremunerative. The real skill of the conveyancer is to know when to speak up and when to shut up.

3. What is Being Looked For?

In examining a title the purchaser's solicitor seeks the answers to the following (not exhaustive) list of questions:

(1) Does the seller own the property, or have power of sale?
(2) Are the real burdens and servitudes acceptable?
(3) Are there any heritable securities?
(4) Has feuduty been redeemed?
(5) Are the searches clear?[4]
(6) Are there any occupancy rights under the Matrimonial Homes (Family Protection) (Scotland) Act 1981?[5]
(7) Have the necessary planning and building consents been obtained?[6]

As he examines the title, the purchaser's solicitor makes notes, called notes on title. Practice varies enormously as to how elaborate these notes in title ought to be. In the olden days, before photocopiers came into use, the practice was to note in detail all the important deeds, for the deeds themselves would soon be returned to the seller's agent, and then, after settlement, to the lender. Nowadays it is quicker to take photocopies, which can then be stapled to the notes. But older solicitors tend to stick to the old style. And there is certainly a danger in using the photocopier, which is that it can become a psychological substitute for actually reading the deeds properly. However the notes on title[7] are set out, they should be clear, should answer the questions set out above, and should identify any problems which need to be taken up. Some agents write in red ink any items which have yet to be seen, such as, for

[4] For this, see chap. 7.
[5] For this, see chap. 8.
[6] For this, see chap. 3.
[7] For an example see J.H. Sinclair, *Handbook of Conveyancing Practice in Scotland*, p. 207. Many agents would nowadays use a rather shorter form.

instance, the feuduty redemption receipt, the matrimonial homes affidavit, and so on. In that way such matters are not forgotten after having been identified. The notes on title will, apart from anything else, form the basis for the letter to the seller's agent raising points about the title.

Once examination of title is complete the titles are returned to the seller's solicitor, with the disposition drafted by the purchaser's agent, and with any observations arising out of the examination.

Question 1: Does the Seller Own the Property or Have Power of Sale?

A purchaser will receive a good title if and only if there is a good title in the seller,[8] or, alternatively, if the seller, though not himself the owner, has power of sale.[9] So the first task is to check the seller's title.

In the normal case one is checking that the seller is the owner. But on occasion the seller may not be the owner but may nevertheless have a valid power of sale. For example, he might be a judicial factor, or a heritable creditor enforcing his security, or a trustee in sequestration. But the principle remains the same. Such a person stands in the shoes of the owner. Thus, if the purported owner has become insane, and the property is being sold by his *curator bonis*, the purchaser's agent still needs to check, in the same way, that the *incapax* is in fact the owner. Of course he will also have to check that the actual seller has been duly appointed by the court and has power of sale.

Suppose that the client, Z, is buying a house from Y. Z will receive a good title if, and only if (1) Y owned the property at the time of Z's registration or (in virtue of the doctrine of accretion) comes to own it subsequently and (2) the disposition by Y to Z is valid (*i.e.* properly executed and so on). Point (2) is easily checked. But what of point (1), namely, whether Y was owner? The answer is that, as for Z, so for Y. Y owned the property if, and only if (1) the person from whom he bought (X) owned the property at the time of Y's registration and (2) the disposition from X to Y is valid.

[8] Or in the consenter, if any.

[9] *Nemo plus juris ad alium transferre potest quam ipse habet*, or, in a briefer version, *nemo dat quod non habet.*

So one must consider X's title, and then W's title (X's author) and then V's title (W's author), and so on. For the problem is that title is derivative. Y has a good title only if X had a good title, whose title in turn depends on W and on V. Where does it all stop? Does one have to go right back to the original Crown grant by Alexander III or James IV? The answer, of course, is no, because of the doctrine of positive prescription.

Positive prescription

The basis of positive prescription was formerly the Prescription Act 1617, but is now section 1 of the Prescription and Limitation (Scotland) Act 1973. Its importance in conveyancing law and practice cannot be overstated. In terms of section 1(1) of the 1973 Act, prescription applies to "interests in land," *i.e.* to real rights in land. The real rights in land are (1) *dominium* (ownership), both *utile* and *directum*; (2) security, *e.g.* standard security; (3) lease; (4) proper liferent; and (5) servitude. But special provision is made for servitudes in section 3 and so[10] servitudes are excluded from section 1. Also excluded are short leases,[11] for by section 1(2) the interest in land must be capable of being recorded in the Register of Sasines, which a short lease is not. This chapter is concerned only with *dominium utile*, but the same rules apply to other interests in land and indeed must be applied in, for instance, the purchase of a superiority title or of a leasehold title, the latter being common in commercial conveyancing. In practice, prescription is almost never encountered with reference to the remaining interests in land, *i.e.* security and proper liferent.

There are two requirements if prescription is to operate. First, there must be an appropriate deed which has been recorded in the Register of Sasines (called the foundation writ or the prescriptive writ). Secondly, the interest in land must be possessed for ten years.

Identifying the foundation writ

The examination of title begins with a bundle of writs, sometimes a very large one, tied up with red tape.[12] Which is the foundation

[10] See the definition of "interest in land" in s. 15(1).

[11] Leases of 20 years or under.

[12] It is one of the mysteries of existence that red tape is pink. And one of the

writ? The rule for prescription is that the 10 years of possession must follow and be *founded* on (hence "foundation" writ) the recording of the deed. So the foundation writ is the first property writ recorded more than 10 years before the current transaction. Thus, if it is now 1993, and Y is selling to Z, and Y bought the property in 1989 from X, and X bought the property in 1985 from W, and W bought the property in 1977 from V, the foundation writ is the disposition of 1977.[13] (If there is a qualifying writ which is not quite 10 years old this can be treated as the foundation writ provided that the ten year period will have expired by the time the client's disposition is recorded.) By "property writ" is meant a deed which conveys the property: usually this will be a disposition or feu disposition, but it may also be[14] a notice of title or a judicial decree having the effect of a conveyance.

Once the foundation writ has been identified, it must be read to ensure that it complies with section 1. For this purpose only the deed itself should be considered[15] and extrinsic evidence is disregarded. This is less straightforward than it sounds. By the deed itself is meant (1) the actual words of the deed and (2) any other words which are formally imported by reference—typically descriptions and real burdens under, respectively, section 61 and section 32 of the 1874 Act. Other deeds which are referred to but are not formally imported are not part of the foundation writ and fall to be disregarded for this purpose. This includes any links in title, also called midcouples, mentioned in the foundation writ for the purposes of deduction of title.[16]

skills to be learned by the novice, apart from trying to find out how the dictaphone works, and where the loo is, is how to tie the writs up again so that they won't promptly spill out all over the floor. (The secret is to tie them up as tight as possible, leaving one out, and then slide that one in.)

[13] The foundation writ can sometimes be very old. One of the authors once acted in the purchase of property from a corporation which had owned it continuously since 1646, when it had effected the purchase. The foundation writ was therefore well over 300-years-old.

[14] See s. 5(1).

[15] s. 1(1): "Sufficient in respect of its terms."

[16] See Halliday, para. 21–06. For instance, suppose that the foundation writ deduces title through a confirmation in favour of the grantor of the deed, but that that confirmation does not include the property in question. That does not affect the status of the deed as a foundation writ.

"Sufficient in respect of its terms"

The deed must be sufficient in respect of its terms to constitute a title to the interest in land or in land of a description habile to include the particular land.[17] To test this, the description given in the dispositive clause must be examined. All that is required is that the words of description are capable of including the land in question, even if this is not the only, or even the most natural, interpretation of the words.[18] For instance, it is common to find that the description is little more than a glorified postal address. In that case, the subjects actually possessed for the prescriptive period will be owned. By contrast, a bounding description excludes land lying beyond the stated boundary. This is the maxim of "no prescription beyond a bounding title." Thus, if the description states a boundary line, and the successive owners have in fact possessed to a line beyond that line, there will be no ownership of the extra land, no matter how long the possession has endured.[19]

Not ex facie invalid or forged

The foundation writ must not be invalid *ex facie* or forged.[20] If a deed is forged it is not a good foundation writ. But apart from that, defects which are not apparent from a visual inspection of the deed do not matter. One is concerned only with *ex facie* validity and, as explained earlier, extrinsic evidence is irrelevant. Thus, so long as the deed looks correct, it does not matter that it is actually fundamentally defective, *e.g.* because it was granted by a non-owner or because an inspection of the midcouples listed in the deduction of title clause would reveal that they are inept or even non-existent. Nor does it matter that such defects are actually known about. The law is concerned only with the appearance of the deed. Good faith is irrelevant in positive prescription. The test is whether, if there were no extrinsic defects, the deed would be sufficient to confer the right in question. If the answer is yes, the foundation writ is good. In marginal cases the test may be difficult to apply, but it appears from the wording of section 1(1A) of the 1973 Act that doubts should be resolved in favour of validity. Only

[17] s. 1(1)(*b*)(i).

[18] *Auld* v. *Hay* (1880) 7 R. 663; *Suttie* v. *Baird*, 1992 S.L.T. 133.

[19] The rule is the same even where it is argued that the land is possessed as a part and pertinent: see *Cooper's Trs.* v. *Stark's Trs.* (1898) 25 R. 1160.

[20] s.1(1A).

a deed bearing clear evidence of its own invalidity fails to make the grade.[21]

The requirement of possession

Possession must follow the recording of the foundation writ. The period is 10 years.[22] The possession must be continuous, by which is meant, not that the possessor must be there all that time, but that he must not have yielded possession to anyone else (*e.g.* a squatter) who does not recognise his title. Possession may be civil, for example through a tenant. In terms of section 1(1)(*a*) of the 1973 Act possession may be "by any person and his successors." So the fact that the property may have changed hands does not matter, so long as the new proprietor or proprietors also took possession. Section 1(1)(*a*) provides that the possession must be exercised "openly" (*i.e.* not just when the neighbour is out shopping), "peaceably" and "without any judicial interruption." By section 1(1)(*b*) possession must be *founded* on the foundation writ, by which is meant that the possession must be "adverse" (*i.e.* attributable to the foundation writ) and not of consent (*i.e.* attributable merely to the consent of the true owner).

Both a foundation writ and 10-years' possession are required for prescription. But while foundation writs are anxiously examined and argued about by solicitors, possession is usually taken for granted and no evidence of possession is required. Whether this is entirely wise seems open to question. But, of course, verifying past possession is difficult. What in practice usually happens is that the purchaser's agent checks the search for the past 40 years. If there is a competing title, this will usually be shown up by the search, and in that case it may be necessary to investigate the history of the possession. There is no magic about the figure of 40 years. It is a practical point. Thus, suppose the foundation writ is 12-years-old, and in fact it was invalid at the time, and someone else owned the property. A 40-year search will, in practice, reveal this fact, and in that case it may be necessary to verify that the seller, or his predecessors, have had 10 years of possession. If a 40-year search

[21] See further J. Burns, *Conveyancing Practice* (4th ed.), p. 201.

[22] In certain questions with the Crown, the period is 20 years: s.1(4). Generally, on the calculation of time, see s. 14.

throws up no competing title, almost certainly there is no competing title.

Effect of prescription

According to section 1(1) of the 1973 Act, the effect of prescription is that "the validity of the title . . . shall be exempt from challenge." This means that even if the foundation writ was voidable or, worse, void, the fact no longer matters, and the title based on that deed can no longer be challenged. Of course, in practice, most foundation writs are perfectly good even without prescription; but the great thing about prescription is that it is not necessary to prove that this is so. Quite simply, it no longer matters. Thus, suppose that it is now 1993, and Y is selling to Z. Y bought in 1989 from X. X bought in 1985 from W. W bought in 1977 from V. The 1977 disposition is the foundation writ. Provided that it is *ex facie* valid (and not a forgery), and provided that there has been possession for at least 10 years back from now (since 1983), the title is good, even if the 1977 disposition was void. Further, any right to challenge the title which is more than 10-years-old may be disregarded. Prescription cuts off any right to reduce the title. But it will not cut off other rights. For instance, the ordinary running of positive prescription will not cut out real burdens or servitudes or heritable securities.[23] (If it did, then anyone with a mortgage more than 10-years-old would be happy.)

A quirk

There is a curious quirk which arises from the law of prescription. Suppose that in 1977 A disponed 50 hectares to B, who recorded his disposition. B took possession, but due to a misunderstanding about boundaries only took possession of 49 hectares, A remaining in possession of the extra hectare. Then in 1987 A would have reacquired, by prescription, title to that hectare. For A would have had ten years of possession and this would be attributable to the deed by which he had (sometime before 1977) acquired the property. Correspondingly, in 1987 B's ownership of that hectare would

[23] Such rights may be extinguishable by negative prescription, but not merely by possession for 10 years.

cease.[24] Although logical, this is an odd result, which appears to offend against the principle that one cannot derogate from one's own grant.

A note on the disposition a non domino

It sometimes happens that someone notices that a piece of ground is unoccupied and apparently abandoned. Using prescription, it is possible to acquire ownership. What happens is that the person gets a friend to grant to him a disposition of the land,[25] and the disposition is recorded. This is called a disposition *a non domino*, *i.e.* from a non-owner. The disponee takes possession, and 10 years later will become the owner. This may seem like theft, but good faith is not a requirement of positive prescription. Moreover, the true owner has 10 years to reclaim his property, and the policy of the law is that if an owner abandons his property he cannot expect the law to protect his rights forever. When purchasing from someone who purports to have acquired ownership in this manner, it is obviously wise to verify that there has been 10 years of possession, unless the acquisition took place long ago, such as more than 40 years ago.

Writs subsequent to the foundation writ

Assuming a good foundation writ followed by 10-years' possession, the title 10 years ago today was fine. But what has happened since? The owner may have been inhibited, or sequestrated, or have died, or have disponed the property to someone else. The task of the purchaser's solicitor is to connect the current seller with the good title of 10 years ago. If the property has not changed hands

[24] See *Wallace* v. *University of St Andrews* (1904) 6 F. 1093 and *Love-Lee* v. *Cameron*, 1991 S.C.L.R. 61.

[25] Sometimes one sees the disposition in the form of a conveyance by X to himself. This may not be valid, because a conveyance which does not purport to convey may not be a valid foundation writ. (To convey is to transfer, and it is difficult to see how one can transfer to oneself. Compare *Kildrummy (Jersey) Ltd.* v. *Inland Revenue*, 1992 S.L.T. 787.) The normal practice is, therefore, to make sure the disponee is someone distinct from the disponer. Of course, the disposition must not appear to be a disposition *a non domino*, for that would be self-defeating, for a foundation writ must not contain evidence of its own invalidity.

during that period, the seller will have been the grantee of the foundation writ, and there is nothing further to be checked in this respect. But in many cases the property will have changed hands. If so, the dispositions or other writs connecting the current seller to the good title of 10 years before must be examined. Such writs must be absolutely, and not merely *ex facie*, valid, for prescription has not yet operated on them. So extrinsic defects matter as much as intrinsic defects, although in practice it may not always be possible to find out about such extrinsic defects. Each title is different and an exhaustive list of things to look out for cannot be given, but some of the more important points are given below.

Each consecutive deed must follow on from its predecessor. This means either that the granter of deed 4 was the grantee of deed 3 or that, the grantee of deed 3 having died or been sequestrated, etc., without having conveyed the property, the property has passed to the granter of deed 4 in some other way, *e.g.* as a result of a grant of confirmation of executors or act and warrant in favour of a trustee in sequestration. In such cases the confirmation, etc., is called a midcouple or link in title and, of course, must be checked. Another example is the special destination. For instance a house is conveyed to A and B and the survivor of them. A dies, and the next deed is a disposition by B alone. These issues are considered elsewhere in this book.[26]

Each deed must be checked for errors, such as the designations of the parties, the description of the subjects, and the mode of execution. (Note that until 1970 deeds had to be signed on each page, and that during 1990 different rules, 3 sets in all, were in force at different times for execution by companies.[27]) In principle, the warrants of registration should be checked, as should the stamp duty, though in practice the Keeper will have been highly unlikely to have accepted a deed with errors of these kinds. The conveyancer should consider whether there is anything in a deed which raises reasonable suspicions and suggests that further evidence is needed. It must be remembered that the deeds after the foundation writ must be absolutely (and not merely *ex facie*) valid. A party who signs as "Postman Pat" is probably under age and unable to convey property. Further inquiries must be made of the seller's solicitors.

[26] Chap. 23 (deaths), chap. 24 (destinations) and chap. 27 (bankruptcy).
[27] See chap. 15.

There is also the possibility that a deed, while not void, might be voidable. Examples of voidable deeds include: (1) Deeds by persons between the ages of 16 and 18 which are "prejudicial" within section 3 of the Age of Legal Capacity (Scotland) Act 1991; (2) Gratuitous alienations and unfair preferences granted by persons when insolvent; (3) Deeds by a party who has been inhibited[28]; (4) Disposals by a spouse within five years prior to a claim by the other spouse for aliment or financial provision.[29]

Voidable titles and good faith

Where a deed within the prescriptive progress is voidable (not void), there are two possibilities. The first possibility is that the purchaser does not know about the problem and has no reasonable means of knowing about it, for example because it appears neither from the deed itself nor from the search. In such a case, he is protected, because voidability does not affect a subsequent purchaser in good faith.[30] Unless the deed is reduced, and the extract decree recorded[31] before the purchaser records his own disposition, there is no danger from a subsequent reduction. The right to reduce is a personal right which does not transmit against successors in good faith.

The other possibility is that the purchaser does know, or ought to know, that the deed is voidable. In that case, the right to reduce will transmit against him, with the result that the seller is not offering a good and marketable title and must take steps to buy off the party with the right to reduce.

Gratuitous alienations

Space allows only a few words about this important subject.[32] A "gratuitous alienation" means, in most cases at least, a donation of property. Gratuitous alienations are generally perfectly valid,

[28] Here, the search should provide the necessary information.

[29] Family Law (Scotland) Act 1985, s. 18.

[30] Stair, IV xl, 21; Erskine, III, v, 10; Hume, *Lectures*, iii, 236–238. See, further, *Stair Memorial Encyclopaedia*, vol. 18, para. 692.

[31] 1924 Act, s. 46(1).

[32] For the law, see McBryde, *Bankruptcy* (W. Green, 1989).

for an owner is free to give away his property if he feels generous. Indeed, donations are common between family members. But if a person is insolvent, he is forbidden by law to give away his property, and if he does so, the donation is voidable by his creditors. Since the donation is voidable only and not void, a third party acquiring for value and in good faith has nothing to worry about. Thus, suppose that a husband gratuitously transfers title to his house to his wife, but is insolvent, and a year later is sequestrated. In the meantime, the wife has sold the property to X. If X was in good faith, his title cannot be reduced by the trustee in sequestration, who in that case can do no more than sue the wife for the value of the property. The trouble is that if the fact that the wife's acquisition was gratuitous appears from the face of the title, which it usually does, X is barred from pleading good faith.[33] So X is at risk, at least in theory. In practice, of course, most gifts are not made by insolvent donors. The law is probably that unless there is some particular ground for suspecting voidability, or unless there is some special clause in the missives, a purchaser cannot object to a title which includes a gratuitous transfer.[34]

Identification of subjects

It is pointless establishing that the seller has a good title, unless it is a good title to the subjects which the purchaser has contracted to buy. But in practice this is easier said than done, not least because missives are themselves often dangerously vague in describing the property. All deeds within a prescriptive period will usually contain the same description, which will normally consist of (a) a general description and (b) a particular description imported by reference from the break-off writ.[35] The general description may not take matters very far. But unless there is a good plan, the particular description may also be of limited help. Old particular descriptions are often either impossibly vague or refer to boundary features which no longer exist, for example:

[33] *Hay* v. *Jamieson* (1672) Mor. 1009; Erskine, IV, i, 36; Bell, *Comm.*, ii, 183.

[34] *Cf. Sibbald's Heirs* v. *Harris* , 1947 S.C. 601, discussed in chap. 5.

[35] In other words, the successive deeds will not normally contain the full description, but refer to an earlier deed by A to B. Clients are often puzzled why the deed in their favour should refer to other people. For descriptions, generally, see chap. 9.

"All and Haill that piece of land part of the said West Mill Hough being the east part thereof now or formerly divided from the west part by a line drawn from the tree standing, or which stood, immediately on the east of the said meadow park, straight across over the acqueduct in a straight line terminating at a holly bush which stood on the south side of the river which bush was the westmost except one at that place having a young plane tree growing up through it."[36]

Modern particular descriptions, at least in housing estates, sometimes employ the dreaded "floating rectangle," *i.e.* a plan showing a plot of ground apparently in the middle of nowhere and which does not include any recognisable and permanent landmarks such as a public road. Even if the plan shows a road, this may not be sufficient. Thus, the plan may show the property next to "the public road from Drumbeg to Balnacraig" with no indication of where on that road (which is 35 kilometres long) the property actually lies.

The situation may be easier if the purchaser's solicitor inspects the property himself, but in practice this is seldom done. Any plan or verbal description should be sent to the purchasing client for confirmation that this is the property which he thinks he is buying. With flats, the client should be contacted to check that the flat he thinks he is buying is the same one as is identified in the deeds. Regrettably, it sometimes happens that title is taken to the first floor south when the client thinks he is buying the first floor north.[37] The notes on title should give a reasonably full summary of the description, or there should be photocopy attached of the deed giving the description.

[36] Compare *Anderson* v. *Lambie*, 1954 S.C. (H.L.) 43, *per* Lord Reid at 51: "The lands were described as 'parts of the twenty-six shilling and eightpenny land of old extent of Blairmackhill' and otherwise were only identified as having been possessed by persons long since forgotten or bounded by other lands apparently now unidentifiable."

[37] In such cases the seller will also typically have been under the same error, and possesses the "wrong" flat which the buyer then blithely moves into. It will be found that the descriptions were muddled up when the individual flats were first sold off 100 years before.

Question 2: Are the Real Burdens and Servitudes Acceptable?

Ensuring that the seller owns the property is the most important part of examination of title. But a number of other things also require to be checked. These take less time and may be dealt with more briefly here.

The first concerns real burdens and servitudes. These are considered in a separate chapter and only a few remarks will therefore be made here. Almost all property is subject to real burdens of one kind or another. Old burdens writs are often long, irrelevant and in deplorable handwriting, but the purchaser's solicitor must wade through them nonetheless just in case something important to the client is lurking there. How does one know which deeds impose burdens? The answer is that one cannot know. The practice is to take the list in the dispositive clause of the most recent disposition as being correct ("but always with and under the burdens, conditions and others specified in. . ."). But since the solicitor will not have before him all the deeds relating to the land since the beginnings of time (although it may feel like it) there is no practicable way of checking that this list is complete. However, cases where a burden has been left off the list in recent writs are in practice almost unknown.

The client is going to have to live with the continuing burdens, so the question must be asked whether they are acceptable. The missives will typically have stipulated that the burdens shall not be "unusual or unduly onerous," the meaning of which is discussed in the previous chapter. Most burdens are not unusual or unduly onerous. This can cause problems if the client wants to use the property for some purpose other than domestic (*e.g.* commercial), and the proposed use turns out to be prohibited by a real burden. Unless the burden is unusual or unduly onerous, the client will be locked into the bargain and must buy a property which he cannot use as he wishes. This is a disaster and might lead to a damages action by the client against his solicitor. The way of avoiding this difficulty is to specify in the original offer to purchase that the particular use proposed by the client is not contrary to the conditions of title.[38]

[38] See further *Armia* v. *Daejan Developments Ltd.*, 1979 S.C. (H.L.) 65.

If there is an objection, it should be made before settlement. Once the disposition has superseded the missives, any subsequent claim rests on the warrandice clause, and can only be made where the purchaser did not know about the burden at the time when the disposition was delivered, which is something that in practice could hardly happen.[39]

Informing the client

Before settlement the purchasing client should be informed what the real burdens are. He needs to know what he is allowed to do and not allowed to do with the property, and what his maintenance obligations are to be.

Servitudes

For servitudes, much the same considerations apply as for continuing real burdens. But it must be remembered that servitudes, unlike real burdens, can be constituted by prescription, that where constituted by writing they need not be recorded, and that even where recorded they may appear in the title of the dominant property only.[40] Hence, it may be that the purchaser's solicitor cannot discover their existence.

Question 3: Are There any Heritable Securities?

Heritable securities, as real rights, are unaffected by a change of ownership of the burdened land. So if a security affects the property in the hands of the seller it will continue to affect the property in the hands of the purchaser, unless it has been discharged. It is thus the duty of the solicitor for the purchaser to ensure that all securities have been discharged, or will be discharged by settlement. The security most commonly encountered is, of course, the standard security. But in property which has not changed hands for many years one still occasionally finds the pre-1970 securities, *i.e.* the bond and disposition in security and the *ex facie* absolute disposition. If the seller is a company there may also be a floating charge, but since a floating charge is not, until crystallisation

[39] Except in the case of certain unrecorded servitudes.

[40] *Balfour* v. *Kinsey*, 1987 S.L.T. 144.

("attachment"), a real right, it will not run with the property and no discharge is necessary, though one would normally require a certificate of non-crystallisation from the chargeholder.[41]

In practice, there is usually a series of old securities accompanied by a matching series of discharges, and also the current security granted by the seller to a bank or building society, and which is to be discharged as part of the current transaction, out of the proceeds of sale. So far as the current security is concerned, the seller's solicitor prepares a draft discharge, and sends it to the purchaser's solicitor for revisal. The engrossed (*i.e.* principal) discharge will then be prepared and sent by the seller's solicitor to the lender for execution. All being well, the discharge will then be delivered at settlement. For old securities, all that need be done is to check that each security deed is matched by an appropriate discharge, and the simplest way to do this is by reading the search, which should generally cover a period of at least 40 years. The search will identify the relevant deeds. Is it necessary to examine the discharges themselves to check that they are valid? In theory the answer is yes, at least as far as *ex facie* validity is concerned.[42] With discharges older than five years, a defect not discoverable from the face of the deed will not affect a purchaser unless he knows about it.[43] So only *ex facie* validity matters. This rule does not apply to discharges within the previous five years, but at common law a *bona fide* purchaser is only affected by defects sufficiently serious to make the deed void (as opposed to voidable), and such defects are usually discoverable from an examination of the deed itself.

Some solicitors make copious lists of securities and discharges in the course of notes on title, but arguably this is a waste of time.

Question 4: Has the Feuduty Been Redeemed?

In a most cases the feuduty[44] has already been redeemed.[45] If it has not been, and is not being redeemed at this sale, the purchaser will have to continue paying feuduty. This will only be the case where

[41] See chap. 26.

[42] Though *cf.* Halliday, para. 21–57.

[43] 1970 Act, s. 41.

[44] The following remarks apply equally to groundannuals, very few of which are now in existence.

[45] Under the 1974 Act.

the feuduty is unallocated. The second question, assuming that it has been redeemed, is whether the redemption money been paid to the superior. If it has not been paid, the purchaser may become liable.[46]

If the feuduty has already been redeemed, then evidence is required that the redemption money has actually been paid. Redemption money is calculated by reference to the market price of $2\frac{1}{2}$ per cent. Consols (a type of Government bond) one calendar month and one day before the date of redemption, and in practice this figure is produced by multiplying the annual feuduty by the feuduty factor for the relevant day. A list of feuduty factors is published monthly in the *Journal of the Law Society*. The factor varies from day to day but is typically around 10.

The rules on evidence of payment depend on whether the original redemption was voluntary or compulsory. Under the voluntary procedure, redemption occurs only on payment being made to the superior, and payment is then acknowledged by a receipt in the statutory form. So the receipt must be seen, and this will normally be found among the title deeds. Under the compulsory procedure (*i.e.* redemption on sale), redemption occurs automatically on the date of entry and without reference to whether the superior has actually been paid or not. For this reason the Act makes no provision for a statutory receipt, but the practice is for superiors to issue receipts. In most cases, therefore, a receipt will be included among the titles. But if there is no receipt there is a danger, at least in theory, that the client will become liable for the redemption money. This is because any unpaid redemption money is secured on the property as a pecuniary real burden.[47] The real burden is temporary. Its normal duration is for a period of two months beginning with the service on the superior of the statutory notice of redemption (or, if later, and provided a notice has been sent, the date of entry). But the period can be extended by the court, subject to the extract decree being recorded within the initial two month period.[48]

What this means in practice is that if there is no feuduty redemption receipt, one requires to see a receipted duplicate notice of redemption (to show that the two month period has been triggered

[46] See, generally, ss. 4 and 5 of the 1974 Act.

[47] 1974 Act, s. 5(5). This is not a real burden in the ordinary sense, but a type of heritable security.

[48] 1974 Act, s. 5(6)-(8).

in the first place) and a Sasine search for the relevant two-month period which does not disclose the recording of an extract decree under section 5(7) of the 1974 Act. If there is no extract decree, then no liability can attach to the purchaser and there is no need for further inquiry.

Occasionally, feuduty falls to be redeemed as a result of the current transaction. If this is the first time that the property has been sold since 1974, then, unless the feuduty is unallocated, the seller must pay the redemption money and obtain a feuduty redemption receipt. In practice, this cannot usually be done until after settlement, in which case the obligation to deliver such a receipt (*e.g.* within four weeks) should be added to the letter of obligation which the seller's solicitor grants at settlement.

If the feuduty is unallocated it cannot be redeemed. But since there is now a statutory right to have feuduty allocated,[49] missives sometimes provide that the seller must exercise this right and thereafter proceed to redemption. In the absence of such a provision there is no obligation to allocate and redeem, and the purchaser would take over liability for feuduty from the date of entry. Feuduty is usually payable twice a year, at Whitsunday and Martinmas, and, for the purposes of apportionment between seller and buyer, is regarded as running evenly from day to day.

Some practical points are worth mentioning. First, the amount of feuduty is often derisory, making the complexity of the redemption provisions particularly irksome. Indeed, nowadays superiors often do not bother to demand payment. Secondly, redemption of feuduty is not redemption of the feu itself.[50] The superior may lose interest in a practical sense, but not in a legal sense. Thirdly, redemption of feuduty has no effect on the overfeuduty, *i.e.* the feuduty due by the superior to his superior; and overfeuduty can in theory be exacted directly from the proprietor of the *dominium utile*. The practice, however, is to ignore overfeuduty. Fourthly, nowadays most feuduties have been redeemed. Fifthly, although in law only allocated feuduties are redeemable, in practice if a feuar sends his superior a cheque for redemption the superior will happily cash it and issue a redemption receipt. Probably this in law amounts to simultaneous allocation and redemption. Sixthly and

[49] 1970 Act, s. 3.
[50] 1974 Act, ss. 4(3) and 5(3).

lastly, since superiors so often do not collect the feuduty, when redemption is made there will be arrears, which will have to be paid off at the same time.[51]

[51] Typically, five years of arrears, earlier sums having been extinguished by the quinquennial prescription: 1973 Act, s. 6.

Chapter 7

SEARCHES AND LETTERS OF OBLIGATION

Introduction

There are four types of search[1]: in the Sasine Register, in the personal register (whose formal name is the Register of Inhibitions and Adjudications) in the Companies Register and in the Land Register. This chapter considers only the first three, the fourth being dealt with later.[2] In this chapter it will be assumed that the searches are being done in connection with a sale. But very much the same applies for other types of transaction, such as a security, or a long lease, so where appropriate "debtor" or "lessor" can be substituted for "seller."

In general, a search is for the benefit of the purchaser, to enable him to be sure that nothing has been registered that might prejudice the title he is getting. But it must not be forgotten that a purchaser is usually granting a security at the same time, and that the purchaser's agent is usually (at least in domestic conveyancing) also the agent for the lender. Thus, the search is also for the benefit of the lender, for if the title is bad the security will be bad too.

An obligation is probably implied by law that the seller[3] shall exhibit or deliver clear searches.[4] The rule seems to be that delivery is required for such searches as relate exclusively to the property conveyed.[5] Missives usually have a clause which repeats the implied rule. Occasionally, a contract will say that the seller need neither exhibit nor deliver a search. That will not of itself free him from

[1] For searches see Halliday, and G.L. Gretton, *Guide to Searches.*

[2] Chap. 20.

[3] The same applies to a borrower on heritable security and indeed to any onerous transaction. But the grantor of a non-onerous deed in general does not need to show good title, and hence need not exhibit searches. Examples are donations and conveyances by an executor in implement of a legacy.

[4] The question of what exactly satisfies the requirement of a "clear" search is considered in chap. 5.

[5] See 1979 Act, s. 16.

an obligation to grant a valid title. It merely shifts the onus on to the purchaser to make the necessary searches himself.

Firms of searchers

The registers are public and so, in theory, anyone can search there. But in practice, legal searches are done by firms of professional searchers,[6] who guarantee the accuracy of their reports. Their services are generally swift, efficient and inexpensive, and they play a vital part in conveyancing practice.

1. The Sasine Search

Normally, the purchaser's agent can expect all relevant deeds which have been recorded in the Sasine Register to be among the deeds which the seller sends to the buyer for examination. But the buyer would be unwise to take this on trust, for in theory there might be one or more other deeds in the Sasine Register which are not among the deeds which the seller produces. This might be as a result of fraud by the seller, or mere inadvertence. Here are some examples.

(1) The estate is a large one and over the years the seller has sold off various small parcels of land. Indeed, this is the norm for large estates. In that case, copies of the break-off deeds should have been put up with the titles. But it can happen that one or more such deed has been overlooked, so from the deeds in the possession of the seller it looks as if he owns rather more than he actually does.

(2) It might be that the seller has granted a standard security without telling his solicitor. This is unusual, but it can happen, and in the last few years there has been an increasing incidence.[7]

(3) There might be an adjudication against the seller. In that case, the seller should know of it, but a copy will not be in the deeds, and the seller may conveniently forget to tell his solicitor.

So a purchaser always insists on a Sasine search, to ensure that he knows of all relevant deeds. The same is true in transactions

[6] Until about 1987 there were also the "official searchers" who were Register House staff.

[7] The seller may not be fraudulent in not telling his solicitor. He may not realise what he has done. Such securities are commonly called "double-glazing standard securities" because they are often presented to the householder for signing for credit deals, such as double-glazing.

other than sale, such as the grant of a new security, or a long lease, and so forth.

The memorandum

A Sasine search is a search of the Sasine Register, based on the search sheets,[8] to identify all deeds registered there within any defined period. In nine cases out of 10 there will be an existing search among the deeds, which was prepared at the time of the last transaction. In that case, the practice is to send this off to the searchers with a request that they continue it to the present. This is called a continuation of search. The letter of request to the searchers is called a memorandum for search, or for continuation of search, and always follows a standard format.[9] The memorandum is drafted by the seller's solicitor and sent to the purchaser's agent for approval and return. The seller's solicitor then extends it (*i.e.* makes a principal copy) and sends it off to the searchers, and it will be returned to them when complete. The seller pays the searchers' fee. Occasionally, there is no existing search and in that case it will be necessary to instruct a new search.

What length of search?

How far back a search should go depends on various factors, but the general rule is that it should go back 40 years or to the date of the foundation writ, whichever is the longer. Some people consider it sufficient to go back only to the foundation writ, since any prior writ will be irrelevant by reason of positive prescription. There are, however, a number of reasons why the standard advice is to go back 40 years. One is that there might be undischarged securities. As a rule of thumb, any security older than 40 years has probably been extinguished by payment or by the long negative prescription. A second is that positive prescription works only if there has been possession. In practice, one does not normally check

[8] The search sheets kept up by the Keeper do not have any statutory basis. There is a sheet for each major interest (*dominium utile*, superiority, long lease) in each property, and the sheet notes briefly all deeds affecting that property, with a reference to where the deed itself can be found in the register.

[9] See Gretton's *Guide to Searches*.

the fact of possession. A 40–year search is a sort of substitute, for if there were a competing title, such a search would almost certainly show it up, and in that event further inquiry could be made.

If there is an existing search, it should be checked back either to the foundation writ or for 40 years whichever is the longer, for the same reasons.

Timing

It is now necessary to consider timing and the relationship of interim and final report. In an ideal world the buyer would want to see the up-to-date search before he settles the transaction. But in practice this is not possible, for two reasons. The first is that the search will be closed off by the searchers when the deed in favour of the buyer is recorded, which will be a few days after settlement has taken place. The second is that delays at the Sasine Register have meant, at least until recently, that it takes several months after anything is recorded for the deed to be fully traceable by the searchers. Hence, a report from the searchers at a given date would only show the state of the Sasine Register as it was some months earlier. If there were any later deeds, they would not be disclosed, because of the information delays within the register. Thus, even if the buyer were happy to get a search which was closed off at the date of settlement, there would still be a "blind period" for the previous few months. However, the position has recently been changing as a result of the computerisation of the Presentment Book.

Computerisation of the presentment book

When a deed is presented for recording in the Sasine Register, brief details of it are at that initial stage entered into a book called the Presentment Book. Hitherto it has not been practical to search this book, with its huge number of unindexed entries. However, in April 1992, the Keeper converted the book into a computer database, which began to be searchable early in 1993. The solicitor submitting the deed completes an application form which is then fed through an optical scanner, the information thereby feeding through to the database. This enables interim reports to be complete up to the previous day, a vast improvement. The system is new and it remains to be seen how it will work in practice. Two points should be noted. The first is that if it is desired that the interim report should cover the Presentment Book, this should be specifically stated in the memorandum to the searchers. It is suggested that this should always be done. The second is that it is not yet clear just how accurate or complete the information is which is retrieved from the database.

Interim reports and letters of obligation

The problem of delay is resolved partly by splitting searches into interim and final, and partly by the use of letters of obligation. Whether this system will be changed in any way by the computerisation of the Presentment Book remains to be seen.

In the first place, the searchers are asked to produce an interim report a day or two before settlement. Traditionally, missives did not expressly stipulate for this, though nowadays it is increasingly common to do so. The interim report will show all deeds recorded up to a few months before, and note any other deeds which, from the pencilled notes on the search sheets, appear to be in the registration pipeline. Where the Presentment Book database is searched, the interim report should be completely up to date. If the interim report is clear,[10] this is a reasonable basis for settlement, for the danger of an unknown deed in the blind period is not large, especially if the Presentment Book has been searched. The final search will come back from the searchers several months after settlement, and will be closed off at the date the deed in favour of the purchaser is recorded.[11] Usually the final report is clear. But there is still the danger of some deed turning up on the final search which was recorded in the blind period. This is unusual but can happen, at least where there has been no search of the Presentment Book. To cover this risk it is the practice for the seller's agents to give a guarantee called a letter of obligation.[12] This covers the blind

[10] Meaning that the report discloses no deeds which the purchaser was not in any case aware of.

[11] The date when the search is closed off is the date beyond which no search is made, so that any later deeds will not be disclosed. It is not, therefore, the date when the search is completed, which is typically several months after the date of closing off.

[12] For a style see J.H. Sinclair, *Handbook of Conveyancing Practice in Scotland*, p. 201. And see the discussion of letters of obligation later in this chapter.

period, and it also covers the settlement-to-recording gap. Thus, if settlement takes place on June 1 and the purchaser records his deed on June 4, it is, in theory, possible for another deed to be recorded on June 2. This normally could happen only by reason of the fraud of the seller. At any rate, the letter of obligation covers this short period too. A letter of obligation normally provides that this period is covered only if the deed is recorded within a stated period, usually 14 days, because there is no reason why the seller's agents should run any risk caused by delay in recording. When the seller's agents get the final search back from the searchers they send it to the purchaser's agents. The latter check it and, assuming that it is clear, send the letter of obligation back marked as implemented. Note that the letter of obligation is granted by the seller's agents. The seller himself is bound in any case to give clear searches by the missives. But the purchaser does not want to rely on this.

Start and close dates for the Sasine search

When preparing the memorandum for the searchers, both the start date and the closing date are given. The start date will be a specific date, normally the day after the close of the existing search. The closing date will not be a specific date, but will list one or more deeds which are to be recorded. These are normally the disposition to the purchaser, the discharge of the old security, and the new security. When the searchers find all these deeds on the register they will then close off the search. Obviously, they need to know the date after which they need not search, for otherwise they could never give a final search report until the Sasine Register finally ends its long life.[13] This date is normally just a few days after settlement, though, as already said, it will take several months for the information to be fully available to the searchers. Note also that when the seller's agents draft the memorandum, they will insert only the disposition to the purchaser and the discharge of the existing security. It is for the purchaser's agents when revising the draft to add the new security deed, assuming that there is to be one.

[13] It will close when all titles are transferred to the Land Register. It was set up by the Registration Act 1617.

2. The Personal Search

The personal search is a search in what is officially called the Register of Inhibitions and Adjudications, but is commonly called the personal register or the diligence register. Whereas the Sasine Register is a register of deeds giving title to land, the personal register is a register of names. The main things it includes are inhibitions and sequestrations. Despite the name, adjudications normally go into the Sasine Register or Land Register and not the Register of Inhibitions and Adjudications. If a person is inhibited or sequestrated then, of course, he will be barred from selling.

Inhibitions

We cannot here enter into any detail concerning the law of inhibition,[14] but will summarise a few leading points. Inhibition forbids the inhibited person from selling or otherwise alienating his heritable property. It also strikes at a subsequent grant of heritable security, and probably a subsequent floating charge in so far as the charge affects heritage. Breaches of inhibition are not void, but are voidable at the instance of the inhibitor. This is done by an action of reduction *ex capite inhibitionis*, though in certain types of case it is possible for the inhibitor to enforce his rights without any action of reduction. An inhibition endures for five years, after which it prescribes.[15] An inhibition can be used not only in execution of a decree but also on the dependence. In the latter case it will become void if the pursuer fails in the action. The sheriff court has no jurisdiction in inhibition, and so if a pursuer wishes to inhibit in such an action he must obtain "letters of inhibition" from the Court of Session. Letters of inhibition can also be used in Court of Session actions, but usually one finds that warrant to inhibit is included in the signeted summons, in which case what will appear on the search will be the words "summons and inhibition."

Inhibition may be discharged voluntarily by the inhibitor, the discharge being registered in the personal register. Or it may be discharged by interlocutor of the Court of Session, this being called

[14] See G.L. Gretton, *Law of Inhibition and Adjudication.*

[15] 1924 Act, s. 44.

a recall. Recalls likewise are registered in the personal register. Partial discharge and partial recall are possible, whereby the inhibition is discharged from certain property or a certain transaction, while retaining its effect as against other property and transactions. Such a partial recall is sometimes called a restriction.

Inhibition simply identifies the person inhibited, without specifying any particular property, for all heritable property in Scotland is automatically affected. It is purely a negative diligence, and confers on the inhibitor no real right. A creditor who wishes to obtain a real right by diligence must use adjudication. Adjudication need not be preceded by inhibition, though in practice it usually is. A decree of adjudication, upon being registered in the Sasine Register or Land Register, gives the adjudger a real right, being a type of judicial heritable security.

Inhibition takes effect on the day when it is registered. However, the inhibitor may first register a Notice of Inhibition.[16] If so, the inhibition takes effect from the date of the registration of the notice, provided that the inhibition itself is registered within 21 days of the notice. If the inhibition itself is registered outwith that period, the notice is void, and the inhibition takes effect from its own date of registration. The reason for the notice procedure is speed: in practice, it is usually possible to register a notice several days earlier than the inhibition itself can be registered.

Sequestration and trust deeds

As will be seen below, there are various types of entry in the personal register. After inhibitions, the most important are sequestrations and trust deeds for creditors.[17] Naturally, a purchaser wishes to be sure that the seller has not been sequestrated, and has not granted a trust deed. In the case of sequestration, what enters the register is normally the "warrant to cite." This does not mean that the person has in fact been sequestrated, but only that there is a petition for his sequestration. However, the warrant to cite, upon being recorded, bars the debtor from alienating his heritable property. Moreover, if the warrant to cite is not followed by registration of an interlocutor dismissing the petition, it is normally a fair infer-

[16] See s. 155 of the 1868 Act.

[17] Bankruptcy (Scotland) Act 1985, s. 14 and Sched. 5(2).

ence that sequestration has taken place. Recently it has come to light that some sheriff clerks are apparently failing to register some warrants to cite in the personal register. The effect of such omission on a bona fide third party is unclear. An alternative source of information on bankruptcies is the Register of Insolvencies,[18] but it is not current conveyancing practice to make a search in that register.

Occasionally, it happens that a seller is sequestrated about the time of the sale, the warrant to cite not appearing on the interim report. In that case there follows what is traditionally called the "race to the register." The trustee in sequestration can complete title, by recording a notice of title, and if he does so before the purchaser has recorded his disposition, the trustee will have won the race. He will be the owner, in trust for the creditors, and the purchaser will have nothing, except a claim in the sequestration. The reason is that at the time when the purchaser records his disposition, the grantor is no longer owner, so that the deed is, by this time an *a non domino* deed. Conversely, if the purchaser records first, he wins the race. In practice, it is difficult for the trustee to act quickly, so that the purchaser strolls home.

Instructing the personal search

The personal search is usually done through a firm of searchers and is handled with the Sasine search, so that the instructions for both go out together and the reports come back together. There is the same pattern of interim and final search. The personal register has the advantage that it is always up to date, so that a search done today will show entries made yesterday.[19] Consequently, the need for the letter of obligation is less. Still, the latter covers the personal register also.

When the seller's agents draft the memorandum for search, they will put the seller's name on it. When the buyer's agents revise it they will normally add the buyer's name. The reason for this is that the buyer will normally be granting a security and the lender will want to know if the buyer is inhibited or sequestrated.

[18] Bankruptcy (Scotland) Act 1985, s. 1.

[19] Register House feeds the entries into a computer, and some search firms compile their own databases. Searching thus means keying in the name to be searched against.

Identifying the person to be searched against

The object of the personal search is to ensure that there are no entries against the person being searched against. The search is by name and address. A danger here is that entries, such as inhibitions, may not have quite the same name as the name stated in the search memorandum. Thus, if a search is instructed against the surname Schiller, it would not throw up an inhibition made against Shiller. (Whether the error in the inhibition would make it invalid is uncertain.) The computer software commonly used will to some extent compensate for this. Thus, the software, when asked to search against Macdonald will also search against McDonald. An instruction to search against Smith will throw up entries against Smythe.[20] But there are obviously limits as to what can be achieved. Another problem is for foreign names. For instance, an inhibition against Mao Tse Tung would be indexed against Tung. But in Chinese usage, the surname is actually Mao, and the search instruction might have been against Mao, not Tung. Hence, with such names the searchers should be asked to search against both Tung and Mao, and also against Tse Tung.

Another problem concerns addresses. If the name is uncommon, the searchers will report entries against it even if the address in the search instruction does not match the address in the inhibition or other entry. But if the name is common (Macdonald, Smith, Campbell, Jones, etc.) they are less likely to do this. A typical danger would be that an inhibition is made against James Campbell at his business address, but the search is instructed against James Campbell at his home address. Or the inhibition might state a previous address. The name is so common that the searchers may not report it. Their guarantee extends only to exact matches. So it is important that all addresses are stated in the memorandum, and solicitors are under a professional duty to find out from their clients all potentially relevant addresses.

[20] However, not all search firms, it is believed, use such software. Some search firms might thus overlook such entries.

Against whom, and how far back?

Against whom should personal searches be made, and for how far back? This will in the first instance depend on what the missives say, so the question really resolves into what the missives ought to say.[21] This is a tricky question and there is no universally accepted answer. The predominant current view is that there should be a personal search against every grantor of every conveyance since (but not including) the foundation writ, the period of search running back for five years from the date when that conveyance was made.[22] In the case of the present seller, that simply means searching back for five years from the present date. Prior parties will normally have already been searched against in the previous transaction, but of course this must be checked.

Thus, suppose that it is now 1993 and Z is buying from Y. Y bought from X in 1989, X bought from W in 1984, and W bought from V in 1977. The foundation writ is the 1977 disposition. Hence Y must be searched against for the period 1988 to 1993, X must be searched against for 1984 to 1989, and W must be searched against for 1979 to 1984. V need not be searched against. As already mentioned, in practice the existing search will normally show searches against these parties (except the current seller) for precisely these periods.

Search against the heritable creditor?

Some agents request a search against a heritable creditor who is discharging a security. Others take the view that there is little point in this since an inhibition against the creditor cannot stop a dis-

[21] Since, however, there is probably a common law obligation on a seller to exhibit clear searches, there is also the question of what the law requires in the absence of contrary stipulation.

[22] The Law Society standard offer at cl. A8(a) requires personal searches "against all parties having an interest in the subjects of sale during the period of positive prescription." It is not clear exactly what this means. If the five-year period runs back from the date of the present transaction, that is probably inadequate. It should run back from the date of each party's divestiture. And if "the period of positive prescription" means 10 years, it again may be inadequate, since the foundation writ will be older than 10 years.

charge from being granted. An intermediate view is that a personal search against a discharging heritable creditor is needed if but only if he is a person capable of being sequestrated, such as an individual. This is because a personal search will disclose sequestration, and sequestration would mean that any discharge would have to be granted by the heritable creditor's trustee in sequestration. The subject is complex and has never been fully examined. Unless and until matters are clarified, it is probably good practice to require such a search. If, however, the discharging lender is, as is often the case, a major institution, such as the Bank of Scotland or the Halifax Building Society, a search would, in practice, be rather pointless.

If the discharging creditor is a company incorporated under the Companies Acts there ought to be a company search to ensure that the creditor is not in liquidation, receivership or administration. This, however, is seldom done in practice, and again the same point applies about major institutions.

Sales by special parties

Where the current seller is a heritable creditor exercising a power of sale, a personal search is necessary against the seller. It is also standard practice in such a case to search against the debtor, though in general no entry in the personal register against the debtor after the date of the creation of the heritable security can affect the creditor's power of sale.[23]

Where the sale is by an executor the practice is to search against both the deceased and against the executor *qua* executor. It is not necessary to search against the executor as an individual since any inhibition or sequestration against him as an individual could not affect his powers as executor. Much the same considerations apply to sales by trustees. If the disposition contains the consent of a beneficiary, the practice is to search personally against that beneficiary as well. Indeed, in all cases where a disposition involves a consenter, the consenter should in general be searched against.[24]

[23] *Cf. Newcastle Building Society* v. *White*, 1987 S.L.T. (Sh. Ct.) 81.

[24] An exception is where the consent is by a spouse so as to waive occupancy rights under the Matrimonial Homes (Family Protection) (Scotland) Act 1981. Another possible exception is where A sells to B on missives and B sells to C, and

If the sale is by a trustee in sequestration, a personal search is probably unnecessary,[25] though, in practice, one is often instructed against the bankrupt, and this may be wise so as to check that the sequestration notice was properly registered, and, if three years have passed, renewed.[26] Where the sale is by a trustee acting under a trust for behoof of creditors, the practice is to search against both the debtor and the trustee, though the latter is probably unnecessary if the trust is "protected."[27]

If the sale is by a liquidator, receiver or administrator the position is unclear.[28] A personal search against the actual liquidator, receiver or administrator himself is probably unnecessary, though sometimes done. A personal search against the company is normally carried out, but the seller will often seek to stipulate in the missives that the purchaser cannot object to the title on the ground of any inhibition. This is probably safe for the purchaser, subject to two qualifications. The first is that it seems not to be safe where the sale is by an administrator, since an inhibition against a company probably, though not certainly, prevents sale by its administrator.[29] The other is that where a company is in receivership, an inhibition against the company registered, not merely prior to the onset of the receivership, but prior to the original creation of the floating charge, will probably prevent sale.[30] Because the law on such matters is not clear, it is especially important to have clear provision in the missives, whatever that provision may be.

the disposition is granted by A to C with B's consent. If *Leeds Permanent Building Society* v. *Aitken Malone & Mackay*, 1987 S.L.T. 338 is correct, an inhibition against B will not affect C's title. However, the practice in such cases is to search against B as well as against A. The point is complex and cannot be discussed further here.

[25] For instance, any inhibition against the bankrupt has no effect on the trustee's power of sale: Bankruptcy (Scotland) Act 1985, s. 31(2).

[26] Bankruptcy (Scotland) Act 1985, s. 14. See also the 1924 Act, s. 44(4) as amended.

[27] Bankruptcy (Scotland) Act 1985, Sched. 5, as amended by the Bankruptcy (Scotland) Act 1993.

[28] The law is governed mainly by the Insolvency Act 1986, which, however, gives no guidance in this matter. See, further, G.L. Gretton, *Law of Inhibition and Adjudication*, chap. 11.

[29] This, at least, is the view expressed in G.L. Gretton, *Law of Inhibition and Adjudication* and it does not seem that a contrary view has been expressed.

[30] Compare *Iona Hotels Ltd.* v. *Craig*, 1990 S.C.L.R. 614.

There are also problems about how a partnership should be searched against. Practice varies, but a standard practice is to search against the firm name and against the names of the persons who hold title for behoof of the firm.[31]

Personal search against the purchaser

The practice is for the purchaser to be personally searched against, as well as the seller, at least if he is at the same time granting a heritable security to finance the purchase. An inhibition would not, however, prevent the inhibited party from purchasing heritable property. Moreover, the purchaser's heritable creditor will normally be protected against any inhibition against the purchaser.[32] More serious is the possibility that the purchaser might be an undischarged bankrupt, a fact which would be disclosed by the personal search.

Inhibition against the seller after missives

Sometimes a seller is inhibited after conclusion of missives but before the purchaser's title is recorded. In that case the inhibition is ineffective because the seller was under an obligation to sell before the inhibition was registered.[33] Nevertheless, in this situation the search is not clear because *ex facie* of the registers the inhibition predates the sale, for the missives are not recorded.[34] In this case, the general view is that the buyer can refuse to settle. In practice, various possibilities are open. The purchaser may choose to settle, carefully keeping the missives as the evidence that the inhibition came too late. Or he may agree to settle only if the seller obtains a title insurance policy. Or he may insist that the seller obtains a discharge or recall of the inhibition, or a consent to the sale by the inhibitor.

[31] See G.L. Gretton, *Guide to Searches*, p. 26.

[32] Because of s. 157 of the 1868 Act. In practice, however, the lender may wish to withdraw if the purchaser is inhibited, partly because the inhibition may throw doubt on the purchaser's solvency and partly because the existence of the inhibition may cause practical problems if the purchaser defaults and the lender has to sell.

[33] Inhibition does not strike at future voluntary acts, *i.e.* acts which the inhibited person was already under an obligation to perform when he was inhibited.

[34] See chap. 5.

Types of entry in the Personal Register

The following is a list (probably not exhaustive) of the various types of entry which may be thrown up by a personal search.

(1) Inhibition, usually in the form of letters of inhibition or summons and inhibition.
(2) Notice of inhibition.[35]
(3) Discharge by inhibitor.
(4) Certified copy interlocutor, or decree, of recall.
(5) Decree of dismissal or absolvitor where inhibition was used on dependence.[36]
(6) Notice of litigiosity, which may take the form either of a summons of adjudication or a summons of reduction.[37] These have an effect similar to inhibition.
(7) Decree of adjudication. However, such decrees are not normally registered here at all, but in the Sasine Register or Land Register.
(8) Notices concerning sequestration.[38]
(9) Trust deeds for behoof of creditors.[39]
(10) Company administration orders and interlocutors refusing or discharging such orders.[40]
(11) Applications for rectification of title.[41]
(12) English bankruptcy orders.[42]

3. The Company Search

If the seller is a company, a company search will be necessary, chiefly to ensure that the seller is not in liquidation or receivership. The same is true if a company has held title during the prescriptive

[35] 1868 Act, s. 155.

[36] This will have the effect of discharging the inhibition.

[37] 1868 Act, s. 159 as amended by the Law Reform (Miscellaneous Provisions) (Scotland) Act 1985, Sched. 2, para. 4.

[38] Bankruptcy (Scotland) Act 1985, s. 14. See also ss. 15(5) and 17(8).

[39] Bankruptcy (Scotland) Act 1985, Sched. 5, para. 2.

[40] Insolvency (Scotland) Rules 1986, r. 2.3(3).

[41] Under s. 8 of the Law Reform (Miscellaneous Provisions) (Scotland) Act 1985.

[42] These are registered if the English trustee so wishes but not otherwise. Their effect is uncertain.

progress. Thus, if Z is buying now from Y, and two years ago Y bought from X Limited, Z will need to check that there was a company search done against X Limited at that time, and that it was clear. If not, such a search must be done now. If the missives have been properly drafted, the purchaser will have the right to demand such searches.[43] Company searches are done by the same searching firms as do other searches. The correct name of the company, and also its registered number, should be put on the memorandum of search.

Scottish companies are registered at the Companies Office in Edinburgh.[44] Each company has its own file there, now held in microfiche form. The file is divided into three parts. There is the G-fiche, which is for general documents, such as the company's memorandum and articles. There is the A-fiche, which is for accounts and annual returns. Lastly, there is the M and MR-fiche. The expression "Register of Charges" means the M and MR-fiche. In this are entered: (1) all company charges which have to be registered there, such as standard securities[45] and floating charges,[46] and (2) receivership. Liquidation and administration orders are registered in the G-fiche, and the latter is also registered in the personal register.[47] Solicitors often request the searchers to search merely in the "Register of Charges," which is an error because such a search will not disclose liquidation or administration. However, in practice searchers will normally report back if there has been a liquidation or administration, even though not expressly so asked.

Length of search

The usual practice is to ask for a search beginning from the date of the company's incorporation, or October 27, 1961, whichever

[43] Probably such a right is implied by law in any case, for the seller must show good and marketable title.

[44] 100–102 George Street.

[45] Standard securities must also, of course, be registered in the Sasine or Land Register. Failure to register in the charges register (which happens all too often) may result in nullity.

[46] Companies Act 1985, s. 410 *et seq*. The Companies Act 1989 replaces these sections with new, though similar, provisions, which will be numbered s. 395 *et seq*. of the 1985 Act, the present s. 395 *et seq* being replaced. However, this part of the 1989 Act is not yet in force.

[47] Liquidation and receivership do not go into the personal register.

is the later,[48] and ending 22 days after the close of the Sasine search.[49] This period is calculated to ensure that anything which has happened before the recording of the disposition will have had time to enter the company file. Of course, if the company being searched against is not the current seller, but, say, a previous owner, it is necessary only to search up to 22 days after the date when the disposition granted by that company was recorded.

What is being searched for?

Standard securities will be disclosed, but they will in any case be known from the Sasine search. Floating charges will also be disclosed, but they, in principle, should not matter since they do not prevent the company from selling, and such sale will automatically discharge the floating charge in relation to the subjects sold.

However, there are two dangers here. The first is that the charge will often contain a clause forbidding the company from selling its heritable property without the consent of the charge holder. No one knows whether such a clause could prejudice the title of a buyer,[50] but equally no one would wish to take the risk of it. The second danger is that the charge might have attached (crystallized) by liquidation or receivership.[51]

The memorandum for search should thus seek information about registered charges, liquidation, receivership, and also about administration. It should further inquire whether the company has been struck off.[52] Lastly, it is quite common nowadays to ask the searchers to report the names of the registered directors and secretary. This is to enable the purchaser to be sure that the disposition

[48] October 27, 1961 is the date when charges became registrable.

[49] It assists the searchers if they are informed of the date when the disposition is recorded.

[50] *Trade Development Bank* v. *Warriner & Mason (Scotland) Ltd.*, 1980 S.C. 74 suggests an affirmative answer.

[51] Companies Act 1985, s. 463; Insolvency Act 1986, s. 53. Where a company is selling, the purchaser will be looking for a certificate of non-crystallization from the charge holder and a certificate of solvency from the directors, points which are dealt with in chap. 26.

[52] Under s. 652 of the Companies Act 1985. Such striking-offs are extremely common. Of course, a dissolved company has no power to sell or dispone.

is signed by persons authorised to sign it.[53] However, this step is not usually taken where the company is a large and respectable one.

Foreign companies

Sometimes the company involved is not Scottish but foreign. It may be English or French or whatever. Sometimes it may be registered in some tax haven, such as the Isle of Man. If it is registered elsewhere in the UK then Scottish searchers can generally do the appropriate search. If it is incorporated outwith the UK the problems become greater: how can one be sure that the seller, a company incorporated in some country so obscure that one is not confident about which continent it is in, is not dissolved or being dissolved or otherwise unable to give good title? And how can one know whether the persons signing the disposition are authorised to do so on behalf of the company? We cannot discuss this issue here, except to say that in such cases it may be necessary to obtain a formal letter from a law firm in the country concerned.

4. Letters of Obligation

A letter of obligation is a formal undertaking by the seller's solicitors that the final search will be clear, and, if there is a security to be discharged, that the recorded discharge will be delivered within a specified time after settlement. It takes the form of a letter adopted as holograph, addressed to the purchaser's solicitors.[54] In effect, the seller's solicitors are acting as guarantors of their clients. There is no legal obligation on the seller's agents to grant a letter of obligation, unless the missives so provide.[55]

[53] For execution of deeds by companies, see chap. 15. Companies must register the names of the current directors and secretary: Companies Act 1985, s. 288. There is an argument that a purchaser in good faith would be protected if the signatories of the disposition were not properly appointed, but the issue is complex and a search on the point is a sensible precaution.

[54] Despite this, any action to enforce it is by the purchaser, rather than his solicitors: *Emslie* v. *James Thomson & Sons*, unreported: see 1991 J.L.S. 349.

[55] The Law Society's standard offer has such a clause. Such a clause probably does not bind the seller's solicitors directly, but rather binds the seller to ensure that his agents grant the obligation.

There has been grave concern in the profession on this subject. Many solicitors object to having to guarantee a title—especially those who have had to pay up as a result. Two factors have made matters worse in recent years. The first is the growth of the backlog at Register House, which has increased the length of the blind period in Sasine searches. The longer the blind period, the greater the risk that it might contain something nasty. However, the computerisation of the Presentment Book should improve matters greatly, and may, indeed, remove most of the risk from letters of obligation. The second reason is the growth of what are commonly called double-glazing standard securities. A company provides goods or services on credit terms. The customer signs on the dotted line. Unknown to him, he has signed a standard security for the amount of the credit. The double-glazing company (or whoever—obviously this problem arises in many types of case) then registers the security. The customer sells the property a few months later and before paying off the debt. He does not tell his lawyer that there is a new security. When the final search comes through, it discloses the security. The customer has by now vanished to a retirement villa in Iraq, and his solicitor has to pay off the security because of the letter of obligation. These sneaky standard securities used to be rare, but no longer, alas.[56]

A fairly new development is that the profession's insurers have now agreed to compensate solicitors for payments under letters of obligation provided that the solicitor took proper steps to minimise risk. Ideally, the seller's solicitor should get a letter signed by his client expressly saying that he has not granted any security and that there has been no adjudication or inhibition against him, that he has not been sequestrated and is not subject to pending sequestration proceedings. But this is a counsel of perfection.

As well as promising a clear search, a letter of obligation may cover other things too, the most likely of which is delivery of a discharge of the old security. But the seller's agent should, for obvious reasons, beware of undertaking to deliver any document unless he can be sure that it will be obtainable. For instance, a letter of obligation should not promise delivery of a retrospective building consent unless the seller's solicitor can be certain that the local

[56] For discussion of the whole subject see 1991 J.L.S., pp. 135, 171, 179, 349, 423 and 450.

authority will issue this. The point may seem obvious, but law firms do sometimes fall into this trap, thereby exposing themselves to a damages action if and when they fail to deliver the necessary document.

It is unclear whether a letter of obligation prescribes after five or 20 years. It may be that it depends on the precise nature of the obligation being undertaken.[57] The prescription point might seem academic, for who would let a letter of obligation lie for five years in the file, unimplemented? But in truth it is all too easy to let things slide. What normally happens is that one just waits for the search to come in from the seller's agents. If the latter find that they cannot implement their obligation, they may do nothing and hope that the other side will forget about it. And this occasionally happens. The buyer's agents have to remember, about a year after the transaction has settled, to chase up the search if it has not yet come in. Naturally, this is easy to forget. One help is that the purchaser's lender may be more efficient, and chase up the purchaser's solicitor for the search.

[57] An obligation to deliver a clear search is arguably an obligation relating to land and so subject to the long negative prescription: 1973 Act, Sched. 1, para. 2(*e*). But other obligations may be subject to the five year prescription. See *Liebermann* v. *G.W. Tait & Co.*, 1987 S.L.T. 585 (obligation to deliver a local authority comfort letter), and *Barratt Scotland Ltd.* v. *Keith*, 1993 G.W.D. 3–205.

Chapter 8

MATRIMONIAL HOMES

Introduction

At common law, where the matrimonial home was owned by just one spouse, the other spouse had no rights in it, and if the marriage broke down, the owning spouse could insist that the non-owning spouse leave. The position was not as bad as it sounds, partly because the ejected spouse could sue for aliment to cover housing costs, or financial provision on divorce, and partly because the great majority of matrimonial homes are owned in common by both spouses, and when two persons own in common, the common law is that neither can compel the other to leave. However, the law was felt to be unsatisfactory, and the Matrimonial Homes (Family Protection) (Scotland) Act 1981 changed the position, giving "occupancy rights" to the non-owning spouse. The Act is important to conveyancers because of the need to ensure, when buying a house, that there are no outstanding occupancy rights.

Occupancy rights

Occupancy rights are conferred by the Act where title[1] is held by only one spouse, and are conferred on the other spouse. The Act calls the spouse who holds the title the "entitled spouse" and the other the "non-entitled spouse." The non-entitled spouse is thus the spouse who is entitled to occupancy rights. The chief element of occupancy rights is the right to occupy the matrimonial home even if the entitled spouse withdraws his consent to such occupation. In other words, if Mr and Mrs Smith live together, and title is held by Mr Smith, he cannot throw Mrs Smith out, except with the consent of the court. Indeed, she can, with the consent of the court, throw him out, for another aspect of occupancy rights is that the non-entitled spouse can obtain a court order excluding

[1] The rights also apply in non-ownership cases, such as leases.

the entitled spouse from the home, this being called an "exclusion order."[2]

The matrimonial home

The Act applies to "matrimonial homes." Although the title of the Act uses the word "family," it is not necessary that there be any children for the Act to apply. "Matrimonial home" is defined as:

> "Any house, caravan, houseboat or other structure which has been provided or has been made available by one or both of the spouses as, or has become, a family residence and includes any garden or other ground or building attached to, and usually occupied with, or otherwise required for the amenity or convenience of, the house, caravan, houseboat or other structure but does not include a residence provided or made available by one spouse for that spouse to reside in, whether with any child of the family or not, separately from the other spouse."[3]

Note three consequences of this definition. In the first place, suppose that Mr and Mrs A live in a flat together. Mrs A then moves out, and buys a house for herself, and lives there without her husband. The house is not a matrimonial home.[4] A has no rights in it. But the flat where her husband is living remains a matrimonial home.[5] She could insist on moving back to the flat, and could apply for an order excluding Mr A from the flat. In general, once a property is a matrimonial home, it retains that status until something happens which takes it outwith the definition, or until something happens to bring the occupancy rights to an end.

[2] There may be a logical problem here. Section 4(1) defines an exclusion order as an order "suspending the occupancy rights of the other spouse." But since only Mrs Smith has "occupancy rights," how can she have Mr Smith's occupancy rights suspended?

[3] 1981 Act, s. 22. Simplicity of drafting is not a feature of this Act. For discussion of this definition see D.I. Nichols and M.C. Meston's annotated (2nd ed.) of the Act.

[4] Hence, she could sell it and give an affidavit (see below) that it was not a matrimonial home.

[5] Thus, in effect he could not sell it without his wife's consent.

In the second place, only something which can be lived in can be a matrimonial home. Thus, the Act can be ignored in, for instance, the sale of a factory. Or again, A grants a standard security to B and B assigns this to C. C need not worry that B might be married, because a standard security cannot be a matrimonial home. (But C may be affected by possible occupancy rights in the house in favour of A's spouse.)

In the third place, only human beings can be married. Suppose that A sells a house to B Limited and B Limited later sell it to C. The house cannot be a matrimonial home in relation to B, though C will still need to be sure that it is not a matrimonial home in relation to A.

Why the Act affects conveyancing

Much of the 1981 Act is of limited interest to conveyancers, and occupancy rights would be of limited interest to them as well, if it were not for the fact that occupancy rights are not only rights by one spouse against the other, but in certain cases can affect third parties, such as a purchaser. This is because section 6(1) of the Act provides that, subject to certain qualifications, a "dealing" by the entitled spouse does not affect the occupancy rights of the other spouse. "Dealing" includes sale, so that if Mr A sells the house (even after Mrs A has moved out), her occupancy rights can survive and be enforceable against the purchaser. In other words, occupancy rights are not purely personal rights but are, to a certain extent, though not fully, real rights. It is because occupancy rights are quasi-real rights that they are important in conveyancing. They are, however, not true real rights because they do not affect certain types of third party. Thus, as will be seen later, they affect some purchasers but not others, some creditors but not others, and so on.

Two other types of right, similar to occupancy rights, deserve brief mention. The 1981 Act gives, in certain situations, rights similar to occupancy rights to cohabitants.[6] But these rights are of little conveyancing importance because they cannot in general affect third parties. Again, rights somewhat similar to occupancy rights

[6] 1981 Act, s. 18.

are created by the Bankruptcy (Scotland) Act 1985[7] in favour of the family of a bankrupt.

Response to the Act—reform

The Act proved to be something of a conveyancing disaster, and even after two rounds of reform[8] much remains that is unsatisfactory from the conveyancer's point of view. The Scottish Law Commission has conceded[9] that the conveyancing aspects of the Act "have proved to be inconvenient and unpopular," and has suggested possible further reforms.[10] However, for the moment conveyancers are stuck with the present system. They have, however, gradually learned to cohabit with the Act.

Restriction and ending of occupancy rights

Occupancy rights are the rights of a spouse as such, and so end when the spouse ceases to be a spouse, which is either by the death of one party or by divorce. In addition, a spouse can renounce occupancy rights, though this is very rare in practice. It is also possible for occupancy rights to be extinguished by prescription. Where occupancy rights exist, and have not been set aside by death, divorce or renunciation, a third party who buys the house, or acquires any rights in it, will normally need the consent of the non-entitled spouse.

If that were all, the Act would not have been such a headache for conveyancers. A purchaser would simply have checked whether the property was subject to occupancy rights, and, if so, asked for the consent of the spouse holding those rights. However, what of the case where there appear to be no such rights, typically the case where the seller is unmarried? Mr X, the seller might say he was unmarried, but might he be lying? It would have, perhaps, been reasonable for the Act to have made no provision for such a case, for purchasers always have to run minimal risks of fraud. Or it

[7] s. 40.

[8] Law Reform (Miscellaneous Provisions) (Scotland) Act 1985 and the Law Reform (Miscellaneous Provisions) (Scotland) Act 1990.

[9] Discussion Paper No. 85 (1990), p. 1.

[10] Scottish Law Commission Report (No. 135) on Family Law (1992).

might have gone further and said that in such an unlikely event a purchaser would be protected by good faith. But in fact it went even further than this, and provided protection for the purchaser provided that he is both in good faith and holds an affidavit from the seller, stating on oath there there are no occupancy rights. Possibly the most sensible response of conveyancers would have been to ignore this strange and complex procedure designed to guard against remote possibilities, especially since purchasers regularly run greater risks (albeit still very remote) all the time.[11] However, since the Act laid down this rigmarole, conveyancers felt obliged to go along with it, and this being universal practice, a solicitor who fails to demand an affidavit in such cases is guilty of negligence.

The three deeds

The conveyancing side of the Act revolves around three deeds, namely the renunciation, the consent and the affidavit. These are sometimes confused (at least by legal typists). One sometimes sees the word "affidavit" on the backing of a deed which, when opened, turns out to be a consent or a renunciation.

In the renunciation a spouse wholly gives up occupancy rights. It can, however, only refer to "a particular property" so that a deed renouncing such rights in any future matrimonial home would be invalid.[12]

In the consent, also called the consent to dealing, a spouse consents to a particular transaction, but does not otherwise give up occupancy rights. Thus, if the husband has sole title, and grants a standard security, and the wife consents, her occupancy rights remain intact as against the husband himself and as against all third parties except the heritable creditor and any parties deriving right from the heritable creditor.

Lastly, there is the affidavit. Whereas the renunciation and consent are deeds which waive occupancy rights, either wholly or partially, an affidavit has a different purpose. It is not a waiver of

[11] *e.g.* the danger of a forgery of a deed in the prescriptive progress, or of the incapacity of the grantor of such a deed, or the danger of non-possession for the prescriptive period.

[12] 1981 Act, s. 1(5).

occupancy rights, but a statement that no such rights exist. (This is typically where the owner is unmarried, but a married owner can sometimes grant an affidavit too, where the property is for some other reason not a matrimonial home.) It is thus an evidential deed rather than an extinctive deed. Another obvious difference is that whereas a renunciation or consent is granted by the owner's spouse, and affidavit is granted by the owner himself. Lastly, whereas a renunciation or consent can clear the way for any type of transaction, an affidavit is relevant only for two types of transaction, namely sale and security. It cannot cover others, such as gift, trust, lease or servitude.

Styles: (1) Renunciations

The renunciation has no prescribed form,[13] except that the renouncer must swear or affirm before a notary[14] that it is made "freely and without coercion of any kind." In practice, the renunciation will have four signatures, namely those of the renouncer, the notary, and two witnesses. There has been some difference of opinion as to whether witnesses are necessary, but it has become standard practice.

In 1985 the Act[15] was amended so that a renunciation can be made outwith Scotland before "any person duly authorised by the law of the country (other than Scotland) in which the swearing or affirmation takes place to administer oaths or receive affirmations in that other country." In England commissioners for oaths are more common than notaries, and all English solicitors are now, *ipso facto*, commissioners for oaths.[16] For renunciations done abroad there is the problem that there is no easy way of checking whether the person administering the oath is duly authorised. (Where can you lay your hands on the current list of notaries in Upper Volta?) Sections 6 and 8 of the Act help by providing that a bona fide purchaser or heritable creditor will be protected if the

[13] See Halliday, para. 21–30 for a style.

[14] Thus, it seems that a justice of the peace could not do this.

[15] s. 1(6).

[16] Solicitors Act 1974, s. 81. There may, however, be a problem here. The Commissioners for Oaths Act 1889, s. 1 says that a commissioner may administer an oath "for the purposes of any court or matter in England." See, further, an article by S. Styles at 1991 J.L.S. 444.

renunciation "bears to have been properly made." It should probably bear the seal of the foreign notary.[17]

Styles: (2) Consents

For the consent, there is a prescribed style.[18] It can either be in a separate deed or incorporated in the deed to which it consents. Both are common and indeed often both are used in the same transaction, that is to say, there is a consent given at the beginning of the transaction followed by a second consent incorporated in the final deed. This double consent is in fact commonly stipulated for in missives. The prescribed style requires attestation, but not a notary.

Styles: (3) Affidavits

There is no prescribed style for affidavits.[19] Though the Act requires a notary for a renunciation, it makes no corresponding provision for affidavits, nor, again in contrast to the provisions for renunciations, is there any provision for execution outwith Scotland. There is thus some uncertainty as to whether an affidavit could be sworn before, say, a Scottish justice of the peace or a Californian notary.[20] There seems to be no requirement for witnessing, but this is usually done. Affidavits are sometimes registered in the Books of Council and Session, in which case witnessing is essential.

The 1985 reforms[21] made no difference to renunciations (except as to execution abroad) or to consents, but they did make changes to affidavits.[22] The Act lays down a style not directly but indirectly. In its original form it provided for "an affidavit sworn or affirmed by the entitled spouse declaring that there is no non-entitled spouse." This was bizarre, for "an entitled spouse" implies a non-

[17] See letter by A. Ferguson at 1992 J.L.S. 10 and article by I. Swinney at 1992 J.L.S. 141.

[18] S.I. 1982 No. 971. See, further, Halliday, para 21–29.

[19] For a style see Halliday, para. 21–31. For the execution of affidavits, see chap. 15.

[20] See D.I. Nichols and M.C. Meston's annotated (2nd ed.) of the 1981 Act, p. 52, and the contributions by Styles, Ferguson and Swinney (above).

[21] Law Reform (Miscellaneous Provisions) (Scotland) Act 1985.

[22] For the background to these reforms, see an article at 1982 J.L.S. 455.

entitled spouse, so that any affidavit in these terms could only be false.[23] The new wording in section 6 is "an affidavit sworn or affirmed by the seller declaring that the subjects of sale are not a matrimonial home in relation to which a spouse of the seller has occupancy rights." This is clearly an improvement. Corresponding new wording was introduced to section 8, for heritable securities. But the changes were not retrospective.

Sections 6 and 8 of the 1981 Act make it clear that an affidavit, unlike a renunciation or consent, can cover only two types of "dealing," namely sales and securities. In particular, gifts, trusts, leases and servitudes are apparently not covered.[24]

Thus, if a married woman gives property to her daughter, the donor's husband can consent. But if the woman is a widow, no matrimonial documentation is possible. Nor is such documentation possible for the grant of a lease by a bachelor, or where a divorced person grants a trust deed for behoof of creditors. In all these cases (and others, such as servitudes) the grantee must just take the chance that there might be a spouse in the woodwork who might have occupancy rights. This seems to be an odd state of affairs, which, equally oddly, seems to have attracted virtually no notice.

What is a dealing?

As has been seen, occupancy rights concern the conveyancer because they can survive "dealings."[25] What then is a "dealing"? It is not a term of art in Scots law, so it is curious that the Act nowhere defines it. Section 6 tells us only that the term "includes the grant of a heritable security and the creation of a trust but does not include a conveyance under section 80 of the Lands Clauses Consolidation (Scotland) Act 1845." That is all. It does not mention sale. It is only by inference that it is clear that a sale is a "dealing," because section 6(3)(*e*) has a provision for the case where "the dealing comprises a sale." So, apart from heritable security, trust, sale, and a conveyance under the 1845 Act,[26] it is a

[23] See the definitions in s. 1 of the 1981 Act.

[24] Nichols and Meston (above) p. 53 say that excambion is covered, but this seems questionable.

[25] s. 6.

[26] Part of the law of compulsory purchase.

matter of speculation as to what is or is not a "dealing." The cautious view is that a "dealing" might be any juridical act which might adversely affect occupancy rights. Thus, gifts, leases and servitudes are probably "dealings." With no case law, the prudent conveyancer must assume that they are.

Agreeing to the shortening of a calling-up notice for a standard security is, perhaps, not a "dealing" since there is specific provision for it in section 20, the effect of which, however, is virtually to make it a "dealing." A sale by a heritable creditor is not a "dealing" because it is not an act of a spouse, but the original grant of the security is a "dealing," so that if the security is itself subject to occupancy rights then the same will presumably be true of any act done by the heritable creditor, which is why a purchaser from a heritable creditor will check the matrimonial documentation produced when the security was granted. Subject to section 12 of the 1981 Act, an adjudication is not a "dealing" since again it is not the act of a spouse. For sequestration, see above.

A borderline case is a further advance on an existing heritable security. Usually there is no difficulty, for usually the spouse will already have consented to the security. But suppose that A, a bachelor, grants a standard security, and later marries. So far so good, because even though the spouse has not consented, the security was a pre-marriage transaction and so cannot be subject to the new spouse's occupancy rights. But what if A then borrows further? This does in a sense put the occupancy rights at risk, for a larger loan must increase the danger of default. So is the further advance a "dealing?" No one knows. The prudent course is therefore to obtain matrimonial documentation for a further advance, though it is impossible to say whether this is legally necessary or not. Of course, in practice such advances are often made without the involvement of a solicitor. But a solicitor nevertheless may be confronted by this question when acting for a purchaser from a heritable creditor. For if the loan on which there was default included a further advance, and this further advance was not covered by matrimonial documentation, the title of the purchaser might possibly be at risk. It is doubtful whether section 41 of the 1924 Act could give protection here. In practice, the problem is usually ignored.

Timing

Sections 6(3)(*e*) and 8(2A) in their pre-1991 form[27] said that a purchaser or heritable creditor is protected against latent occupancy rights if both (a) he is in good faith and (b) "at or before" the time of the transaction there is produced a renunciation or consent or affidavit. This meant that retrospective affidavits were worthless, and this fact caused a good deal of bother in practice.[28] The Law Reform (Miscellaneous Provisions) (Scotland) Act 1990[29] changed this so as to remove the "at or before" clause. Retrospective deeds are thus now competent, though the general view is that on this point the 1990 Act is not itself retrospective, so that retrospective affidavits are possible only for dealings on or after January 1, 1991.[30]

Common ownership

Where title is in the name of both spouses (as is usual nowadays) there are, it seems, no "occupancy rights."[31] Any deed granted by just one spouse could have no effect on the rights of the other spouse, not because of anything in the Act, but simply because of common law. The Act[32] does, however, give the court a discretion to refuse or postpone decree in an action of division and sale raised by one spouse.[33]

Consider, next, the case where title is held in common by two persons who are not married, at least to each other, and likewise the case where title is held by three persons, two of whom are spouses. In such cases the Act has virtually no conveyancing implications, because of section 6(2), which defines "entitled spouse" for the purposes of the section thus:

[27] *i.e.* prior to the coming into force of the Law Reform (Miscellaneous Provisions) (Scotland) Act 1990.

[28] See an article by G.L. Gretton at 1990 J.L.S. 412.

[29] Sched. 8, para. 31, effective from January 1, 1991.

[30] See, *e.g.* a letter from the Keeper at 1991 J.L.S. 179.

[31] See the definition scheme in s. 1, and an article by G.L. Gretton at 1981 S.L.T. (News) 297. The amendments to the Act do not seem to have affected this point.

[32] s. 19.

[33] Arguably, there is a loophole here. A spouse might convey his half share to a nominee, who would then raise an action. But this is speculative.

> "entitled spouse" does not include a spouse who, apart from the provisions of this Act,—
>
> (*a*) is permitted by a third party to occupy a matrimonial home; or
>
> (*b*) is entitled to occupy a matrimonial home along with an individual who is not the other spouse, whether or not that individual has waived his or her right of occupation in favour of the spouse so entitled."

This provision is convoluted and hard to grasp. What it apparently means is that where there is common ownership involving a party other than the spouses, there can be no "entitled spouse" for the purposes of section 6, and hence a spouse has no protection against a "dealing." In other words, in the case of common property, occupancy rights do not affect successors, and are purely personal. Thus, if two sisters own a house in common and sell it, there is no need for affidavits (if they are spinsters) and no need for renunciations or consents (if they are married). However, the provision quoted is to be found only in section 6 (protection to purchasers) and not in section 8 (protection to lenders). The practical result of the omission has been that where in such a situation the parties wish, not to sell the property, but to grant a heritable security, matrimonial documentation is often demanded. This practice is understandable but, it is thought, not necessary. Broadly speaking, section 6 does three things. (1) It says that occupancy rights are unaffected by "dealings." (2) It states exceptions to this rule, including the common ownership exception. (3) It has specific provisions for sales. The first two of these are of general application, and are not confined to sales. Section 8 deals with heritable securities but its provisions correspond only to what is here called part (3) of section 6. Parts (1) and (2) of section 6 apply equally to heritable securities, and indeed to all "dealings." (Poor drafting, perhaps.) Hence the conclusion, that in the common ownership situation, a heritable creditor does not need to be protected by matrimonial documentation. It is understood that the Keeper takes the same view. However, if a lender insists on the documentation, then it must be done.

Lastly, cohabitants. If both parties are infeft, the case is the same as before. Matrimonial documentation is not required. If one party only is infeft, section 18 may apply to confer occupancy rights on the non-entitled cohabitant, but this is purely a personal right. It cannot survive a "dealing" and so it is not normally of interest to conveyancers.

Prescription

The Act in its original form had no provision for the prescriptive extinction of occupancy rights. The Law Reform (Miscellaneous Provisions) (Scotland) Act 1985 introduced a quinquennial prescription.[34] The importance of prescription to the conveyancer is where there has been a "dealing" which has not been supported by matrimonial documentation. The provision applies only where both (1) the entitled spouse has ceased to be entitled to occupy the house and (2) starting from that date, five years have passed during which the non-entitled spouse has not occupied the house. The first of these can, in most cases, be easily established as being the date of sale. But the second is not so easily established. Thus, suppose it is now 1993 and X is selling to Y. Y notices that when X bought in 1988 from W no matrimonial documentation was obtained. It is clear that as far as W is concerned the first requirement was met in 1988. But one also needs to know that since 1988 the house has not been occupied by anyone who might have been a spouse of W. There is no easy way to prove this. The practice has developed of getting X to swear a (non-statutory) affidavit that during that period no one has occupied the house who might have been a spouse of W. This seems a reasonable procedure, though it is doubtful whether Y could be required to accept it, unless there was a stipulation to that effect in the missives. It appears that the Keeper is prepared to accept such an affidavit for land registration purposes. The five year period, though an improvement, is still long. The Scottish Law Commission suggest that the period might be reduced.[35] As they say, "the object of the Act is to protect spouses from eviction or the threat of eviction, not to enable them to evict others from houses which were formerly the matrimonial home."

[34] 1981 Act, s. 6(3)(*b*), as amended.
[35] See pp. 73 and 82 of their Discussion paper (above).

Dispensation

The Act[36] empowers the court to dispense with the consent of a spouse to a dealing. The three main grounds are (1) that the spouse cannot be traced; (2) that the spouse is *incapax*; (3) that the spouse has unreasonably withheld consent. There are problems as to the exact meaning of the last of these, but we will not deal with dispensation to any extent since it is mainly a matter for court practitioners rather than conveyancers.[37] Mention must, however, be made of *Fyfe* v. *Fyfe*.[38] Here the husband wanted to sell the house but his estranged wife refused to consent. He applied for a dispensing order. The court refused, on the ground that dispensation is competent only in relation to a specific transaction, and marketing a property is not a specific transaction. Just how specific one has to be is not clear from the case. Possibly the stage of concluded missives must be reached, or perhaps it is only necessary that a formal offer has been received. But whatever the exact rule may be, the effect is that dispensation is likely to be a pointless exercise. For the missives would have to be conditional upon the obtaining of the dispensing order, and few buyers would be prepared to wait while an action, whose outcome must be uncertain, drags its way through the courts.

Curators, attorneys, executors, trustees

Some people argue that a "dealing" by a *curator bonis* falls outwith the Act because it is not something done by a spouse. This may be right but the question is perhaps an open one. At a policy level it is not clear why a wife should cease to be protected when her husband suddenly realises that she is an undercover Venusian in the pay of the well-known intergalactic conspiracy to populate the Highlands with six million Andromedan terrorists. The cautious approach is to assume that a "dealing" by a *curator bonis* may be covered by the Act. So if the *incapax* is married, the spouse should consent. If the *incapax* is unmarried, there is a problem, for it

[36] s. 7.
[37] For procedural problems see *Longmuir* v. *Longmuir*, 1985 S.L.T. (Sh. Ct.) 33.
[38] 1987 S.L.T. (Sh. Ct.) 38.

seems pretty clear that a *curator bonis* could not swear an affidavit. But this is just one of several cases where no matrimonial documentation is possible. If the incapacity affects the spouse whose consent is needed, again there is a problem because although a dispensation is competent, there is the *Fyfe* v. *Fyfe* problem (above).

The general, but not universal, view is that it is not competent to include in a power of attorney a power to swear an affidavit. Opinion is rather more divided as to whether it is competent to include a power to sign a consent or a renunciation. Practice does not seem to be settled on either point and there seems to be no authority.

The 1981 Act did not make it clear how a transaction by an executor or other trustee is to be treated. Clearly, no one could have occupancy rights against a trustee *qua* trustee. But might a beneficiary's spouse have occupancy rights? Under section 1, occupancy rights arise not merely where the entitled spouse is owner but where he is entitled to occupy, with the consequence that a right less than ownership can be a ground for occupancy rights. Thus, if a beneficiary is entitled to occupy, his spouse might have occupancy rights. But that of itself does not prove that a purchaser, say, from the executor or other trustee needs to obtain matrimonial documentation. For section 6 says that occupancy rights will survive a "dealing" only where the "dealing" is done by the "entitled spouse." It could be argued that a sale or other transaction by an executor or other trustee is done only by the trustee and not by the beneficiary, so that no documentation would be required, since no occupancy rights could survive the transaction. A strong example would be where a trust deed directs the property to be sold. Such a sale could hardly be a "dealing" by the beneficiary. Another strong example would be if the sale is necessary to raise funds to pay off debts. Arguably, a transaction is never a "dealing" by the beneficiary except where his consent to it is necessary. But because of the uncertainties, the safe course, and the one generally adopted, is to obtain matrimonial documentation in relation to the beneficiary, *i.e.* either an affidavit from the beneficiary himself or a renunciation or consent from his spouse. Thus, suppose a man dies with sole title, and leaves a widow, who is his sole legatee and executor, and she sells *qua* executor, an affidavit from her *qua* beneficiary should be obtained. (She might have remarried.)

Often the beneficial interest will be vested in more than one person. In that case section 6(2)(*b*) will apply and there will be no need for matrimonial documentation. But if there is any room for doubt, documentation should be obtained.

Land Register practice

The 1979 Act (as amended) provides that occupancy rights are overriding interests. But rule 5(*j*) of the Land Registration (Scotland) Rules requires the Keeper to add a note that there are no subsisting occupancy rights of spouses of former owners if he is satisfied that this is the case. (If not satisfied, he will qualify the note.) Naturally, the occupancy rights of the existing owner's possible spouse are not covered. The Keeper's note is not conclusive as to occupancy rights. As overriding interests they either exist, or do not exist, independently of what he says. The advantage of the Keeper's statement that there are no such rights is simply that if it turns out to be incorrect he will be liable to pay compensation. At first sight it would appear that such compensation is not available because section 12(3)(*h*) of the 1979 Act excludes liability where "the loss arises in respect of an error or omission in the noting of an overriding interest." But the view generally taken, and taken by the Keeper himself, is that the Keeper would be liable because a statement under rule 5(*j*) is, strictly speaking, not a "noting of an overriding interest." This seems correct.

Missives

Some offers make no provision at all about matrimonial documentation. This is presumably on the view that such documentation will have to be produced anyway because of the general obligation to produce a good and marketable title. Doubtless this is correct, but the usual practice is to have a clause in the offer dealing with the matter.

There are two common errors in such clauses. The first is to use the prefatory words: "Where the subjects are a matrimonial home within the meaning of . . . " The trouble with this is that matrimonial documentation is normally required whether or not the property is a matrimonial home. Thus, if the seller is a spinster, the property cannot be a matrimonial home, but the purchaser still wants to get an affidavit. The other error is that such clauses sometimes stipulate for documentation from the seller but forget to require that documentation be produced for prior transactions.

Two other points about missives. The first is that in operational areas it seems wise to add a provision that the land certificate will contain an unqualified statement in terms of rule 5(*j*). This is not always done in practice. The second is that in some cases the qualified acceptance should make it clear that full documentation will not be available. Thus, suppose that a widowed mother gives a house to her daughter. No documentation is possible because affidavits are not available for gifts. When the daughter comes to sell, the qualified acceptance should make it clear that no matrimonial documentation is available in relation to the acquisition. As a matter of fact the title offered is probably good anyway, since a purchaser can hardly object to the lack of documentation under the Act in a situation where the Act itself prevents any documentation from being obtained. But if the missives are clear the need for argument is avoided. In other cases, documentation which should have been obtained is absent. Again, it is wise to mention this in the qualified acceptance. Agreement can then be reached, before conclusion of missives, as to whether the purchaser will accept the situation or not. It may be that the missives as finally adjusted will provide for a title insurance policy.

CHAPTER 9

DISPOSITIONS

Deeds of constitution, transfer, and extinction

Conveyancers traditionally distinguish three classes of deed. First, a deed of constitution, or creation, creates new real rights which did not previously exist. Examples are feu dispositions, leases and standard securities. In all these cases the grantor retains a real right of some sort, but the grantee also acquires a real right of some sort, newly created. Secondly, a deed of transfer, or transmission, simply transfers from one person to another an existing real right. Dispositions and assignations are the main examples. (If A leases land to B, that is a deed of constitution, but if B assigns the lease to C, that is a deed of transfer.) Thirdly, a deed of extinction extinguishes some real right. Examples are renunciations of leases and discharges of standard securities. This chapter deals with one type of deed of transfer, the disposition, which, of course, is the most important single type of conveyancing deed.

Dispositions

A disposition[1] is the deed used to transfer ownership of land,[2] whether *dominium utile* or *dominium directum*. So if A sells a house to B, the sale is effected by a disposition[3] by A in favour of B and registered in the Sasine or Land Register. This is a standard disposition. What is happening is that A is selling all that he owns.

[1] In feudal terms, a disposition is a conveyance *a me de superiore meo*, or *a me* for short, *i.e.* away from me (the grantor) to hold of the grantor's superior. This is feudal substitution. By contrast a feu disposition is a conveyance *de me et successoribus meis*, or *de me* for short, *i.e.* a conveyance to hold of the grantor and his successors, so that the grantee becomes vassal of the grantor.

[2] Subject to minor qualifications, ownership of corporeal moveables is transferable without any deed.

[3] However, if the missives so provide, the sale could be effected by a feu disposition.

There can also be a break-off (or split-off) disposition, in which A sells part only of what he owns. He sells part of a house or field or estate and retains the rest. Break-off dispositions carry all the terms of a standard disposition as well as a number of additional terms.

Unlike many other deeds, there is no statutory form of disposition, although certain individual clauses have prescribed statutory forms. In theory, therefore, one is free to use whatever form one wishes, provided that it is clear. In practice, there is a standard method of drafting a disposition which, with minor local and personal differences, is in universal use. This is not a pretty deed. It is written in the first person, and, although long, is usually all one sentence, the different parts of the deed being marked off by a battery of colons, semi-colons and commas. Some of it is redundant, mere empty words of style. The language is to some extent archaic.[4] The client may not understand it, and may, not unreasonably, wish it to be explained. The deed is unilateral in form—only the granter signs—but bilateral in effect: the grantee is considered bound by its terms when he accepts delivery at settlement.[5] There are two forms of disposition in current use, namely dispositions of Sasine land (*i.e.* land not yet registered in the Land Register), and dispositions of property already registered in the Land Register. They are similar but not identical. The latter are dealt with later in this book in Chapter 20. The present chapter is concerned with Sasine dispositions only.

Structure of the disposition

A disposition is divided into several clauses. There can be some variation in practice, but in a typical modern disposition of property in the Sasine Register these are: (1) the *narrative* clause, also called the *inductive* clause, stating the parties and the cause of transfer; (2) the *dispositive* clause, with words of conveyance, and identifying the property; (3) the *burdens* clause, stating the real burdens, existing or new[6] (4) the *entry* clause, stating the date when

[4] Conveyancing deeds often have a long history. The disposition has been evolving for more than 800 years.

[5] See, *e.g.*, *Hunter* v. *Boog* (1834) 13 S. 205.

[6] The burdens clause is strictly speaking part of the dispositive clause, but in practice conveyancers usually speak of it as a clause in its own right. Sometimes

the disponee is to take possession; (5) the *warrandice* clause, whereby the disponer warrants the title; (6) the *non-supersession* clause, declaring the missives not to be superseded; (7) the *testing* clause, which is to say, the clause of attestation. After the testing clause comes the warrant of registration, but this is not classified as a clause of the deed. Where exemption from stamp duty is being claimed, there should be a *stamp* clause before the testing clause. In some cases there has to be a clause of *deduction of title* after the entry clause. Until recently there were three other clauses, namely the *writs* clause, the *rents* clause and the *relief* clause, which came before the warrandice clause, but these are now implied[7] and are thus usually omitted.

A simple example will illustrate the clauses:

> [Narrative] I, James Jameson, residing formerly at forty-two Sauchiehall Square, Glasgow and now at five Frances Street, Stornoway, heritable proprietor of the subjects hereinafter disponed, in consideration of the price of forty thousand pounds (£40,000) paid to me by Alan Dewar Johnston and Clare Janet Macleod or Johnston, residing together at thirty-two Fairlie Drive, Dundee, of which I hereby acknowledge receipt . . .
>
> [Dispositive] . . . do hereby dispone to and in favour of the said Alan Dewar Johnston and Clare Janet Macleod or Johnston equally between them All and Whole that area or plot of ground with the dwelling-house erected thereon and garden ground effeiring thereto known as five Frances Street, Stornoway, in the County of Ross and Cromarty being the subjects more particularly described in and disponed by Disposition by James Chalmers Campbell in favour of Donald Macleod dated first and recorded in the Division of the General Register of Sasines applicable to the County of Ross and Cromarty on eleventh both days of May in the year nineteen hundred and thirty-five, together with (primo) the fittings and fixtures (secundo) the parts and pertinents and (tertio) my whole right title and interest present and future . . .

other individual parts are also called clauses, such as the "parts and pertinents clause."

[7] 1979 Act, s. 16.

[Burdens] . . . But always with and under in so far as valid subsisting and applicable the burdens conditions and others specified and contained in the said Disposition by James Chalmers Campbell in favour of Donald Macleod dated and recorded as aforesaid. . . .

[Entry] . . . With entry and actual occupation as at the fourth day of October nineteen hundred and ninety-three . . .

[Deduction of title—not applicable here as grantor is infeft]

[Warrandice] . . . And I grant warrandice . . .

[Stamp] . . . And I certify that the transaction hereby effected does not form part of a larger transaction or of a series of transactions in respect of which the amount or value or the aggregate amount or value of the consideration exceeds sixty thousand pounds. . . .

[Non-supersession] . . . And the missives of sale which I have concluded with the said Alan Dewar Johnston and Clare Janet Macleod or Johnston and which are constituted by letters dated fourth, sixth and twelfth June nineteen hundred and ninety-three will form a continuing and enforceable contract notwithstanding the delivery of these presents except in so far as fully implemented thereby, but the said missives shall cease to be enforceable after a period of two years from the date of entry hereunder except in so far as they are founded on in any court proceedings which have commenced within the said period. . . .

[Testing] . . . In witness whereof these presents are subscribed by me at Stornoway on the first day of October in the year nineteen hundred and ninety-three in the presence of Elspeth Marie Macdonald and Andrew Matheson Christie both trainee solicitors at fourteen Pinwherry Gardens, Stornoway. . . .

After the signatures appears the warrant of registration:

Register on behalf of the within named Alan Dewar Johnston and Clare Janet Macleod or Johnston in the Register of the County of Ross and Cromarty.

This warrant is signed by the solicitors for the Johnstons, with the words "Dundee, Agents" added, if Dundee is where their office is situated.

1. Narrative Clause

Obviously, the parties to the deed must have legal capacity. (The same issue also arises at the stage of concluding missives.) Specialities in deeds granted by executors, trustees, partnerships and by companies are considered elsewhere in this book. A disposition by a person lacking capacity is void. Thus, if a person who is *incapax* (e.g. senile) is to dispone land, this should be done on his behalf by a *curator bonis* or other person with authority to act on his behalf. However, when examining a title it is seldom possible to know that a deed is void because of lack of capacity.

A child can own land. But a person under 16 has no capacity to grant a disposition.[8] This must be done by the child's guardian. A child under 16 can, of course, be the grantee of a disposition, but if this is by way of purchase the consent of the guardian is necessary, and the same is arguably true even in the case of a gift or legacy.[9] A person under the age of 21 may make application to the court to set aside a transaction which he entered into between the ages of 16 and 18 and which is a "prejudicial transaction."[10] One should therefore hesitate before taking a disposition from such a person since the possibility of reduction (however remote) will remain until the granter reaches the age of 21. Title insurance may be advisable.

Trustees and executors generally have full capacity to transfer trust property. Even if the disposition is in breach of trust, that is not a question of *capacity*, and the disposition is not void. Indeed, a disposition in breach of trust will often not even be voidable

[8] Age of Legal Capacity (Scotland) Act 1991, ss. 1 and 2.

[9] Section 1(3)(*e*) of the Act says that a child under 16 is not prevented by the Act "from receiving or holding any right title or interest." However, to acquire ownership of land is more than merely to "receive." Some action is necessary, if only to instruct a solicitor to sign the warrant of registration. Moreover, landownership may involve obligations, which a child under 16 could hardly fulfil without its guardian's consent.

[10] Age of Legal Capacity (Scotland) Act 1991, s. 3.

because of the protection given to the disponee by section 2 of the Trusts (Scotland) Act 1961.[11]

Where the granter is a juristic person, rather than a natural person, there are two possible limitations on full capacity. First, the granting of the disposition may be *ultra vires*; and secondly, the natural person acting on behalf of the juristic person in negotiating and signing the disposition may be exceeding his authority. An *ultra vires* deed is void at common law. A deed granted beyond an agent's actual authority is valid only if it falls within the agent's ostensible authority. These issues as they relate to companies are considered elsewhere.[12]

Consenters

Where some third party has, or may have, an interest in the property being conveyed which is potentially damaging to the position of the grantee, it is generally necessary that he signs the deed as a consenter. Most dispositions do not have consenters, but if there is one the relevant details are given in the narrative clause. The intended effect of the consent may be expressly stated in the deed itself. A common example is where a heritable creditor consents to the effect of discharging the security. Or again the effect may be defined by statute. An example is a consent given by the spouse of the disponer in terms of the Matrimonial Homes (Family Protection) (Scotland) Act 1981.[13] These are the simple cases. In other cases there are two, mutually exclusive, effects of signing as consenter. In the first place, if it turns out that the consenter, and not the granter, was the true owner of the land, the fact that the consenter signed is sufficient to transfer ownership to the grantee. That at least is the view of Stair[14] and of *Mounsey* v. *Maxwell*.[15] Erskine,[16] however, argues that there is no transfer of ownership, although the consenter is under a personal obligation to grant a new disposition. The debate is discussed by Hume in his report of

[11] Note that this provision does not require good faith on the part of the disponee. A disgruntled beneficiary must pursue a personal remedy against the wicked trustee.

[12] chap. 26.

[13] s. 6(3)(*a*)(i).

[14] II, xi, 7.

[15] (1808) Hume 237.

[16] II, iii, 21.

Mounsey, who concludes that Erskine's view is incorrect. In the second place, if the consenter is not owner but has some other real right in the land,[17] or, alternatively, if he has only a personal right in relation to the land, he cannot thereafter exercise the right to the prejudice of the grantee or (probably) the grantee's successors. A common example is where A sells on missives to B and B resells to C and the disposition is from A to C with B's consent. Another example is where a trustee dispones with the consent of a beneficiary. Unless otherwise stated in the deed, the consenter corroborates only the conveyance of the land contained in the dispositive clause. His consent does not touch the other clauses, *e.g.* the warrandice clause.

Designation

All parties to a deed—granter, grantee and consenter—must be designed. But other people mentioned in a deed need not be designed: thus, there is no need to design the granter and grantee of deeds which are referred to for real burdens. Where designation is required, the approved technique is to design a party on the first occasion in which he appears in the deed and thereafter to refer to him as "the said Alan Dewar Johnston."

The test of a successful designation is that the party in question can be identified. The normal practice is to provide the full name and address. Some solicitors also add the party's occupation, although strictly this is only necessary where two people of the same name live at the same address (*e.g.* father and son).

In the usual case the granter of the present disposition will be the grantee of the immediately previous disposition of the same property (or, in the case of Land Register titles, the person listed in the title sheet). But his address will typically have changed. In the older disposition he will be designed as living at his former address. It is good practice to link up the two deeds by giving both addresses—as in the style above. This demonstrates that the James Jameson who was designed as living in Sauchiehall Square is the same James Jameson who now lives at Frances Street.

Where a married woman adopts her husband's name, it is usual to give her maiden name as well, as in "Clare Janet Macleod or

[17] *e.g.*, a lease or a heritable security.

Johnston." This, apart from anything else, can assist indexing at Register House. Where a party acts in a representative or fiduciary capacity, such as a trustee or as a liquidator, this fact should be added to designation together with details of his appointment. Thus, for an executor the designation will refer to the confirmation in his favour, mentioning its date and the court which issued it. For a trustee in sequestration the reference will be to the act and warrant, its date, and the court issuing it. In the case of a trustee under a deed of trust, the deed of trust must be identified, typically by reference to the Books of Council and Session where it will have been registered.

Juristic persons such as companies are designed by reference to registered office and to the statute under which they are incorporated. Some solicitors add the company's registration number, and this is good practice. The reason is that it is easy for a company to change its name, and indeed a company can have a name which was formerly possessed by another company. Only the registration number is an unchangeable birthmark by which the identity can be unambiguously determined.

Heritable/uninfeft proprietor

It is standard practice to follow the name and designation of the granter with either the words "heritable proprietor" or the words "uninfeft proprietor." "Heritable proprietor" means that the granter is infeft in the land, *i.e.* that he is, or claims to be, the legal owner of it. "Uninfeft proprietor" means that the granter, while not actually infeft, holds the land under an unregistered conveyance. Strictly, of course, "uninfeft proprietor" is a contradiction in terms: if you are uninfeft, then you cannot be proprietor. Nonetheless the usage, if illogical, is sanctioned by long-standing custom, and is convenient, for an uninfeft proprietor, although not owner, can grant a valid disposition, provided that he holds an unregistered conveyance (a "midcouple") and provided that he deduces title in the disposition.[18]

[18] 1924 Act, s. 3. See chap. 22. In Land Register conveyancing it is not necessary to insert a clause of deduction of title: 1979 Act, s. 15(3).

Cause of granting, and consideration

The cause of granting is stated in the narrative clause. In most cases the cause is sale. The price paid for the land (less any moveables) is usually given in the narrative clause. This is to comply with the Stamp Act 1891,[19] which requires that "all the facts and circumstances affecting the liability of any instrument to duty . . . are to be fully and truly set forth in the instrument." Conveyancing law does not actually require the price to be stated in the deed, and so it can be omitted (though this is rare) provided that it is disclosed to the Inland Revenue.[20]

Where the disposition is a gift, the traditional form is to narrate that the deed is granted for the "love, favour and affection" borne to the grantee.[21] A disposition by an executor or trustee will usually narrate the will or deed of trust, explaining that the grantee is a beneficiary. Occasionally one sees the formula "for certain good and onerous causes and considerations." This is a legalistic way of saying that the reason for the deed is not being stated. But silence is lawful. It is not necessary to say why a deed is being granted.

There can be many reasons, apart from sale, why a disposition is granted. While silence is possible, it is normal to explain, and sometimes this becomes something of a story. Indeed, one could begin by narrating the creation of the heaven and the earth, getting on, at about page 4, to the bit about Almighty God feuing Scotland to Adam and Eve and the survivor of them.[22] It is a matter of judgment how much to include. If in doubt, include it, because the effect is to preserve evidence as to what may have been some com-

[19] s. 5.

[20] Halliday, para. 4–22.

[21] These words acquire a certain irony where the disposition is part of a separation agreement on marital breakdown.

[22] In fact, we have it on good authority that God did not convey Scotland to Adam and Eve. "In the 28th verse [of the first chapter of *Genesis*], God saith to Adam and Eve, 'increase and multiply, and replenish the earth, and subdue or subject the same, and have dominion over the fishes of the sea, the fowls of the heaven, and all living things which move upon the earth.' This gift, therefore, could not be to Adam and Eve, who could neither replenish the earth nor subjugate nor subdue it; but it was to mankind which then was in their persons only; and it did not import a present right of property, but only a right or power to appropriate by possession, or *jus ad rem*, not *jus in re*": Stair, II, i, 1.

plex transaction. Sometimes there have been conveyancing problems in the past which the present deed is intended to correct, and if so it is helpful to outline the background.

While in practice the seller will not release the disposition until payment is made, the buyer ought nonetheless to have a formal receipt. This is achieved by including words such as "of which I acknowledge receipt." A receipt in this form raises a strong presumption that payment has been made.[23]

2. Dispositive Clause

The dispositive clause is introduced by the words "do hereby dispone." "Dispone" means "transfer," so "hereby dispone to the said Alan Dewar Johnston and Clare Janet Macleod or Johnston" has the effect (once the deed is registered) of transferring the property to the Johnstons. At common law "dispone" was a magic word, without which ownership could not pass. Synonymous terms were unavailing. By statute this rule has been abolished,[24] and all that is now needed is some term that makes the intention plain. But in practice the word "dispone" continues to be used.

Common property or joint property

The only case where heritage can (and indeed must) be held in joint property is where it is held by trustees. All other cases of *pro indiviso* ownership are cases of common property.[24a] It should be observed, however, that ownership in common is often referred to, loosely, as ownership "in joint names." That, for example, is the terminology that clients generally use. It is not usual to specify in the disposition whether the multiple ownership being conferred is common or joint. The law is clear. But since common property, unlike joint property, can involve shares of different sizes, it is good practice to specify the size of individual shares ("to the said Alan Dewar Johnston and Clare Janet Macleod or Johnston *equally between them*"). If the shares are intended to be equal, which is generally the case, this is not strictly necessary, for if the size of the shares is not stated, the law will presume that equal shares are intended.

[23] Ersk., II, iii, 22.
[24] 1874 Act, s. 27.
[24a] *Stair Memorial Encyclopaedia*, vol. 18, para. 34.

Description

The principal task of the dispositive clause is to describe the property being conveyed. The description is introduced by the words "All and Whole,"[25] words of great antiquity and considerable obscurity. According to Craig[26]:

> "The words 'all and whole' are exegetical and mean that the subject is conveyed as a complete unit with all its parts. In ordinary language the word 'all' is used with reference to things differing in kind, and the word 'whole' with reference to things of the same kind. Anyhow, the effect of these words is to show that the entire or universal subject is carried by the disposition. For the person who sells an estate or transfers it for some onerous cause is bound in law to hand it over complete and perfect, clear of all burdens, servitudes, and encumbrances whatsoever."

Only in a break-off disposition—where land is being conveyed as a separate unit for the first time—is it necessary to prepare a new description. This is fairly unusual. In most cases the land being conveyed has already been conveyed as a separate unit many times before and all one needs to do is to copy out the description from the most recent disposition, unless it is so woefully inadequate that redrafting is required.[27]

Land may be described in two different ways. First, it may be described by reference to its boundaries. This is a particular, or bounding, description. Secondly, land may be described simply by name (*e.g.* a postal address), without reference to boundaries. This is a general description. In practice, most modern dispositions contain both a general and a particular description, though usually the particular description is by reference to an earlier deed where the description is set out in full. (For descriptions in the Land Register, see chapter 20.)

[25] Formerly, in good Scots, All and Haill, the Latin original being *totas et integras*.
[26] *Jus Feudale*, II, iii, 23.
[27] In which case the best course is to have a surveyor make a plan, which will be annexed to the disposition.

General description

The following are typical general descriptions:

(1) Detached house: "All and Whole that detached dwelling-house number twelve Cherrytree Lane, Aberdeen."

(2) Tenement flat: "All and Whole that flatted dwelling-house[28] entering by the common passage and stair number fifteen Montrose Crescent, Dumfries being the southmost dwelling-house on the second floor above the ground floor."[29]

(3) Estate: "All and Whole the lands of Cottown of Fetterletter, Ardlogie, Little Gight, Blackpool, Little Milbrex, North Faddonhill, Bruckleseat, Letherty, Myre of Bedlam, Moss of Blackhillock, West Auchmaliddy, Dens, Middlemuir, Belnagoak, Gowanwell, Middlethird, Backhill of Ardo, Merdrum, Cairnorrie, North Arnybogs, Auchencrieve, Auchnagatt, Skilmafilly, Mains of Inkhorn, Quilquox, Mains of Schivas, Greenness, Lethen, Mill of Crichie Den, Hornscroft, Flobbets, Milton of Fochel, and Redmoss in the County of Aberdeen."[30]

How detailed need a general description be? The standard is modest. The description must be sufficient to distinguish the land conveyed from all other land. But extrinsic evidence is permitted,[31] a rule which allows great vagueness in the original description. Thus, in *Murray's Trustee* v. *Wood*[32] the description was: "All and Whole that piece of ground fronting Baker Street of Aberdeen, in the burgh and county of Aberdeen." Since it could be established by extrinsic evidence that the granter owned only one property in

[28] "Flatted dwelling-house" is the standard expression. Not "flat" since "flat" traditionally means "floor."

[29] Care has to be taken to avoid ambiguity. Some people call the ground storey the first storey. Moreover, in some tenements the bottom floor is a basement below street level.

[30] An actual example, abbreviated, in Aberdeenshire. John Rankine (*Land-Ownership* (4th ed., 1909) p. 101) wrote disapprovingly of descriptions by " a string of uncouthly-spelt names." This was the standard form of description for estates in the old days, and is sometimes still encountered, with no plans to help. To those interested in place names or local history, these deeds are poems.

[31] Which is just as well, for otherwise the traditional type of estate title would be invalid.

[32] (1887) 14 R. 856. See also *Cattanach's Tr.* v. *Jamieson* (1884) 11 R. 972 where the court looked for help in other parts of the deed.

Baker Street, this was held to be a sufficient description. "All my property" would also be a sufficient description.[33] The fact that a description is sufficient in law does not, however, guarantee that it is acceptable for the purposes of registration, an issue which is discussed below.

Particular (or bounding) description

When property is first conveyed as a separate unit (a split-off or break-off) it is necessary[34] to have a particular description defining the boundaries. (This may also be desirable even where the disposition is not a split-off, where the existing description is obscure.) There is, however, one case where a property being conveyed for the first time as a separate unit does not need a bounding description. Suppose that a part of a field is split off. That deed will need a bounding description. But when the remainder comes to be conveyed later on, the description of the original subjects can be repeated, "under exception of" the subjects already split off, which are defined by a reference to the earlier break-off deed.

Plans

Where a particular description is necessary, it is good, and today almost invariable, practice, to have a surveyor draw up a plan, which is annexed to the deed and recorded with it. Several points should be noted. First, the plan should show a scale and boundary measurements. Secondly, surveyors often mark different areas by colouring.[35] This is useful, but has the drawback that at Register House the deed will be registered in black and white only. Future confusion can be avoided if the colour words are written in on the plan, or if different sorts of hatching are used instead of, or in addition to, colours.[36] Thirdly, the north point must be shown. Fourthly, often two plans are needed, one a detailed plan and the other a "location plan" showing where the detailed plan fits into the surrounding area. Lack of a location plan can lead to what is

[33] The Keeper would not accept such a deed for registration, but it could be the basis of a notice of title.

[34] In practice.

[35] For instance, the subjects conveyed are shown red, the areas owned in common with the neighbours are shown green, and a line of servitude access is shown blue.

[36] *e.g.*, north-west to south-east hatching, vertical hatching, cross-hatching, etc.

commonly called the "floating rectangle" which shows only that Fergus Matheson owns 1.23 hectares of a certain shape somewhere or other in Angus. The plan needs to tie in with some publicly identifiable and permanent point in the landscape. "Point" not "line," because knowing that Fergus's land adjoins, for instance, a burn called Water of Pitdoune is of limited value if the Water of Pitdoune is nine kilometres long.

Verbal description

Nowadays, property is often described by a postal address followed by reference to the plan, the plan thus constituting the particular description. But traditionally, and this is still common, there is, in addition to the plan, a detailed verbal description of the boundaries. Here, the conveyancer mentally stands in the middle of the plot, and turns round clockwise, describing the boundaries and their lengths as he mentally sees them from the central point, usually though not necessarily starting from the northern boundary. Since the conveyancer does this in practice on the basis of the surveyor's plan, and since a verbal description is generally less precise than a plan, it will be seen that the verbal description is often really superfluous. Indeed, it can be worse, because it is very easy to make a mistake in a verbal description. However, the verbal description can clarify points which a plan may leave unclear. A typical example is whether the boundary follows the nearside, middle line, or farside of a boundary feature such as a wall.

Measurements (nowadays usually metric[37]) are followed by the words "or thereby" since absolute accuracy is not normally attainable. It is usual to give the measurement in both figures and words. Decimals are worded thus: "along which boundary it extends seven metres and eighty-five decimal or one-hundredth parts of a metre (7.85 m) or thereby." Or "seven metres and eight decimal or one-tenth parts of a metre (7.8 m) or thereby." This is perhaps inelegant and sometimes is misunderstood, but it is standard practice. It is usual, though not invariable, to have a statement of superficial area: "extending to one hectare and two hundred and twenty-five decimal or one thousandth parts of a hectare (1.225 ha) or thereby."

[37] Under EC Directive 80/181/EEC, new conveyancing descriptions will have to be in metric form from January 1995. See 1992 J.L.S. 463.

Where the boundary has a physical existence, such as a road or a wall, the description ought to state whether the legal boundary is the nearside or farside or middle line (*medium filum*). If the deed is silent on the point, the expression "bounded by" will generally be construed as meaning the nearside, so that, for example, a boundary wall itself so described would not be part of the subjects.[38] But there are exceptions, and the expression "bounded by a road" means, where the road is public, that the boundary is the *medium filum*.[39]

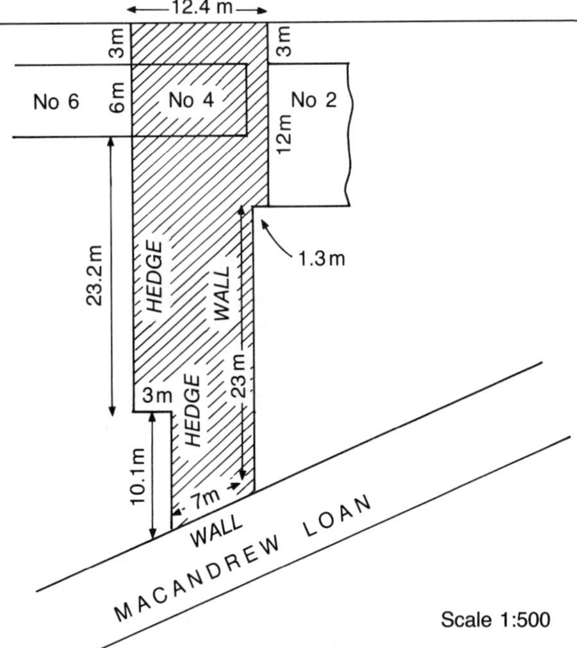

The following is an appropriate verbal description to accompany the plan shown:

[38] See Halliday, para. 18–11.
[39] *Magistrates of Ayr* v. *Dobbie* (1898) 25 R. 1184. See also Gordon, paras. 4–35 and 4–36.

"ALL and WHOLE that plot of ground with the semi-detached dwelling-house erected thereon known as Number Four Torduff Road, Dalry, Selkirkshire, extending to four hundred and thirty square metres or thereby, all as the said plot is shown hatched on the plan annexed and signed as relative hereto, and is bounded as follows: On or towards the north by the southern edge of Torduff Road aforesaid along which it extends twelve metres and four decimal or one-tenth parts of a metre (12.4 m) or thereby; on or towards the east by other subjects known as Number Two Torduff Road aforesaid, along which it extends in a southerly direction following the centre line of a brick wall three metres (3 m) or thereby, again in a southerly direction following the outer or western face of the house erected on said adjacent subjects at Number Two Torduff Road aforesaid along which it extends twelve metres (12 m) or thereby, then in a westerly direction following the centre line of a brick wall along which it extends one metre and three decimal or one-tenth parts of a metre (1.3 m) or thereby, again in a southerly direction following the middle line of a stone wall along which it extends twenty-three metres (23 m) or thereby, until it meets Macandrew Loan; on or towards the south by the outer or southern face of a stone wall separating the said plot from Macandrew Road aforesaid along which it extends seven metres (7 m) or thereby; on or towards the west by other subjects known as Number Six Torduff Road aforesaid, along which it extends in a northerly direction along the middle line of a holly hedge ten metres and one decimal or one-tenth part of a metre (10.1 m) or thereby, then in a westerly direction following the middle line of said hedge along which it extends three metres (3 m) or thereby, then in a northerly direction following the middle line of said hedge along which it extends twenty-three metres and two decimal or one-tenth parts of a metre (23.2 m) or thereby, then in a northerly direction following the middle line of a mutual gable wall between the house erected on the plot hereby disponed and the house erected on the said adjacent subjects at Number Six Torduff Road aforesaid along which it extends six metres (6 m) or thereby, then in a northerly direction following the middle line of a wooden fence along which it extends three metres (3 m) or thereby until it reaches Torduff Road aforesaid."

A note on old measures

The imperial measures are: 1 mile = 8 furlongs; 1 furlong = 10 chains; 1 chain = 22 yards; 1 yard = 3 feet; 1 foot = 12 inches. One yard is about 0.91 metres, and a mile is about 1.6 kilometres. As to superficial measure, 1 acre = 4840 square yards, i.e. a furlong by a chain. An acre is thus about 0.4 hectares. The acre was also divided into 4 roods, and each rood into 40 poles, a pole thus being 30.25 square yards.

The old Scots measures are occasionally still encountered. Without giving a full account, the Scots fall was about 5.65 metres, and the Scots chain was 4 Scots falls. The Scots acre was about 5086 square metres. It was divided into 4 roods. Each rood was divided into 40 falls (i.e. square falls).

Discrepancies—"demonstrative" and "taxative" plans

The verbal description and the plan are to be read together. But occasionally there are irreconcilable discrepancies between them. If the deed declares the plan to be "taxative," that means that in the event of such inconsistency, the plan is to be deemed correct, while if the plan is stated to be "demonstrative" that means that the verbal description is to prevail. A plan should be stated to be demonstrative where it is only a sketch. This used to be common, but good modern practice is always to have an accurate plan drawn up by a surveyor. The other case where a plan should be declared demonstrative is in a new development where the plan shows some features as already existing but other features which are not yet built, the possibility being that the developer might depart to some extent from his current intentions. In other cases the plan should normally be declared taxative, since a plan prepared by a trained surveyor is likely to be more accurate than a verbal description. Some conveyancers, however, routinely declare a plan to be "demonstrative not taxative" as words of style. This is unwise. The declaration should be considered and deliberate. Occasionally, a deed is silent as to the point. In that case the resolution of the discrepancy can be difficult.[40]

[40] For the reported decisions on such cases, see Halliday, para. 18–13 and Gordon, para. 4–08.

Description by reference

When a piece of land is first broken off as a separate unit, the break-off conveyance will almost always contain a new particular description. In future dispositions of that unit it is not necessary to repeat verbatim the terms of that description. Instead the relevant part of the break-off disposition can be incorporated into the later deed by reference. At common law it is competent to incorporate into a deed all or part of any other deed provided that the deed so incorporated is adequately identified. But for descriptions by reference there is a special statutory procedure set out in the 1874 Act[41] and the 1924 Act.[42]

The statutory form of words is: "All and Whole the subjects in the County of [insert county] described in [name deed]." Many practitioners like to accompany the reference to the deed with a rhetorical flourish, such as "described in disponed by and delineated red on the plan annexed and subscribed as relative to" the deed in question. Note that the deed referred to must itself contain a full particular description, and not merely another description by reference.[43] Also note that Schedule D to the 1924 Act requires a reference to the county, which, according to Halliday,[44] means the traditional geographical county and so not the post-1975 local government area or the registration county, though the registration counties do generally coincide with the traditional counties. But problems can arise because over the years there were occasional adjustments to county boundaries. A radical example is the county of Cromarty, which was in various bite-sized chunks scattered through Ross-shire, the two counties being united in the nineteenth century: is the conveyancer supposed to make the distinction, or not? If so, he will need to consult a local historian. Even apart from this problem, stating the county is not strictly necessary, so long as the identity and location are clear.[45]

[41] s. 61.

[42] s. 8 and Sched. D.

[43] 1874 Act, s. 61. But by s. 8(1) of the 1924 Act the particular description incorporated may, and in practice commonly does, contain a description by reference to the larger area of which it formed part.

[44] para. 18–16.

[45] As Halliday observes at para. 18–14.

Registration requirements

Even though a description is valid as a matter of law, it may still not be sufficient to satisfy the Keeper of the Registers. In the Sasine Register the position is regulated by *Macdonald* v. *Keeper of the Registers*.[46] There, the Keeper was held entitled to reject a deed with the description "the house in No. 140 McDonald Road, Edinburgh, the title to which is in my name" on the basis that, since No. 140 was a tenement building, he could not tell which flat was being conveyed. It is true that, standing *Murray's Trustee* v. *Wood* ,[47] the description, and hence the disposition itself, was valid; but it was said that the Keeper has a broad discretion to reject deeds in the interests of the purity of the register.

Where a description is good in law but not acceptable for registration, all is not lost. The disposition is still valid. The grantee, as uninfeft proprietor, has the possibility of making up title or of selling on, using the deduction of title procedure.

"Under exception of"

Where parts of a property have been split off, and the remainder of the property then comes to be disponed, it is common for the full original description to be repeated, adding that the conveyance is under exception of the various split-off areas, which are then described by reference.

Part and portion clause

In a break-off conveyance, after the description there follows a clause identifying, by reference, the larger subjects of which the present subjects were hitherto a part. This is convenient for future conveyancers examining the title and is also important for Register House, and the search firms, to keep track of what has happened.[48]

[46] 1914 S.C. 854.

[47] (1887) 14 R. 856, discussed above.

[48] Thus, on a split-off, Register House will open a new search sheet. They mark it as having been broken off from the search sheet for the larger subjects, and that search sheet will be correspondingly marked.

The clause runs: "Which subjects hereby disponed form part and portion of the subjects in the County of . . . described in . . . "[49]

Parts and pertinents

The description is concerned with the land conveyed. But the grantee receives more than the bare land. The generic term for the extras which also pass to the grantee is "parts and pertinents." In so far as there is any sustainable distinction between "parts" and "pertinents" it is that "parts" are those rights which are exercisable over the land itself, while "pertinents" are those rights exercised in association with the land but beyond its boundaries.[50]

"Parts"

Land is owned *a coelo usque ad centrum* (from the heavens to the centre of the earth). Anything built on or lying underneath the land is a part of the land. So houses and trees and minerals are parts. But this is subject to the exception of legal separate tenements,[51] *i.e.* property reserved from the land by legal implication. Of the legal separate tenements, two (gold and silver, and oil and gas) are the property of the Crown. Coal is the property of British Coal. The remaining separate tenements are: the right to fish for salmon; the right to gather mussels and oysters; and the right to collect free teinds. Of these, only salmon fishings are important today. Originally in Crown ownership, salmon fishings are now very often in private hands. Teinds[52] are obsolete although they are sometimes mentioned in dispositions.[53] Minerals are conventional separate tenements, that is, they are not reserved by legal implication but are capable of being reserved—and hence owned separately from the land—if the parties so wish. In practice, minerals are very often

[49] 1924 Act, Sched. D, note 3.

[50] See *Stair Memorial Encyclopaedia*, vol. 18, paras. 199–206.

[51] *Tenementa separata*. See *Stair Memorial Encyclopaedia*, vol. 18, paras. 207–213.

[52] See Gordon, chap. 10.

[53] Teinds were burdens on land. So if a title to land included its own teinds, that was a benefit, since the landowner was the owner of his own teind. However, the benefit was modified to the extent that teinds themselves were burdened with stipend.

reserved by the superior when land is feued. If they have been reserved, then they do not pass as a part of the land.

"Pertinents"

Pertinents form a miscellaneous ragbag. Whereas parts are parts by necessary implication, this is only true of pertinents in two cases. One is real conditions such as real burdens and servitudes: if Blackmains has a servitude right over Whitemains, then that right is inseparable from Blackmains and passes in any conveyance thereof. The other is a speciality of the law of the tenement: in a flatted building each individual flat has as a pertinent a right of common property in respect of the common passage and stair. These two cases apart, a pertinent is usually another, and smaller, piece of land which is subordinate in some way to the principal land. A garage or cellar are examples. In practice, land A only becomes a pertinent of land B by express grant or by positive prescription.[54]

The wording of the parts and pertinents clause

In an ordinary disposition the granter dispones all that he owns. Nothing is retained. Accordingly, new pertinents cannot be created, for there is no retained land in respect of which a valid grant can be made. So an ordinary disposition is simply a disposition with the existing parts and pertinents. Since parts and pertinents, by definition, pass with the land, no clause is actually necessary. "A grant of the lands of A . . . is as extensive as a grant of A with parts and pertinents."[55] Nonetheless, a clause is usually included as a matter of style. At one time the clause was very long. Craig[56] offers the following:

> "along with the houses, buildings, woods, plains, muirs, marshes, ways, paths, rivers, streams, lakes, meadows, pastures, and pasturages, mills, multures and the sequels thereof, fowlings, huntings, fishings, peat-mosses, turbaries, rabbits, rabbit-warrens, doves and dove-cots, gardens, orchards, smithies, malt-kilns and brew-houses, brooms, woods, forests, and coppice, timber, quarries of stone and lime, courts and

[54] On the latter see *Cooper's Exrs.* v. *Stark's Trs.* (1898) 25 R. 1160.

[55] *Gordon* v. *Grant* (1850) 13 D. 1 at 7.

[56] *Jus Feudale*, III, iii, 30.

their suits, herezalds, bloodwites, and merchets of women, together also with grazings, free ish and entry, and all other liberties, conveniencies, profits, easements, and pertinents whatsoever, named as well as unnamed, under the ground as well as above the same, pertaining, or which may in any manner whatsoever lawfully pertain in the future, to the foresaid lands, including the castle, mills, parts, pendicles, and pertinents thereof, freely, fully, quietly, wholly, honourably, happily and in peace, without any impediment, revocation, contradiction, or obstacle whatsoever."

Modern practice is, alas, more restrained. A typical clause is:

"Together with (One) the fittings and fixtures (Two) the parts, privileges and pertinents, and (Three) my whole right, title and interest, present and future, in and to the subjects hereby disponed."

The reference to "fittings" is odd. In *Jamieson* v. *Welsh*[57] Lord Kinnear justly commented that " a sound conveyancer in framing a disposition . . . will not think it necessary to insert a futile conveyance of the *moveables* which would carry nothing."

The reference to "whole right, title and interest" is to cover accretion: if the granter does not own the property at the time of the grant but comes to own it later, ownership will accresce automatically to the grantee. But in fact the same effect is achieved by the clause of absolute warrandice.[58]

If the grantor owns the salmon fishings or any other legal separate tenement, these will not pass to the grantee unless expressly mentioned, this usually being done in the pertinents clause.[59]

The parts and pertinents clause is likely to be different, and more extensive, in a break-off conveyance. Here, it is often necessary to confer on the grantee rights over land being retained by the granter, and these rights appear either directly in the pertinents clause, or sometimes in a separate Deed of Conditions which is then incorporated by reference into the pertinents clause. Typically the rights are servitudes, such as a right of way or a right to lead pipes and

[57] (1900) 3 F. 176 at 182.

[58] Stair, III, ii, 2; Bankton, III, ii, 16 and 18; Ersk. II, vii, 3. For accretion, see *Stair Memorial Encyclopaedia*, vol. 18, para. 677.

[59] *McKendrick* v. *Wilson*, 1970 S.L.T. (Sh. Ct.) 39.

cables. Once a pertinent has been created, it remains a pertinent. So new rights appearing in the pertinents clause of a break-off disposition need not be repeated in detail in future dispositions, although it is helpful to make reference to the deed or deeds which created them.[60] A future conveyancer examining the title can thus readily discover what the pertinents are.

Burdens

The creation of new real burdens and servitudes is discussed in chapter 10. Here we consider the conveyancing practice where there are existing burdens, which is usually the case. The existing burdens must be referred to in the disposition.[61] This is partly to avoid the possibility of irritancy.[62] Partly, too, it is to avoid claims in warrandice: in granting warrandice the granter guarantees the terms of the dispositive clause, and if the dispositive clause makes no reference to burdens, the granter is taken as guaranteeing that there are none.[63] A third reason is purely practical: when faced with a bundle of title deeds it is difficult to know which writs contain real burdens. The list in the disposition saves time and energy.

Existing burdens are almost never repeated in full. All that is required is an incorporation by reference.[64] The usual method of referring to burdens is: "But always with and under the burdens, conditions and others, so far as valid, subsisting and applicable, specified in . . ." [then list the deeds in which the burdens appear]. This is a slight adaptation of the statutory style.[65] The significance of "so far as valid, subsisting and applicable" is that real burdens can become spent, and the grantee does not wish to be committed to the proposition that all the burdens in the title remain live and

[60] "Together with the servitudes and other rights contained in . . ."

[61] Except for dispositions of registered land: 1979 Act, s. 15(2). The reason is that the burdens are all on the title sheet.

[62] Some deeds imposing burdens require future deeds to refer to them, on pain of irritancy. The enforceability of such an irritancy is perhaps arguable. If a burden has been omitted, the matter can be put right under s. 9 of the 1924 Act.

[63] However, if the grantee knows of, or is deemed to know of, the burden, there will be no remedy in warrandice.

[64] 1874 Act, s. 32 and Sched. H, replacing s. 10 of the 1868 Act, which, however, has never been repealed. See also s. 8 and Sched. D of the 1924 Act.

[65] 1874 Act, Sched. H.

enforceable. In practice, the list is simply copied from the immediately preceding disposition. But if a burden is obviously spent it can safely be omitted. Typically there are two or three deeds listed. All deeds older than 1858 will be instruments of sasine, because until that year dispositions and feu dispositions could not be registered directly and their contents were summarised in the instrument.

Reservations

The dispositive clause also includes details of anything which is being reserved to the granter. In feu dispositions the granter usually reserves the minerals. In an ordinary disposition the most that is likely to be reserved — and that only in a break-off disposition — is a servitude over the land disponed in favour of the land retained by the granter. In a complex deed it can sometimes be unclear whether some item is being disponed or reserved. In such cases the practice is to say something like "together with by way of grant not exception" or vice versa.

3. The Implied Assignations

The narrative and dispositive clauses are the two most important clauses in a disposition. But there are also a number of ancillary clauses. Two of these (neither of which is usually of much importance) are the clause of assignation of writs and the clause of assignation of rents. Until the passing of the 1979 Act these clauses were set out in full.[66] But by section 16 of the Act these two clauses[67] are now implied and need not be mentioned. These clauses are "assignations" since what they transfer is incorporeal, intimation being effected by registration.[68]

Assignation of writs

The assignation of writs has two effects. The first is the transfer of certain personal rights. Conveyances contain a number of contrac-

[66] In the form prescribed by s. 8 and Sched. B of the 1868 Act.
[67] Together with the clause of relief, for which see below.
[68] *Paul* v. *Boyd's Trs.* (1835) 13 S. 818; *Edmonds* v. *Magistrates of Aberdeen* (1855) 18 D. 47; (1858) 3 Macq. 116.

tual obligations by the granter to the grantee, the two most important being the obligation of warrandice and the obligation of relief.[69] These obligations can sometimes be enforced by successors of the original grantee. Suppose that A dispones to B, B dispones to C, and C dispones to D. In the dispositions A, B and C will have entered into certain obligations. But since these are personal, not real, they can, on general principles, be enforced only by B, C and D respectively. Unless, of course, they are assigned. By section 16(1) of the 1979 Act the implied assignation of writs imports "an assignation to the grantee of the title deeds and searches and all deeds not duly recorded." What this appears to mean is that some, but not all, of the obligations in dispositions are assigned. In past times this was important (*e.g.* for unexecuted precepts of sasine, procuratories of resignation, and other antiquarian exotica). Today what it all appears to mean is that (a) obligations of warrandice are assigned[70] and that (b) obligations of relief are not. Why both should not be treated in the same way is a mystery.[71]

The practical effect is this. In the above example, when A dispones to B, A grants warrandice. So B has a right against A. When B dispones to C, B in turn grants warrandice to C. So C has a right of warrandice against B. But he also has a right of warrandice against A, for B's former right has passed to C by the assignation of writs. Similarly, when C dispones to D, D comes to hold three rights of warrandice, against A, B and C.

The second aspect of the assignation of writs concerns the delivery of the title deeds. Section 16(1) of the 1979 Act places the granter under certain obligations as to the title deeds, including the obligation to deliver all titles relating exclusively to the land conveyed. Since the title deeds are normally delivered at settlement,[72] along with the disposition, the section 16 obligation is usually fulfilled at precisely the same moment as it is incurred! Any lingering obligation under section 16(1) — for example, in relation to deeds not relating exclusively to the land conveyed — flies off

[69] See below.

[70] Stair II.iii.46.

[71] Similar difficulties apply to s. 8 of the 1868 Act.

[72] The only common exception is in a break-off disposition, where the granter may retain them.

if and when land is first registered in the Land Register without exclusion of indemnity.[73]

Until 1979 dispositions usually included, as an appendix, an inventory of writs listing the principal title deeds. This practice, never required by law, has now virtually disappeared.

Assignation of rents

The clause of assignation of rents, though included, expressly or by implication, in all deeds, is relevant only if the property disponed is tenanted. Its object is twofold. In the first place, it enables the disponee to draw the rents as soon as the disposition has been delivered and its terms intimated to the tenant. This point was important long ago when a disponee might be slow in completing his title. Nowadays, when disponees complete title immediately, this aspect no longer matters. The other purpose of the clause is to arrange, as between disponer and disponee, the point in time after which the rents payable will go to the disponee. For instance, if the disposition is granted in August, and the rent is payable twice a year, in May and November, is the disponer to keep the May rent, and the disponee to take the November rent? Or should the rent for May to November be divided? And so on.

Before the 1979 Act, the disposition could either have a detailed clause, or could simply say "I assign the rents," the meaning of which expression was defined by statute.[74] Under section 16 of the 1979 Act the assignation of rents is implied.[75] However, the implied statutory meaning is extremely hard to understand,[76] involving as it does problems about forehand rents, backhand rents, arable farms, pastoral farms, conventional terms, legal terms, and so on.[77] Con-

[73] Except in relation to land and Charge Certificates. See the 1979 Act, s. 3(5). This is because after registration the prior titles are (or are said to be) irrelevant.

[74] 1868 Act, s. 8.

[75] 1979 Act, s. 16. The meaning of this implied clause is very similar to the meaning defined in s. 8 of the 1868 Act.

[76] See J. Rankine, *Law of Leases* (3rd ed., 1916) and G. C. H. Paton and J. G. S. Cameron, *Landlord and Tenant* (1967).

[77] An example will illustrate the sort of problems that can be encountered. A pastoral farm is let with the rent one term backhand. The landlord sells with entry at August 1. The rent "conventionally" payable at Martinmas is "legally" payable at the previous Whitsunday. Therefore, by the statutory provisions it goes to the disponer, even though actually paid when the disponee is already the owner.

veyancers who are unwilling to take a month off to investigate the law should avoid the statutory provisions by making express, detailed and clear provision as to how the rental income is to be apportioned as between disponer and disponee.

4. The Contractual Obligations

As well as being an executory deed, conveying the land (and the writs and rents), a disposition is also a contract imposing obligations, usually on the granter. As personal rights, these obligations do not transmit for the benefit of future owners unless assigned. Whereas ownership passes to the disponee only on registration, the contractual obligations generally take effect immediately, on delivery of the disposition. The contractual obligations are: (1) Entry; (2) Warrandice; (3) Obligation of relief; and (4) Non-supersession clause. Here we deal only with the first and third of these, the others being considered elsewhere.[78]

Entry

Entry is the date at which the granter is bound to yield possession to the grantee. There is a statutory clause of entry[79] which, slightly modernised, reads: "With entry on[80] twenty-second November Nineteen hundred and ninety-three." In a sale the date of entry will already have been contracted for in missives. The date of entry must be distinguished from the date of the disposition, from the date when the disposition is delivered, and from the date of entry with the superior.

The "date of the disposition" is the date of execution (signature) or, if there is more than one signature, of last execution. This date will be found from the testing clause. It has little legal significance. Usually it is before the date of entry. If it is after the date of entry (*e.g.* because something has gone wrong with the transaction and settlement is delayed) it is usual to add to the entry clause the words "notwithstanding the date hereof," which indicates that the unusual sequence is not just a typing error. It sometimes happens

[78] See Chap. 19.

[79] 1868 Act, s. 5 and Sched. B.

[80] Or sometimes "as at."

(*e.g.* with gifts or with sales to sitting tenants) that entry is to be on the same day as the deed is executed, and in that case the entry clause reads "with entry at the date hereof."

The "date of delivery" is, in a sale, the date of settlement, the date at which the transaction actually settles, that is, when the disposition is handed over in exchange for the price. In a normal sale the date of entry and date of settlement are the same day. But if things go wrong (*e.g.* the purchaser cannot come up with the money) the date of entry may pass without the transaction being settled. Before delivery, the disposition has no effect. After delivery, but before registration, its effect is limited, since at this stage ownership has yet to pass. But the deed still has various effects. Its contractual clauses have full effect, and the disponee, though not infeft, has the status and privileges of an uninfeft proprietor.

The grantee must "enter with the superior." Until 1874 this meant the grantee had to obtain a further deed,[81] from the superior, accepting him as the new vassal. This was "feudal entry." But feudal entry now occurs automatically on registration of the disposition.[82]

Entry (in the non-feudal sense) is the date at which the granter must yield possession. But possession may either be natural (*i.e.* physically by the owner) or civil (through another person, such as a tenant) and the entry clause in its statutory form is satisfied by either. This means that a purchaser who arrives with his removal van only to find that the property is tenanted has no redress under the statutory clause. And nor does he have redress under the warrandice clause.[83] The solution is to contract specifically for vacant possession, thus: "With entry and actual occupation[84] on twenty-second November Nineteen hundred and ninety-three."

The meaning of vacant possession or actual occupation has occasionally caused problems. In *Stuart* v. *Lort-Phillips*[85] cattle belonging to a neighbour was found grazing on about one-third of the subjects of sale. The neighbour claimed he had an agricultural

[81] Usually a charter of confirmation, though the alternative, the charter of resignation, was sometimes used.

[82] 1874 Act, s. 4. Nothing, therefore, is now required of the superior.

[83] *Lothian & Border Farmers Ltd.* v. *McCutcheon*, 1952 S.L.T. 450, though the soundness of this decision is doubtful.

[84] Or "vacant possession."

[85] 1977 S.C. 244.

tenancy. Both facts were held to be a breach of the obligation to give vacant possession. This was so even although the claim to the tenancy might (and in fact did) turn out to be spurious.[86]

If an express entry clause is omitted, it is implied that entry is at the next term of Whitsunday or Martinmas.[87] But in practice the clause is never omitted.

Obligation of relief

An owner of land has certain obligations *qua* owner, the main ones being (a) feuduty, (b) real burdens, (c) (non-domestic) rates, (d) council tax, and (e) statutory notices, *e.g.* notices served by the local authority under the Civic Government (Scotland) Act 1982, section 87 requiring the repair of buildings and empowering the authority to carry out the work itself and recover the cost from the "owner."[88] Difficult questions can arise as to when these obligations pass to the grantee, and to what extent the grantee has relief against the granter.

When does the grantee become liable to third parties?

For feuduty (if payable), council tax[88a] and rates, the grantee becomes liable on taking entry. For real burdens and, probably,[89] for statutory notices also, the grantee becomes liable on acceptance of delivery of the disposition. Usually entry and acceptance of the disposition occur on the same day, *i.e.* on settlement. Where repair work has already been done in implement of a real burden, a grantee will not, it seems, be liable for it.[90]

When does the granter cease to be liable to third parties?

The fact that the grantee becomes liable does not necessarily mean that the granter ceases to be liable. In fact, there is continuing liability in the granter, and hence concurrent, joint and several

[86] See also *Scottish Flavour Ltd.* v. *Watson*, 1982 S.L.T. 78 where it was held that the presence of rubbish was too trivial.

[87] 1874 Act, s. 28.

[88] For statutory notices see Chap. 3.

[88a] Local Government Finance Act 1992, s. 75.

[89] *Pegg* v. *Glasgow District Council*, 1988 S.L.T. (Sh. Ct.) 49.

[90] *David Watson Property Management* v. *Woolwich Equitable Building Society*, 1992 S.L.T. 430.

liability in both granter and grantee, in the following circumstances. First, until the grantee registers the disposition the granter remains owner, and as owner continues to be liable in respect of real burdens.[91] Secondly, until a notice of change of ownership is sent to the superior,[92] the granter remains liable for any feuduty and real burdens due to that superior. This requires some explanation. Up until 1874 active steps were required of a grantee to take feudal entry with the superior. Usually dispositions were granted *a me vel de me*, followed by base infeftment, and entry with the superior occurred on the granting of a charter of confirmation. The 1874 Act dispensed with express feudal entry. By section 4(2) of that Act entry occurs by implication whenever the disposition is registered. But this carried the practical disadvantage that the superior would no longer know when his vassal had changed. To meet this point section 4(2) provided for a notice of change of ownership to be sent to the superior. Until the notice is sent the granter remains liable for the prestations of the feu, *i.e.* for feuduty and for real burdens. In practice, however, the feudal system being in terminal decline, the notice is almost never sent, and cases where a superior seeks to rely on section 4(2) seem to be unknown in practice.

Thirdly, where an obligation constituted as a real burden became prestable during the granter's ownership, he continues to be liable even after his ownership has ceased. Thus in *Marshall* v. *Callander & Trossachs Hydropathic Hospital Ltd.*,[93] it was held that a real burden requiring the re-building at enormous expense of property which had been destroyed by fire could not be avoided by disponing the land to a company without any assets.[94]

Does the grantee have a right of relief?

It may happen that the grantee meets expenses or fulfils obligations for which the granter is wholly or partially responsible. Can the cost then be recovered from the granter? The answer depends on the nature of the debt. For feuduties, council tax and rates the

[91] *Hyslop* v. *Shaw* (1863) 1 M. 535.

[92] 1874 Act, s. 4(2).

[93] (1895) 22 R. 954.

[94] A fourth possibility is that a person who was the original grantee of a conveyance imposing real burdens continues to be liable in contract even after ceasing to be the owner.

position is that the grantor is liable up until the date of entry. If, in the event, the grantee elects to meet the granter's liability by paying the superior or local authority, he has a right of relief in terms of the obligation of relief clause. This clause, formerly express, is now implied by the 1979 Act, to the effect of imposing on the grantor an obligation to relieve the grantee of all feuduties, ground annuals, annuities and public, parochial and local burdens exigible prior to the date of entry.[95]

For statutory notices the position is less clear. There is some authority to suggest that the term "public, parochial and local burdens" includes statutory notices.[96] But in any event the missives should, and normally do, make provision for liability as between seller and purchaser.

The obligation of relief clause does not extend to real burdens. But in the cases identified earlier of concurrent, joint and several, liability in granter and grantee, a right of relief exists on general principles, although its extent will depend on the liability of the parties *inter se*. Unfortunately there is no authority on this question. Thus, if a superior secures implement by the grantee of a real burden which became prestable during the granter's ownership, there is a right of relief against the granter. But how much of the cost can the grantee recover? The law is unclear.

Environmental law liability

An area of law which has grown in importance at an exponential rate in recent years is environmental law. Its relevance to conveyancing is obvious, and nowadays missives for commercial property often have very extensive provisions as to such matters. But because the subject is so complex, and is mainly concerned with commercial conveyancing, we do not propose to deal with it here.[97]

5. Testing Clause

Probative deeds finish with a testing clause giving details of execution. Although the testing clause appears above the signatures, it is not possible to prepare it until the deed has been signed. When

[95] 1979 Act, s. 16(3).

[96] *McIntosh* v. *Mitchell Thomson* (1900) 8 S.L.T. 48.

[97] See *Scots Law and the Environment: Liability for Contaminated Land*, by Brodies, W.S.

a deed is being prepared for signature it finishes with the words "In witness whereof." Granters are then asked to leave a substantial gap between the end of the deed and their signatures so that the testing clause can be added. The law and practice of execution of deeds is considered in Chapter 15.

6. Excambions

An excambion is a disposition where A dispones land to B and B dispones other land to A. In other words it is a swap. The deed[98] is usually called a "contract" of excambion, a somewhat misleading term since in fact it is a two-way disposition and will normally have been preceded by a contract, typically by missives. Of course, it is possible to have two separate dispositions instead of an excambion. Excambions may be used in all sorts of cases but the typical one is where two adjacent landowners agree to swap certain areas, perhaps so as to straighten out a zigzag boundary.

7. Section 19 Agreements

If there is a boundary dispute on account of uncertainties in the deeds, and the parties come to an agreement, the agreement can be given effect to by the use of a disposition, or two dispositions, or an excambion. Alternatively, a section 19 deed can be used.[99] This is available where the title boundaries of neighbouring properties are mutually inconsistent, and the parties agree on a solution. A deed is registered with an agreed plan, and the matter is thus settled.

8. Revisions and Alterations

By convention dispositions are drafted by the grantee's solicitor. This is because the disposition will be the grantee's title and the grantee has the stronger interest in ensuring that it is correct. However, in large developments, such as housing estates, the granter's solicitor will usually produce a *pro forma* style of disposition to be used by all grantees. In feu dispositions the deed is by convention drafted by the superior's solicitor.

[98] For a style see Halliday, para. 22–67.

[99] 1979 Act, s. 19. For a style see Halliday, para. 18–85.

Once a deed has been drafted it is sent to the solicitor acting for the other party to be revised, that is to say checked for errors, both legal and clerical. The revising solicitor marks "revised" on the draft, and adds the firm name and the date. The deed is then returned to the original solicitor who prepares an engrossment, which is a fair copy typed on deed paper. This process is usually sufficient to eliminate both drafting and clerical errors.[1] Nonetheless it may sometimes happen that an engrossed disposition requires to be altered.

Alterations

Before execution there is no restriction on alterations. Minor alterations can be made by interlineation, marginal addition or erasure (known collectively as vitiations) or — more simply in the age of word processors — by reprinting the offending page. If a vitiation is made, the testing clause must contain a declaration that it was made prior to execution. Otherwise — subject to section 39 of the 1874 Act — it is *pro non scripto* (*i.e.* not part of the deed).

After execution a deed cannot lawfully be altered. Alteration amounts to the crime of forgery.[2] But in practice deeds occasionally are altered by one of the solicitors involved, the alteration being cheerfully and dishonestly declared in the testing clause as having been made before subscription. The most brazen case of alteration is the substitution of one page for another — which is possible now that the granter does not have to sign each page.[3] Such dishonesty cannot be condoned. It may be added that errors are often trivial, in which case they do not need to be corrected. If an error does require attention, it may be possible to have a fresh deed prepared. But in practice errors often do not come to light until the property is being resold, by which time the original granter may have disappeared or become unwilling to cooperate.

Judicial rectification

Section 8(1)(b) of the Law Reform (Miscellaneous Provisions) (Scotland) Act 1985 provides that:

[1] Word processors have helped to eliminate clerical errors.
[2] Hume, *Commentaries*, i, 159.
[3] 1970 Act, s. 44.

> "where the court is satisfied, on an application made to it, that . . . a document intended to create, transfer, vary or renounce a right . . . fails to express accurately the intention of the granter[4] of the document at the date when it was executed, it may order the document to be rectified in any manner that it may specify in order to give effect to that intention."

This provision deals with obvious and spectacular cases of error in expression, such as where the wrong subjects are conveyed.[5] In *Bank of Scotland* v. *Graham's Tr.*[6] it was held that a standard security could be rectified to the effect of including the name of the grantor, which had been left out by mistake. The First Division took a wide view of section 8, though indicating that it could not be used to cure absence of signatures. As now interpreted, section 8 is a vitally important lifeline for conveyancers when all other attempts to make good a drafting error have failed.

For the purposes of an application under section 8, parole evidence is admissible to show the granter's intention.[7] Consequential amendments to other deeds may also be ordered. Rectification is retrospective, an idea which is problematic in the creation of real rights. Section 9 contains the important limitation that rectification is excluded where third parties have acted in reliance on the unrectified deed.

9. Interpretation

Each clause in a disposition has its own recognised function, and in all questions involving that function the clause is treated as the principal provision. If therefore there is a repugnancy between the principal clause and the rest of the deed the principal clause prevails. But if the principal clause is ambiguous, that ambiguity may be resolved by reference to the rest of the deed.

Orr v. *Mitchell*[8] is a well-known example of the latter point.

[4] One wonders why the intention of the grantee is not also relevant.

[5] See *M.A.C. Electrical and Heating Engineers Ltd.* v. *Calscot Electrical (Distributors) Ltd.*, 1989 S.C.L.R. 498; *Oliver* v. *Gaughan*, 1990 G.W.D. 22–1247 *Aberdeen Rubber Ltd.* v. *Knowles & Sons (Fruiterers) Ltd.*, 1993 G.W.D. 21–1301. See also *Rehman* v. *Ahmed*, 1993 S.L.T. 741.

[6] 1991 S.L.T. 879; *affd.* 1993 S.L.T. 252.

[7] s. 8(2).

[8] (1893) 20 R. (H.L.) 27.

Here the granters of a disposition owned a mixed estate, that is an estate part superiority and part *dominium utile*. It was unclear from the dispositive clause (the principal clause for this purpose) whether the granter was disponing all that he owned or whether the disposition was confined to the superiority interest. But the rest of the deed made clear that only the superiority was being conveyed.

Extrinsic evidence cannot be used to modify or add to the terms of a written deed.[9] But extrinsic evidence is not wholly excluded, and may be used to explain words which are contained in the deed. What it may not be used for is to add new words or to delete existing ones. There are two main examples of the explanatory role of extrinsic evidence. The first is to link up words used in the deed to physical objects or people. For example, no description can dispense entirely with extrinsic evidence. To say that a property is "bounded on the south by the road known as Buchanan Street, Glasgow" might require extrinsic evidence as to the location of Buchanan Street. The second is to resolve ambiguity. If a word is ambiguous, extrinsic evidence may be led to explain its meaning. But this meets the important exception that extrinsic evidence is not permissible to explain ambiguities in words constituting real burdens. The whole of a real burden must be contained within the four corners of the deed. If a word is ambiguous, it is simply interpreted *contra proferentem* (that is, against the superior or other dominant proprietor seeking to enforce it). This subject is explored further in the next chapter.

10. Effect of Delivery of Disposition

Before delivery of the disposition, the right of the purchaser is purely a personal right under the missives. Under the missives the seller has a personal right to be paid, and the purchaser has a personal right to receive a valid disposition. At settlement the parties perform their respective obligations — payment and delivery. But the purchaser at this stage still does not have ownership. Ownership is a real right and can be obtained only by infeftment, which involves registration in the Sasine Register or Land Register. Until the purchaser is infeft, the seller remains infeft, and thus the seller

[9] Subject to the statutory provisions as to judicial rectification, referred to above.

is still the owner. Of course, the interval between the delivery of the disposition and its registration is short — seldom more than a few days. In this period the purchaser is in theory at risk simply because the seller is still the owner. Thus, the seller could fraudulently convey the property to someone else (X). In that case there would be a "race to the register" between X and the purchaser, and whoever registered first would win.[10] Much the same would apply if the seller were to be sequestrated.[11] During the interval between delivery and infeftment the disponee is technically called an uninfeft proprietor, which is to say that, while uninfeft, he can obtain infeftment at his own hand, simply by taking a taxi to Register House.

[10] Though X, if in bad faith, would be subject to the "offside goals rule." See further, *Stair Memorial Encyclopaedia*, Vol. 18, paras. 695 *et seq*.

[11] See G. L. Gretton, "Delivery of Deeds and the Race to the Register," 1984 J.L.S. 400.

Chapter 10

REAL BURDENS AND SERVITUDES

Introduction[1]

Real burdens and servitudes are very similar, both being examples of what are sometimes called real conditions.[1a] In each there is a burdened property (or servient tenement) and a property in favour of which the burden exists (the dominant tenement or benefited property). Both the benefit and the burden run with the property, so that successive owners of the servient property are bound, and successive owners of the dominant property are benefited.

However, the two types of real condition differ in a number of important respects. Servitudes are a limited class, such as the servitude of way, of pasturage, of piping, and so on.[2] By contrast, real burdens are not of any fixed types, though in practice the commonest real burdens are (1) amenity conditions, such as a prohibition of commercial use[3] and (2) upkeep obligations, such as obligations to maintain boundary walls or the structure of a tenement building. A burden must have "praedial benefit," that is it must benefit the dominant subjects themselves and not merely its owners personally. Another difference between the two types of real condition is that real burdens can only be created by entering the infeftment of the servient property.[4] Servitudes are not so restricted. A deed of servitude may be valid even though unrecorded.[5] Or again, it is possible

[1] This chapter cannot attempt a complete account of what is a very complex area of law. See, further, Gordon, chaps. 22 to 25 and vol. 18 of the *Stair Memorial Encyclopaedia*, paras. 375–493.

[1a] For real conditions see the *Stair Memorial Encyclopaedia*, vol. 18, paras. 344–353.

[2] For a list see Gordon, paras. 24–22 and 24–23.

[3] "No trade business or profession" is the usual wording.

[4] However, a real burden created under s. 17 of the 1979 Act arguably does not enter the infeftment.

[5] Or it may appear only in the infeftment of the dominant subjects: *Balfour* v. *Kinsey*, 1987 S.L.T. 144.

to have both implied servitudes and also servitudes by prescription. None of these is possible for real burdens. A last salient point of difference is that the courts adopt a far more restrictive approach to the construction of real burdens than to that of servitudes.

Like so much in property law, our law of servitudes is borrowed from the law of Rome. Real burdens by contrast are home-grown.[6] It is sometimes supposed that real burdens grew out of the feudal system, but this is only a half truth. It is true that in practice a majority of real burdens are created in feu dispositions, so that the dominant property is the superiority.[7] But this is not a requirement of law. It is perfectly competent to create a real burden in a disposition.[8]

When are servitudes and real burdens needed?

The need for real conditions arises mainly when property is split off. This applies to servitudes, to amenity burdens, and to upkeep burdens. Thus, suppose that an owner of a house surrounded by a hectare of land sells half the land, the buyer intending to build a house there. The seller may require the use of a septic tank lying in the area sold. This can be achieved by the servitude of "sinks".[9] Again, the seller may wish to continue to use a path through the land being sold, which will be implemented by a servitude of way. The seller may wish to impose an upkeep real burden, for instance an obligation to share equally in the maintenance of a common boundary wall. He may also wish to impose amenity burdens, to protect the amenity of his retained property. For instance, he may impose an obligation not to build more than one house,[10] and not to use the sold property for commercial purposes. Of course, if he wishes to impose such servitudes and burdens, he should so specify in the missives. The general principle of law is that if missives do

[6] Though equivalent institutions are to be found in other legal systems.

[7] Though the neighbouring properties may also be benefited and have a right to enforce.

[8] Indeed, the most famous case on real burdens, *Tailors of Aberdeen* v. *Coutts* (1834) 13 S. 226; 1837 2 Sh. & Macl. 609; (1840) 1 Rob. 296 was a case of a non-feudal real burden.

[9] The curiously named servitude right to discharge "foul water"—to use the polite term—into another person's land.

[10] This could also be achieved by a servitude *non aedificandi*.

not provide for the imposition of real conditions, a purchaser can refuse to accept such imposition.[11]

The classic example is the tenement building. When a block of flats is built, it will be in unitary ownership—that of the builder. It may remain in unitary ownership, with the owner renting out the flats rather than selling them. But if the flats are sold off individually either after construction or at some later stage, it is normal to insert real burdens. The main reason is that the common law of the tenement as to upkeep is generally regarded as unsatisfactory in various respects, especially because it imposes the sole obligation to maintain the roof on the owners of the roof, who, at common law, are the top flat owners.[12] Therefore, in the original split-off conveyances of individual tenement flats there are normally upkeep real burdens and also amenity burdens, especially those forbidding commercial use.

Another standard case is where a volume builder such as Barratts develops a housing estate. Upkeep burdens will be imposed for such things as mutual boundary walls, but in addition there will be amenity burdens. Why do Barratts impose such burdens? After all, when they have sold all the houses they no longer have any commercial interest. The reason is that such burdens actually increase the attractiveness of the estate to potential purchasers. Of course, as far as a purchaser's own house is concerned, he would in theory prefer it to be burden-free. But he wants burdens on the other houses, to keep up the amenity of the area. The price he pays for the burdens on the other houses is that he accepts burdens on his own.

Real burdens and planning law

The question is sometimes asked, why amenity burdens continue to be used when modern planning law protects amenity. For example, if your neighbour in Edinburgh's Heriot Row wishes to turn his house into a nuclear reprocessing factory, you need not worry, because he will not get planning consent.

[11] *Corbett* v. *Robertson* (1872) 10 M. 329. *Cf. Morris* v. *Ritchie*, 1991 G.W.D. 12–712, 1992 G.W.D. 33–1950.

[12] Except for the portion of the roof over the common passage and stair, which is owned in common by all the tenement proprietors and is, therefore, at common law, their mutual responsibility.

There are three answers to this question. The first is that amenity burdens can cover points which could not be covered by planning law. For instance, in new housing estates there is sometimes a burden forbidding the parking of caravans in the front drive. Planning law could not prevent that. The second answer is that the planning authorities often fail to enforce planning law, especially in respect of minor infringements. The third reason is that the planning authority can always grant planning consent, leaving the outraged neighbour fuming but powerless. These two latter points arise from the fact that planning law is part of public law. It is enforced or waived by a public authority. Neighbours have a right to voice their objections, but the planning authority makes up its own mind. The value of real burdens is that they are part of private law, and can be enforced by the owner of the dominant property. This is true even if planning consent has been given. If planning consent is given to convert a dwelling-house into a public house, but there is a real burden forbidding any "trade business or profession," and the dominant property is the neighbouring property, the owner of that neighbouring property can interdict use as a pub, notwithstanding the grant of planning consent.[13]

Importance of use in practice

Whenever there is a break-off conveyance, it should be instinctual for the conveyancer to consider the possible need for servitudes and real burdens. This applies to both parties to the deal, for it is not only the seller but also often the buyer who may need such conditions to be imposed.[14] The clients may not have thought about this question clearly, and so an active approach is necessary. A site visit is desirable. This will, for example, reveal if there is a path to the public road from the retained subjects over the subjects to be

[13] The fact that planning permission has been granted may, however, help the burdened owner in an application to the Lands Tribunal for variation. See E. Young, 1988 J.L.S. 434.

[14] The buyer may wish conditions to be imposed on the seller's retained property, for precisely the same sort of reasons as vice versa. A burden purportedly imposed, in the disposition, upon the retained subjects would be ineffectual (except contractually) since it would enter the infeftment only of the dominant subjects. Hence, in such a case a deed of conditions should be used under s. 17 of the 1979 Act.

sold. Or it will reveal similar problems about pipes and cables. Or it will indicate the existence of a boundary wall which will need to be kept up.[15] And so forth. In addition to upkeep burdens the clients must be asked about amenity burdens which they may wish to have.

Occasionally, split-offs happen where the lawyers involved have failed to do these things. Such failure can cause problems to the clients in future years and may even give rise to a negligence action against the solicitors involved. Sometimes, however, the bacon can be saved by arguing that a servitude exists by implication, or, after 20 years, by prescription. Note, however, that real burdens cannot arise either by implication[16] or by prescription.

Dominant and servient subjects

In both servitudes and real burdens it is necessary that there be two identifiable subjects: the burdened or servient property and the benefited or dominant property. Real conditions are praedial, that is to say they affect land rather than persons, or, in other words, affect persons only in their relation to land. Real conditions are thus "real at both ends." When drafting real conditions it is vital that both subjects be clearly identified. This is not often a problem for the burdened or servient property, because a real burden must enter the infeftment of that property itself, and servitudes, though they need not enter the infeftment, in practice usually do so. However, even as far as the servient property itself is concerned, imprecision as to the identity of the burdened property can sometimes occur, and if it does occur it will be fatal to the validity of the condition. In one case,[17] a burden was imposed on an area "occupied as the lawn." Though this may have been clear enough at the time, and so perhaps valid as a contractual burden, it could not be a valid real burden because of the intrinsically transient nature of

[15] If there is no boundary wall there may be a need to impose a burden requiring one to be built and maintained.

[16] A type of real condition called common interest does, however, arise by implication. The main example in practice is the implied common law rules as to maintenance obligations in a tenement building.

[17] *Anderson* v. *Dickie*, 1915 S.C. (H.L.) 79. See also *Scottish Temperance Life Assurance Co.* v. *Law Union & Rock Insurance Co.*, 1917 S.C. 175.

the definition. As Lord Kinnear said,[18] future parties interested in the title "cannot be sent . . . to seek for a real burden in sources so remote from the title as the memory of gardeners."

Much more common is failure to identify the dominant subjects. The problem arises particularly with real burdens, which far too often identify the burdened property but not the benefited property. Yet there can be no real burden without an identifiable benefited property.[19] The law, leniently, will sometimes imply the benefited property. Thus, in a feu disposition, it will be implied that the superiority is the benefited property, and where land is split off by disposition, it is implied that the retained land is the benefited property.[20] In certain other cases, however, the implied dominant subjects may be wider, a typical example being where a developer sells all the houses in an estate on identical terms. Here, not only the superiority but also the neighbouring feus may be by implication benefited: this is the case of the so-called *jus quaesitum tertio*.[21] However, the law in this area is one of immense complexity,[22] and the task of proving an implied benefited property is often extremely difficult. The practical lesson, therefore, is that whenever a real burden is created, it should specify fully and without vagueness or ambiguity which property or properties are benefited. For example, in a new housing scheme it should be stated (if that is the intention) that all the neighbouring properties are benefited. A suitable clause would run: "Declaring that the real burdens hereby created are for the benefit of the following subjects . . . and shall accordingly be enforceable by the proprietors for the time being of those subjects."

One particular problem which sometimes crops up is whether,

[18] At p. 86.

[19] There have been cases where a burden which failed to identify the dominant property has been upheld, such as *Lawson* v. *Wilkie* (1897) 24 R. 649, but in such cases the point has not been at issue. The law remains that the benefited property must be identifiable.

[20] *J.A. Mactaggart & Co.* v. *Harrower* (1906) 8 F. 1101.

[21] The leading case is *Hislop* v. *MacRitchie's Trs.* (1881) 8 R. (H.L.) 95. In a tenement, it is generally assumed that the burdens on each flat are for the benefit of the others, and so enforceable by those other owners, but there seems to be no authority confirming this.

[22] See A.J. Mcdonald, "Enforcement of Title Conditions," in D.J. Cusine (ed.), *Scots Conveyancing Miscellany: Essays in Honour of Professor J.M. Halliday*, and vol. 18 of the *Stair Memorial Encyclopaedia*, paras. 399–404. Because of the full treatment in these sources, the subject will not be further discussed here.

on the division of the dominant subjects into separate plots, a servitude of way or for piping or a real burden enures to the benefit of all the various plots which now make up the dominant subjects. A farmer who happily granted a servitude of way for a neighbouring farmer may be less happy if he finds that instead of the occasional tractor there are countless cars driving up and down day and night because the neighbouring farm is now a housing estate.[23] Because of uncertainties in the law, the ideal is to make clear provision on the point in the servitude itself, either allowing such future use or alternatively forbidding it.

Making a burden real

A burden is not real[24] unless it is made clear that it binds not merely the present owner of the servient property but future owners as well.[25] "Words must be used in the conveyance which clearly express or plainly imply that the subject itself is affected, not the grantee and his heirs alone, although it is not essential that any *voces signatae* or technical form of words should be employed."[26] The usual way to make the intention clear is to have a clause at the end of the burden, or list of burdens, expressly declaring the burdens to be real burdens. Such a clause is not strictly necessary, but if it is absent it will be a question of interpretation whether the burden was intended merely as a contract between the parties to the deed, or as a real burden. Another formula which is equally good is to make the burden binding on the grantee "and his successors as proprietors of" the subjects in question. One often comes across the formula that a burden binds the grantee "and his foresaids." This is a reference to the destination clause. If the destination was to "X and his heirs[27] and assignees" there is a potential

[23] *Keith* v. *Texaco Ltd.*, 1977 S.L.T. (Lands Tr.) 16 indicates that such a servitude could not be expanded in this way. There were, however, special factors in that case which may mean that it did not lay down any general rule. See also *Alba Homes Ltd.* v. *Duell*, 1993 S.L.T. (Sh.Ct.) 49.

[24] There are theoretical problems about whether real burdens are fully "real" in the strict sense of that term, but this is not the place to discuss these issues.

[25] A burden which is not real will still in most cases be enforceable as between grantor and grantee as a matter of contract law.

[26] *Tailors of Aberdeen* v. *Coutts* (1840) 1 Rob. 296, *per* Lord Corehouse at 306–307. *Voces signatae* means technical terms of law.

[27] Or executors.

problem in that this phrase probably does not mean future owners generally.[28] However, this will probably not be fatal if there is a clause expressly declaring the burdens to be real burdens.

Creation of real burdens: deeds of conditions

At common law a real burden could be created only as part of a conveyance—whether disposition or feu disposition—of the subjects to be burdened. Moreover, the burden had to be stated *ad longum*. Where a developer wanted to impose identical burdens on all the properties to be sold, this meant repeating the burdens in full in each split-off deed. This was inconvenient, and the position was changed to some extent by section 32 of the 1874 Act which authorised the use of deeds of conditions. The developer could record a deed of conditions setting forth the burdens, and each split-off deed could then impose burdens simply by a reference to the recorded deed of conditions.

This was an improvement but did not change the basic rule that the burden could be created only as part of a conveyance. For the recording of the deed of conditions did not of itself burden the land to which it related. This fact was often an inconvenient one. Suppose, for instance, that A owned a hectare of land and sold half to B. It was mutually agreed that both areas should have a real burden forbidding commercial use. This burden could be inserted only in the title of the half hectare being disponed (or feued). The other half, the retained half, could not be burdened because there was no conveyance of it. All that could be done was to have a contract obliging the owner of the retained half (the seller) to impose the burden as a real burden when, in the future, he came to dispose of it. Provided that he did so, everything worked out. But the contractual obligation could easily be forgotten, especially after several years. Or it might be consciously breached. Or the owner in question might be sequestrated and the trustee would then be free to sell in disregard of the contract. What was needed, therefore, was a method by which an owner of land could create a real burden over it in favour of neighbouring land outwith the context of a conveyance. That this should be possible is natural enough, for a servitude can be so created. Matters were put right

[28] For authorities on this question see G.L. Gretton at 1984 J.L.S. 103.

by section 17 of the 1979 Act which provides that an owner can use a deed of conditions so as to burden his land immediately.[29] Of course, neither section 32 of the 1874 Act nor section 17 of the 1979 Act make the use of deeds of conditions compulsory. Real burdens can still be created in the common law way, namely *ad longum* provision in a conveyance of the land to be burdened.[30]

A real burden cannot take effect unless there is some other property which is the benefited or dominant property.[31] This fact places limits on the operation of section 17. Suppose that a developer has five hectares on which he intends to build 80 houses. He records a deed of conditions imposing amenity burdens. The intention is that the burdens on any one plot will enure to the benefit of the other plots. But at the moment when the deed of conditions is recorded, all the plots are still owned by one and the same person, the developer. Hence, at this stage no real burdens yet exist. But as soon as the developer dispones the first plot, not only will that plot be burdened, but all the other plots, at that stage still owned by the developer, will also be burdened.

The common law rule that a real burden must enter the infeftment of the servient property[32] is largely unaffected by the introduction of deeds of conditions. The rule is an important one in many contexts. The classic example is where a top flat in a tenement is purchased. The title is duly examined and it is found that there is a burden imposing a share, say an eighth, of the upkeep of the roof. But this of itself means nothing. For at common law the top flat is liable for the whole upkeep of the roof over that flat. This obligation cannot be varied by a *burden* in the top flat title. What the purchaser needs to check is that the titles of the *other* flats in the block have burdens imposing shares of the roof upkeep. Indeed, in missives for top flats it is the practice to have a clause obliging

[29] Section 17 provides that this immediate burdening always happens unless the deed of conditions otherwise provides.

[30] This is done after the description. The introductory words are typically: "But always with and under the following real burdens." If the deed already makes reference to existing burdens, which will usually be the case, the clause creating the new burdens comes after the references to the existing burdens, and is typically introduced by the words: "And also with and under the following additional real burdens."

[31] This, of course, is the same rule as for servitudes: *nulli res sua servit*.

[32] See, *e.g.*, *McLean* v. *Kennaway* (1904) 11 S.L.T. 719; *Jolly's Exr.* v. *Stonehaven*, 1958 S.C. 635.

the seller to produce evidence of this, which will normally be done by producing quick copies of the burdens writs[33] of the other flats.

Deeds of conditions often specify what are to be the parts of the development to be owned in common by the purchasers, *e.g.* parking areas. However, a deed of conditions cannot actually convey the common parts. This must be done by the conveyance(s). Hence, in such cases it is necessary for each subsequent split-off conveyance to say not only that the property is subject to the burdens in the deed of conditions, but also that the conveyance includes the appropriate share in the common areas specified in the deed of conditions. In other words, the deed of conditions needs to be referred to twice, once for the burdens and once (in the parts and pertinents clause) for the common parts.

Burden must appear in full

A real burden must appear in the Sasine Register (or Land Register) in full. It is incompetent to create a real burden by reference to another deed whether registered or unregistered.[34] The leading case here is *Aberdeen Varieties Limited* v. *James F. Donald (Aberdeen Cinemas) Limited*[35] where the terms of a real burden were made by reference to the contents of an Act of Parliament. This was held to be invalid. Thus, one sometimes comes across real burdens which cannot be interpreted without referring to the Town and Country Planning (Scotland) Acts. Such burdens are, it seems, void. In older deeds one sometimes comes across real burdens which refer to prior articles of roup. These again are void. However, extrinsic evidence is not absolutely excluded, for burdens have to be construed according to the physical facts on the ground.[36]

Creation of servitudes

Although a servitude can be created by unregistered deed, the standard practice is to use a registered deed. If the servitude is being imposed on property being split off, it is simply inserted in

[33] Which will typically be the original split-off writs.
[34] Apart from deeds of conditions: 1874 Act, s. 32.
[35] 1939 S.C. 788; 1940 S.C. (H.L.) 52.
[36] *McLean* v. *Macwhirn Developments Ltd.*, 1976 S.L.T. (Notes) 47.

the split-off conveyance itself. If the servitude is in favour of the split-off property and is over the property being retained, the practice is sometimes to insert the servitude once again in the split-off conveyance itself, though of course as a right rather than as a burden. This is perfectly competent,[37] although it gives rise to the practical difficulty that the existence of the servitude cannot then be ascertained merely from an examination of the title of the servient property. This difficulty can be avoided by having a separate deed of servitude which is then recorded or registered with reference to the title of the servient property. In that way, a search of the title of the servient property will reveal the existence of the servitude.

Of course, it is also convenient to have the existence of the servitude noted in the title to the dominant property, not because this is a formal requirement but because it should be possible from an ordinary examination of a title to discover what rights are included. This is commonly done by mentioning the servitude in a "together with" clause after the description.[38]

Probably the commonest servitude is that of way. In practice there are two types: pedestrian and vehicular. It is important in drafting to specify which type. To avoid any doubt as to whether vehicular access includes pedestrian access, the phrase "pedestrian and vehicular" should be used. If the nature of the servitude has not been specified, a court will, it seems, construe the servitude on the basis of actual usage.

Creation of servitudes by implication and by prescription

The creation of a servitude by implication is almost always the mark of conveyancing negligence. If a servitude is needed, it should be created expressly. Because of this we do not propose to discuss here the creation of servitudes by implication.[39] Servitudes by prescription are, again, only marginally a conveyancing matter and so

[37] *Balfour* v. *Kinsey*, 1987 S.L.T. 144.

[38] This, however, is seldom done for real burdens, *i.e.* in relation to the title to the dominant property.

[39] See Gordon, paras. 24–34 to 24–41 and the *Stair Memorial Encyclopaedia*, vol. 18, paras. 452–457 for discussion and authorities. Some important cases are *Cochrane* v. *Ewart* (1861) 23 D. (H.L.) 3; *Gow's Trs.* v. *Mealls* (1875) 2 R. 729, *Murray* v. *Medley*, 1973 S.L.T. (Sh. Ct.) 75 and *King* v. *Brodt*, 1993 G.W.D. 13–886.

will not be discussed here. The relevant prescriptive period is 20 years,[40] and it should be noted that only positive servitudes, and not negative ones, are capable of prescriptive creation.

Reference to burdens and servitudes

If a property is burdened by servitudes or burdens, it is convenient if all these conditions are listed in each conveyance of the burdened property, so that anyone can tell at a glance what the burdens are. In practice, this is done after the description. A clause is added beginning with such words as: "But always with and under, in so far as valid subsisting and applicable, the following real burdens conditions servitudes and others namely . . . " The list then refers to the various recorded deeds which created the burdens or servitudes.[41] Those deeds, or photocopies of them, will commonly be among the titles themselves. If one examines a title and finds that copies of some of these burdens writs are not available, they should be obtained, typically by getting a "quick copy" from Register House.

Deeds creating burdens often impose an actual obligation to make reference to the burdens in all future conveyances, and sometimes this obligation is backed up by an irritancy clause. It is not quite clear why draftsmen like this approach, because a real burden does not cease to be valid and enforceable merely because it is not referred to in the latest disposition. Moreover, it is not clear whether clauses of this sort are enforceable. However, on the assumption that they are enforceable there is a statutory mechanism whereby failure to make reference can subsequently be put right.[42]

Reference to burdens should also be made in notices of title,[43] but not in standard securities.[44] Nor is such reference necessary in deeds concerning subjects registered in the Land Register.[45] The reason is that the title sheet and land certificate list such burdens

[40] 1973 Act, s. 3.

[41] 1874 Act, s. 32 and Sched. H. See chap. 9.

[42] 1924 Act, s. 9(3) and (4). These provisions are, however, rarely encountered in practice.

[43] 1924 Act, Sched. B.

[44] 1924 Act, s. 9(1) as applied by s. 32 of the 1970 Act.

[45] 1979 Act, s. 15(1).

in any case. However, a deed inducing a first registration should refer to burdens in the same way as a Sasine writ.

Restrictions on the content of real burdens

There are restrictions on the content of real burdens. There must be "praedial benefit" to the dominant property, *i.e.* it must benefit the property as such.[46] A real burden cannot forbid the performance of ordinary juristic acts in relation to the property, such as the grant of a lease,[47] or subfeu,[48] or disposition,[49] or subdivision of title.[50] However, pre-emption rights are lawful.[51] A real burden cannot impose a permanent obligation to pay money, other than an upkeep burden.[52] Even an upkeep burden might arguably be invalid if it takes the form of an obligation to pay an indefinite sum of money, as opposed to a direct obligation to maintain.[53] A burden will also be invalid if contrary to public policy, though case law here is sparse.[54]

[46] See *Aberdeen Varieties Ltd.* v. *James F. Donald (Aberdeen Cinemas) Ltd.*, 1939 S.C. 788; 1940 S.C. (H.L.) 52, though this is not the main thrust of that case. The distinction is a fine one. See also *Phillips* v. *Lavery*, 1962 S.L.T. (Sh. Ct.) 57 and *Cooperative Wholesale Society* v. *Usher's Brewery*, 1975 S.L.T. (Lands Tr.) 9.

[47] *Moir's Trs.* v. *McEwan* (1880) 7 R. 1141 at 1145. As Lord Young said, "you cannot make a man proprietor and yet prohibit him from exercising the rights of proprietorship." See also *Calder* v. *Police Commissioners of North Berwick* (1899) 1 F. 491 at 493. However, restrictions on use can go very far. A prohibition of any building has been recognised since Roman times as a valid servitude (*non aedificandi*) and in *Lees* v. *North East Fife District Council*, 1987 S.L.T. 769 a real burden forbidding all use except that of a swimming pool was upheld.

[48] 1874 Act, s. 22; Conveyancing Amendment (Scotland) Act 1938, s. 8.

[49] Tenures Abolition Act 1746, (20 Geo. II, c. 50), s. 10.

[50] This seems to follow from the general incompetency of restrictions on disponing and subfeuing. Section 8 of the Conveyancing Amendment (Scotland) Act 1938 expressly invalidates restrictions on subdivision by feu. Prohibition of subdivision in the sense of use or structure rather than title is not, in principle, incompetent.

[51] See *Matheson* v. *Tinney*, 1989 S.L.T. 535 and authorities there cited. They are, however, subject to restrictions: Conveyancing Amendment (Scotland) Act 1938, s. 9 as amended.

[52] 1974 Act, s. 2.

[53] *Tailors of Aberdeen* v. *Coutts* (1840) 1 Rob. 296; *Magistrates of Edinburgh* v. *Begg* (1882) 11 R. 352; *Tennant* v. *Napier* (1888) 15 R. 671; *Wells* v. *New House Purchasers Ltd.*, 1964 S.L.T. (Sh. Ct.) 2; *David Watson Property Management* v. *Woolwich Equitable Building Society*, 1992 S.L.T. 430.

[54] See *Campbell* v. *Dunn* (1825) 1 W. & S 690; (1828) 6 S. 679 for discussion, and also *Moir's Trs.* v. *McEwan* (1880) 7 R. 1141.

Interpretation[55]

Real conditions are construed according to the *praesumptio pro libertate*, the presumption for freedom. In other words, land is presumed to be free of burdens. If the validity of a condition is doubtful, it will generally be construed as invalid,[56] while if its scope is doubtful, it will generally be construed according to its narrowest possible meaning,[57] and the courts are very reluctant to extend the scope of a burden by implication. Hence, the vital importance when drafting new burdens of accuracy. For example, an obligation to build cannot be extended to imply an obligation to maintain.[58] In one case an obligation to build a house "which may include a garage" was held not to imply a prohibition on building a second garage.[59] An obligation to supply water was held not to imply an obligation that it be drinkable.[60] By contrast, where there was an obligation to maintain a boundary fence it was held that it could fairly be implied that the fence should be stockproof.[61] A common burden is one which restricts use to that of a private dwelling-house, but this has been held not to prevent use as an orphanage.[62] Another common burden is that the dwelling-house

[55] On interpretation, see the *Stair Memorial Encyclopaedia*, vol. 18, paras. 415–422; Gordon, paras. 22–41 to 22–50; Halliday, paras. 19–30 to 19–33.

[56] But in practice it can be difficult to predict what a court would say. Thus, in *Lothian Regional Council* v. *Rennie*, 1991 S.L.T. 465; 1991 S.C.L.R. 709 two judges held a burden to be ineffectual as being hopelessly imprecise in its scope, while the third judge thought that its meaning was perfectly clear.

[57] For illustrative examples, in addition to the cases cited below, see *Graham* v. *Shiels* (1901) 8 S.L.T. 368, *Shand* v. *Brand* (1907) 14 S.L.T. 704, and *The Walker Trustees* v. *Haldane* (1902) 4 F. 594. But the court will not adopt a narrow reading unless it is a reasonable one: *Cochrane* v. *Paterson* (1882) 9 R. 634 at 638; *Frame* v. *Cameron* (1864) 3 M. 290 at 294.

[58] *Peter Walker & Son (Edinburgh) Ltd.* v. *Church of Scotland General Trustees*, 1967 S.L.T. 297. Contrast *Clark* v. *Glasgow Assurance Co.* (1854) 1 Macq. 668. Though a House of Lords case, it is out of line with current judicial attitudes.

[59] *Carswell* v. *Goldie*, 1967 S.L.T. 339. And see *Ross* v. *Cuthbertson* (1854) 16 D. 732 and *Buchanan* v. *Marr* (1883) 10 R. 936.

[60] *Anstruther's Trs.* v. *Burgh of Pittenweem*, 1943 S.L.T. 160.

[61] *Church of Scotland General Trustees* v. *Phin*, 1987 S.C.L.R. 240. This case, like some others cited, shows that it can be difficult to predict how stringent a court will be.

[62] *Brown* v. *Crum-Ewing's Trs.*, 1918 1 S.L.T. 340.

must be "self-contained." But in a series of cases the courts have held that this refers to structure not use. Thus, such a burden does not prevent division into flats, provided that the structure remains capable of use as a single dwelling-house.[63] An obligation to erect buildings of a certain type does not imply a prohibition of additional buildings of a different type.[64]

The terms "conventional dwelling-house"[65] and "buildings of an unseemly description"[66] have both been held to be too vague as the basis of real burdens. But it has been held, perhaps incorrectly, that "not of a class inferior to the houses some time ago built by" is valid as the basis of a real burden.[67] An obligation to erect houses[68] is invalid as a real burden if no time limit is expressed.[69] Where a burden forbids a certain use, it is presumed not to forbid use of the same kind which is merely ancillary. For example, a prohibition of commercial use would not prevent a house being used commercially provided that its main use continued to be that of a dwelling-house.[70] Because of this rule, it may be desirable when drafting a burden to add a clause expressly forbidding ancillary use, and this is sometimes done.

[63] The distinction seems odd but is well supported by authority, *e.g.*, *Moir's Trs.* v. *McEwan* (1880) 7 R. 1141; *Buchanan* v. *Marr* (1883) 10 R. 936; *Miller* v. *Carmichael* (1888) 15 R. 991; *Porter* v. *Campbell's Trs.*, 1923 S.C. (H.L.) 94.

[64] *Cowan* v. *Magistrates of Edinburgh* (1887) 14 R. 682; *Fleming* v. *Ure* (1896) 4 S.L.T. 26. For whether the burden implies a prohibition of altering the buildings see *Cochrane* v. *Paterson* (1882) 9 R. 634, *Thom* v. *Chalmers* (1886) 13 R. 1026, and *Johnston* v. *MacRitchie* (1893) 20 R. 539.

[65] *Lawson* v. *Hay*, 1989 G.W.D. 24–1049.

[66] *Murray's Trs.* v. *Trustees for St Margaret's Convent* (1906) 8 F. 1109; 1907 S.C. (H.L.) 8.

[67] *Morrison* v. *McLay* (1874) 1 R. 1117. This was arguably too vague, judged in the context of other reported cases. See also *Middleton* v. *Leslie* (1894) 21 R. 781.

[68] Burdens of this nature were once very common. The superior wanted to keep up the value of the land as a security for his feuduty. Clauses requiring insurance and rebuilding in the event of destruction were common for the same reason. Such clauses (except in so far as they might protect amenity) are now pointless in a feu disposition since feuduty cannot now be imposed. (In the old days, the feuduty might represent the whole capital value. Land was sometimes sold for feuduty alone, with no grassum or price.)

[69] *Gammell's Trs.* v. *The Land Commission*, 1970 S.L.T. 254, distinguishing *Anderson* v. *Valentine*, 1957 S.L.T. 57.

[70] *Colquhoun's C.B.* v. *Glen's Tr.*, 1920 S.C. 737; *Low* v. *Scottish Amicable Building Society*, 1940 S.L.T. 295.

It is common to find burdens forbidding "nuisances." There is only one reported case[71] where such a clause has been challenged as too vague. In that case the burden forbade:

> "any soap work candle work tan work slaughter house cattle mart skin work dye work oil work lime work distillery brewery or other manufacture or chemical process of any kind, nor to deposit nauseous materials thereon nor to lay any nuisance or obstructions on the roads or streets adjoining said ground nor to do any other act which may injure the amenity of the said place of the neighbourhood for private residences."

The challenge failed. Clauses of this sort are often to be found in older deeds.[72] The modern tendency is simply to forbid any "trade business or profession" and there can be little doubt that this expression is acceptably precise. Reference to "nuisance" as such is rare in modern burdens. One interpretative problem is that "nuisance" is a delict against neighbours in any case.[73]

In practice, the approach to be taken to the interpretation of burdens depends very much on the situation one is in. Sometimes a person has concluded missives to buy, and his agent must decide on the acceptability of the burdens. Here, a cautious approach needs to be adopted. It is not enough that the burden is probably invalid, or, though valid, probably does not strike at the use proposed by the purchaser. Probability is not enough for a purchaser. He wants certainty, or something near it. By contrast, suppose that an owner is using his property in a certain way, and the owner of the benefited subjects objects on the ground that the use is in breach of a burden. Here the law agent for the owner will be only too glad to seize upon any argument that will tend to show that the burden is invalid or is to be construed in a narrow sense. And the same, of course, applies if litigation takes place. A probable argument once accepted by a court becomes a certainty.

The above remarks apply to the interpretation of real burdens. The approach to servitudes is different. Although the *praesumptio*

[71] *Mannofield Residents Property Co. Ltd.* v. *Thomson*, 1983 S.L.T. (Sh. Ct.) 71.

[72] "The usual grotesque enumeration of noxious and offensive businesses and trades"—Lord Shaw in *Porter* v. *Campbell's Tr.*, 1923 S.C. (H.L.) 94.

[73] On nuisance as a delict see the *Stair Memorial Encyclopaedia*, vol. 14, para. 2001 *et seq.*

pro libertate applies in principle to servitudes also, in practice the latter are more liberally construed.[74]

Interest to enforce

The benefited owner must not only have a title to enforce, namely that he must be the owner of property which is the dominant property, or one of the dominant properties, but he must also have an interest. This really comes down to the proposition that there must be praedial benefit. Thus, the two properties must be either neighbouring or at least reasonably near each other.[75] Where the dominant property is the superiority there is a strong presumption of interest to enforce.[76]

Land Register

The common law rule that a real burden must enter the infeftment of the servient subjects applies equally in land registration cases. The Keeper inserts the real burdens in the title sheet. His practice is to copy the original wording, even though this may be archaic or unclear or verbose.[77] Any burdens not so entered cannot be effective as real burdens.[78] However, the fact that a real burden does appear in the title sheet does not necessarily imply that the burden is valid.[79] Entry in the title sheet is a necessary condition of validity, but not a sufficient condition. If a burden appearing in the title sheet turns out to be invalid, no compensation is payable by the Keeper.[80] The common law rule that servitudes need not enter the infeftment is maintained in land registration practice by

[74] See, *e.g.*, *Alvis* v. *Harrison*, 1991 S.L.T. 64.

[75] In *Aberdeen Varieties Ltd.* v. *James F. Donald (Aberdeen Cinemas) Ltd.*, 1939 S.C. 788; 1940 S.C. (H.L.) 52 a distance of half a mile was found to be too great. But everything will turn on the facts of the case. Suppose that there is a burden forbidding industrial use, and it is proposed to build a nuclear reprocessing plant. In such a case, half a mile would presumably not be excessive.

[76] *Earl of Zetland* v. *Hislop* (1882) 9 R. (H.L.) 40.

[77] See 1979 Act, s. 6(2).

[78] This is the effect of s. 3(1)(*a*) of the 1979 Act.

[79] See, *e.g.*, *Brookfield Developments Ltd.* v. *Keeper of the Registers of Scotland*, 1989 S.L.T. (Lands Tr.) 105.

[80] 1979 Act, s. 12(3)(*g*).

the rule that they are classified as overriding interests[81] and as such can be effectual even though not appearing in the title sheet. However, the Keeper will note servitudes on the title sheet of the servient property where their existence is known to him.[82] As already mentioned, conveyances of registered property need make no reference to existing burdens.

Discharge, variation, acquiescence, and the Lands Tribunal

A servitude can be discharged by unrecorded deed, though in practice a recorded deed should always be used. A real burden is discharged by a recorded minute of waiver[83] or, much less commonly, by charter of novodamus.[84] A servitude can be prescriptively extinguished *non utendo*, *i.e.* by non-use for 20 years.[85] The same is probably true of real burdens.[86] Both servitudes and real burdens can also be limited or extinguished by acquiescence. For instance, if the dominant owner in a servitude of way acquiesces in the building of a wall across the way, the right is lost. It is well settled that acquiescence transmits against the successors of the dominant owner.[87] This fact is often useful in examining burdens writs. Suppose, for instance, that there is a feu disposition of 1893 which feued plots of ground to builders for the erection of tenements. The feu disposition will have imposed various real burdens. Some, such as restrictions on use, are likely still to be enforceable. But suppose that one of the burdens concerned the building line. For instance, it may have provided that there should be no building nearer than four feet from the inner line of the pavement. This is unlikely to be important now in 1993. For if the builder in fact built up to three feet from the pavement, acquiescence will long ago have barred any objection.[88] As a general rule, acquiescence

[81] 1979 Act, s. 28.

[82] 1979 Act, s. 6(4).

[83] See s. 18 of the 1979 Act.

[84] Applicable only where the burden is in favour of the superior.

[85] 1973 Act, ss. 7 and 8.

[86] The point, however, is arguable. Compare Gordon, paras. 22–82 and 23–30 with the *Stair Memorial Encyclopaedia*, vol. 18, para. 431.

[87] *Ben Challum Ltd.* v. *Buchanan*, 1955 S.C. 348, the leading modern case in this area.

[88] The burden might, however, still be important if the tenement were now to

requires the servient owner to have altered his position, such as spending money on building operations. It seems that acquiescence cannot take place merely on the basis of change of use.[89]

Under the 1970 Act the Lands Tribunal has an equitable power to waive or vary "land obligations," a term which includes both servitudes and real burdens. Applications are frequent, mainly in relation to real burdens. Because the jurisdiction is essentially discretionary,[90] the outcome of such applications is often difficult to predict.[91]

Feu dispositions almost always contain real burdens, and a superior, who is typically the superior of numerous feus, will often receive applications for minutes of waiver. He will generally make a charge for his consent, such as £500. If, however, waiver is needed for an expensive development, the superior may hold out for a much larger sum. One limitation on the self-interest of the superior is that if he asks for too much money the owner may decide to make an application to the Lands Tribunal, and if he is successful the superior may be paid nothing at all.[92]

An owner seeking a minute of waiver must be sure to identify all the persons entitled to enforce.[93] There is no point in obtaining a minute of waiver from the superior only to find that the neighbour seeks and obtains an interdict. In some cases, where numerous parties are benefited owners, it may be that obtaining the signature of all of them to a minute of waiver is impracticable, in which case an application to the Lands Tribunal may be unavoidable. Note, however, that some feu dispositions are so drafted that although both the superior and neighbours have the right to enforce, if the superior grants a minute of waiver that will bind the neighbours also.

be demolished, and new building to take place. The new building would have to be at least four feet from the pavement. (On the assumption that such burdens are not invalid under the rule of *Anderson* v. *Dickie*, 1915 S.C. (H.L.) 79.)

[89] *Johnston* v. *The Walker Trustees* (1897) 24 R. 1061.

[90] Guidelines for the exercise of the discretion are laid down in s. 1(3) of the 1970 Act.

[91] However, there is now a large body of reported cases which give some guidance. See Halliday, chap. 19 and Gordon, chap. 25 for a survey of some of the case law.

[92] Under s. 1(4) of the 1970 Act the Tribunal can order that the superior be paid compensation, but in practice it is common for no compensation to be ordered.

[93] See *Dalrymple* v. *Herdman* (1878) 5 R. 847.

Transmission of liability

A real burden binds future owners. Thus, if there is an upkeep burden, the future owner will have to pay for future repairs. But the question of the transmission of liability for current or past repair work, which has not yet been paid for, has traditionally been less clear. The decision of the House of Lords in *David Watson Property Management* v. *Woolwich Equitable Building Society*[94] appears to hold that once the work has been done and payment is due, liability does not transmit. However, some uncertainty still attaches to the situation where ownership passes at a time when repair work is outstanding, and perhaps has been begun, but at all events has not been completed or invoiced.[95] The standard practice is, as far as possible, to cover such matters expressly in missives.

[94] 1992 S.L.T. 430. The case deals with transmission of liability against a heritable creditor in possession, but its *ratio* seems to be of more general applicability.
[95] See further the *Stair Memorial Encyclopaedia*, vol. 18, para. 412.

Chapter 11

THE MORTGAGE MARKET AND THE MORTGAGE PACKAGE

Introduction

This and the following chapters do not seek to give a complete account of the law of heritable security.[1] The emphasis is on the practical aspects. Securities over non-residential property are not covered, except incidentally. With some trepidation, and with apologies to linguistic purists, we will often use the term "mortgage." This is the word that the client understands, and will also often be used by others such as insurance companies, the Inland Revenue, etc. In formal writing, of course, one always uses the correct term—heritable security or standard security.[2] A further terminological point is that the typical client uses the word "mortgage" to mean the whole package, not just the security. Thus, he includes the loan, the life policy and so on. The average client will also say that "the Abbey National gave me a mortgage." It must be remembered that in law the opposite is true. The lender gives a loan. The debtor gives the security.

This chapter is concerned with the mortgage market and the mortgage packages available. The next chapter gives an account of the law of heritable security, while chapter 13 examines the role of the solicitor in preparing the security documentation.

Sources of funds

Before the last war, house purchase loans were often obtained privately, typically by the solicitor putting two clients in touch with each other, one with money to lend, and the other with a house to

[1] For which see Halliday, and D.J. Cusine, *Standard Securities* (Butterworth, 1991).

[2] Heritable security is the generic term. Under modern law there is only one species of that genus, which is the standard security.

buy, though, of course, institutional lending was also common. Nowadays, private lending is rare. Not counting local authorities, there are about 200 mortgage lenders at present in the market. The main lenders are the building societies.[3] Their share of the market varies, but is always over 50 per cent. Insurance companies are mainly involved in the mortgage market by providing life policies, but some also lend. So do local authorities, who traditionally have lent mainly on cheaper properties to poorer borrowers. Since the introduction of the right-to-buy legislation[4] they also often lend to council house buyers, and indeed normally must do so if requested.[5] The banks traditionally were not involved in the domestic mortgage market at all, but this began to change during the 1970s, and they are now active in this field. Their percentage of the market fluctuates but around 20 per cent of domestic mortgages are now with the banks. A new type of lender has appeared on the market in recent years, known as the centralized lenders, such as the Mortgage Corporation, the Household Mortgage Corporation, Chase Manhattan, the Sumitomo Bank, and Banque Nationale de Paris. These are distinguished by the fact that they do not have a high street network. The centralized lenders tend to be less flexible than the others. Thus, they will seldom offer a 100 per cent. mortgage and some will not offer a repayment mortgage.

The normal practice is to obtain all the finance from a single lender. This is worth mentioning because in some other countries it is common to obtain a cocktail of loans from different lenders, each lender taking security, the whole package making up the total amount needed. When a house is sold, the modern practice is for the seller to redeem the existing mortgage (from the proceeds of sale) and for the buyer to set up his own mortgage. It is in theory possible for the buyer to take over the existing mortgage. This was common in the nineteenth century, but today is almost unknown. The mechanism for doing it is the bond of corroboration and discharge.[6] Again, in some countries it is the norm for the buyer to

[3] Collectively, they are huge institutions. At present the amount advanced by the Halifax on mortgages is about £48,500,000,000.

[4] Currently contained in the Housing (Scotland) Act 1987.

[5] Housing (Scotland) Act 1987, s. 216. Purchasers are, of course, free to obtain finance elsewhere.

[6] See the next chapter.

take over the existing mortgage (a fact reflected in the price) and obtain a top-up mortgage as required.

Choosing the mortgage package

The choice of mortgage package is for the client to make. Often he has already arranged finance before he sees his solicitor.[7] But often he has not yet done this. In England the solicitor will, in such a case, often tell the client to go off and arrange the finance himself, the solicitor merely doing the paper work,[8] but in Scotland the solicitor is normally willing to do this himself, as part of the Scottish philosophy of providing the client with a complete service. The mortgage market is sophisticated and rapidly changing, and the solicitor will check leading lenders for the terms of their various packages. If, as is usual, the mortgage is to be an endowment one, then not only will a loan have to be chosen but also a life assurance policy. Note that a solicitor must give "best advice" so as to comply with the rules of the Financial Services Act 1986.

Solicitors are in a competitive market, and other people will be trying to set up the financial deal, especially banks, building societies and estate agents. (The main incentive is the commission obtained by arranging the endowment policy.) Solicitors argue that they do this job better than others. Most banks and building societies are tied agents under the Financial Services Act which means that they will sell life policies only for one life office.[9] For instance,[10] the Halifax are tied to Standard Life, which means that if a client arranges an endowment mortgage with the Halifax, he will obtain a Standard Life policy. So if a client goes direct to the Halifax, he will not be offered a choice.[11] Likewise, the Dunfermline are tied to Scottish Life, the Bristol & West to Eagle Star, the Abbey

[7] Even if this is the case the solicitor should check its suitability. If unsuitable it should, if still possible, be changed.

[8] A survey in England in 1989 showed that most solicitors gave their client no financial advice at all. However, this has recently begun to change, with many English law firms now following the Scottish approach.

[9] Some banks have independent arms which are not tied, but the average borrower will not be put in touch with the independent arm, unless he insists.

[10] The examples to be given are illustrative only. The position changes with time.

[11] This does not, however, mean that all endowment mortgages with the Halifax involve a Standard Life policy. A solicitor may arrange a Halifax mortgage with a policy with some other life office.

National to Friends Provident, Royal Bank of Scotland to Royal Scottish, and so forth. Only a fairly small minority of lenders are independent, such as the Bradford & Bingley and the Clydesdale Bank. Solicitors are independent and can thus fix the client up with any life office. A solicitor will also be willing to advise a repayment mortgage, which is less lucrative to himself, since in general no commission will be obtained. Banks, building societies and estate agents will seldom do this. All these have come under criticism in recent years for not looking after the client's interests, but instead trying to maximise their commission. Solicitors generally offer informed and impartial advice. (Unfortunately not everyone realises this.) So the client who reaches the solicitor's office without already having been set up with a mortgage package is lucky. For the solicitor, every client is, hopefully, a permanent client, in whose long-term prosperity he has an interest. This is not so true for others in the market.

There also exist firms called mortgage brokers, for instance John Charcol. What they do is arrange mortgages, as brokers, not principals. They do not usually charge for the service, but make the profit on the commission on the endowment policy. But in some cases (*e.g.* where the customer wants a repayment mortgage) they will charge a fee of about one per cent. of the loan.

The world of mortgages is all too often a world in which the borrower is regarded as fair game. Few clients really understand the various packages on offer. These packages have multiplied over the years. Twenty years ago, no one had heard of deferred-interest mortgages, PEP, PPP mortgages, ECU mortgages, LIBOR mortgages, equity release mortgages and so forth. The task of the adviser is correspondingly harder, and the role of the solicitor in offering genuinely independent and impartial advice is more important than ever.

The mortgage market is sometimes tight and sometimes flush. If the latter, it is easy to get a loan, subject to financial status, etc. But if the market is tight, it may happen that a building society will only lend to existing customers, and so forth. In a very tight market a "mortgage queue" develops, which means that it takes some time (*e.g.* three months) for the loan to be made available, even for the best customers. This may necessitate bridging finance. When the market is tight, the client obviously has less choice, and his solicitor's contacts with lenders become even more important. A solicitor generally has good contacts with local banks, building societies and so on, and so is able to fix up a loan. But it has been many years since a really tight mortgage market has existed.

A note on building societies

Building societies are non-profit cooperatives, unlike banks, though, with the consent of their members, they can convert to being profit-making companies under the Companies Acts.[12] They are corporations whose members are their depositors and borrowers (with a few exceptions). Thus, if one has a mortgage with the Halifax, one is a member, and so, for instance, one can vote at general meetings, etc. In theory, therefore, a building society has no interest in exploiting its borrowers.

Under the older law, a building society could lend only on a first-ranked mortgage on residential property, but the law has now changed to a certain extent. The Building Societies Act 1986 identifies three classes of loans. (1) Class 1 loans are to individuals secured by first mortgage on residential property. At least 90 per cent. of lending must be by way of Class 1 loans. (2) Class 2 loans may be on postponed security and need not be to individuals. (3) Class 3 loans are unsecured loans to individuals only. One consequence of this is that it is not easy (and it used to be impossible) to obtain a second mortgage[13] with a building society.

Types of mortgage—general

A heritable security secures a loan. It is important not to confuse the loan element with the security element. The security itself is always of one type: a standard security under the 1970 Act. The main qualification to this remark is that a lender may ask for additional security, *i.e.* security over and above the standard security on the house itself. The usual example in this connection is a security over a life policy. Occasionally, the lender will also require a guarantee from a third party.[14] The real variables come

[12] Building Societies Act 1986, s. 97. The Abbey National did this.

[13] *i.e.* a postponed secured loan.

[14] *e.g.* where the borrower is young and with a low income, a guarantee from his parents. Another example is the mortgage indemnity guarantee, for which see later.

not in the security element but in the loan element, for lenders offer loans of every type imaginable. In what follows we shall look at some of the variables, but it must be remembered that the total number of permutations is vast.

Interest

In the old days, interest was normally payable twice a year at Whitsunday and Martinmas, but nowadays it is almost always payable monthly. Again in the old days, mortgages were usually fixed-interest, in which the rate was fixed at the outset and could not change. This made sense when market interest rates were fairly stable from year to year. But nowadays market rates fluctuate, often wildly. Thus, if the mortgage rate is fixed, it may soon be much above or much below market rates. Nowadays lenders do not like to take the risk of being locked into a below-market rate, so that fluctuating-rate mortgages are now the norm. For if the rate is fixed, and market rates fall, borrowers will be likely to pay off the loan and take out a new mortgage at a lower rate, whereas if market rates rise, borrowers will stay with the loan. The risk is thus a one-way bet in favour of the borrower. There are two ways by which lenders can avoid this danger, where the rate is fixed. The first is to have a clause in the contract forbidding early redemption. Such clauses are competent[15] but in practice are seldom used.[16] The alternative is to allow early redemption only on payment of a penalty. Such clauses are common, but are used to protect the lender only for mortgages where the rate is fixed only for a certain period. In current practice mortgages where the rate is fixed for the whole period are almost unknown.

Where the rate is a fluctuating one, how is it determined? The reasonable approach would be to refer to some independently-determined rate. This is common in commercial loans, where the rate is often tied to LIBOR.[17] In domestic mortgages the traditional way of setting the fluctuating rate was for the loan contract to refer

[15] Redemption of Standard Securities (Scotland) Act 1971, s. 1.

[16] In some countries, where fixed-interest mortgages are the norm, such clauses are widely used.

[17] London Inter-Bank Offered Rate. This is the constantly changing rate at which banks lend to and borrow from each other on the London Money Market. A commercial loan might thus be set at, for instance, LIBOR +2.

the rate to the Commissioners on the Rate of Interest on Landed Securities in Scotland. This venerable body, organised under the auspices of the W.S. Society, meets twice a year and sets a rate for the next six months, at the current market rate. Their rate is published in the legal press. However, nowadays few mortgages are tied to this rate. The vast majority of domestic mortgages have a clause allowing the lender to fix the rate. The lender can do this at any time and simply writes to the borrower to notify changes. In theory this is risky to the borrower, for what happens if the lender fixes the rate at 1,000,000 per cent.?[18] In practice, of course, this does not happen. The lender sets the rate to keep in line with market rates. Sometimes a maximum and minimum is preset, *i.e.* a cap and collar mortgage. The cap is the maximum and the collar is the minimum. It is also possible to have the one without the other.

A change of rate sometimes comes into effect the month after it is announced. More common nowadays is annual adjustment. Thus, the rate is adjusted every April or whatever. The benefit to the borrower is that his payments are fixed for 12 months at a time. Note that although the rate *payable* is adjusted annually, the rate *chargeable* is normally adjusted whenever the general rate changes. For example, suppose that in October the Halifax cuts its rate from 11 per cent. to 10 per cent. The borrower continues to pay at the old rate until April. During the interval he is thus overpaying, and this is taken into account at the annual adjustment.

Very common nowadays is the low-start or deferred-interest system whereby the rate payable is for the first so many months (*e.g.* 24) both (1) fixed and (2) below market rates. Using this method it is possible to cut the initial cost of a mortgage by 30 per cent. or more. The purpose is to help people who are short of money now but hope to be in a better position in a couple of years or so. The low fixed rate means the rate payable not the rate chargeable. The balance (chargeable but not payable) is added on to the capital. So after the grace period, not only does the borrower start to pay full rate, but also his total loan will have increased.[19] So after the grace period, to the end of the mortgage, he will be paying more than he would have done if he had opted for a conven-

[18] We are unsure of the answer.

[19] *i.e.* the unpaid interest is "rolled up."

tional mortgage. Clients often do not properly understand all this so it is important to explain it to them carefully. There are various sub-types of low-start mortgage. Thus, the length of the grace period is variable,[20] and also many schemes provide for graduated increases in the payment level until, after a set time, the full rate is reached. Lastly, as well as the rolled-up interest there are often other hidden costs. Thus, there is often an "administration fee"[21]; the deferred interest is often charged at a higher rate, such as one per cent. higher; and often a costly Mortgage Indemnity Guarantee[22] is required. Sometimes, someone who is experiencing difficulties in paying his existing mortgage switches into a low-start mortgage. This has the benefit of an initial reduction in monthly outgoings, but often it just means getting deeper into debt, so that doomsday is merely postponed, and when it comes, is even more catastrophic.

Mention should be made of large mortgages. Once upon a time building societies were run for the benefit of the poorer members of society—the so-called working and lower-middle classes. They were classic self-help organisations. So large mortgages were not encouraged, since a large mortgage means someone who is economically better off. So either they were refused or only granted at a higher rate of interest. This was ideology prevailing over market forces, because a large loan is, on a pound-for-pound basis, cheaper to administer than a small one, so should, on market principles, command a slightly lower rate. Nowadays almost all the building societies have abandoned the traditional ideals and offer lower rates on larger mortgages. They have various names for these, such as "premier" mortgages. The same applies to other lenders. The starting point is usually around £60,000. This can lead to odd results. Thus, with some lenders a loan of £60,500 is actually cheaper than a loan of £59,500.

As has been said, true fixed interest mortgages have more or less disappeared. However, so-called fixed interest mortgages are common. The name, however, is misleading. What happens is that

[20] Typically, between one and five years.

[21] *e.g.* £150.

[22] See later.

[23] Contrast the deferred-interest mortgage, mentioned above, where the rate is also fixed for a period, but what is fixed is the rate payable, but not the rate chargeable.

the rate is fixed for a stated period, sometimes as little as 12 months and sometimes as long as five years. After that, the rate floats. During the first period the rate is truly fixed, *i.e.* the fixed rate is not only the rate payable but also the rate chargeable.[23] During the fixed period, there is a risk to each party. If market rates rise, the lender loses money, while if they fall, it is the borrower who loses. In the latter event, the borrower would wish to bail out by paying off the mortgage and obtaining a new one elsewhere at a lower rate. If this were possible then obviously the system would not work, so what happens is that there is a stiff financial penalty for early redemption, such as six months of interest.

In some market phases lenders offer a lower rate for a period (generally one year) to first-time buyers, while others offer something similar to any new customer. At the time of writing there are rate discounts on offer from one per cent (Bradford & Bingley) up to one and three-quarter per cent. (several lenders) with the Halifax offering a discount of two point three five per cent. on certain deals.

Lastly, when comparing interest rates it is important to look at the APR.[24] The APR is a standardized way of calculating an interest rate. For instance, at the time of writing the Bradford & Bingley is offering a rate of "6.9%" while the Royal Bank is offering "9.7%." But in APR terms the first of these is 10.49 per cent. and the second 11.1 per cent. Of course, even comparing the APR is not enough, for (as in this example) the details of the schemes will often differ, so that the lowest APR is far from being the only consideration.

The term

The term means the length of time the mortgage is to run. This is negotiable,[25] but for domestic mortgages the usual periods are multiples of five years, the commonest term being 25 years. Different lenders have different maximums. For instance,[26] the maximum for the Bristol & West is 25 years, for Lloyds Bank 30, for the

[24] The annual percentage rate as calculated in terms of the Consumer Credit Act 1974.

[25] And can sometimes be renegotiated later, *e.g.* if the borrower gets into financial difficulties. A lengthened term can mean reduced monthly payments.

[26] We repeat that the examples are purely illustrative.

Abbey National 35 and for the Alliance & Leicester 40 years. A lender will seldom agree to a term which would run beyond the borrower's retirement age. This is simply because beyond that age the borrower is unlikely to have an income level sufficient to pay off a loan. Obviously, in most cases the loan is redeemed much sooner than the term, by the sale of the property. The average lifespan of a domestic mortgage is only about seven years.

Loan agreements—whether backed by security or not—almost always have an "acceleration clause" whereby the lender is entitled to demand repayment in full, ahead of term, if there is an "event of default" such as a failure to pay an instalment timeously. Such clauses will be found in almost all domestic mortgages. But paradoxically there is often also a clause tucked away saying that in any case the whole loan is repayable on demand irrespective of any default. We say "paradoxically" because an on-demand loan does not need an acceleration clause: indeed the two things contradict each other. Loans are either repayable on demand, or they are not. They cannot be both. But this contradiction is found in many domestic mortgages nowadays. The legal effect is untested. But arguably an on-demand clause added to a term loan contract is void. It may be added that the inclusion of an on-demand clause in a loan which is intended to be a term loan seems an act of bad faith by the lender. Fortunately, lenders in practice do not usually rely on such clauses.

Capital-and-interest and interest-only mortgages

In a term loan, there are in essence two ways to repay the capital. The first is "amortisation" which means that the borrower pays, every month or whatever, (1) the interest due and (2) a small part of the capital. The amount of the latter is calculated so that the whole capital will have been repaid by the end of the term. In domestic mortgages this is called the "repayment"[27] or "annuity" or "capital-and-interest" method. The alternative is to pay interest only during the term, thus keeping the capital constant. The capital is then paid off in a lump sum at the end of the term. These are sometimes called "bullet" loans or "balloon" loans. Both methods are common in domestic mortgages. Traditionally, lenders were

[27] An odd expression, since all loans must be repaid!

reluctant to offer interest-only mortgages since it means tying up the whole capital for the whole term,[28] but nowadays most mortgages are interest-only.

The repayment mortgage, or annuity mortgage, where the loan is amortised, was once the standard method, but today only about 10 per cent of new mortgages are of this type. There is a monthly payment which stays constant throughout the term (apart from interest changes and certain tax aspects). Part of each payment represents interest, and part capital. In the early years most is interest. As the years go by, more and more of the capital is paid off and so the total annual interest bill falls. As it falls, more and more of the monthly payment can be ascribed to capital. Near the end of the life of the mortgage, almost all the monthly payment is of capital. The monthly payment is mathematically calculated to ensure that the loan will be fully paid off at exactly the term. The calculations are quite complex in theory but in practice there are preprinted tables. Each year the lender sends the borrower a statement showing how much capital has been repaid.

The alternative is for interest only to be paid during the term, no repayment of capital being made until the end, when the whole capital is repaid in a lump sum. In this case, the lender will insist that the borrower joins some savings scheme which will ensure that the amount needed will be accumulated. There are various ways to do this, but the most common is the endowment mortgage.[29] At this point it will be necessary to digress in order to explain the basics of life assurance.

Life assurance

There are many different sorts of life assurance available. But the basics are as follows.

(1) Term assurance. If the life assured dies within the next 15 years (or whatever period is agreed) the life office will pay the sum assured. But if he dies even one day later, nothing is payable. This is the cheapest form, in terms of premiums,[30] for the simple reason

[28] Indeed, it used to be the case that lenders would offer this package only at a higher rate of interest than for a repayment mortgage.

[29] For others, see later.

[30] Life assurance premiums are generally paid monthly.

that in most cases the life office never has to pay out a single penny. A slightly cheaper variant is the reducing term assurance, in which the sum assured declines as the years pass, to zero at the end of the term.[31]

(2) Whole of life assurance. This means that the policy matures on death, whenever that is. This is more expensive in terms of premiums because no one is immortal, and so the life office has to pay out one day.

(3) Endowment assurance. This means that the policy matures on death, but if the assured is still alive at a stated date (often his 65th birthday) the policy matures anyway. This is, in premium terms, the most expensive form of assurance.

In the first two types, the sum payable on death is almost always a predetermined sum stated in the policy itself. But in the third, this is not usually the case.[32]There are two main types of endowment policy where the sum payable is flexible. In the traditional "with-profits" endowment, the policy states a fixed sum which is the minimum which will be paid. But over the years "bonuses" are added to the policy, the amount of which will depend on the investment success of the life office. When the policy matures, the sum payable will normally be well in excess of the guaranteed minimum. These endowment policies are a popular way of combining life assurance with savings. A common variant nowadays is the "low-cost with-profits" endowment. Here the minimum sum payable at the maturity date is less than the minimum sum payable at death. However, the policy holder hopes that the bonuses to be added over the years will more than make up the difference.

These are only the basic types. In practice, there is a myriad of different endowment options, and only an insurance broker can really advise. One variant which is worth mentioning is the low-start, low-cost, with-profits endowment, where the monthly payments to the life office are in the early years lower than they would otherwise be, and higher in the later years.

[31] Such policies are widely used as "mortgage protection policies." See later.

[32] If it is, the endowment policy is a "without profits" policy. These are very rare.

Obviously, the level of premium depends on various factors, including the age and health and sex of the life assured. Alex, aged 40, a heavy drinker, smoker and drug abuser, who works as a mercenary in central Africa, will not get such favorable terms as Tom, a healthy 21–year-old who avoids all drugs and hazardous activities, such as sexual intercourse, except under medical supervision. Mother nature (not father nature) decrees that most men live shorter lives than most women, so that women pay lower premiums than men, since the risk to the life office is lower.

The life assured is the person on whose death the policy will become payable. The policy holder is the person to whom, or to whose representatives, the money will be payable on maturity. This is usually in the first instance the same person as the life assured, but need not be. Thus, a woman might take out a policy on her husband's life: he would be the life assured but she would be the holder. Joint policies are possible, and sometimes are used by couples. There are two main types: those payable on the first death and payable to the survivor, and those payable on the first death and payable to the estate of the first to die. Joint policies payable on the second death are possible but rare.

A life policy is normally assignable,[33] which is to say that the holder can transfer it to someone else, by sale or otherwise. The assignee then becomes the legal holder, and if the policy matures will be the person paid by the life office. As we shall see, such assignations are common. It must not be forgotten that every assignation requires intimation, *i.e.* notice to the life office.

Life policies acquire a capital value as time goes on. Some people find this idea puzzling. Suppose there is an endowment policy with a maturity value of £50,000, which will mature next year when the life assured is 65. The present value of the policy is therefore of a similar figure. For instance, the life office would be prepared to pay a large sum to be freed of their liability to pay this money next year. This is called the surrender value. In practice, however, the surrender values offered by the life offices are not generous, and a better price can usually be obtained by selling the policy.[34] In the USA a gruesome business has developed of buying life pol-

[33] See chap. 14.

[34] Life policies are regularly auctioned in London (*e.g.* by Messrs. Foster and Cranfield), and there are some companies which buy policies on a private basis.

icies from AIDS sufferers. The seller gets cash to spend before he dies, and the buyer gets cash as soon as he does die.

Life assurance and mortgages

Life assurance interacts with domestic conveyancing in two ways. The first is that for repayment mortgages the lender will usually insist that the borrower takes out what is called a mortgage protection policy. This is simply term life assurance where the term is the life of the mortgage and the maturity value is the mortgage debt. If the mortgage is of the repayment type, the policy is often of the reducing type,[35] so that at any stage the amount covered by the policy will be the current amount of capital due, which, in a repayment mortgage, is a steadily declining figure. The idea is simply that if the borrower dies during the life of the mortgage, there will be a fund out of which the loan can be paid off. It may be asked why the lender insists on this, since the lender is secured anyway by standard security. One reason is that if the property market has fallen, a forced sale might fail to recover the loan. Another reason is that lenders wish to avoid enforcement action because it is costly in administrative terms and results in bad publicity, especially if it means putting a widow and children out on the street. A mortgage protection policy makes the need for enforcement in the event of the death of the borrower much less likely.

The other impact of life assurance is on endowment mortgages.

Endowment mortgages

In an endowment mortgage the borrower takes out an endowment policy with a life office and a loan with the lender. The maturity period of the policy is the same as the term of the loan. Thus, if the borrower dies during the term, the policy matures and pays off the loan. If he survives to term, the policy matures at exactly the right moment to pay off the loan. Unless it is a non-profit endowment (which is rare) there will usually be bonuses as well, so that after the loan has been paid off there will be a useful surplus.

[35] However, level term assurance is also often used. This would mean that if, for example, the borrower died 15 years into a 25–year mortgage, there would be a surplus left after repaying the loan.

During the life of the mortgage the borrower pays the lender interest only. He thus has two monthly payments to make, one to the lender, of interest, and the other to the life office, of premiums.

In an endowment mortgage the policy is usually assigned to the lender.[36] This works as additional security. If there is default the lender could surrender the policy to the life office or auction it, though this seldom happens. (Usually, of course, the lender would simply sell the house.) If the borrower dies, the whole maturity value is paid by the life office to the lender because the latter is the legal holder, even if the amount involved is greater than the debt, which is likely because of accumulated bonuses. The lender then deducts the amount of the loan and pays the balance to the executor or whoever is entitled to the reversion to the policy.[37] Usually, of course, the borrower does survive till his 65th birthday or whenever. If so, well and good. The life office pays the maturity value to the lender, who then pays any free balance to the borrower.

If the life policy is a low-cost, with-profits endowment,[38] the minimum sum guaranteed to be payable on death is not less than the capital of the debt. But, unlike a conventional endowment, the sum payable at maturity at the end of the term is not so guaranteed.[39] The borrower simply hopes that the accumulated bonuses will be enough to pay off the loan at that stage. Generally that is a safe bet, and indeed the total amount is in practice often enough to pay off the loan twice over. But there does exist a risk here, which, however remote, must be explained to the client.

Most mortgages are either endowment or repayment so one needs to have some idea how they compare with each other in practice. In an endowment mortgage the monthly payment to the lender is smaller than it would be in the case of a repayment mortgage,[40] but this does not mean that the endowment mortgage is

[36] However, recently there has been a trend by lenders not to require assignation. For some discussion see a letter by A.C. Sampson at 1991 J.L.S. 424.

[37] This can cause complexities in succession law, for a partial exploration of which see articles by G.L. Gretton at 1987 J.L.S. 303 and 1988 J.L.S. 141.

[38] A majority of endowment mortgages nowadays are of this type.

[39] In a typical low-cost, with-profits endowment mortgage of £30,000, the sum payable on death would be £30,000, but the minimum sum guaranteed at maturity would be around £9,000 to £11,000.

[40] Because in an endowment mortgage the borrower pays only interest to the lender.

cheaper, because there are the assurance premiums to take into account too. But as against this the person with a repayment mortgage must also pay premiums on his mortgage protection policy, though because this is term assurance only the premiums will be fairly low.

The following example is based on a £30,000 loan for a 25–year term at 10 per cent. The borrower is aged 30 and in good health. The figures are approximate. (1) Low-cost, with-profits endowment mortgage: (a) Interest payment to lender—£187 after tax relief. Add (b) Policy premium—£38.[41] Total—£225 monthly. (2) Repayment mortgage: (a) Payment to lender of both interest and capital—£224 after tax relief. Add (b) Policy premium—£9. Total—£233 monthly.

So which is better? Nowadays endowment mortgages are much more common, but this does not prove that they are better. For building societies, banks, estate agents and mortgage brokers have an interest in getting borrowers to take up for these mortgages because of the attractive commissions from the life office.[42] It is difficult to say which is better, but some points of comparison are worth noting.

In the first place, endowments (other than without-profit endowments) include a savings element. Full-cost endowments are significantly more expensive than lost-cost endowments. They are accordingly appropriate where the borrower wishes to include a large savings element. However, with low-cost endowments there is a small danger that they will fail to pay off the mortgage at term—*i.e.* negative saving.

Full-cost endowment mortgages will involve higher monthly outgoings than a repayment mortgage. But the comparison in this respect between lost-cost endowments and repayment mortgages is mathematically quite complex. In our example, the monthly outgoings on the low-cost endowment were about £8 less than for the repayment mortgage. When interest rates are low, low-cost endowment mortgages usually involve slightly lower monthly outgoings than repayment mortgages, with the converse when interest rates are high.

Endowment mortgages can be less flexible than repayment mort-

[41] The exact amount will depend on the insurance company selected.

[42] A few life offices give no commission.

gages in a number of respects. Early repayment of an endowment mortgage may be harder because capital has not declined. To release the capital value of the endowment policy, sale or surrender is required, which can be complicated and which may not realise a fair value.[43] Changing the mortgage term is harder in an endowment mortgage because it normally involves renegotiating the life policy. Again, whereas it is usually easy to convert from repayment to endowment, the converse is more difficult, both for practical reasons and because if an endowment policy is surrendered, a loss usually results. So once into the endowment system, the borrower tends to be locked in. Again, the investment element in an endowment mortgage is inflexible in that the borrower is tied to a single company for 25 years or whatever.

Endowment mortgages, like other interest-only mortgages, have a tax advantage in that the borrower gets the full benefit of tax relief throughout the term, whereas in a repayment mortgage the interest element declines over the years, so that the tax relief also declines.

It is difficult to say which of the two is better. In 1991 the chairman of the SIB,[44] David Walker, launched a fierce attack on endowment mortgages. His points were (1) that endowment policies are a highly illiquid form of investment, in that they cannot be converted into cash before maturity except with difficulty and at a penalty; (2) that they are complex with the result that investors and perhaps even their professional advisers will find it difficult to assess how good they are as investments; (3) that the "industry"—meaning banks, building societies, life offices, etc.—knows perfectly well that a large proportion of endowment policies will in practice be surrendered or allowed to lapse long before maturity, with consequent heavy loss to the customer but profit to the life offices and to those who get commission on policy sales; (4) that the public simply does not realise the enormous profits being made on commissions; (5) that the public is being subjected to excessive

[43] Early repayment in order to sell the existing house and to buy another, of the same or greater value, presents no difficulty in an endowment mortgage, for the policy can be used to finance the new mortgage. However, problems may arise if the owner wishes to sell but not to buy another house (*e.g.* he wishes to emigrate or to rent), or wishes to buy another house but of a lower value.

[44] Securities and Investment Board, established under the Financial Services Act 1986.

pressure to take out endowment mortgages. Most of these points are strictly speaking applicable to any endowment policies, not just to endowment mortgages, but in practice most policies are issued in this connection.

In general, life offices have a rule whereby if a life policy is surrendered or cancelled within a certain period, the commission, or part of it, is repayable. That is fair enough. Some people who sell life policies, however, often include in the small print a clause whereby if this happens the customer will pay the commission personally. Dishonest Joe cheats you by selling you a policy you do not need and cannot afford. You then cancel it at considerable loss to yourself, for effectively you are writing off the premiums you have paid, or most of them. Dishonest Joe then sues you for his commission.

Lastly, endowment mortgages are sometimes sold on the footing that it is a sort of transferable mortgage, which can be continued when the owner needs to move house. The following quotation from a customer illustrates this:

> "I will probably move in a couple of years, and then who knows? I don't want to have to take out a new mortgage every time I move up the ladder. With an endowment, you can top it up to cover the extra borrowing and it will still be repaid 25 years after you bought your very first house. This system seems more sensible in this day and age."[45]

There is very little in this. On moving house a client must "take out a new mortgage" regardless of what type of mortgage his old house was on. It is just as easy to "move up the ladder" in the repayment system as in the endowment system. Those hoping to gain commission by selling endowment policies nevertheless say the sort of things just quoted.

Unit-linked endowment mortgages

A variant on the endowment mortgage is the unit-linked endowment. The life office invests in a unitised, three-way fund[46] and the

[45] "Which Mortgage" magazine, September 1992, p. 21.

[46] A three-way fund is invested in a mix of equities, property and gilts.

maturity value is the value of the units at maturity.[47] These schemes are relatively new, and have a higher risk/reward ratio than conventional endowments. If the investments do well, the customer does better than in a conventional endowment, and vice versa. At the time of writing, the poor performance of the stock markets is causing speculation in the financial press that many of these schemes will fail to pay off the mortgages they are designed to cover. It is essential that clients be advised carefully, and in writing, of the risks inherent in this type of scheme. However, some unit-linked endowments have a bonus system which gives the borrower protection.

Unit trust, investment trust, and PEP mortgages

Unit trust, investment trust, and PEP[48] mortgages are all interest-only mortgages, in which the borrower agrees to take out a regular savings plan which is designed to achieve a sufficient sum to repay the loan at maturity. Because they are not very common, and because their advantages and disadvantages are matters for investment law and practice rather than conveyancing, we will not discuss them further here. But it should be noted that, like unit-linked endowments, they have a high risk/reward ratio and therefore are only for clients with a certain degree of financial sophistication. In these schemes there is no assignation to the lender.

Pension mortgages

A PPP[49] mortgage is interest-only with lump sum repayment at term, as in an endowment mortgage. But instead of an endowment policy, the saving mechanism is a personal pension scheme which matures at retirement age (which will be the same date as the term of the loan). Part of the pension will be commuted into a lump sum which pays off the loan. The rest of the pension remains to give a regular income. There is no assignation to the lender, since

[47] As with lost-cost, with-profit endowment, there is a life assurance element whereby if the borrower dies, the life office guarantees as a minimum to pay off the loan.

[48] Personal equity plan.

[49] Personal pension plans, regulated by the Income and Corporation Taxes Act 1988, Pt. XIV, Chap. III.

pension funds are non-assignable. The borrower will also have to take out a mortgage protection life policy as in the case of a repayment mortgage. The attraction of the pension mortgage is that pension schemes receive favorable tax treatment. Disadvantages are that the system may compel retirement at the agreed time, and that there is no surrender value. The law on PPPs is complex and cannot be dealt with here.

Foreign currency mortgages

A foreign currency mortgage is one denominated in a foreign currency such as German marks or Japanese yen or Swiss francs. In other words, though the house is in Scotland the loan is in marks, or whatever, and must be repaid in marks. There is no law compelling people to transact in sterling. One can, for example, open an account with the Bank of Scotland in dollars or marks. The attraction of a foreign currency loan is that interest rates will often be lower than for sterling loans. The drawback is if interest rates in currency A (*e.g.* sterling) are higher than in currency B (*e.g.* Swiss francs), this is generally because the financial markets believe that in the longer term there is a strong possibility that currency A may be devalued against currency B. Thus, if one borrows in yen to buy a house, one benefits for the time being from a lower interest rate, but the risk is that a year later, or five years later, sterling will fall against the yen, which will of course mean that the outstanding capital of the loan will increase (in sterling terms). Foreign currency mortgages, therefore, have a strong element of risk and so are only for financially sophisticated clients.

An ECU mortgage is one denominated in ECUs.[50] These used to be unknown but now have a niche in the market, and there are several firms specialising in them such as the Executive Mortgage Corporation, the ECU Group, and the Instituto Bancario San Paolo di Torino.

A multi-currency mortgage is where a money broker is used to swap the loan from one currency to another, to get the benefit of foreign exchange fluctuations. If it works well, the borrower finds that the capital of his loan falls in sterling terms. But it is highly

[50] The currency of the EC.

speculative and the borrower could also find the capital value increasing in sterling terms.

Indexed mortgages

An indexed mortgage is one where the capital of the loan is index-linked, so that the total debt increases with inflation. The benefit to the borrower is that because his capital is secure in real terms the lender can afford to charge a lower rate of interest. To this extent the idea is similar to that of a foreign currency mortgage. They are, however, rare. The Building Societies Act 1986 authorises building societies to lend on this basis.

Equity share mortgages

An equity share mortgage is where the borrower and lender are owners in common of the house. The borrower has a mortgage only in respect of his share. Thus, this is cheaper for him. The contract provides for the transfer of the other share to him in slices, until he owns it all. The price payable for each slice is fixed by an index or arbitration. The idea is to help poorer people who could not afford to take a mortgage over the whole property. Such mortgages are not very common. Deals of this sort can sometimes be set up with a housing association. The buyer pays the association rent for the slice not (yet) owned by him. A variant of this idea is where the seller sells only a 50 per cent. (or whatever) share, with the other 50 per cent. to be bought by the buyer after (say) five years, or sooner at his option, at a value to be fixed by an independent valuer. The buyer needs initially to get a loan only to cover the 50 per cent. For instance, some of the companies in the Barratt group offer this.

Builders' schemes

Volume house builders often offer special mortgage deals as an incentive, especially when the market is weak. The last paragraph refers to one such type of deal. Often the builder will offer to subsidise a more conventional mortgage by, for example, paying the mortgage for six months. These schemes are often tied to a particular lender. Of course, in economic terms what is happening is that the builder is cutting the price of the house, but instead of doing so directly is channelling the discount into a mortgage subsidy.

Non-status (self-certification) mortgages

Non-status mortgages, also called self-certified mortgages, are where the lender relies on the borrower's own statement of his financial circumstances. They are typically used for self-employed borrowers. Some lenders will accept pure self-certification while others will ask for an accountant's letter. Normally in a non-status loan the maximum borrowable is only around 70 per cent. of the property value. In addition to this ordinary use of non-status mortgages, loan sharks offer non-status mortgages (usually remortgages) to people in financial difficulties, often at very high rates of interest.[51] Such people are tempted because their financial problems destroy their credit status, thus making conventional borrowing harder. In this type of case a non-status remortgage is often the last stage before bankruptcy. Such people should be advised to restructure their lives rather than go for an ultra-high interest loan.

Non-purchase mortgages

This chapter deals with mortgages for house purchase. But a person may already own a house and wish to use it as security for a loan for some other purpose. We will not discuss such mortgages here, apart from certain particular aspects. Note that in such cases the loan will not normally be provided by a building society, for reasons already explained.

Remortgages

A remortgage is where a new mortgage is taken out and the proceeds used to pay off the old one. This is done where for one reason or another the borrower prefers the terms of the new mortgage. Alternatively, he may be able to renegotiate the terms of his existing mortgage in which no new mortgage will be required. The prefer-

[51] The advertisement may say "CCJs welcome." A CCJ (county court judgment) is roughly the equivalent in England of a sheriff court decree, the point being that such lenders are prepared to lend to people already in debt.

ence for change will have to be fairly strong because of the costs involved. These involve: (1) resurvey fee (2) "administrative charge" by new lender and (3) legal costs. The first two may amount to, say, £250, depending on circumstances. If the old mortgage was a house purchase mortgage then the new one will be considered as the same (except in so far as the new loan may be larger than the old one) both for the purposes of building society law and also for tax law.

Further advances

A further advance is where the borrower borrows more money from the same lender. This is common for home improvements. Lenders are usually willing to make a further advance for this purpose, so long as there is sufficient equity.[52] Likewise a further advance is usually easily obtainable to pay for a large but unexpected repair, since the lender has an interest in ensuring the good condition of the property. Because the original standard security will almost invariably have been for all sums due and to become due it automatically covers the new advance.[53] Note that loans for home improvement do not now qualify for tax relief. Lenders will wish to know the purpose for which the further advance is sought, and will often impose restrictions, especially in the case of building societies.

Second mortgages

A second mortgage is where there is a further secured loan which, for whatever reason, is not from the existing lender. There are some institutions which specialise in these, *e.g.* First National Bank. A second mortgage will not normally attract tax relief, since it will not normally be for the purpose of home purchase. As a postponed heritable security, it ranks second. A notice of second charge should be sent to the first lender under section 13 of the 1970 Act.

[52] Equity in this context means market value of the property minus secured debt.
[53] Subject to s. 13 of the 1970 Act—see below.

Equity release mortgages

By the time a person has reached the age of, say, 70 he will normally have paid off his mortgage and retired. But his pension may not be very good. Why live in poverty while he is sitting on a valuable asset, which, when he dies, will merely enrich his heirs? Why not release some of the equity and spend it while still alive? This is the reasoning behind what are called equity release mortgages or home income mortgages. The way it works is that the old person borrows and secures the debt on his house. Interest only is payable, the capital being repayable at death. The proceeds of the loan are used to buy an annuity. Part of the income from the annuity is used to pay the interest on the loan. The rest is free extra income. When the person dies, the capital is repaid. The net effect is that the value of the estate at death is less than it would otherwise have been. The money has, instead, been spent by the owner while still alive. The insurance companies offer annuities, and some have prepackaged equity release schemes. Because the cost of an annuity depends on life expectancy at commencement, these schemes only make sense for older people. The amount of the loan is typically about 25 per cent. of the value of the property. Thus, most of the value is still available to the heirs.

There are many variants on the market. One variant is actually not in the form of a mortgage at all. In this, there is a sale and lease-back. The company thus becomes legal owner, and the old person becomes tenant, at a nominal rent of say £5 per annum, the lease lasting to death. Sometimes the owner sells only a share of his property, *e.g.* 50 per cent. The price paid by the reversionary company will not be the current market price, but a discounted figure, discounted to reflect the fact that the company does not recover its investment until the death of the planholder.

Such schemes can be a good way of rescuing an old person from unnecessary poverty. In recent years they have become quite common. But they can have drawbacks too. For in the first place, if the person dies soon after the scheme is set up, the annuity company makes a whopping profit, the heirs suffer a whopping loss, and the old person only gets little benefit. This, of course, is a risk inherent in any annuity deal. And of course it can work the other way round, as with any annuity: if the person lives to 110, the annuity company suffers a whopping loss, and the old person can die happy in the knowledge that he has done what was probably the best business deal of his life. Secondly, the estate is less than it would otherwise be. Whether this matters or not depends on the circumstances. If the old person has no children, this may be no problem. But if he wants to leave a good estate to his heirs, this scheme may be inappropriate. Finally, the interest rate on the loan will normally be variable whereas the annuity is normally fixed. This is fine if interest rates fall, but can be a disaster if they rise. Old people often do not really understand variable interest rates. In 1989–1990, when interest rates went through the roof many old people suffered badly by being locked into one of these schemes. It is vital that the point is fully explained.

The tax aspects of such schemes are complex. The interest payments on the loan are generally deductible for income tax,[54] while the annuity income is notionally split, with part of the annuity being deemed income, and so taxable, and part being deemed a partial return of capital, and so non-taxable.[55]

How much can be borrowed?

Here, as before, only house purchase mortgages are dealt with. Two factors determine how much can be borrowed. The first is the status of the borrower, and the second is the value of the house. But exactly how these factors will be applied varies from lender to lender, and also varies from one year to another. So what follows is only a general picture.

The lender will take details about the borrower, especially about his income. In general, a lender will advance up to about three times the gross annual income, calculated before deductions for tax, national insurance and so forth. Often there are joint borrowers (*e.g.* husband and wife) both with incomes. In that case the practice is to lend about three times the larger income plus the smaller income. Extra income, such as overtime, is usually included at half its amount. Thus, suppose the husband earns £14,000 per annum basic gross plus £4000 per annum overtime gross and the wife earns £10,000 per annum gross. The maximum which would be offered based on status would thus be about:

[54] Income and Corporation Taxes Act 1988, s. 365. The qualifications are similar to those which apply to other mortgage tax relief, *e.g.* the £30,000 ceiling.

[55] Income and Corporation Taxes Act 1988, s. 656.

(3 × £16,000) + (£10,000) = £58,000

But practice varies. At the time of writing the Halifax were offering a multiplier of three and a quarter for one borrower or two and a half for the combined income of joint borrowers, and the Alliance & Leicester two and three-quarters for one borrower and for joint borrowers two and three-quarters for the first income and one for the second income. Lenders generally seek confirmation of income, either by being authorised to contact the salaries department of the borrower's employer, or by asking to see wages slips.

The other factor determining the amount borrowable is the value of the property. Once again, practice varies, with some lenders prepared to offer up to 90 per cent. of value, others 95 per cent. others 100 per cent. while yet other figures may be encountered. Thus, at the time of writing, Barclays were offering 90 per cent. the Halifax 95 per cent., and the Nationwide 100 per cent. This figure is calculated, not on the purchase price, but on the valuation obtained by the lender from their surveyor. Often the valuation figure is lower than the final purchase price, since a lender's surveyor takes a cautious approach. This point is important since it is often not appreciated by clients, and so must be explained to them. Thus, if a 90 per cent. loan is available, and the property is valued at £50,000, but bought for £55,000, the purchaser will then have to find £10,000 in cash.

There are thus two maximum figures, one based on status and the other on value. Which applies? The answer is, whichever is the lower. Thus, suppose that the couple in our earlier example wish to buy a house which the surveyor values at £70,000. And suppose that the lender is prepared to lend only up to 80 per cent. of valuation, *i.e.* £56,000. The status-based maximum was £58,000. So the building society will lend only the lower of these two figures. If the house is in fact bought for £73,000, the clients will have to find out of their own pockets £17,000, plus, of course, the various expenses and outlays involved in house purchase.

Some mortgage lenders have an absolute maximum which they are prepared to lend, but this is seldom a problem. Most have no limit, and for those that do the limit is usually very high, such as £250,000 or £500,000. One or two have lower limits. Thus, at the time of writing some of the smaller lenders, such as the Ecology Building Society and the Catholic Building Society (not major players!), had limits of £100,000, while one or two others had a limit as low as £60,000. These limits reflect the old ideology of building societies, namely self-help institutions for the lower and middle classes, not banks for the rich. Nowadays, most building societies have abandoned the old traditions.

Borrowers tend to assume that if the lender is prepared to lend a given figure, then they can afford to meet the repayments on that loan. It is easy for the solicitor to make the same assumption. But the rules used by lenders for determining maximum loans based on status are mechanical and may be inappropriate to the individual borrower, who may in fact not be able to afford the loan which the lender is prepared to give. It is the duty of the solicitor to give proper advice based on the individual circumstances of his client. He must discuss with the client whether he will be able to keep up the mortgage payments, especially with first time buyers. And clients must always be warned that interest rates may rise.

Sometimes, if the lender will not offer enough, it may be possible to obtain a top-up loan from a second lender, secured on the property on a postponed basis. Banks or insurance companies may be willing to offer this. Of course, the interest rate for a top-up loan will be higher, and may impose on the borrower monthly outgoings greater than can be afforded.

Mortgage indemnity guarantee

If a lender gives a loan at a high percentage of valuation, it may insist that a guarantee be obtained from an insurance company. This is called a mortgage indemnity guarantee (MIG). Currently, most lenders will insist on a MIG where the loan exceeds 75 per cent. of valuation.[56] The reason for this is, of course, that high percentage loans involve a greater risk to the lender, for if there is default there is a greater danger that the forced sale of the property will not recoup the whole loan. For an MIG a one-off premium is payable by the borrower, called a mortgage indemnity premium. The cost of this depends on the circumstances, and varies considerably from lender to lender, but can be expensive. For instance, for an 80 per cent. loan on a £60,000 house the premium will be typically between £100 and £400, for a 90 per cent. loan, from

[56] At the time of writing the only major lender which did not insist on this was the Royal Bank of Scotland.

£250 to £800 and for a 100 per cent. loan, from £1,000 to £2,000. This premium is, of course, payable by the borrower. It comes as a shock to many borrowers, and clients must be warned in advance. In addition, if there is default and the insurer has to pay, the insurer is subrogated and so can sue the borrower. Thus, a MIG is purely for the benefit of the lender, and not for the borrower. It may be added that a MIG is often required in low-start mortgages too.

MIGs are big business. During the current recession the companies issuing these policies have suffered large losses. Thus, on August 22, 1991 Eagle Star announced losses of £121 million on MIG policies and their losses for 1991–1992 are estimated at £350 million. As a result premium rates are rising.

CHAPTER 12

HERITABLE SECURITIES

The pre-1970 securities

Before the 1970 Act, there were four ways of constituting a heritable security. First, there was the pecuniary real burden, whereby in a disposition by A to B a real burden was inserted to secure a debt due by B to A. This was not often used. It is uncertain whether it was made incompetent by the 1970 Act. Probably it remains competent. The other three types were all abolished by the 1970 Act, though securities in those forms already in existence were unaffected. They were the bond of cash credit and disposition in security, the bond and disposition in security, and the *ex facie* absolute disposition. Virtually all examples of the two types of disposition in security were discharged long ago, and so one seldom needs to know anything of them in modern practice. But a surprising number of the last type are still in existence or have recently been discharged, so it is still necessary to know something about them.

Though the two types of disposition in security were called "dispositions," they did not in fact operate as dispositions. The grantor remained legal owner, vest and seised as of fee. The creditor was infeft only in a subsidiary real right, of security. There were thus two infeftments, and two real rights, in the same property. Essentially, the same is true of the modern standard security. This double real right is a hallmark of the heritable security in the strict sense of the term. By contrast, in the *ex facie* absolute disposition, legal ownership was transferred to the creditor, with the borrower, although the real owner in a functional sense, merely having a personal right against the lender. This entitled him to live in the property, provided he did not default, and to have the property disponed to him on repayment. Thus, there was only one real right, that of the creditor.

By definition, an *ex facie* absolute disposition is simply a disposition. How can one identify it, therefore, as being different from an ordinary disposition? There are tell-tale signs, the main one being that in the narrative clause the cause of granting is simply stated to be "for certain good and onerous causes and considerations." Another sign is that the disponee is a financial institution, though of course this sign is not sufficient in itself, since financial institutions also buy property in the ordinary way. Moreover, where there is an *ex facie*, one will normally find among the titles a loan contract.

A true heritable security, such as the bond of cash credit and disposition in security, the bond and disposition in security, and the standard security, can be discharged by a unilateral deed of discharge. There is no place for a reconveyance, since the debtor (or, by this time, the ex-debtor) is already the legal owner. But when the loan secured by an *ex facie* is paid off, a reconveyance is obviously necessary. The lender simply dispones back to the borrower, or to someone nominated by the borrower. In practice, the latter was very common. Thus, if A had a house with an *ex facie* to the Halifax, and A sold it to B, A would pay off the loan from the proceeds and the Halifax would dispone direct to B. Indeed, B would often buy through the same method, so the Halifax would dispone not to B at all but to B's building society or other lender, such as the Leeds. Thus, if A sold to B the disposition would typically not be by A to B at all, but by the Halifax to the Leeds. A and B (the real seller and buyer) would appear in these deeds simply as "consenters."

In a straightforward redemption, however, the lender would simply dispone to the borrower. In this deed the narrative clause narrates that the original disposition, though *ex facie* absolute, was truly in security of a loan, and that the loan has now been repaid. This form of discharge is still competent and is still used. The 1970 Act, section 40, introduced an alternative and optional form of discharge of the *ex facie*. This innovation was perhaps not very well judged.[1] A section 40 discharge is declared by the statute to have the effect of a common law reconveyance which contains "all necessary and usual clauses" and which is deemed to be in favour of "the person entitled thereto." Taking the latter point first, for it is the more important of the two, it will be observed that a section 40 discharge does not *name* the deemed disponee. This is

[1] For the background to this complex subject, see G.L. Gretton at 1986 J.R. 51 and 192.

most curious. On this principle, one might as well adopt a system of conveyancing in which all deeds affecting title to land are in favour of "the person entitled thereto." Who is "the person entitled?" The borrower? His widow? His executor? The man he sold the property to in the pub? Section 40 does not say. It is a guessing game. Of course, in the majority of cases where a section 40 discharge has been used one can make a fair guess at the identity of "the person entitled." But in a minority of cases real problems exist. One of the authors was involved in a case where the borrower had died. A section 40 discharge was then recorded, with the warrant of registration in favour of the widow. But was she the "person entitled"? She had in fact died shortly before the recording of the discharge. Was "the person entitled" then the son, who was the father's executor? What about the fact that the executor had omitted the property from the confirmation? Or was the "person entitled" the residuary legatees, who were two other sons? Or was it the family business to whom the father had sold the property, but only on missives? Or was it the local council who had recently served a compulsory purchase order but had not got as far as a general vesting declaration? The other point is about the "necessary and usual clauses." This also often causes trouble. Take this case. Mr and Mrs X buy a house in 1968 with a survivorship clause. In 1969 they grant an *ex facie*. In 1984 Mr X dies. In 1985 a section 40 discharge is recorded. In 1993 Mrs X dies. Her executor wants to sell. But he can sell only if Mrs X died owning the whole property. Did she? Do the "necessary and usual clauses" mean that the section 40 discharge revived the survivorship destination? This may seem an esoteric problem but such cases have arisen times without number and continue to do so. The moral is never to use a section 40 discharge, and that if one has already been used, to put on one's thinking cap to see if there are problems caused by it.

Standard securities

We now turn to standard securities which have, since the 1970 Act, been the only competent method of securing a debt over land. A standard security secures a loan. A loan needs a loan contract. The two things are quite distinct: the loan, and the security for the loan.[2] The 1970 Act[3] states that the loan contract (the personal obligation or bond[4]) can either be combined with the security or be contained in a separate unrecorded document which must then be referred to in the security itself. (For a security must state what it secures.) A standard security containing the loan contract is known as a Form A security, while a standard security which refers to but does not contain the loan contract is called a Form B security. Either form can be used. In domestic mortgages, Form A is the norm, while in commercial cases Form B is the norm. The meaning and effect of Form A are defined in section 10 of the 1970 Act. One point to be noted from section 10 is that where Form A is used the loan is presumed to be an on-demand loan. So if Form A is used for a term loan, this must be stated expressly.

Form A is not perfectly drafted. But strict compliance with this and the other styles is not necessary. As Halliday says[5]: "Section 53(1) of the 1970 Act makes it clear that precise adherence to the actual words of the prescribed forms is not essential."

Pro forma standard securities

Most lenders use preprinted forms of standard security, in which the task of the solicitor is simply to fill in the blanks.[6] These *pro forma* securities generally make reference to a Schedule of Variations which the lender will have registered in the Books of Council and Session. This schedule lays down the standard conditions of loan for that lender, and technically operates as a variation of the standard conditions in the 1970 Act. The borrower is thus presented with a contract of adhesion—take it or leave it. There is virtually no possibility of negotiation of terms.[7]

The debt secured: all sums?

A standard security can either be for a fixed amount, or for all sums due or to become due. The latter is almost invariable in practice. This is convenient because it means that if at a later stage

[2] The 1970 Act can perhaps be criticized for sometimes failing to observe the distinction properly.

[3] ss. 9 and 10 and Sched. 2.

[4] "Bond" means loan contract, but in practice the word is sometimes extended to mean the security itself.

[5] Para. 37–11.

[6] Examples can be found in Halliday, and in D.J. Cusine, *Standard Securities*.

[7] That is to say, in ordinary domestic mortgages.

there is a further advance, that will be automatically covered by the security. Without this system, lenders would be more reluctant to make a further advance, or would have to insist on a new standard security, which would be slow and expensive. Whether a standard security is for all sums or not is determined by the wording of the bond element. Sometimes a Form A security will state the loan as a fixed sum, and later have a clause stating that the security is to be good not only for the loan but for all sums. Alternatively a Form A security may not state the loan at all, but merely have words obliging the grantor to pay to the grantee all sums, for which obligation the security is granted.

Interest rate

Form A requires the interest rate to be stated. As true fixed-interest loans are rare, this creates a problem. The old practice was to state the rate in force at the time the security was entered into, with a further provision to the effect that it was variable. Nowadays the usual practice is not to state the initial rate, but merely that the rate is variable. It is generally accepted that this is sufficient compliance with Form A. Details about interest will then be given in the Schedule of Variations, which is referred to in the security itself.[8]

Description and burdens

The property subject to the security must of course be identified by an ordinary conveyancing description.[9] In the case of the Land Register, this must include the title number, though this will not be possible in a first registration, since no title number will yet have been allocated. If a standard security is being granted over subjects which are being split off at the same time, there does not yet exist a ready-made description. The usual way of tackling this is for the description in the standard security to refer to the description in the break-off disposition "recorded of even date with the

[8] For a valuable account of common clauses dealing with interest, see D.J. Cusine, *Standard Securities*, para. 4.29.

[9] 1970 Act, Sched. 2, Note 1. For a potential problem here see D.J. Cusine at 1990 J.L.S. 98.

recording of these presents."[10] There is no need to refer to the burdens.[11]

Deduction of title

The 1970 Act allows[12] title to be deduced in a standard security. But the borrower could always complete title first, and in practice a lender always insists that he does so. Thus, this provision is virtually a dead letter.

The standard conditions

Schedule 3 of the 1970 Act sets forth the "Standard Conditions" which, except in so far as expressly varied, apply to every standard security. The idea is to provide a sort of ready-made contract to save people the bother of making their own.[13] These conditions can be varied in any particular standard security, and usually are so varied. Most institutional lenders have a Schedule of Variations which is long and tedious—but important.[14] These variations can be embodied in the standard security itself but the normal practice is to register them in the Books of Council and Session so that they do not have to be recited *ad longum*. Instead, each standard security simply refers to the registered schedule. Although it is generally true that the standard conditions can be varied, section 11 of the 1970 Act says that the provisions about redemption, sale and foreclosure cannot be varied.[15]

One clause often seen in a Schedule of Variations is that the loan is payable on demand. As was seen in chapter 11, this clause may be at variance with what the client understands to be the case. Lenders who use such a clause do not normally mean to rely on it. But it must be drawn to the client's attention nevertheless.[16] Sometimes such a clause occurs in a Schedule of Variations which elsewhere clearly contemplates that the loan is to be a term loan.

[10] For Land Registration cases see ROTPB, para. G 3.22(d).

[11] 1924 Act, s. 9(1), as applied by the 1970 Act, s. 32.

[12] s. 12.

[13] *Cf.* the standard form articles of association in company law.

[14] For an example see D.J. Cusine, *Standard Securities*, chap. 4.

[15] It is, therefore, perhaps curious that these provisions are in the standard conditions rather than in the body of the Act.

[16] It may be that there is no express on-demand clause, but if the lender is using Form A, such a clause will be implied unless excluded: 1970 Act, s. 10.

This is a simple self-contradiction. A loan is either a term loan or an on-demand one. It cannot be both. Sometimes a Form A security has a Schedule of Variations which says nothing about the loan being a term loan, but makes reference to the original offer of loan. In that case the provisions of the offer of loan have contractual effect except in so far as subsequently modified, and in practice the offer of loan will have specified that the loan is to be a term loan.

Another clause often seen in a Schedule of Variations is one saying that the borrower may neither transfer ownership nor grant any second security, unless with the lender's consent. This clause originated in commercial mortgages, where it may have some point. In domestic mortgages it is arguably pointless. A standard security as a real right would be unaffected by any such transaction. If the borrower breaks this condition, the lender could in theory accelerate the loan. Arguably, the transfer or second security would be voidable.[17]

Transfers subject to security

This point, however, raises another one, which perhaps deserves brief mention. In the absence of the sort of clause referred to above, a borrower is perfectly free to transfer ownership, by sale or otherwise, to another person. The effect is that personal liability for the loan remains with the borrower. Real liability stays with the property. Thus, in the event of default the house could be sold even though in new ownership, but the new owner is not personally liable for the loan.[18] Occasionally, it is desired to transfer ownership to another person, keeping the loan and security in place, and for the outgoing owner to be freed of liability and for the incoming owner to take on liability. The way to do this is to have a bond of corroboration and discharge.[19] This is a tripartite deed, signed by the old owner, the new owner, and the lender. "Corroboration" means that the new owner is accepting personal liability under the loan contract. "Discharge" means that the lender is discharging the old owner of any personal liability. In addition, of course, there

[17] *Cf. Trade Development Bank* v. *Warriner and Mason (Scotland) Ltd.*, 1980 S.C. 74.

[18] Subject to the 1874 Act, s. 47 and the 1924 Act, s. 15.

[19] Such a deed is now classifiable as a "variation" within the meaning of s. 16 of the 1970 Act.

must be the disposition. The old owner cannot be quit of personal liability merely by disponing the property, nor by the fact of another person assuming liability. Discharge requires the consent of the lender. Such arrangements, when they happen, are generally family transactions. An example would be where the husband owns the house, and as part of a separation agreement is to transfer title to his wife.

An example of a slightly different arrangement is where a woman owns a house and marries, and the couple agree on common ownership. A simple disposition of a half share will achieve this, though if the standard security has a prohibition on transfer then the consent of the lender will be required. But even then the result would be that while ownership was shared, the woman alone would be the debtor. Hence it is usual in such a case to have a deed of variation of the standard security whereby the husband assumes joint and several liability for the loan.

Joint borrowers

Often there are two borrowers, typically husband and wife. Both own the house in common, so both grant the security. Both also are bound by the same loan contract, and as between them and the lender their liability is joint and several.[20] Normally, a joint standard security creates no special problems, but it can do so on occasion. Take, for example, a case one of the authors had to advise on. There was a joint mortgage, and the house was worth £500,000. The amount outstanding on the loan was £150,000. The couple split up, and they wished to redeem the mortgage. The idea was that the wife was to get the house free of mortgage. They offered £150,000 to the bank. The bank refused to discharge the security because the husband owed them another £200,000 on another loan,[21] to which the wife was not a party. The husband

[20] Their liability *inter se* is not normally a problematic issue. If it were to arise, the presumption would be for equal liability. There are, however, some complex issues here. For instance, suppose that a husband and wife have a joint mortgage, and the husband is employed while the wife keeps house. The husband pays the mortgage. Could he turn round five years later and demand from his wife half of what he had paid? We cannot discuss such problems here.

[21] The issue of a lender refusing to grant a discharge of a security because of the existence of another outstanding loan is discussed in chap. 13.

could not raise the £200,000 at that time. Could the wife insist that the bank accept the redemption at the £150,000 level? The issue is too complex to be analysed here, but the solicitor needs to be conscious of such possible problems.

Matrimonial Homes Act

Domestic mortgages normally require the appropriate documentation under the 1981 Act.[22] The point is that the lender needs to be protected against latent occupancy rights. The documentation will be a renunciation or a consent, or an affidavit, as appropriate.

Variations

By "variations" is here meant not the variations of the standard conditions, which are stated in the original security itself, but subsequent variations, made after the security has already been registered. The subject is covered in section 16 of the 1970 Act. This states that variation is not appropriate where discharge, or restriction, or assignation would be appropriate. Where what is to be varied is a term which is contained in the original standard security as registered, the variation must itself be registered, but if the term to be varied is itself not registered, the variation need not be registered. For example, in a Form B security, a variation of a term in the (unregistered) loan contract would not have to be registered. Where the variation has to be registered, this can be done either by a new deed (a deed of variation) or by endorsing the new terms on the original standard security, and re-registering that deed.

But it is unclear what the sanction is for failing to register a variation. An unregistered variation would still be binding contractually as between debtor and creditor. Presumably, therefore, the sanction would be that third parties would not be affected. But it is not easy to think of an illustrative example, especially as section 16(4) provides that even a registered variation does not affect real rights acquired by third parties prior to the variation.[23]

Such matters as further advances and changes in interest rate can be handled by a deed of variation, but in practice are not so

[22] See chap. 8.
[23] If this is the true meaning of that subsection.

handled. As to the first, virtually all standard securities are for all sums, and as for the second there is normally a provision for a floating interest rate, whereby changes are made informally. Hence, deeds of variation are rare. Sometimes a deed of variation is used when a couple split up, and one of them takes on the whole property and also the loan. It is also sometimes used when a single owner marries and the spouse, as well as taking a half-share of the title, also becomes jointly liable for the loan.

Assignation of standard securities

Assignations of standard securities are dealt with in section 14 of the 1970 Act. An assignation is where the lender transfers the loan and the security for it to a third person, for whatever reason. The assignation must be recorded. Once that is done, the assignee is substituted for the original creditor in all the rights, both personal and real. The rule *assignatus utitur jure auctoris* applies, as it generally does in assignations of any type, so that any defence which the debtor could have pled against the cedent (assignor) can equally be pled against the assignee. Thus, suppose that the price paid by the assignee is based on the assumption that a certain amount is still due under the security, and that assumption turns out to be false, and that the true sum is lower. In that case the debtor cannot be liable for more than the true amount, even though the assignee was in good faith.[24] Assignation is simple enough in the case of a fixed-sum standard security, but such securities are rare. As has been said,[25] "while there is no theoretical objection to assigning a standard security for a fluctuating amount, there are practical problems which make it undesirable." These problems are complex and cannot be discussed here.

It is quite common for a lender to sell a mortgage portfolio, meaning, for instance, £25,000,000 worth of mortgages. The seller, the original creditor, thus obtains a lump sum, and the buyer takes over the rights under the mortgages. The price for such a sale is a matter for negotiation. But when a mortgage portfolio is sold, there are normally no assignations of the individual mortgages. This

[24] In which case, the assignee will normally have a claim against the cedent in warrandice.

[25] D.J. Cusine, *Standard Securities*, para. 6.11.

would generally be too costly and inconvenient. So legally the seller remains the heritable creditor and the borrower can ignore the fact that the mortgage has been sold. Indeed, he may not even know that it has been sold. Thus, for instance, he keeps up payments to the same party, who then passes on such payments to the buyer. In other words, the sale is simply a contractual arrangement between the two financial institutions. This is technically called sale by sub-participation.[26]

There can be no question of an assignation of a standard security by the debtor. Only rights can be assigned, not obligations. [27] The debtor can transfer his ownership of the property,[28] but that transfer is by disposition not assignation.

Security over a standard security

Occasionally it happens that the creditor in a standard security wishes to use his rights as a security for a debt. Thus, suppose that A borrows from B and grants to B a standard security. B then wishes to borrow from C and use his (B's) real right as a security in favour of C. Can this be done? It might be thought that B could assign the standard security to C, as a security, the standard security to be reconveyed to B when B's debt to C is repaid. If B defaults to C, then C could appropriate the debt due by A and if necessary enforce the standard security against A.

However, this is incompetent. Under section 9(8)(*b*) of the 1970 Act a standard security is an "interest in land" and by virtue of section 9(3) a security over an interest in land can be created only by standard security. Therefore, an assignation in security of a standard security is incompetent, and the only permissible method is to have a standard security over the standard security, as indeed is envisaged by section 9(2).

A standard security over a standard security is a strange animal. If B defaults to C, C has no claim against A or against A's land. Instead, C can enforce his (higher level) standard security by selling the (lower level) standard security. The buyer of the latter would

[26] See E. Ferran, *Mortgage Securitisation* (1992) for a full study.

[27] Otherwise, a debtor would assign the debt to a tramp, and so be free of his debt!

[28] Subject to what has been said above.

then be substituted for B. If C could not find a buyer, he could become the holder of the (lower level) standard security by the foreclosure procedure.

Restrictions

A restriction[29] is where the lender agrees that part of the property is disburdened, with the remainder continuing to be subject to the security. It is, thus, a sort of discharge. Obviously, it is uncommon. An example is where X sells a slice of garden to his neighbour. The latter would insist on a deed of restriction from X's building society, for otherwise the title to the slice of garden would be encumbered. Whether a lender will require payment for such a deed is a matter for negotiation. A commercial example of restriction is where a building company develops a site and puts up, say, 40 houses. There is a commercial mortgage over the whole site securing a loan which is financing the development. As each house is finished it is sold, but each buyer will insist on an unencumbered title. So the bank will grant a deed of restriction for that house. This will have been envisaged in the original contract between the builder and the bank. The contract will normally say that in return for the deed the bank must be paid, say, 75 per cent. of the sale price, thereby ensuring that as the extent of the security is reduced the outstanding loan is also reduced.

Restriction can be effected by a deed of restriction, duly registered. It is more common, however, for the lender to execute the disposition as a consenter to the effect of restricting the security.[30]

Discharges

Discharges are regulated by section 17 of the 1970 Act. On complete repayment the lender must grant a discharge to the borrower, which is then registered. The expense of this falls on the borrower. The statutory style[31] is far from perfect. It requires that the discharge state that it is "in consideration of £ . . . being the whole

[29] Regulated by s. 15 of the 1970 Act.

[30] The 1970 Act makes no provision for effecting a restriction in this way, but there can be no question of its validity, under the common law of heritable security.

[31] Sched. 4, Form F.

amount secured by the standard security aftermentioned." But it can be difficult to know what sum to fill in. Thus, suppose a company grants a standard security for its current account, which is sometimes in overdraft. Ten years later the company decides to change its bank, at a time when the account happens to be in credit. A discharge is required. What sum can be filled in? There never was a principal sum. There was, instead, just an account with many thousands of credit and debit entries. Another case where the style is inappropriate is where the lender agrees to discharge the security without repayment of the loan.[32] It is hard to see, in any case, why a clause of this sort is required. The common law of deeds is that it is not necessary to state the reason or cause of granting. So why the statute requires such a clause in a discharge is obscure, let alone a clause which is inappropriate in many types of case. In practice, draftsmen often depart considerably from the statutory style, and indeed there can be little doubt that a discharge which wholly omitted the consideration clause would be valid. But it is wise to adhere to the official style as nearly as is reasonably possible.

Usually, the security being discharged is an all-sums security. Here, a peculiarity of the official style must be noted, namely that the all-sums aspect not only must be mentioned, but in fact affects the wording of the discharge at two separate points. In the following the words which are underlined must be inserted for an all-sums security: "in consideration of . . . [33] *being the whole amount secured by the standard security aftermentioned* paid by . . . hereby discharge a standard security *for all sums due or to become due*."

The discharge is normally a separate deed. But it can alternatively be indorsed on the original standard security, and some standard securities have a preprinted form of discharge at the end. Where this is done, the security will be registered again, by way of discharge. In addition, the discharge can be incorporated as part of a disposition. Thus, if A wants to dispone to B, and the plan is to discharge a standard security which X has, X could execute the disposition as well as A, as consenter, to the effect of discharging the security.[34]

[32] Which, of course, is unusual, but can happen for various reasons.

[33] In a domestic standard security there is inserted here the loan figure stated in the original security deed.

[34] As with restriction, the 1970 Act does not expressly authorise this, but once again there can be no doubt of its competency under the common law.

Section 18 makes provision for the case where the lender fails to grant a discharge. This, again, is inadequately drafted, for various reasons, including the fact that it assumes that repayment of the loan is being offered at the same time. This is the same mistake as before: by the time the discharge is wanted there may be no outstanding loan.

A standard security, like any security, is purely an accessory right, meaning that it can have no existence separate from the debt which it secures. Hence, once the debt is gone, the security secures nothing, and so is implicitly discharged.[35] Therefore, the discharge is simply evidential. The (ex) debtor wishes it to be granted simply as proof that his property is now unencumbered. However, this is true in an unqualified way only of fixed-sum standard securities. By contrast, suppose that a standard security is granted for an overdraft. Over the years the account is sometimes in debit and sometimes in credit. It must not be supposed that the moment the debit balance disappears, the security is discharged. Therefore, in the case of all-sums standard securities, the discharge is more than merely evidential.

Death

If the debtor dies, normally the debt will be repaid immediately from the proceeds of a life policy which will have been taken out to cover that contingency. In the unlikely event that this does not happen, whoever takes over the property (the spouse, or a legatee, etc.) must undertake, as a condition of taking the property, to pay off the loan. For the purposes of succession, the debt is deemed a burden on the heritable estate, and thus does not, for example, diminish *jus relictae*. However, if the debt is secured not only by the standard security but also by an assignation in security of a life policy, the debt is, for succession purposes, notionally ascribed both to the land and to the policy.[36]

The death of the creditor is much less usual, because the creditor is seldom an individual. If he is, then the security and the loan which it secures simply forms part of his estate to be administered

[35] *Cameron* v. *Williamson* (1895) 22 R. 393.

[36] *Graham* v. *Graham* (1898) 5 S.L.T. 319, and see an article by G.L. Gretton at 1987 J.L.S 303.

by his executor and transferred to a beneficiary, or sold. The debt (which, from the creditor's viewpoint, is an asset) is deemed heritable in the succession to the creditor's estate.[37]

Consumer Credit Act

A loan which is under the limit (£15,000 currently) may be a "regulated agreement" under the Consumer Credit Act 1974. The impact of this on conveyancing is that if a standard security is granted to secure a regulated agreement, the standard security itself falls under the statutory regime, with various implications, including the format of the documentation and the rights of the parties, including rights and procedures on default.[38] However, in practice not many standard securities are affected, for the following reasons. First, most standard securities are for sums over £15,000. Secondly, if the lender is an exempt institution such as a building society or a local authority, the statutory provisions do not apply. Next, the provisions do not apply if the borrower is a registered company. Finally, they do not apply if the lender is a purely private lender. Thus, if a client gets a loan of £10,000 from his aunt, the statutory provisions do not apply, unless she is a professional moneylender. Because of these factors, we will not deal further with securities regulated by this Act.[39]

Ranking

The subject of ranking[40] is vast and only certain aspects can be dealt with here. Ranking is partly dealt with by the 1970 Act itself and partly by the common law.

The most important fact about a standard security is that it is a

[37] Subject to certain qualifications contained in s. 117 of the 1868 Act. See M. Meston, *The Succession (Scotland) Act 1964* (4th ed., W. Green, 1993) for discussion.

[38] For instance, on default the lender must first serve a "default notice" prior to calling up, etc. This default notice under the Consumer Credit Act 1974 must not be confused with the notice of default under the 1970 Act itself. There are cases where a default notice must be followed by a notice of default.

[39] See, further, Halliday, paras. 37–47 to 37–53.

[40] See Halliday, paras. 42–27 to 42–41 and D.J. Cusine, *Standard Securities*, chap. 7.

real right, and, like most other real rights, will obey the rule *prior tempore potior jure*.[41] So the first to be registered ranks first. Thus, if lender A has a first-registered standard security for a loan of £50,000, and lender B has a second-registered security for a loan of £25,000, and there is default and the house is sold for £60,000, after deduction of expenses, A takes £50,000 and B takes the balance of £10,000. If, however, the two securities were registered at the same time they would rank *pari passu* so that A would receive £40,000 and B £20,000. Moreover, creditors are free to enter into a ranking agreement, the meaning of which is self-explanatory. Such agreements, though common in commercial cases, are rare in domestic cases.

Account must also be taken of section 13 of the 1970 Act. If the first security is for all sums, a potential problem exists. For after the second security is granted, the first creditor might lend further sums, which would have the effect of eating up the equity[42] on which the second creditor had relied. So common law developed a rule[43] whereby if the first creditor knew that a second security had been granted, any further advance by him could not prejudice the second security. The substance of this rule is given statutory force by section 13. Note that only voluntary further advances by the first creditor are so affected. Thus, interest accumulating is unaffected. And if the further advance had already been contracted for, it is unaffected.[44] The knowledge of the first creditor of the existence of the second security is a matter of actual knowledge. No formal notification procedure is laid down. But the practice is for the second lender, or his solicitor, to send what is commonly called a notice of second charge to the first creditor. It is vital to do this when acting for a second creditor. Section 13 is not very clearly drafted and there has been controversy as to its exact meaning. The main issue is this: if the first creditor, after receiving notice, does make a further advance, is that advance secured *tertio loco* or is it unsecured? It is difficult to see any clear answer.[45]

[41] Earlier by time, stronger by right.

[42] Meaning, in this context, market value minus secured debt.

[43] See *Union Bank* v. *National Bank* (1886) 14 R. (H.L.) 1.

[44] This would be rare in domestic cases. But commercial loans are often "drawn down" in "tranches."

[45] See articles at 1980 J.L.S. 275 and 1981 J.L.S. 26 and 280 for discussion.

Drafting postponed securities

When a postponed standard security is granted, Schedule 2, Note 5 to the 1970 Act says that it should refer to the prior security, and repeat this statement in the warrandice clause. This is sensible from a practical point of view, but even if such a clause were omitted the security would still have a postponed ranking simply by virtue of being created later than the first security. If, however, two securities are being created at the same time, one of which is to be postponed to the other, it is vital that the postponed security contains wording clearly postponing it. If this is done, it does not matter that the two securities are registered on the same day or even if the postponed security is registered first. But if the words of postponement are omitted, and the securities are registered the same day, they will rank *pari passu*, or if the security intended to be postponed is registered first, it will rank first. If that happens, the problem will have to be resolved by a ranking agreement.[46]

Insurance

The lender will insist on property insurance.[47] Most lenders will offer the borrower a choice of, say, six insurance companies. The level required is normally reinstatement value rather than market value. The cover should be increased to keep in line with inflation. Many policies have an automatic annual increase linked to inflation. Some lenders pay the premiums themselves and charge the borrower, while others leave it to the borrower to make the payments. Sometimes the policy is in the joint names of the lender and the owner, sometimes in the name of the lender, sometimes in the name of the borrower, and sometimes in the name of the borrower with the name of the lender endorsed on the policy. All these raise difficult theoretical questions as to the respective interests in the policy of the two parties, and also as to insurable interest.

[46] If, in such a situation, the holder of the security intended to rank second proves uncooperative, it may be possible for the other security holder to have a remedy against him based on the prior agreement between them, assuming that such an agreement could be proved.

[47] See 1970 Act, Standard Condition 5. For a useful discussion of the practice of leading mortgage lenders, see D.J. Cusine, *Standard Securities*, para. 5.18.

The lender is not concerned with contents insurance so the client must be reminded of the need for this.

Sickness and unemployment insurance

The lender normally insists that the borrower has life assurance cover to not less than the amount of the loan. This ensures repayment in the event of death. But the borrower may also run into problems by reason of sickness or unemployment, either of which may make it difficult to keep up the monthly mortgage payments. It is possible to obtain insurance cover against these risks. Lenders do not insist on such cover, but generally offer it through an associated insurance company. The solicitor should check with his client whether he wishes to have this cover. Of course, the premiums will increase the monthly outgoings. Combined sickness and redundancy cover will typically cost around six per cent of the monthly mortgage cost, so that if for instance the monthly mortgage payments are £300 this cover would cost about £18 per month.

Acceleration

If the loan secured is an on-demand loan, the creditor can insist on repayment at any time, though section 19 of the 1970 Act provides that he cannot enforce his rights under the security itself without first serving a calling-up notice. If the loan secured is a term loan, the contract, if properly drafted, will have an acceleration clause. This is a clause, standard in all term loan contracts, secured or unsecured, whereby if the debtor defaults in a defined way (such as being in arrears for more than 21 days on any instalment) the creditor may, at his option, convert the loan into an on-demand loan and call for repayment of the whole debt at once. For obvious reasons, no acceleration clause is needed in an on-demand loan.

Sometimes term loans have no acceleration clause. This might cause problems. Take this example. X lends Y £50,000, and the loan contract says that it is repayable in two equal instalments, the first after two years and the second after four. The contract is silent as to acceleration. A standard security is granted for the loan. After the two years no payment is made. The lender enforces by sale. How much can he take from the sale? £50,000? Or just £25,000? The argument for the latter is that at the time of the sale only

£25,000 was due and resting owing. Section 27 of the 1970 Act, which deals with what is to happen to the sale proceeds, simply says that the lender is paid "the whole amount due under the standard security," which in this context is perhaps ambiguous. The matter seems never to have been tested in court, and it seems that there has been no discussion in the literature either. In practice, everyone assumes that where a term loan is secured by standard security, a right of acceleration is implied, so that in our example the creditor could take the whole £50,000. And there is also an argument that common law implies a right of acceleration in every loan contract for any breach which amounts to a material or repudiatory breach. This may be right but it is largely unexplored territory.

Mortgage arrears

Mortgage arrears can arise for all sorts of reasons. The main ones are loss of employment and marital breakdown. In practice, solicitors are not often called on to advise a borrower who is in arrears, since such people do not usually turn to their lawyer. But sometimes they do. It can be wise, in that event, to suggest to them that they visit the Citizens Advice Bureau, or a debt counsellor.

Mortgage problems do not exist in isolation from the rest of the client's affairs. A mortgage problem simply means a debt problem. The solution may be a change of lifestyle. But in what follows we will look specifically at ways of cutting the mortgage payments.

The client should contact the lender. Most lenders are reluctant to take enforcement action at an early stage. Such action involves administrative costs and can bring bad publicity. Some lenders have ethical standards and wish to give borrowers a chance to get back on their feet. So, although they may not say in so many words that they are prepared to put up with some arrears on a temporary basis, in practice they sometimes are so prepared. The theory is that they will be more understanding if the borrower gets in touch with them to explain his problems. This is true of creditors in general. Debtors who are in financial trouble are naturally reluctant to contact their creditors, but it is often wise to do so. This may delay enforcement action, and in some cases a deal can be struck. This at least is the theory, but in practice this approach works better with some creditors than with others.

If the financial problems are likely to be temporary, some sort of renegotiation of the mortgage may be advisable. The lender may agree to a payment holiday and a period of reduced payments with arrears payable over an agreed period. Another possibility is for payments to be put on an interest-only basis for several months. But this is possible only for repayment mortgages, for in others the monthly payments to the creditor are already interest-only. However, sometimes it is possible to arrange for the endowment policy to be put on ice for a period. But even for repayment mortgages this scheme is often not of much use, since in the early years, when the problems are most likely to arise, most of the monthly payment is interest anyway. A common tactic for cases where the problems are likely to be temporary is to switch to a new mortgage, where the initial monthly payments will be lower. The new mortgage may be of the low-start or deferred-interest type. By doing this it is sometimes possible to cut monthly outgoings dramatically. But this is appropriate only where the borrower's finances are likely to recover later. For in a low-start mortgage payments will go up to full level after a set period. But worse than that, the unpaid interest is accumulated during the grace period and added to capital, so that thereafter the borrower will be paying substantially more than he would have done under a more conventional mortgage. A low-start mortgage can thus get the borrower further into debt. This can make sense, or it can be a disaster. Careful thought is needed.

In some cases the social security system will help pay the mortgage. The rules are complex, but in essence the interest element will be covered, but not any capital repayments, and in addition for the first 16 weeks only 50 per cent of the monthly payments will be met by the system.[48] The client should be told to contact the local social security office.

If the problems are not short term, the best advice may be to cut the mortgage payments by selling the house and buying a cheaper one, with a smaller mortgage. Though this advice is obvious, it is too seldom given. If the worst comes to the worst and the borrower is put out on the street by the lender, he will normally qualify to be rehoused by the local authority under the homeless persons

[48] The rules are currently to be found in the Income Support (General) Regulations 1987 (S.I. 1987 No. 1967), as amended.

legislation.[49] If this looks like happening, the debtor should be told to get in touch with the local housing department without delay.

Negative equity

The "equity" in a house is the market value minus secured debt. If the secured debt is greater than market value, the property is said to have negative equity. This can happen where a high mortgage (*e.g.* 95 per cent) is followed by a market slump, or of course where a lower mortgage has been followed by a second mortgage. The effect of the property slump which emerged in the late 1980s has been that numerous homes now have negative equity. In 1992 the Bank of England estimated the number in the UK at about one million, while other estimates put the figure even higher. Fortunately, the problem is much less widespread in Scotland than in England.[50] Negative equity is a problem for both lender and borrower. It is a problem for the lender because if the borrower defaults, sale of the property will not pay off the debt. It is a problem for the borrower partly because it may mean that he has become insolvent.[51] Moreover, where there is negative equity the owner will find it difficult to sell the house and buy a new one, for the simple reason that the sale will not generate enough cash to pay off the existing mortgage.

Borrowers sometimes ask if they can walk away from a mortgage, that is to say, hand the keys to the lender and give up the property and thereby be freed of the debt.[52] The legal answer is that such an action does not free the borrower of the debt. A borrower is personally liable for any shortfall suffered by the lender after a sale.[53] In practice, however, a lender may write off the short-

[49] Currently contained in the Housing (Scotland) Act 1987.

[50] Because the property slump has been less severe here. Moreover, there is some evidence that in Scotland the risky practice of "mortgaging up to the hilt" has been less common than in England.

[51] The value of his total assets now being less than his total liabilities. Of course, negative equity does not necessarily imply insolvency. The borrower may have other assets. Moreover, the fact of insolvency does not necessarily imply bankruptcy. The borrower may still be able to meet his monthly mortgage payments, and as and when market prices go up, solvency will then re-emerge.

[52] This question is asked only where there is negative equity. No rational person would wish to walk away from a property which had positive equity.

[53] Under Scots (and English) law. In some legal systems the rule is different.

fall. But the borrower's name may go down as a bad risk with the credit reference agencies.

Enforcement[54]

In the overwhelming majority of cases the question of the enforcement of a standard security does not arise. Lenders in general are careful to lend only to those whom they believe to be creditworthy. But enforcement, though unpleasant, is sometimes necessary. Without the possibility of enforcement the mortgage system would not work, and most people agree that the mortgage system is a good one, because it enables people to buy their homes when they otherwise would be unable to do so.

In most countries the sale process is supervised by the court and takes a good deal longer than it does with us, with the result that it takes longer to get the debtor out of the property. There is a good deal to be said on this subject. It could be argued that our system in fact gives a reasonable deal to the debtor. While the legal systems of some other countries try to confer rights on the debtor, such rights often backfire in practice. This is especially true on the question of getting the best price. The debtor hopes that the best price will be realised, so that his debt is reduced as much as possible, or wholly paid off, with as much free proceeds as possible. And, of course, if there are other creditors they too have an interest that a good price will be obtained. But the selling creditor is concerned only to get the debt paid off. Thus, if the debt is £40,000, the creditor would be happy to sell for £41,000, even though the fair market value might be £60,000. In Scotland, this problem is dealt with better than in many countries. Apart from the statutory rule[55] that the selling creditor is under an obligation to get the best price reasonably obtainable, in our system, unlike many, the property is marketed like any other property. Thus, if one looks at the property pages of the local newspaper, some of the properties will be creditor sales, but there is no way to tell which. The effect is that a fair market price is normally obtained. By contrast, many

[54] For a good account see D.J. Cusine, *Standard Securities*, chap. 8. In practice, conveyancers are not often involved with enforcement, since this tends to be handled by court lawyers, though the eventual disposition on sale will, of course, be done by a conveyancer.

[55] 1970 Act, s. 25.

countries have a system in which potential buyers know that it is a creditor sale, so that many potential buyers back off, for the same reasons that most people would not bid at a warrant sale. There is something ghoulish about buying at a creditor sale.[56] Our system, thus, usually works for the debtor's benefit. However, there is one criticism of our system which has some force, namely that the sale can go ahead too quickly. But not everyone would agree. The subject is a large one and cannot be considered further here.

So much for policy. Now for technicalities. The law of enforcement is a subject of great, and perhaps unnecessary, complexity. Part of the law is in the 1970 Act (itself divided between the body of the Act and the standard conditions), part is common law, and one or two bits are in the Heritable Securities (Scotland) Act 1894.[57] That latter Act is not of much importance today because most of it was superseded by the 1970 Act. The enforcement parts of the 1970 Act are, perhaps, not well drafted. The creditor has a whole battery of remedies, including personal action, summary diligence, poinding of the ground, adjudication, removing the debtor and letting the property, maills and duties, and so forth. But to a large extent these remedies are of theoretical interest only since in practice the creditor will almost always opt for sale. So that is what we will deal with here.

The three roads to sale

There are three roads which lead to sale, namely calling up, notice of default, and a section 24 application.

The calling up process is covered by section 19 of the 1970 Act. The creditor serves a calling-up notice which requires repayment of the whole debt within two months. If the two-month period expires without payment, the power of sale emerges automatically. The Act does not say what circumstances justify the service of this notice. There is no problem if the loan is an on-demand one, or if, though a term loan, there is an acceleration clause which has been activated. In practice, one or other of these will virtually always be the case. But as we saw earlier, if there is a term loan with no

[56] In domestic cases. Commercial cases are different.

[57] Yet others are in the Consumer Credit Act 1974, if the mortgage is regulated by that Act, which, however, is not generally the case.

acceleration provision, there is a question mark as to whether arrears entitle the lender to accelerate.

Notices of default are governed by sections 20 and 21 of the 1970 Act. The notice states what the default is, and calls upon the debtor to cease to be in default within one month, failing which the enforcement powers emerge. The Act uses the word "default" in different ways and there has been some controversy about exactly what it is supposed to mean in different contexts.[58] But it is clear that failure to make a payment to the lender is a "default" under Standard Condition 9(1)(*b*), and thus entitles the creditor to issue a notice of default. A key difference between this procedure and a calling-up notice is that the latter requires repayment of the whole debt, whereas a notice of default requires only that arrears be brought up to date. The debtor can, if he wishes, challenge the notice in court.[59] It is curious that no parallel provision is made for the calling-up process, although a debtor who thought that a calling-up notice was unlawful (*e.g.* he might claim that there had been no default in payment) could presumably raise a common law action of declarator, suspension and interdict. The notice of default should not be confused with the default notice which is needed in cases under the Consumer Credit Act 1974. If the standard security is regulated by that Act, a default notice will be needed in addition to the calling-up notice or notice of default.

Lastly, there is the section 24 application. This is an application by the creditor to the court stating that the debtor is in default and asking for permission to sell. When is this route used? Probably the only case where it *has* to be used is where the creditor wishes to sell, not because of any failure to pay, but because the debtor has become insolvent.[60] This is not very common. But section 24 is also available, as an option, for cases under Standard Condition 9(1)(*b*), namely any breach of the security. The section does not cover Standard Condition 9(1)(*a*), namely failure to comply with a calling-up notice, but it could still be used in such a case, because failure to comply with such a notice must also imply a breach under Standard Condition 9(1)(*b*).[61] In practice, creditors often adopt a

[58] For an interesting discussion see D.J. Cusine, *Standard Securities*, para. 8.14.

[59] 1970 Act, s. 22.

[60] Standard Condition 9(1)(*c*).

[61] All this seems unduly complex. Even the account in the text has been heavily simplified.

belt-and-braces approach. They issue either a calling-up notice or a notice of default and then, if the money is still not forthcoming, also apply under section 24. In practice, section 24 applications are seldom defended. The benefit of obtaining a section 24 decree, as opposed to relying solely on a calling-up notice or notice of default that has not been complied with, is that the creditor's remedies have been judicially declared and so there can be no dispute as to the right to exercise them. Where the debtor is a company in liquidation, the issue of a section 24 warrant for sale prevails over the rule[62] that any disposition of the property of a company in liquidation is void.[63] If the creditor can prove that the statutory requirements are met, the court has no discretion to refuse a section 24 warrant.[63a]

The actual power of sale emerges when: (1) a calling-up notice has not been complied with at the end of the two months; or (2) when a notice of default has neither been complied with nor challenged in court within the one month period; or (3) when a notice of default has been challenged but the challenge has been unsuccessful; or (4) where a sale warrant has been granted under a section 24 application.

To sell, the creditor will need to get the debtor out of the property. Often the debtor flits of his own accord. But if he does not, court procedure will be required. This issue has caused great difficulty in recent years because of the obscurities of the Act.[64] Matters have, however, now been clarified by an Act of Sederunt,[65] and the current position seems to be as follows. If the creditor has issued a calling-up notice or notice of default which has not been complied with, he should seek ejection of the debtor under section 5 of the Heritable Securities (Scotland) Act 1894. If he makes a section 24 application without seeking ejection, the application is a summary one. But if (as is usual) he wishes to combine a section 24 application with a warrant to eject, he can do so, but the action must proceed as an ordinary action. A heritable creditor in possession

[62] Now contained in the Insolvency Act 1986, s. 127.

[63] *UDT Noters*, 1978 S.L.T. (Notes) 56; *UDT* v. *Site Preparations Ltd.*, 1978 S.L.T. (Sh. Ct.) 14 and 21.

[63a] *Halifax Building Society* v. *Gupta*, 1993 G.W.D. 14–948.

[64] See, *e.g.*, an article by George Jamieson at 1989 S.L.T. (News) 201.

[65] S.I. 1990 No. 661.

is not liable for upkeep costs which the debtor had failed to pay.[66]

A problem about section 24

The 1970 Act does not lay down a style for a section 24 application, and in practice therefore the style suggested by Halliday[67] tends to be followed. This seeks (1) declarator that the pursuer (creditor) has the right to enter into possession, (2) an order requiring the defender (debtor) to flit, and (3) declarator that "the pursuer has right to exercise in relation to the said subjects all other powers competent to a creditor in lawful possession of the said subjects by virtue of the Conveyancing and Feudal Reform (Scotland) Act 1970." It can be argued that a decree in such terms does not authorise sale. The Act confers various powers on a creditor in lawful possession, but it seems that the power of sale is not among them. The wording of the Act suggests that the power of sale is distinct from the powers consequent upon lawful possession. Hence, it would seem wise, in a section 24 application, to seek express declarator of the power of sale as well. That does not necessarily mean that a creditor who has a section 24 decree in the above terms does not have power of sale. It means merely that, if this argument is correct, he does not have power of sale by virtue of the decree. He may still have power of sale if there is an expired calling-up notice or notice of default.

The sale

Once the power of sale has emerged and possession has been obtained, the property can be sold. Sometimes this is done by an in-house solicitor for the lender, and sometimes by an outside firm. The marketing happens in the same way as for any other property: as has already been said, a prospective purchaser will not normally know that this is a creditor sale.

If there is more than one security, it is possible for the postponed creditor to sell. If both creditors wish to sell, the law makes no

[66] *David Watson Property Management* v. *Woolwich Equitable Building Society*, 1992 S.L.T. 430.

[67] Para. 39–61.

provision as which is to do it. The custom, however, in such cases is that the first-ranked creditor will do the sale unless otherwise agreed. And in one case[68] it was held that where a first-ranked standard security holder had taken possession, he could interdict a second-ranked heritable creditor from selling.

Section 25 of the 1970 Act imposes a duty to advertise and a duty to get the best price reasonably obtainable. These come to much the same thing. If the creditor advertises properly then he should get the fair market price, while conversely a fair market price is unlikely to be achieved without proper advertising. The 1924 Act, section 38 contained detailed provisions as to advertisement in relation to bonds and dispositions in security, but these were not repeated in the 1970 Act. In practice, however, the 1924 rules are often followed, to avoid any dispute about the sufficiency of the advertising. Halliday so recommends.[69] But estate agents are sometimes feeble about advertising. Sometimes they do not even put in a newspaper advertisement at all but merely list the property in their free handout. In land registration cases the Keeper appears to take the view that this is sufficient, but many would disagree. Difficulty may arise when the purchaser's solicitor asks for evidence of proper advertisement. The normal practice is to get from the newspaper publisher a certificate of advertisement, whereby the publisher confirms that such and such an advertisement appeared in the paper on such and such days.

It has been explained above that there is an obligation to obtain the best price reasonably obtainable. If the ex-debtor can prove that the lender has failed in this respect, he is entitled to damages.[70] However, in practice the burden of proof in damages actions of this sort is a fairly high one.[71] It has been held that the debtor cannot interdict sale on that ground.[72] It probably also follows that the ex-owner could not reduce the sale on that ground, though this is not quite certain.

Missives are concluded in the usual way. Usually no moveables will be included, since the creditor normally has no right to sell

[68] *Skipton Building Society* v. *Wain*, 1986 S.L.T. 96.

[69] Para. 39–41. See also D.J. Cusine (ed.), *The Conveyancing Opinions of Professor J.M. Halliday*, p. 314.

[70] *Royal Bank of Scotland* v. *Johnston*, 1987 G.W.D. 1–5.

[71] *Dick* v. *Clydesdale Bank*, 1991 S.L.T. 678.

[72] *Associated Relays* v. *Turnbeam*, 1988 S.C.L.R. 220.

the moveables.[73] However, some lenders include in their standard conditions a right to sell any moveables in the premises. In that case they will be selling not as security holders but as agents. There are some technical problems in this connection, and where such a sale of moveables happens the selling creditor will not warrant title to the moveables. A selling creditor will indeed be more reluctant than an ordinary seller to warrant certain other things, such as that the central heating is in good working order.

The disposition is granted by the creditor. It is, thus, in a sense a disposition *a non domino*. For a style see Halliday,[74] though for some reason this contains clauses which are now unnecessary, as a result of the 1979 Act, such as the assignation of writs and rents. It should be observed that the disposition does not have a clause deducing title through the standard security. The practice is for the selling creditor to grant fact and deed warrandice personally and to bind the debtor in absolute warrandice. It is, however, arguable that this practice is unreasonable. If it turns out that there is a problem about the title, the debtor will normally not be worth suing.[75] It is arguable that the selling creditor should grant absolute warrandice. But a purchaser who wanted this would have to stipulate for it in the missives.

A search should be made against the property and the seller and also against the debtor though it is unlikely that any entry in the personal register could affect the sale. Thus, an inhibition against the debtor after the security was created but before the sale is irrelevant.[76]

Might the buyer find his title reducible by the former owner on the ground of some invalidity in the sale? There are few definite answers here. There is a statutory provision in section 41 (as amended) of the 1924 Act[77] which says that a buyer will be protected by good faith. However, the actual wording of the section is obscure and leaves open many issues. Some people take a fairly robust view while others fear that the protection given by section

[73] Unless the creditor has resorted to the diligence of poinding of the ground, which is occasionally done, though more often in commercial than in domestic cases.

[74] Para. 39–45.

[75] If he were fully solvent, there would have been no forced sale.

[76] *Newcastle Building Society* v. *White*, 1987 S.L.T. (Sh. Ct.) 81.

[77] As applied by s. 32 of the 1970 Act.

41 may be very limited. No one knows. The safe course to take when acting for a purchaser is the cautious one. In particular, it is necessary to insist on certificates of advertisement and on the calling-up notice or whatever other steps were used to lead to the sale, including any decrees. Moreover, these need to be kept because a subsequent buyer will wish to check them too, until such time as they become irrelevant by prescription. In many cases the creditor will have obtained a decree under section 24. In that case there is usually no question as to his right to sell,[78] though there may still be questions as to the exercise of that right. The purchaser should, of course, see the decree and take a copy of it.

Documentation under the 1981 Act is not required in relation to the selling creditor (in respect of whom the house could never be a matrimonial home) but is still required in respect of the debtor. This should have been obtained at the time the security was granted in the first place.

A theoretical point

A standard security is a *jus in re aliena*, that is to say a real right, but not a real right of ownership. The debtor has the real right of ownership. Though this is generally well understood, a common mistake is to suppose that the creditor becomes owner as soon as he takes possession. This is not correct. The debtor remains the owner until the moment when ownership passes to the buyer, which, of course, is at the moment when the disposition in his favour is registered. The creditor never becomes owner, unless there is a decree of foreclosure[79] which is extremely rare.

When is the right of redemption cut off?

Up to what point does the debtor still have the right to pay off the debt and so save the property? The issue is seldom of importance, for if the debtor could pay he would have done so at an earlier stage. But the point is worth a few words. Section 23(3) of the 1970 Act says that under the notice of default procedure the debtor has the right to redeem right up to the moment when missives of

[78] Subject to the wording of the decree: see above.
[79] 1970 Act, s. 28.

sale are concluded. This is very sensible, but no parallel provision exists for the other two roads to sale. A guess would be that the same rule would apply, since it is the only reasonable rule. However, it may be that in such a case the debtor would have to serve a notice of redemption.[80]

What happens to the proceeds of sale?

The distribution of the proceeds of sale is governed by section 27 of the 1970. The creditor holds the proceeds in trust, first for payment of the expenses of sale, secondly for payment of any prior secured debt, thirdly for payment of his own secured debt and any other secured debt having an equal ranking, fourthly for payment of any postponed secured debt, and fifthly, for payment to the debtor.[81] Of course, payment at any of these levels can be made only to the extent that there are funds remaining from the previous levels. In *Halifax Building Society* v. *Smith*[82] the Sheriff Principal[83] said: "Professor Halliday in his commentary on the Act . . . suggests that the tabulation in s. 27 represents one of the better characteristics of modern draftsmanship. If this is so the terms thereof seem nevertheless to have sown a considerable amount of doubt and confusion."

In complex cases the creditor will not want to take the risk of distributing the fund himself, but will instead raise a multiplepoinding, so that the court can decide who gets what. In some cases, especially if there is an arrestment, he will generally have little choice but to take the multiplepoinding route.

If the sale fails to pay off the whole debt, the debtor remains personally liable for the balance.

Diligence[84]

Sometimes another creditor of the debtor has inhibited before the sale. This will not normally affect the secured creditor's power of

[80] See *A. Dunlop & Sons' Judicial Factor* v. *Armstrong*, 1993 G.W.D. 2–127.
[81] This text is a rough paraphrase of the statutory wording.
[82] 1985 S.L.T. (Sh. Ct.) 25.
[83] Caplan.
[84] See G. Maher and D.J. Cusine, *Law and Practice of Diligence* (Butterworth, 1990); G.L. Gretton, *Law of Inhibition and Adjudication*, and vol. 8 of the *Stair Memorial Encyclopaedia*.

sale.[85] Whether it will give the inhibitor any right to share in the proceeds of the sale has been a matter of controversy and conflicting decisions.[86] If, however, a creditor has used the diligence of adjudication, and has recorded or registered the decree of adjudication, then that creditor falls to be treated as a secured creditor with a ranking determined by the date of registration.

Quite often another creditor will seek to arrest in the hands of the selling creditor. This is because upon sale, where a surplus emerges, the debtor—creditor relationship is reversed, and the (ex) debtor becomes a creditor and the (ex) creditor a debtor.[87] Thus, suppose that X has a mortgage with the Halifax on which £40,000 is outstanding, and there is default, and the Halifax sells and, after deduction of expenses, has £50,000 in its hands. X is no longer the Halifax's debtor for £40,000 but the Halifax's creditor for £10,000, and this is an asset which is arrestable by his other creditors. The arrestment must be in the hands of the selling creditor, not the selling creditor's solicitors.[88] The arrestment must obviously be laid on, at latest, before distribution has taken place. There is some uncertainty as to how early the arrestment can take place, but it has been held[89] that it is competent as soon as the selling creditor has taken possession, *i.e.* well before missives of sale will have been concluded, let alone the price received.

Disburdenment

Section 26 of the 1970 Act provides that on the sale by the creditor the property is disburdened automatically of the security and of any postponed or *pari passu* security. Prior securities are not discharged, but this is really a theoretical point. For one thing, if there is more than one security the sale is normally by the first-ranked creditor anyway. Moreover, if the sale were by a postponed creditor, the proceeds would have to be paid in the first instance to the first creditor in terms of section 27, so that security would be discharged by payment.

[85] *Newcastle Building Society* v. *White*, 1987 S.L.T. (Sh. Ct.) 81.

[86] See G.L. Gretton, *Law of Inhibition and Adjudication* for discussion and reference to cases.

[87] Assuming that there is a surplus on sale.

[88] *Lord Advocate* v. *Bank of India*, 1991 S.C.L.R. 320.

[89] *Abbey National Building Society* v. *Barclays Bank plc*, 1990 S.C.L.R. 639. It is, perhaps, open to argument whether this decision is correct.

CHAPTER 13

PREPARING THE SECURITY DOCUMENTATION

The role of the solicitor

The lender needs a solicitor, firstly to check the title to the property and secondly to ensure that the security documentation is properly prepared. Does the lender use the borrower's solicitor or someone else? This is for the lender to decide but in practice for domestic house purchase mortgages the lender normally uses the borrower's solicitor. The benefits are that matters are speeded up because the papers do not have to go back and forth between two separate lawyers, and that it works out cheaper because things are checked only once. The latter benefits the borrower too because he is liable to reimburse the lender for legal fees.[1] It is important to bear in mind that where the borrower's solicitor is also acting in this way for the lender, he has two clients, not one, and owes duties, contractual and professional, to both. Sometimes, the solicitor feels loyalty to his "real" client, the borrower, and is tempted to overlook his duties to his other client, the lender. This temptation must be resisted. For instance, suppose that it emerges that the title to a property is open to question. The purchaser/borrower is prepared to go ahead. Fair enough. But the lender's interests are at stake too. If there is default and the lender has to sell, a defect in title may cause problems, in which case the lender will expect the lawyer to compensate him for any consequent loss.

Setting up the mortgage

Sometimes the client already has a mortgage informally agreed with a lender before he comes to see his solicitor. If so, well and good,

[1] 1970 Act, Sched. 3, para. 12. Under general law, the lender is normally liable to the solicitor for the fee for the security, with the right to recover from the borrower. But some lenders nowadays have a clause in their letter to the solicitor disclaiming such liability, so that the solicitor must recover his fee, if at all, from the borrower direct.

though one should still check that he really knows what he is doing. For instance, he may have been persuaded to take on an endowment mortgage without really knowing what that means. If he does not yet know where he is to obtain his loan, it is for the solicitor to set one up for him, through the latter's knowledge of the current mortgage market.

The lender may want to see the borrower in person, and in any event will ask him to fill in a form giving personal and financial details. As to the latter he will usually either have to produce recent payslips or authorise the lender to contact his employer's wages office. Assuming that all is well, the lender will indicate, informally, willingness to lend up to a figure based on status.

At the first or second meeting with the client the financial details should be gone through, so that both agent and client are quite clear how the figures are going to work out. This will usually involve the sale of his present house too. Once the solicitor has worked out how much the client can afford to offer, he notes interest in the house and phones the lender to instruct a valuation survey.[2] This will be reported back to the solicitor by phone usually next day[3] and a written copy normally follows, bristling with liability disclaimers. The survey report will contain comments about the property and will conclude with a valuation. The client has to pay for this survey of course, but will do this direct.[4] If the offer is successful, the solicitor notifies the lender, who then issues a formal offer of loan to the client. Note that this is not issued until the offer for purchase has been made and accepted and so in theory there is a risk that the client might be committed to the purchase without having a guarantee of finance. But this risk is slight. In practice, the only case where a lender refuses to go ahead after informally agreeing is where it turns out that the client has misled the lender as to his financial position.

The formal offer of loan may be sent by the lender direct to the client, or may be routed through the solicitor. The client then accepts it and posts it back to the lender. The solicitor should check that the client has returned it to the lender. There are, however, some lenders who do not bother with a formal offer at all. At

[2] There is a useful treatment of mortgage surveys in D.J. Cusine, *Standard Securities*, chap. 1.

[3] The "verbal report" or "verbal" for short.

[4] The client may also wish to have his own survey done.

about this time the lender also sends, either direct to the client or through the solicitor, the MIRAS form.[5] This is the tax form which the lender will process and then send on to the Inland Revenue. Once again, the solicitor will not normally be involved directly in this.

The lender will then write to the solicitor formally instructing him to act. It is from this moment that the solicitor has two clients, not one. This letter contains various bits and pieces. One is the letter of instruction itself. Next there is a Report on Title with blanks to be filled in. After examining the title, the solicitor completes the report and returns it to the lender. Next, there is a standard security with blanks. The standard security is preprinted in the lender's preferred form. Thus, a solicitor does not very often have to draft complete standard securities himself. This standard security is usually in duplicate. One is used as a draft and the other for the final version. Next, if this is to be an endowment mortgage there will be a preprinted assignation of the life policy, with blanks, once again in duplicate. Then there will be a copy of the lender's Schedule of Variations. This means variations to the standard conditions, for which see below. This should be examined and passed on to the borrower. Next, there is, in the case of a building society, a copy of the Rules of the Society. This is important because the borrower will automatically become a member, with voting rights, etc. Again, this should be passed on to the borrower. Lastly, there will be a Schedule of Writs. This is a bit of paper, mainly blank, on which will eventually be entered a list of all the title deeds. This is sent to the lender with the deeds after completion of the transaction. A copy should be retained, so that the file will show what deeds are held by the lender. Sometimes, depending on the circumstances, other documentation may also be needed. For instance, the lender might require a guarantee from a third party.

The solicitor must check the documentation on behalf of his client, and bring to his attention anything which is significant, especially anything which he might one day blame the solicitor for not telling him. For instance, if the mortgage provides for an early redemption penalty[6] it is important that the client be told this. It

[5] Mortgage interest relief at source. The current form is MIRAS 70.

[6] *i.e.* a surcharge payable if the borrower wishes to pay off the loan before the end of the term. See chap. 11.

is also a good idea to draw to the client's attention other matters, such as that letting the property is not allowed without the consent of the lender.[7]

At this stage there is normally a quiet period on the security front. Missives may not even have been completed by the time that the lender's letter of instruction is received. If the title has yet to be seen, it will not be possible to draft the standard security. In addition, the endowment policy has very likely not yet been issued so that the assignation cannot be drafted yet. These things are done as soon as they can be done. A delay in the issuing of the endowment policy can cause problems, so if necessary the solicitor must chase up the life office. During all this time the solicitor is, of course, progressing the conveyancing.

Once the standard security and, if applicable, the assignation have been drafted and then engrossed, the engrossments are sent to the client for execution.[8] This should be done several days before settlement. Neither the standard security nor the assignation need to be executed by the lender, perhaps surprisingly. A few days before settlement the completed Report on Title is sent to the lender. This states that the title is good (if it is good), and draws attention to any points which the solicitor thinks the lender should know. Payment of the loan is requested at the same time. This is called requisitioning the loan cheque, since in practice the loan is generally released by cheque. The lender sends the cheque to the solicitor not to the borrower, and the cheque is drawn in favour of the solicitor. The cheque will normally come back by return of post. The cheque is paid into the firm's account and the proceeds credited to the client. Now settlement can take place. It is important to note that if after requisitioning the cheque a major problem crops up, such as a significant delay in settlement, the solicitor must notify the lender. Thus, if there is a delay in settlement for more than a few days the lender will want the money back again for the period until settlement does take place.

After settlement the standard security[9] must be sent off without delay for registration, together with the disposition. The fee

[7] 1970 Act, Sched. 3, Standard Condition 6.

[8] It is preferable, if possible, to have the client come to the office to sign deeds. This ensures that mistakes are not made in the execution.

[9] With a completed warrant of registration, except in Land Register cases.

charged by Register House for a standard security is smaller if the security accompanies a disposition. If there is an assignation of a life policy, the formal intimation must be sent to the life office. This too must be done immediately after settlement.

Some lenders wish to receive the title deeds at this stage. But nowadays many lenders are happy to wait until all the deeds are available. The point is that the disposition, the standard security and the search will all take several months—maybe even a year—to come back from Register House. So instead of getting things in two instalments, many lenders are prepared to wait until everything can be sent at once. The letter of instruction from the lender will have made clear which procedure the lender prefers. If at some future stage the deeds are needed again, they can be borrowed from the lender. In Land Register cases, the lender should be sent the land certificate and the charge certificate.

Procedure for other types of mortgage, such as second mortgages and commercial mortgages, is rather different. There the work is normally divided between the borrower's solicitor and a separate solicitor instructed by the lender.

Searches

Searches are dealt with in chapter 7, but a few points are specifically connected with standard securities. In a typical conveyancing transaction the personal search[10] covers both the purchaser and the seller. Usually, if a problem arises it is because there is something in the search affecting the seller, but the purchaser's solicitor needs to check the search against his own client as well as against the seller. The reason is that he has to make sure that the lender is going to get a good security. It occasionally emerges that the purchaser is an undischarged bankrupt, surprising though this may seem, and has failed to disclose this fact to his solicitor. Naturally, no lender will go ahead and make a loan to an undischarged bankrupt. So when acting for a buyer it is important to check the interim report in relation to the buyer/borrower as well as the seller. For the same reason, if the borrower is a company, a company search, including interim report, will be needed.

One particular issue is whether a fresh personal search should

[10] Or its land registration equivalents—Forms 10 to 13.

be made for a further advance. The counsel of perfection is that it should be. There is some uncertainty as to whether a supervening inhibition could affect a further advance,[11] but at all events if there is an inhibition the agent for the lender will wish to know that fact. And, obviously, if the borrower has been sequestrated, the further advance must be refused. The personal search will disclose sequestration as well as inhibition. If the party seeking a further advance is a company, a new company search should preferably be obtained for similar reasons. However, in practice a new search is often not obtained prior to the release of a further advance. Indeed, very often the advance is made without the lender using a solicitor at all.

Finances of moving house

In a typical case a seller has to pay: (1) the price of the new house; (2) the outstanding loan on old house; and (3) expenses such as legal expenses and flitting costs. Into his hands will be coming two sums: (1) the price of old house, and (2) the loan for new house. One of the tasks of the solicitor is to ensure that the two sides will balance.

In a majority of cases the mortgage on the old house is an endowment mortgage. If the client is buying a more expensive house, this will normally entail obtaining a top-up endowment policy to make up the difference. Thus, X in 1983 gets a 25–year endowment mortgage for £30,000. In 1993 he wants to move and take on a £40,000 mortgage. In that case he will normally need to buy an additional endowment life policy for a cover of £10,000 with a 15–year maturity. He could, of course, switch to a repayment mortgage but the financial realities usually preclude this.

Mortgage interest tax relief[12]

Public policy is that home ownership should be encouraged, and this is done by tax relief. Of course, this is a matter of political

[11] For discussion see G.L. Gretton, *Law of Inhibition and Adjudication.*

[12] The current statutory provisions are ss. 353 to 379 of the Income and Corporation Taxes Act 1988. Note that some of the rules have changed over the years and some older mortgages continue to be governed by repealed provisions. In the text, we state the law for mortgages currently being taken out.

controversy, and the modern view tends to be that tax relief is a bad idea. In effect, it is being phased out by keeping the ceiling for relief at £30,000. Ten years ago most mortgages were within this limit. Nowadays most exceed it. In other words, inflation is being allowed to reduce the tax perk. Some people want to see mortgage tax relief abolished outright. The following is a mere outline and fuller accounts will be found in specialist texts on revenue law.

Only mortgage interest is tax deductible, and not capital repayments. For this reason an interest-only mortgage, such as an endowment mortgage, is rather more tax-efficient than a repayment mortgage, at any rate in the later period of the loan. The mortgage must be for the taxpayer's main residence, so that, for instance, commercial property and second homes receive no tax benefit. The loan must have been taken out for the purchase of the house, and so a loan for home improvements will not qualify.[13] Relief is limited to £30,000. If a client's mortgage is £25,000, he gets full relief, while if it is for £35,000, he gets relief on the interest payments which relate to the first £30,000. The £30,000 ceiling applies to the property itself. Thus, suppose that a husband and wife buy a house in common and both are liable under the mortgage. They cannot claim the relief twice over. Tax relief is confined to basic rate liability (25 per cent.), so that in effect the interest is set off against that part of a borrower's income which is taxed at the basic rate. (Most borrowers do not pay higher rate tax anyway.) If proposals contained in the 1993 Budget speech are implemented, tax relief will be reduced to 20 per cent. from 1994–1995.[13a]

In the old days the system was that the borrower paid the lender whatever was payable and then looked to the Inland Revenue for the relief. The relief would normally be given in the form of lower PAYE. But in 1982 the system was changed when MIRAS[14] was introduced. Under the MIRAS system the relief is built into the monthly payments to the lender. So the monthly payments are smaller than they would otherwise be. Hence, the relief does not appear in the calculation of PAYE. The lender is thus being under-

[13] If the loan is partly to finance the purchase and partly for other purposes, tax relief is available on the former element.

[13a] The plan is to introduce this change in the 1994 Finance Bill.

[14] Mortgage interest relief at source.

paid, but the Revenue makes a compensating payment to the lender. The net result is the same as before 1982, but is achieved in a different way. Not all lenders participate in the MIRAS scheme but most do. If the lender is not in MIRAS, the tax relief is given in the pre-1982 manner. A simple example will explain the system. Suppose that a client has a £50,000 mortgage at a 10 per cent interest rate. The annual interest payable on the first £30,000 is £3,000. Tax relief at 25 per cent on this is £750. He therefore pays each year £2,250 on this element and the full £2,000 per annum on the balance, a total annual payment of £4,250. The lender receives an annual payment of £750 from the Inland Revenue.

Gross-profile and constant-net

In a repayment mortgage, the amount of tax relief will decline over the years, because the relief is available only on the interest element and not on the capital element. Hence, the net monthly repayment figure, after tax adjustment, rises over the years. This is called a gross-profile repayment mortgage. However, this arrangement is now unusual, and many lenders no longer offer it, though it can be of value to the client who wishes to keep his repayments low in the early years. Most repayment mortgages are now of the constant-net type. Here, the monthly repayment is constant throughout the term (apart from changes in the interest rate.) In the earlier years the amount is higher than in a gross-profile mortgage, and in the later years it is lower. The mathematical calculations are complex, but lenders have computers to do the job. The distinction is relevant only to repayment mortgages, for in other types tax relief remains constant.

Leaseholds

Few residential properties are held on leases of substantial duration, and indeed since 1974 it has been effectively impossible to create long leases of residential property.[15] But a small number of older properties are held on leasehold title. The term "leasehold," though strictly an anglicism, means a long lease (over 20 years) registered in the Sasine Register or in the Land Register.[16]

[15] 1974 Act, Pt. II.
[16] Registration of Leases (Scotland) Act 1857, as amended.

A mortgage over a leasehold title is created by standard security, just as with a *dominium utile*.[17] Obviously the lender's agent must check the terms of the lease, on such matters as length, onerous conditions, irritancy, landlord's consent to transactions, and rent. (The latter is usually nominal for residential long leases.) Normally, there is no need to verify the validity of the landlord's title, because even if it was defective when the lease was granted the leasehold title will itself normally have been fortified by positive prescription. Because mortgages of residential leaseholds are uncommon we will not deal with them further. In commercial conveyancing, standard securities over leases are common.

What about tenants?

Sometimes an owner wants to let to a tenant. There are two pitfalls here. One is that he might thereby lose his tax relief on his mortgage in as much as the property might cease to be his principle residence.[18] The other is that the lender must approve.[19] In practice, however, this latter requirement is often ignored. A tenancy given without the heritable creditor's consent is voidable.[20]

Redemption

Redemption usually happens on a resale, but can occur in two other ways. One is that the borrower may one day find himself with enough money to pay off the loan early. The other is that the mortgage runs for its envisaged duration (25 years or as the case may be) and is thereby paid off.

On redemption, a discharge of the standard security must be drafted and engrossed and sent to the lender for execution. It is then returned and sent for registration. If there is a life policy still in the hands of the lender, a retrocession (*i.e.* reassignation) must also be executed by the lender, and a formal intimation of retrocession must be sent to the life office.

If the mortgage is, as usually happens, being redeemed before

[17] See the 1970 Act, s. 9(2) and s. 9(8)(*b*).

[18] There is also the danger that he might lose CGT exemption for a similar reason.

[19] 1970 Act, Sched. 3, Standard Condition 6.

[20] *Trade Development Bank* v. *Warriner and Mason (Scotland) Ltd.*, 1980 S.C. 74.

term, a statement must be obtained from the lender stating the amount outstanding. This is called a redemption statement.[21] Normally it is produced by the lender's computer. Sometimes there is a delay in redemption, in which case it may be necessary to ask for an updated redemption statement. The lender may make a surcharge for redemption before term, such as, for example, three months extra interest. This depends on which lender and which type of mortgage. Such a surcharge should not come as a surprise to the client, for he should have been told about it by his solicitor when he took on the loan.

In the typical case where the redemption is on resale, the purchaser's solicitor will want to see a draft of the discharge before it is engrossed. This is one of the standard seller's drafts which the seller's solicitor will send off as soon as missives are concluded. On the other hand the purchaser's solicitor will not want to see the retrocession (if applicable) because that has nothing to do with the title to the house.

Although the endowment policy will be retrocessed on redemption, in most cases it will have to be assigned again in connection with the new mortgage on the new house. The practice is to go through this rigmarole even if the same lender is involved in both mortgages.

If the redemption is on sale, there is a theoretical problem. The purchaser will not settle unless the existing mortgage is discharged, since he is entitled to a property free of incumbrances. On the other hand the lender will not discharge the mortgage until the loan is paid off, and the loan cannot be paid off until the price has been received from the purchaser, because the price will be the fund from which redemption can be made. So how is the circle squared? The usual solution is that the seller's agent has the discharge executed by the lender in advance of settlement, but holds it on behalf of the lender, so it is for the moment undelivered. At settlement he shows it to the purchaser's solicitor and includes in the letter of obligation an undertaking to register it. Alternatively, he delivers it to the purchaser's solicitor who then registers it. The loan is then repaid the same day from the proceeds of sale.

Section 18 of the 1970 Act has a provision whereby the debtor

[21] Occasionally, where there is acute time pressure, the solicitor relies on a statement given by phone, but this is obviously risky.

serves a notice of redemption on the creditor intimating that he intends to redeem, the notice period being two months. The meaning and effect of these provisions are unclear. The timetable for repayment is a matter for agreement, and if the debt is paid off in accordance with the agreement no question of serving any notice can arise. If the debtor wishes to repay earlier than has been agreed, it is for the creditor to decide whether or not to accept such early redemption. The debtor cannot compel him to accept it, for at common law a debtor cannot, any more than the creditor, insist on early repayment.[22] Either way round, it is not easy to see where a notice of redemption could be applicable. Equally, if the security is for an on-demand loan, the common law is that the debtor can repay at any time. These theoretical considerations receive practical support from the fact that notices of redemption are, it seems, never used.

Redemption—a trap

It would be natural to suppose that if the client pays the lender the amount outstanding on the mortgage, plus any early redemption penalty, the lender will discharge the security. And in 99 cases out of 100 that would be right. But occasionally one finds that the client owes money to the same lender under another contract. For instance, the client might have a mortgage with a bank and also have an overdraft. The standard security will in practice be so devised as to secure the overdraft as well as the mortgage debt.[23] Hence, if the bank is offered the amount due under the mortgage, it can still refuse to discharge the security so long as the overdraft remains in existence. Usually where this happens the amounts due under the other contract are not large, and either they can be paid off, or the lender can be persuaded to discharge the security anyway. Indeed, usually lenders in this situation are happy to cooperate, though they will often insist that the new mortgage (on

[22] There are provisions for early repayment under the Consumer Credit Act 1974. In practice, however, creditors are usually happy to accept early payment, regardless of whether they are so obliged. The Redemption of Standard Securities (Scotland) Act 1971 made it clear that the right to redeem is subject to the agreement between the parties.

[23] Because the standard security will cover all sums due by that debtor to that creditor.

the new house) is with them as well. The reason for this is that the new standard security will then cover the existing overdraft or whatever in addition to the new mortgage loan. But occasionally problems crop up, most often where the client is in business, and so likely to have borrowed from the lender to finance his business. A creditor is normally entitled to refuse to discharge a security not only if there is an additional debt, such as an overdraft, but also if the client is liable to the lender on a guarantee (bond of caution). For instance Smith is director and chief shareholder of Smith Ltd. Smith Ltd. has an overdraft with the bank, for which Smith has—as is usual in such cases—given the bank a guarantee. The bank would (subject to certain qualifications) be entitled to refuse to grant a discharge of the security for Smith's mortgage so long as the overdraft was in place.

Ideally, one should therefore (1) ask the client whether he has any other debts to the lender, apart from the mortgage, or any guarantees, and (2) when asking the lender for a redemption statement ask them to confirm that there are no liabilities other than the mortgage debt.

Chapter 14

ASSIGNATIONS

Introduction

Assignation means the transfer of incorporeal property. For instance, debts, intellectual property rights and insurance policies are transferred by assignation. Some types of assignation are subject to special rules. Thus, there are special rules on the assignation of standard securities.[1] There are also special rules on the assignation of intellectual property rights,[2] of leases,[3] and of company shares, the latter being regulated by the Stock Transfer Act 1963.[4] This chapter considers the general law of assignation, and also the special rules applying to the assignation of life policies. Mandates will also be mentioned.

Assignation is a conveyance, and the reasons for it are as varied as for any other type of conveyance. Thus, it may be in implement of a sale contract, where the holder of the right sells it to another person, or by way of gift and so forth.

General law of outright assignation[5]

Assignation has two steps, namely the deed of assignation and the intimation. The deed of assignation should be probative and should contain words of conveyance, such as "do hereby assign." There is a statutory style in the Transmission of Moveable Property

[1] See chap. 12.

[2] See vol. 18 of the *Stair Memorial Encyclopaedia.*

[3] See Halliday, vol. 3.

[4] Though such transfers are not called "assignations," they are in fact a special type of assignation. A new system for the transfer of shares in quoted companies (the TAURUS system) was to be introduced pursuant to s. 207 of the Companies Act 1989 but has recently been abandoned.

[5] This chapter cannot give a full account of this complex area of law. See Halliday, chap. 7; W.W. McBryde, *Contract*, chap. 17; and *Stair Memorial Encyclopaedia*, vol. 18, paras. 652–662.

(Scotland) Act 1862[6] which is optional but which is in general use. But case law shows that the courts have a lenient attitude as to the style.[7] The question of how intimation is made is a complex one, but in practice the postal method authorised by the 1862 Act is used.[8] The 1862 Act says that to the intimation there should be attached a copy of the assignation. Nowadays, this can be a photocopy.[9] The intimation need not be probative and in practice normally is not. The intimation is made by the assignee or by his solicitors.[10] The 1862 Act does not give a style. In practice, the style is much the same as for intimations of assignations of life policies, for which see below. Because of the importance of intimation, evidence of it is desirable. The usual course is to ask the debtor to acknowledge receipt of the intimation.

The right assigned legally passes at the time of intimation.[11] Thus, suppose that Mary gives Peter a personal bond for £10,000 and Peter assigns this to Anne on June 1. Anne intimates to Mary on June 3 but on the previous day Henry, a creditor of Peter, arrests in the hands of Mary. At the date of the arrestment the bond still belongs to Peter and so the arrestment attaches it, and thus prevails over the right of Anne. This is a vitally important principle.

Another vitally important point is the rule *assignatus utitur jure auctoris*, which means that the debtor (Mary in our example) can plead against the assignee (Anne) any defences which she could have pled against the cedent or assignor (Peter). Thus, if Peter obtained the bond from Mary by fraud, Mary could plead the fraud as a defence to Anne, even though the latter took the bond from Peter for value and in good faith.

In many cases it is preferable to embody a debt obligation not in a personal bond but in a negotiable instrument such as a promis-

[6] s. 1. See Halliday, paras. 7–07 to 7–11 for examples based on this statute.

[7] See, *e.g.*, *Laurie* v. *Ogilvy*, 6 Feb. 1810, Fac. Coll.; *Carter* v. *McIntosh* (1862) 24 D. 925; *Brownlee* v. *Robb*, 1907 S.C. 1302

[8] To what extent informal intimation is valid is, as Professor McBryde says, "one of the long slow burning questions in the law." (McBryde, *Contract*, para. 17–110.)

[9] The Act says that the copy must be "certified as correct" but does not say by whom. In practice, intimations are usually by the assignee's solicitors, who do the certification.

[10] It can, however, be made by the cedent: *Libertas-Kommerz GmbH* v. *Johnson*, 1977 S.C. 191. But this may be questioned.

[11] Stair, III, i, 6.

sory note or a bill of exchange. The main reasons are that intimation of transfer is not necessary, and that the *assignatus utitur* rule does not apply. Thus, in the first example, if Mary had given Peter a promissory note, Anne's right would prevail over Henry's. And in the second example, if this had been a promissory note, Anne would be unaffected by Peter's fraud, assuming that she was in good faith.[12]

General law of assignation in security

Incorporeal property can, as well as being assigned outright, be assigned in security. The idea is that the assignee holds the property as a security for a debt owed to him by the cedent. If the debt is repaid, the assignee will assign the property back to the cedent: this is called retrocession. If the debt is not repaid, the assignee realises the property. Thus, suppose in the example that Peter assigned the bond to Anne as a security for a debt owed by him to her. If he defaults, Anne could enforce the bond against Mary. Or Anne could sell the bond. An assignation in security makes the assignee the legal holder of the incorporeal. The cedent is legally divested.[13] Thus, suppose that the bond provides for repayment by instalments. Mary would pay these instalments to Anne, not to Peter, for as long as Anne continued to be the legal bondholder. Of course the assignee in such a case is under a duty to account to the cedent for moneys received, for the assignee cannot recover more than he is owed by the cedent. Thus, if a bond for £10,000 were assigned in security of a debt for £7,000, and the assignee is paid the £10,000 by the debtor in the bond, the assignee must return the excess of £3,000 to the cedent.

Assignations in security are nowadays not very common except for life policies, for which see below. The form of an assignation in security is similar to that of an outright assignation.

Assignations of life policies

Like other rights, life policies can be assigned either absolutely or in security. There is a simple statutory style in the Policies of Assur-

[12] Because she would be a holder in due course: Bills of Exchange Act 1882, ss. 29 and 38(2).

[13] Contrast, *e.g.*, a standard security, where, despite the security, the debtor remains legally the owner of the property.

ance Act 1867,[14] which is optional, but in practice is followed. The Act calls the intimation "notice of assignment" but does not give a style.[15] It does, however, require the life office to issue written acknowledgement of receipt of intimation on payment of a fee of 25 pence.[16] The usual practice is to send the intimation in duplicate, asking the life office to return one copy with an acknowledgement of receipt on it.

An assignation is security, whether of a life policy or not, can be either in the form of an outright assignation, (*i.e.* an *ex facie* absolute assignation coupled with a separate document setting forth that it is truly only an assignation in security[17]) or an assignation expressly in security.[18] The latter seems more common in practice, at least for life policies.

Retrocession

Life policies are frequently assigned in security in connection with endowment mortgages.[19] When the loan is paid off the policy is then retrocessed. It must not be overlooked that the retrocession requires to be intimated in the same way as the original assignation. In most cases, the mortgage loan is paid off not on maturity, but on a sale, and the seller will be using the same policy as a security for his next mortgage. So the retrocession will have to be followed immediately by a new assignation. This is done even where the same lender is involved in both the old and the new mortgage. Thus, the Halifax may retrocess a life policy to Mr Smith, with intimation to Standard Life, immediately followed by a new assignation by Mr Smith to the Halifax, with a new intimation to Standard Life. All this must be done in the right order. In principle, there is no reason why it should be done this way. If the lender remains the same it seems perfectly safe to leave the policy in its original assigned state, provided that the original assignation is so framed

[14] s. 5. For an example based on this style see Halliday, para. 7–31.

[15] For a style see Halliday, para. 7–35 and D.J. Cusine, *Standard Securities*, para. 2–07.

[16] This figure has not been increased since 1867 and nowadays, being trivial, is not charged.

[17] See Halliday, para. 7–60 for an example.

[18] See Halliday, paras. 7–58 and 7–59 for examples.

[19] See chaps. 11 to 13.

as to cover all debts, present and future, due by Mr Smith to the Halifax. But the practice is to retrocess and then assign once again.

Implications of divestiture

Where incorporeal property is assigned in security, the assignee becomes the legal holder and owner of the property. This can be a significant point in a number of contexts. Two will be mentioned here. In the first place, suppose that Mr Smith is "gathered to his fathers" while the mortgage is still outstanding. In that case the policy matures. Standard Life owe the whole maturity value, bonuses and all, to the Halifax. This is so even if, as will normally be the case, the total maturity value is greater than the mortgage debt due by Mr Smith to the Halifax. The Halifax will pay themselves what they are owed out of the proceeds. The surplus value is then owed by them to Mr Smith's executors.[20] Thus, although the surplus value belongs to Mr Smith's estate, it is not owed to the estate by Standard Life. Standard Life owe nothing to Mr Smith's estate because although Mr Smith was the life assured, he was not the legal holder of the policy. The surplus value is owed to Mr Smith's estate by the Halifax. And of course they will pay it over to the executor[21] without fuss.

The second point concerns postponed securities. Mr Smith (whom we will now suppose to have recovered from his life-threatening illness) is not now the policy holder. He only has a reversionary right. But his reversionary right itself has a value, namely, the surplus value over and above the mortgage debt. Mr Smith may wish to assign this reversionary right to X, and he may wish to do this either outright or in security. Since the reversionary right is itself incorporeal property, it can be assigned. To whom should intimation be made? Not to Standard Life. Why? Because Mr Smith is not, technically speaking, assigning the policy. He is not, at present, the owner of the policy, so of course he cannot assign it. He is assigning his reversionary right, which is a personal right not against Standard Life but against the Halifax. Therefore intimation should be made to the Halifax.[22] Assignations of rever-

[20] Assuming that the reversionary right to the policy was vested in Mr Smith at his death.

[21] Once he has been confirmed by the sheriff.

[22] See *Ayton* v. *Romanes* (1895) 3 S.L.T. 303.

sionary rights are not common but they are occasionally encountered. The effect is to vest the reversion in X. For example, suppose that Mr Smith assigns to the Halifax, and later assigns the reversion to X in security of a debt due by Smith to X. Smith then succumbs to the grim reaper. The policy has a final maturity value of £80,000. The mortgage debt is £50,000. The debt due by Smith to X is £20,000. What happens is as follows. Standard Life pay £80,000 to the Halifax. Standard Life are now out of the picture. The Halifax take £50,000. The surplus of £30,000 they pay over to the owner of the reversion, X. The Halifax are now out of the picture. X takes £20,000. X then pays over the value of the sub-reversionary right, namely £10,000, to Mr Smith's executor. Everyone is now happy, including, presumably, the late Mr Smith.

Personal bond aspect

An assignation in security is a security for a debt, and so, of course, there should be a bond setting forth the terms of the loan contract. This can be done *in gremio* of the assignation itself,[23] but usually the loan contract will be in another document, such as a personal bond or a 1970 Act Form A standard security. In that case the assignation should simply refer to that other document.[24]

Enforcement clause

If Mr Smith lives and keeps up his payments,[25] the question of enforcement does not arise. Nor does it arise if Mr Smith dies, for in that case the maturity value is paid direct to the creditor. The question of enforcement arises if Mr Smith, while alive, defaults on his payments to the Halifax. In that case the Halifax will, in all probability, not seek to enforce its security over the policy, but will enforce the standard security over the house, by sale. This will normally pay off the debt, and the policy can then be retrocessed. But the Halifax wish to have the possibility of enforcement against

[23] See, *e.g.*, Halliday, paras. 7–58 and 7–59.

[24] See, *e.g.*, J.H. Sinclair, *Handbook of Conveyancing Practice* (2nd ed.), p. 215.

[25] *i.e.* the payments secured by the assignation in security. This will typically secure all sums due. Failure to keep up the premiums to the life office is typically made an event of default.

the policy, for otherwise they would not have insisted on the assignation in the first place. This would be important if, for instance, the market value of the house proved to be smaller than the debt due. A security over a life policy can be enforced in two ways, by surrender and by sale. In a surrender, the policy holder (the Halifax) renounces the policy and in exchange the life office makes a payment, called the surrender value. In a sale, the policy is auctioned. Someone will buy it as an investment, taking the benefit when eventually Mr Smith dies.

The right to enforce by surrender or sale is implied in an assignation, but in most cases these rights are also conferred expressly.[26] Obviously, enforcement cannot happen unless the borrower defaults on the loan, but normally one would wish to ensure that the right to sell or surrender the policy did not emerge instantly upon default. Otherwise a borrower might be one day late in making his monthly mortgage payment and find that the next day, without telling him, the lender had sold his policy. A warning period, such as seven days, is thus sometimes written in. In practice, however, assignations are often silent on the matter, but the risk is small, because lenders are seldom in a hurry to sell or surrender a life policy.

Mandates

The term "mandate" has a number of meanings. In conveyancing practice it usually means an instruction by a client (A) to his solicitor (B) to pay, out of moneys belonging to A which come into B's hands, to C, who is a creditor of A. For example, suppose that A is buying a house and there is a delay in obtaining his building society loan. A arranges with his bank (C) for bridging finance. As a condition of this, the bank has A sign a "mandate," which is a letter signed by A and addressed to B (A's solicitor), requiring B to pay to C the proceeds of the building society loan as and when this is received by B.[27] This gives the bank a certain degree of

[26] It will often be found that these provisions are written into the Schedule of Variations attached to the standard security. The assignation of the policy then simply has a short clause referring to the Schedule of Variations.

[27] The building society will make over the loan moneys not directly to A but to A's solicitor.

security that they will be repaid. Or the bank may obtain a mandate for the payment of the proceeds of the sale of the old house. The mandate will be expressed to be irrevocable without the consent of the bank (C). Sometimes the bank will ask the solicitor to confirm that he will honour the mandate, but in general this request should be resisted, since it comes close to being a cautionary obligation on behalf of the client.

An obvious question is whether such mandates amount to an assignation of the future proceeds of the building society loan or of the sale. The question can arise in a number of circumstances. One example would be where another creditor of the client served an arrestment on the solicitor, thereby attaching funds held for the client. The answer to this question is far from clear.[28] To avoid the difficulty, some banks use a document which is in the form of an assignation,[29] rather than a mandate.[30] If a mandate has been used, and a problem arises as to its effect (*e.g.* where there has been an arrestment), the solicitor should refuse to release any money except on the basis of an agreed settlement between all interested parties. If such agreement cannot be arrived at, a multiplepoinding may be unavoidable.

[28] The subject is highly complex. For an introduction, see *National Commercial Bank* v. *Millar's Tr.*, 1964 S.L.T. (Notes) 57. If the mandate amounts to an assignation it will still not defeat an arrestment unless it has been intimated prior to the arrestment.

[29] In particular, using the words "do hereby assign."

[30] Although this is intended to avoid the difficulty, it runs into further problems about whether a future thing (*i.e.* the proceeds of a loan not yet in the hands of the solicitor) can competently be assigned. On this see G.L. Gretton at 1993 J.R. 23.

CHAPTER 15

EXECUTION OF DEEDS

Introduction[1]

The general principle is that the creation, transfer or extinction of real rights in land must be done by formally executed deeds, and moreover contracts (such as missives) for such deeds must themselves be in formal writing. As far as ordinary execution by individuals is concerned,[2] there are two basic methods, namely attestation (signature of the grantor and of two witnesses) and holograph (signature of the grantor, and the deed itself in his handwriting.)

Attestation

Attestation is governed by what are called the authentication statutes, namely the Subscription of Deeds Acts 1540, 1579 and 1681, and the Deeds Act 1696. Though the first two of these statutes remain nominally in force, they were effectively superseded by the 1681 Act, which provides that: "only subscribing witnesses . . . shall be probative . . . and that all such writs . . . wherein the writer[3] and witnesses are not designed shall be null . . . and . . . no witness shall subscribe as witness to any party's subscription unless he then know that party and saw him subscribe . . . or that the party did at the time of the witness subscribing acknowledge his subscription."

The witnesses must be fully *capax*.[4] It is no objection that the

[1] On this subject see Halliday, vol. I, chap. 3; A.G. Walker and N.M.L. Walker, *Law of Evidence in Scotland*; the Scottish Law Commission Consultative Memorandum No. 66 (1985) on *Constitution and Proof of Voluntary Obligations and Authentication of Writings* and their subsequent Report No. 112 (1988) on *Requirements of Writing*. For some practical aspects see K.G.C. Reid at 1987 J.L.S. 148.

[2] Execution by companies and delegated execution are considered later.

[3] The need to name the writer of the deed was abolished by s. 38 of the 1874 Act. Nowadays, of course, deeds are typed or word-processed.

[4] In the case of young people, this now means aged 16 or over: Age of Legal Capacity (Scotland) Act 1991, s. 1(1)(*b*). For the definition of "transaction" see s. 9.

witness is married to or related to the grantor, and in the case of a will it is no objection that a witness is a beneficiary.[5] The witnesses must know the grantor, but the standard here is not high.[6] A witness must either see the grantor sign or hear him later acknowledge that the signature is his.[7] It is perfectly proper for one witness to do the former and the other the latter. Thus, the witnesses might never meet. The witness must sign immediately[8] after the event which he has witnessed, although very short delays will not be fatal. If the acknowledgement route is taken, there is no time limit between the grantor's signature and those of the witnesses: in such a case the time limit is as between the acknowledgement and the signature of the witness. The witness is witness only to the fact of subscription and not to the content of the deed, of which, indeed, he is in practice often ignorant.

The Act of 1681 requires that the witnesses be designed. This is normally done in the testing clause, but the designations can also be added after the signatures at any time before the deed is founded on in court or registered for preservation.[9] A sufficient designation is the full name and address.[10]

The grantor and witnesses must sign on the last page. Formerly, the grantor (but not the witnesses) had to sign each sheet,[11] but this is now necessary only for wills.[12] There is, it seems, no requirement that plans or schedules be signed, but in practice they are signed by the granter (only), and this is a convenient way of identi-

[5] *Simsons* v. *Simsons* (1883) 10 R. 1247. In practice, however, it is preferable that the witnesses have no special connection with the grantor or with the subject matter. This is to reduce the danger of various sorts of fraud.

[6] *Brock* v. *Brock*, 1908 S.C. 964.

[7] Occasionally a solicitor will, after a client has left, ask a clerk or a trainee to sign a deed as witness. This is quite improper, and the request should be refused.

[8] See *Thompson* v. *Clarkson's Trs.* (1892) 20 R. 59 (delay of an hour). In *Walker* v. *Whitwell*, 1916 S.C. (HL) 75 signature by the witness after the grantor's death was held invalid.

[9] 1874 Act, s. 38.

[10] The test of designation is whether the person can be identified. In *Grant* v. *Keir* (1694) Mor. 16913 the designation "indweller in Edinburgh" was sustained.

[11] Deeds Act 1696. The rule was signature on each sheet, and not, as is sometimes supposed, signature on each page.

[12] 1970 Act, s. 44. Because of this change, it is possible to substitute any page except the last. This is the crime of forgery, even if done for some innocent reason, such as to rectify a clerical error.

fying them ("being the subjects delineated in red on the plan annexed and signed as relative hereto"). It is normal to have a short docket above the signature, *e.g.* "This is the plan referred to in the foregoing disposition."

Signature

An Act of 1672[13] provides that parties should "subscrive their Christned names or the initiall letter therof with their Sirnames."[14] In 1672 no one had more than one forename, and modern practice is that it is not necessary to subscribe all the forenames, or initials.[15] But it appears that this Act is permissive and not imperative.[16] In one modern case signature by surname only was upheld,[17] and execution simply by initials has also been sustained.[18] The signature need not be legible,[19] though exactly how this squares with the rule that a mere mark is insufficient is arguable.[20] The approach taken in the case of holograph wills is even more lenient.[21]

The authorities are chiefly on the subscription of the grantor rather than of the witnesses, and it is thought that the courts may be less forgiving where the signature of the witness does not conform to the Act of 1672.

Where the signature does not contain all the forenames or initials it is common practice for the testing clause to state this fact. For instance: "and by Patricia Alice Macdonald subscribing her usual signature, 'P. Macdonald'." But such a statement in the testing clause is not required by law. Nor is it required where the signer uses some standard diminutive of the forename, such as Jim or Jas. for James. Indeed, it seems that the validity of a signature must be

[13] Lyon King of Arms Act 1672.

[14] It also provides that noblemen may subscribe by their titles.

[15] *Stirling Stuart* v. *Stirling Crawfurd's Trs.* (1885) 12 R. 610.

[16] See the Scottish Law Commission Report No. 112 (1988), pp. 68–69 for a good account of the law and an exhaustive survey of the authorities.

[17] *American Express Europe Ltd.* v. *Royal Bank of Scotland (No. 2)*, 1989 S.L.T. 650.

[18] *e.g., Ker* v. *Gibson* (1693) Mor. 16805.

[19] *Stirling Stuart* (above).

[20] In certain types of document, execution by mark has been upheld, but not for conveyancing deeds.

[21] See the celebrated cases of *Draper* v. *Thomson*, 1954 S.C. 136 and *Rhodes* v. *Peterson*, 1971 S.C. 56, the execution in the latter case being "lots of love, Mum."

judged without reference to what is or is not stated in the testing clause.

Testing clause

Strictly, a testing clause, or clause of attestation, is not required, except where alterations in the deed need to be declared. In practice, one is almost always used, and it contains the designations of the witnesses, and the date and place of execution.[22]

Since the testing clause contains details of execution, it cannot be added until after the deed has been signed. What happens in practice is that when the final version (the engrossment) of a deed is prepared it finishes with the words "IN WITNESS WHEREOF," the first three words of the testing clause. In the case of a disposition, the deed will have been typed by the buyer's solicitors, who then rules out the deed thus:

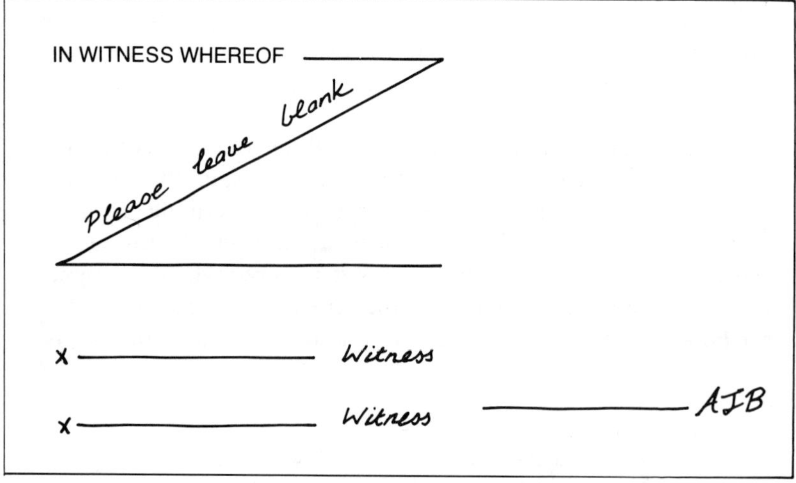

"AJB" is the grantor's initials. The ruling is done in pencil so that it can be rubbed out later. The disposition is then sent to the seller's solicitor, along with a signing schedule.[23] The seller's solicitor then

[22] In practice, the place is given only in broad terms, *e.g.* "at Glasgow." It seems that in law there is no actual requirement that either date or place be stated.

[23] A form on which the date and place of signing, and the designations of the

arranges execution of the deed.[24] Once signed it is retained by the seller's solicitor until settlement, when it is handed over to the buyer's solicitor. It is only then that the testing clause is added, by the buyer's solicitor, using the information in the signing schedule. The deed is then complete and can be sent to the Stamp Office and thereafter to the Register.

It will be obvious that this method of adding the testing clause is open to abuse. Because of the view that the testing clause, although added later, ought to appear above the signatures, as if it were part of the deed,[25] the granter is asked to sign a deed which contains a large gap between the end of the writing and the place marked out for his signature. There is nothing to stop someone adding new material into this gap. Rather more of a risk in practice, there is nothing to stop someone "correcting" a deed by adding, *e.g.* an interlineation in the body of the deed, which can be falsely "declared" in the testing clause as having been added before subscription. The system works on the generally justified assumption that solicitors are trustworthy.

Probativity

"Probative" is an ambiguous word. Sometimes it is used to mean validly executed or validly attested.[26] A more restrictive meaning, and the one used in this book, is that a deed is probative is if it is in such a form as to raise a presumption that it is validly executed.[27] In other words, any writing which is *ex facie* validly attested is probative. The benefit of probativity in this second sense is obvious. For instance, it can be difficult to prove that a document bearing to be signed by someone now dead was in fact signed by him. If, however, the document was in probative form, it is presumed to

witnesses, are to be filled in. Its only role is to enable the testing clause to be completed, after which it can be torn up.

[24] Ideally, the client should call in to the office to do this, to avoid errors. A letter requesting the client to "sign where your initials are marked in pencil" has on at least one occasion been met by a signature in pencil.

[25] Originally, this was to meet the requirement of the Subscription of Deeds Act 1681 that the designations of the witnesses be "in the body of the writ." But s. 38 of the 1874 Act now allows designations to be added below the signatures.

[26] *e.g.* in s. 38 of the 1874 Act.

[27] The point is discussed more fully by K.G.C. Reid at 1985 J.L.S. 308.

have been so signed, and the burden lies on anyone who disputes the fact to prove that it was not so signed.[28] Probativity does not raise a presumption that the whole deed is valid, only that it was validly executed. Virtually all attested deeds are probative, but not all probative writings are validly executed. Probativity is a matter of the appearance of a deed.

The basic rule is that a document which bears to be signed and witnessed in accordance with the authentication statutes is probative. This does not mean that it is, in fact, validly executed. It might be a forgery. Thus, a deed could be probative but not validly executed.[29] Equally, it is possible for a document to be validly executed but not probative, such as a holograph writing[30] or a section 39 deed.[31]

Holograph deeds

A document is holograph if written by hand by the grantor and signed by him. A document not in his handwriting (*e.g.* typed) has the same status if at the end there is a statement in the grantor's handwriting that he accepts the document as if it were in his handwriting, this statement being signed. The usual formula is "adopted as holograph." We do not propose to discuss this form of execution in detail since it is not used in conveyancing except for missives and letters of obligation.[32]

In practice, missives are always adopted as holograph.[33] So are letters of obligation. It has been held[34] that a signature on behalf

[28] Note also that a probative writ cannot prescribe until 20 years: 1973 Act, Sched. 1, para. 2(1): n.b. the definition of "probative" in para. 4(6).

[29] In the strict sense of "probative."

[30] Though in the other sense of "probative," a holograph writing is sometimes treated as probative.

[31] See s. 39 of the 1874 Act, discussed below.

[32] The various statutory styles of conveyancing deed contemplate attestation. Whether or not at common law a conveyancing deed could be holograph is arguable.

[33] There is a theoretical problem here. A firm has no holograph since it is not a physical person, so logically it should be impossible for a firm to adopt as holograph. But this practice is too well established to be questioned.

[34] *Littlejohn* v. *MacKay*, 1974 S.L.T. (Sh. Ct.) 82.

of a firm of solicitors must be by a partner and not merely by, *e.g.*, a qualified assistant.[35]

Section 39 of the 1874 Act

A section 39 deed is an attested deed which has gone wrong, but not too badly wrong, for it must contain the subscription of the grantor and of two witnesses, and these must have been appended according to the requirements of the authentication statutes.[36] The classic example is a will subscribed at the end but not on all the other sheets. A section 39 deed is perfectly valid but it is improbative. Section 39 provides that the court can declare the deed to be validly executed. Such a declarator does not validate the deed, which is already valid, but resolves any difficulty caused by the fact that it was improbative.

Vitiations[37]

A vitiation is an alteration made to a deed after it has been typed. It involves either (1) the deletion of words, whether by erasure or by scoring out or (2) the addition of words, whether by writing over words previously erased or by interlineation or by marginal addition, *i.e.* additional words written in the margin of the deed. The law is concerned to avoid deeds being tampered with after they have been executed. A deed with vitiations looks as if it has been tampered with. Accordingly, the law presumes the vitiation to have been added after execution, with the result that it is not part of the deed and falls to be ignored. Thus, deleted words are reinstated, and added words are deemed *pro non scripto*. But this presumption can be rebutted in one of two ways. Whether it is worth rebutting will depend on the importance of the words inserted or deleted.

The usual method of rebutting the presumption is by an express declaration in the testing clause that the vitiation in question was added *before* execution. Naturally, the declaration must be true.

[35] The correctness of this decision has been doubted by D.J. Cusine and J. Pearson at 1991 J.L.S. 73.

[36] *Walker* v. *Whitwell*, 1916 S.C. (H.L.) 75.

[37] Vitiations are also mentioned in chap. 6.

Vitiations written after execution are not part of the deed and cannot be cured. In the case of marginal additions the practice is for grantors to authenticate the addition by signing their forename or initials on one side of the addition and their surname on the other. The theory here is that a marginal addition is outside the body of the deed and so needs a separate and additional signature. Whether this is really so is very doubtful, but it is wise to follow the traditional practice. The marginal addition must, of course, also be declared in the testing clause.

The other way of overcoming the presumption that the vitiation was added after execution is to raise a petition under section 39 of the 1874 Act, but this is almost unknown in practice.[38]

Until the 1980s, vitiations were quite common. Now, with word processors in almost universal use, they are rare, although not unknown. They are particularly likely to be found in *pro forma* deeds such as standard securities where the blanks are still filled in with an ordinary typewriter.

Powers of attorney

A person can authorize someone to sign a deed on his behalf. This is just an application of the law of agency. Common examples are where a person is going to be out of the country for some time, or where a person is becoming physically or mentally frail.[39] Once authorization has actually been granted, it is unaffected by the subsequent mental incapacity of the granter.[40]

The usual way of authorizing another person to sign, at least on behalf of natural persons, is by executing a deed usually known as a power of attorney.[41] Powers of attorney are normally registered in the Books of Council and Session. It is important to note that powers of attorney are restrictively construed.[42] The agent has

[38] Strictly there is no need to go to court, because the vitiations are valid under s. 39. But a decree cures the problem of improbativity.

[39] Not too mentally frail, for an *incapax* cannot do any juristic act, and thus cannot grant a mandate or agency.

[40] Law Reform (Miscellaneous Provisions) (Scotland) Act 1990, s. 71, though this provision does not apply retrospectively.

[41] This is the English term, which has recently come into general use. The traditional term is factory and commission. For styles see Halliday, paras. 13–12 to 13–21.

[42] Halliday, para. 13–03.

power to do only such things as the deed clearly envisages, and where a deed is signed under a power of attorney, the power must be examined to establish that the agent was acting lawfully. Where a conveyancing deed is executed under power of attorney, this power should be expressly granted in the power of attorney. A person holding a power of attorney cannot normally donate the estate, since to do so would be contrary to his duty to act in the interests of his constituent.

The *Encyclopaedia of Scottish Legal Styles*[43] gives two different methods of drawing up a deed which is to be signed by an attorney. One is to have the deed run in the name of the attorney ("I, AB, attorney of CD, conform to power of attorney in my favour, etc."). In that case, the testing clause runs "IN WITNESS WHEREOF these presents are subscribed by me as attorney foresaid." The other method is not to mention the attorney in the deed, which then runs in the name of the principal, but to say in the testing clause "IN WITNESS WHEREOF these presents are subscribed by me the said CD *per* my attorney AB (design) acting under Power of Attorney, etc." In this case the curious practice has grown up for the attorney to sign, not only his own name but the name of the principal, thus: "CD *per* his attorney AB." But no doubt it would be sufficient if the attorney signed his own name only.

Notarial execution

Sometimes a grantor cannot sign because of physical disability, or cannot know the contents of the deed because of blindness or illiteracy. Whether such a person could verbally authorize another person to sign a conveyancing deed is very doubtful.[44] At any rate,it is never attempted in practice, if only because of the difficulty of proving the existence of the verbal authority. In such cases, therefore, there is a mechanism whereby the verbal authority can be given to a notary public. Execution by the notary gets round the problem, in that it is presumed that the notary has acted properly.

[43] vol. 4, p. 166.

[44] The general rule may be that where a document must be formally signed, an agent can do this only if his agency is formally constituted. However, if this is the rule, there are exceptions. Thus, a client can give verbal authority to a solicitor to make an offer to buy land.

The current law is contained in section 18 of the 1924 Act. Although it can be used for deeds of all kinds, the typical case of notarial execution is the execution of a will on behalf of a very old and frail testator.[45] The agent is usually a notary public (hence "notarial" execution). But section 18 also empowers law agents,[46] justices of the peace and, for wills only, ministers[47] acting in their own parish. The point is that such persons can be trusted to follow the instructions of the person in question and not to take advantage of the opportunity for fraud.

The procedure, which must be strictly adhered to, is as follows. (1) The notary attends with two witnesses. (2) The deed is read to the grantor. (3) The grantor authorizes the notary to sign. (4) The notary writes in his own handwriting the docquet prescribed in Schedule I to the 1924 Act or "words to the like effect." (5) The notary subscribes. (6) The two witnesses subscribe.

All six steps must be one continuous process. In *Hynd's Trustee* v. *Hynd's Trustees*,[48] where steps (4) to (6) were not done until the notary returned to his office, the deed was held to be invalid. It may also be that the six steps must be carried out in the precise order set out above. In *Hynd's Trustee* there is some discussion about the relationship between steps (4) and (5).

Although the 1924 Act does not say so, the notary must not stand to gain from the document either directly or indirectly. If he does stand to gain, the whole deed, and not just the part affecting him, is void, which is a harsh rule.[49] An example is where the deed executed is a will and a member of the notary's firm is appointed executor with power to charge professional remuneration.

Affidavits

Certain other deeds receive notarial execution, especially affidavits.[50] The proper procedure is for the notary to read over the

[45] Of course, the person must be *capax*. Wills are often made by the dying, who, at this final stage of mortal existence, are no longer physically capable of writing.

[46] Defined in s. 2(6).

[47] Of the Established Church. Ministers of "dissenting" churches such as the Roman Catholic or the Episcopalian (Anglican), cannot do this.

[48] 1955 S.C. (H.L.) 1.

[49] For a review of the authorities, see an article by A.G.M. Duncan at 1979 S.L.T. (News) 173.

[50] Also called depositions.

affidavit to the deponent, and then administer the oath to him.[51] The deponent and notary then sign. The notary should also affix his seal. Sealing is not always done, and its omission is probably not fatal. But it should always be done where the document is for use outwith Scotland, because in most countries notarized deeds must be sealed. It appears that witnesses are not required for affidavits, but they are commonly used. The notary is under a duty to satisfy himself of the identity of the deponent, and also that the deponent understands the document.

A typical affidavit would begin: "At Dundee on the tenth day of November in the year nineteen hundred and ninety-three compeared[52] Mungo Park of 41 St Mary's Road Milnathort in the County of Kinross who being solemnly sworn and examined hereby depones" and ends "all which is truth as the deponent shall answer to God."

Execution by companies

Since December 1, 1990 execution of deeds by companies has been regulated by section 36B of the Companies Act 1985 as inserted by section 72(1) of the Law Reform (Miscellaneous Provisions) (Scotland) Act 1990. This replaced an earlier and quite different version of section 36B which, introduced on July 31, 1990, was withdrawn from December 1 in the same year as a result of serious criticisms. Prior to July 31, 1990 execution of deeds by companies was regulated by section 36(3) of the Companies Act 1985, which provided yet another set of rules.[53]

From December 1, 1990 the key provisions on execution by companies are contained in subsections (3) and (4) of section 36B of the Companies Act 1985 (in its current form). These read as follows:

[51] There is no set form. "I swear by Almighty God that to the best of my knowledge and belief the statements in this document are true" is a common form. The deponent may affirm instead of swearing. Without the oath (or affirmation) the affidavit is null: *Blair* v. *North British and Mercantile Insurance Co.* (1889) 16 R. 325.

[52] *i.e.* appeared.

[53] For the background to this confusing history see an article by K.G.C. Reid at 1990 S.L.T. (News) 369, which also gives a table of the different methods of company execution in force at different times.

"(3) For the purposes of any enactment or rule of law relating to the authentication of documents under the law of Scotland, a document is validly executed by a company if it is subscribed on behalf of the company by—

(*a*) two of the directors of the company;

(*b*) a director and the secretary of the company; or

(*c*) two persons authorised to subscribe the document on behalf of the company,

notwithstanding that such subscription is not attested by witnesses and the document is not sealed with the company's common seal.

(4) A document which bears to be executed by a company in accordance with subsection (3) above is, in relation to such execution, a probative document."

Subsection (3) deals with formal validity, and subsection (4) with probativity. Three alternative methods are prescribed for formal validity, and all are declared to confer probativity. Neither the company seal[54] nor witnesses are required. Note also that the methods in subsection (3) are mutually independent, and that they cannot be mixed. Thus, a deed signed by an authorized person and by a director would not be validly executed, unless the director happened also to be an authorized person.

The probativity conferred by subsection (4) does not appear to extend to authority to act, so that it is necessary to check that the person signing as director or secretary or authorized person really was a director, secretary or authorized person. A list of the directors and secretary can be obtained as part of a company search. Typical evidence of authorization to sign on behalf of a company (*i.e.* the third method) is a power of attorney or a minute of a meeting of the board of directors.

Section 36B is without prejudice to other methods of executing deeds by companies,[55] and, in fact, there is one other method. Under general principles of the law of agency a company can authorize someone to sign on its behalf. Since this method of execution is valid, not under the Companies legislation, but under the Subscription of Deeds Act 1681, it requires the subscription of two witnesses.

[54] Indeed, companies no longer need seals, and sealing would seem to add nothing to a company deed, though in practice its use continues to be widespread.

[55] s. 36B(8)(*a*).

Section 36B applies to all companies incorporated under the Companies Acts which require to execute deeds according to the law of Scotland. Thus, it applies equally to English-registered companies executing conveyances of land in Scotland. (Conversely, Scottish-registered companies executing conveyances of land in England require to follow the rules of English law.[56])

Other juristic persons

There are many other juristic persons, such as corporations incorporated by private Act of Parliament (*e.g.* the Bank of Scotland) or by Royal Charter, building societies, local authorities, nationalized industries, industrial and provident societies, universities, and so on. Sometimes the Act establishing the corporation provides a method of execution.[57] But often it does not, in which case the Subscription of Deeds Act 1681 applies, so that execution requires (1) the subscription of a person or persons authorized, by power of attorney or other means, to sign on behalf of the corporation (often the authorization requires sealing as well) and (2) the subscription of two witnesses. The same rules apply to foreign companies executing conveyances of land situated in Scotland.[58] In practice, it is sometimes difficult to say whether a deed granted by a non-company corporation is properly executed.

Execution of discharges: a practical problem

Banks and building societies have to grant one type of formal deed in vast numbers, namely discharges of standard securities. To make things easier for themselves they often send back the executed deed signed by "authorized signing officers" or persons said to hold some sort of "power of attorney" or "board authorization." However, the evidence to prove such powers is seldom forthcoming. In theory, this is unsatisfactory. But in practice solicitors generally accept such executions without query. However, the importance of verifying the execution is greater for other types of deed such as a disposition.

[56] s. 36A.

[57] *e.g.*, the Local Government (Scotland) Act 1973, s. 194.

[58] See the Scottish Law Commission Report (above) pp. 87–96.

Reform

The Report of the Scottish Law Commission already mentioned recommends a major overhaul of the law of execution of deeds. Briefly, the Commission proposes that, for natural persons, simple subscription by the grantor should be sufficient for formal validity. This would greatly simplify the law, abolishing the present categories of holograph deeds, deeds adopted as holograph and section 39 deeds. But while such a deed would be formally valid, it would not be probative unless attested by the signature of one witness. Thus, an abbreviated form of attested writings would survive as a means of achieving probativity, and deeds would continue to be attested. There are equivalent proposals for execution by juristic persons. Indeed, it was an attempt to give effect to these proposals for companies, ahead of the rest of the pack, which led to the flawed provisions which were in force, briefly, from July 31 to November 30, 1990. At one time it seemed as if the Commission's proposals would be implemented quickly. A Bill based on the proposals was given its first reading by the House of Commons on April 26, 1989 as a Private Member's Bill with Government support. Unfortunately, the private member in question did not arrive to move the second reading, the Bill failed, and since then no Parliamentary time has been found for it.

CHAPTER 16

STAMP DUTY

Introduction

Stamp duty dates from 1694. It prompted the Boston Tea Party and the subsequent loss of the American colonies. Its unpopularity continues undiminished. The current legislation is contained in the Stamp Act 1891 (heavily amended over the years) and in numerous Finance Acts.[1] The principal charging section is section 1 of the Act of 1891, which provides that: "From and after the commencement of this Act the stamp duties to be charged . . . upon the several instruments specified in the First Schedule to this Act shall be the several duties in the said schedule specified."

As this indicates, stamp duty is a tax on "instruments" and not on transactions. The word instrument includes every written document.[2] So if there is no instrument, no tax is payable. Hence, oral transactions are not liable to stamp duty. Schedule 1 of the Act lists the heads of charge to stamp duty. Instruments not listed in the schedule are exempt from duty. The trend of recent Finance Acts has been both to reduce levels of duty and to exempt an increasing number of documents which were previously chargeable. Of the items in Schedule 1, the most important for conveyancing purposes are: (1) conveyance or transfer on sale; (2) exchange or excambion; (3) lease or tack; and (4) miscellaneous fixed duties. These will be considered in turn.

1. Conveyance or Transfer on Sale

This head is defined[3] as including: "every instrument, and every decree or order of any court[4] or of any commissioners, whereby

[1] The legislation in collected and amended form is available from commercial publishers. A standard text is Sargeant and Sims, *Stamp Duty*. Stamp duty is administered by the Inland Revenue at the Stamp Office, 15 Picardy Place, Edinburgh, tel. 031–556 8511.

[2] Stamp Act 1891, s. 122(1).

[3] Stamp Act 1891, s. 54.

[4] *e.g.* decree of foreclosure. See s. 6 of the Finance Act 1898.

any property . . . upon the sale thereof is transferred to or vested in a purchaser, or any other person on his behalf or on his direction."

In principle, stamp duty catches the sale of any property, heritable or moveable, corporeal or incorporeal, but only where the transfer is in writing. Corporeal moveables are transferred without writing, so that the stamp duty is not payable on the price of moveables included in the sale, such as carpets. It should be noted that for subsidiary real rights, such as lease and security, the charge to duty under the head of conveyance on sale is not for the original grant of the security or lease but for its subsequent assignation. Stamp duty on leases is considered below. There is no duty chargeable on the original grant of heritable securities.

The tax is borne by the instrument, in general the deed carrying out the actual transfer. So in the purchase of a house it is the disposition which requires to be stamped and not the missives.

Rates of charge

Conveyance on sale duty is *ad valorem*, *i.e.* based on the value of the sale consideration. The rates have changed over the years. There is a view that in examining the title to land it is necessary to check that each deed in the prescriptive progress has been properly stamped. But in practice this is often not done, and indeed the consequences of improper stamping are very limited.[5]

The rates operative from 1984 to 1993 are set out in the Finance Act 1963, section 55(1) as amended by the Finance Act 1984, section 109(1). They apply to all instruments stamped on or after March 20, 1984 provided they were executed on or after March 13, 1984.[6] The applicable rate depends on whether or not the consideration exceeds £30,000. The 1993 Finance Bill will change this

[5] In practice, the Keeper will not record or register a deed unless properly stamped, so it is almost certain that deeds accepted by him have been properly stamped. Moreover, if he has in fact accepted such a deed which has not been properly stamped, stamping will be necessary only if the deed needs to be founded on in court. For the penalties for late stamping, see below.

[6] Note, however, that under the Stamp Duty (Temporary Provisions) Act 1992 the zero-rated ceiling was £250,000 between December 20, 1991 and August 20, 1992. This was an (ineffectual) attempt to inject some adrenalin into a weak housing market.

to £60,000 for instruments stamped on or after March 23, 1993, provided they were executed on or after March 16, 1993. The new figure is adopted in this book.

Consideration £60,000 or less

If the consideration is £60,000 or less, no duty is payable provided that the instrument contains a certificate in the form prescribed by the Finance Act 1958, section 34(4). The certificate should be included as part of the instrument, although by Inland Revenue concession it may be added later, after execution. In practice, it usually appears at the end, before the testing clause. The form is as follows: "I/We certify that the transaction hereby effected does not form part of a larger transaction or of a series of transactions in respect of which the amount or value or aggregate amount or value of the consideration exceeds £60,000."

The purpose of the declaration is to prevent evasion of duty by packaging a large transaction into a series of small transactions, the consideration for each part being less than £60,000. So if A sells B a house for £200,000, duty cannot be avoided by having four separate dispositions of one quarter *pro indiviso* shares, each with a consideration of £50,000. The difference between "larger transaction" and "series of transactions" appears to be the difference between a single contract between the parties and a series of contracts. Where the same parties enter into a series of contracts it is unclear what criteria are regarded as making these a "series of transactions" within the meaning of the Act.

Consideration over £60,000

Stamp duty is paid by the purchaser, and it is essential to warn the client of this in advance. The rate of conveyance on sale duty is £1 for every £100, *i.e.* 1 per cent., but rounded up to the nearest £100. So duty on a disposition for £93,002 is £931.

Value Added Tax

In cases where VAT is payable on the consideration, the consideration is grossed up for stamp duty purposes to include the VAT. Thus, in a sense there is a tax on a tax. Value Added Tax is payable in two main types of case. The first is the sale of new, non-domestic property, and the second is the sale or lease of older non-domestic property if the seller, or lessor, has waived exemption to VAT which would otherwise apply. Although VAT is an important question in conveyancing, it is essentially a matter for commercial conveyancing, and so will not be further dealt with here.

Sale of house with contents

Where a house is sold together with moveable items such as carpets, the moveables are excluded from the consideration for stamp duty purposes. This is because ownership of goods does not pass by "instrument."[7] Therefore, only that part of the price applicable to the heritage should be given as the consideration in the disposition. Missives often provide how the total price in a sale should be apportioned as between heritage and moveables. The temptation may be to overstate the value of the moveables, so that duty is reduced or even (if the figure can be brought below £60,000) eliminated. This temptation should be resisted for several reasons. In the first place, any such arrangement requires the cooperation of the seller, who may not be willing to help. Secondly, in *Saunders* v. *Edwards* [8] it was said that a contract containing false apportionment of the price as between heritage and moveables might not be enforceable, as being contrary to public policy. Thirdly, it is a criminal offence[9] to execute or prepare a false instrument, although the fine (£10) is now derisory. At common law there may also be fraud against the Crown. Fourthly, as *Saunders* indicates, a false apportionment is probably professional misconduct on the part of the solicitor.

Sale of a business

In commercial cases, different types of property may be sold in the course of the same transaction, for example land, goodwill, receivables, stock in trade, and so on. Stamp duty is payable except

[7] At common law it passes by delivery, and under the statutory rules for sales it passes by "intention": Sale of Goods Act 1979, s. 17.

[8] [1987] 2 All E.R. 651. See, in particular, Nicholls L.J. at 665.

[9] Stamp Act 1891, s. 5.

on stock in trade which, as corporeal moveable property, is exempt.

Subsale

If A concludes missives for the sale of a house with B and B immediately resells to C, so that the disposition is granted directly by A to C, duty is payable only on the price paid by C to B, even if less than the price paid by B to A.[10] But there is an anti-avoidance provision,[11] namely that the rule does not apply where the price on the sub-sale is less than the value of the property. Where two dispositions are used, *i.e.* where A dispones to B and B then dispones to C, duty is, of course, payable twice.

Building plots

In the purchase of a house in the course of construction, it is important to know whether duty is payable on the value of the land alone or on the value of the land plus the house. This situation is the subject of an Inland Revenue Statement of Practice.[12] In summary, the rules are that if the house (or other building) is being built either by the purchaser or by some third party who is wholly independent of the seller, duty is payable on the value of the land only. But if, as happens more commonly, the house is being built by the seller or some connected person, the outcome depends on whether there are two separate contracts (*i.e.* a contract of sale and a contract to build) or a single unitary contract. In determining whether there is one contract or two, nothing turns on whether the parties employ two separate documents. The Inland Revenue ask this question: what, in terms of the contract/s, has to be paid in exchange for the disposition? If only the price of the land is payable, there are said to be two separate contracts. Stamp duty is then payable on (1) the value of the land and (2) the value of however much of the building was already in existence[13] at the date of conclusion of missives. If, however, the full price is payable,

[10] Stamp Act 1891, s. 58(4).
[11] Finance Act 1984, s. 112(1).
[12] Statement of Practice No. 87, and see Halliday, para. 22–34.
[13] And therefore part of the land, by accession.

there is said to be a unitary package, and duty is payable on the full amount. In practice, builders will not normally release a disposition without payment of the full price. Where a purchaser seeks to pay a reduced amount of duty, the various contracts must be submitted with the deed so that the Inland Revenue can assess the position.

Company exemptions

Certain exemptions from stamp duty exist in respect of (1) transfers between associated companies, and (2) company reconstructions.

2. Exchange or Excambion

"Exchange" and "excambion" are synonyms. Where A and B agree to excamb land this can be effected by two separate dispositions, or by a single deed, known as a contract of excambion, in which A conveys to B and B conveys to A. An agreement under section 19 of the 1979 Act is a type of excambion.

In cases of a straight exchange the duty is only 50 pence. Where, however, the values of the properties are different and one party makes an additional cash payment, then (in the case of land) conveyance on sale duty is paid on that cash payment.[14] In practice, the cash payment will often be less than £60,000, so that no duty will actually be payable provided that the deed contains a certificate of value. It follows that excambions are very advantageous from the point of view of stamp duty. They are also more common than might be supposed. For example, some builders allow purchasers of one of their houses to swap it for another of their houses.

3. Lease or Tack[15]

In cases of leases, stamp duty is payable *ad valorem*, based on the annual rent rounded up to the nearest £50. But if the rent is not to be constant throughout the lease, then duty is calculated on the average annual rent, again rounded up to the nearest £50. The current rates apply to all instruments executed on or after March 21, 1982. They are set out in Schedule 1 (as amended) to the Stamp

[14] Stamp Act 1891, s. 73.
[15] Tack is the old term for lease.

Act 1891, and depend on the length of the lease. In summary the rates are these:

Duration of 0–7 years	1 per cent.
Duration of 7–35 years	2 per cent.
Duration of 35–100 years	12 per cent.
Duration of over 100 years	24 per cent.

But no duty is payable where the annual rent does not exceed £500.

In addition, conveyance on sale duty[16] is paid on any grassum[17] for the lease. The £60,000 exemption applies only where the annual rent is so small (£600 or less) that the *grassum* is the principal consideration.

It will be seen that leases for more than 35 years attract high rates of duty. One possible method of avoiding these is to have a lease for a shorter period with an option to extend, although this carries the risk that the option will not in fact be exercised.

There is a special stamp duty regime for leases of furnished dwelling-houses for less than a year. Here, there is a fixed duty of £1. But since such leases do not require to be constituted in writing in the first place, there may be no deed to stamp.

In practice, a lease often takes the form of missives of let, which may or may not ultimately be followed by a formal lease. The rule is that where missives of let are entered into it is the missives which must be stamped.[18] A subsequent formal lease should then carry a denoting stamp.[19]

4. Fixed Duties

Schedule 1 to the Stamp Act 1891 also contains a number of fixed duties, as opposed to *ad valorem* duties. At one time these were very numerous. Indeed, until 1985 all deeds not specifically exempted were liable for a fixed duty of 50 pence. This is no longer so. Nonetheless a number of deeds continue to bear a fixed duty of 50 pence. The most important are:

(1) Conveyance or transfer of any kind not hereinbefore described.

[16] See above.

[17] Or in English terms, a premium, *i.e.* a lump sum payable for lease.

[18] Stamp Act 1891, s. 75 and Finance Act 1984, s. 111.

[19] See below.

In effect, this means conveyances in implement of donations (gifts). Until the Finance Act 1985,[20] all *inter vivos* gifts were liable for conveyance on sale duty calculated on the value of the property. This fiscal constraint on generosity has now been removed, and all donations of land bear a fixed duty of 50 pence.

(2) Declaration of trust.

(3) Disposition in Scotland of any property or of any right or interest therein not described in this Schedule. For the most part this appears to overlap with (1). But it seems that the second part of this head of charge ("disposition . . . of any right or interest therein") may be intended to refer to the creation of subordinate real rights and so would catch, *e.g.*, deeds of servitude.

(4) Duplicate or counterpart of any instrument chargeable with any duty. Bilateral deeds, notably leases, are often executed in duplicate so that both parties can have a copy. Only one copy (notionally the principal) attracts full stamp duty. The other copy is stamped at 50 pence,[21] and must also carry a denoting stamp.[22]

(5) Exchange or excambion. This has already been discussed, above.

In certain cases falling within (1) and (3) above, even the 50 pence duty can now be avoided by virtue of the Stamp Duty (Exempt Instruments) Regulations 1987.[23] The 1987 Regulations exempt a number of different categories of deeds (categories A to M). The most important are: (1) deeds of assumption and conveyance of new trustees; (2) transfers out of a trust or executry estate; (3) transfers in connection with divorce; (4) grant of a servitude for no consideration; and (5) conveyance for no consideration (*i.e.* a donation or gift). In order to obtain the exemption the deed must contain a certificate in the form prescribed by the 1987 Regulations, regulation 3. This reads: "I/We hereby certify that this instrument falls within category [one of A to M] in the Schedule to the Stamp Duty (Exempt Instruments) Regulations 1987."

Even after the 1987 Regulations, a number of fixed duty charges remain. It is difficult to see why. The revenue involved is derisory. And from the point of view of the parties to the deed the requirement of stamping is a nuisance where it is not actually overlooked.

[20] s. 82.

[21] Where, however, the principal is exempt, so is the copy.

[22] Stamp Act 1891, s. 72. For denoting stamps see below.

[23] S.I. 1987 No. 516.

5. Payment

In imposing timelimits for payment, section 15 of the Stamp Act 1891 distinguishes between *ad valorem* duty and fixed duty. Most *ad valorem* duties must be paid within 30 days of the execution of the deed, or, where executed abroad, within 30 days of its arrival in the UK. Inland Revenue practice, however, is to calculate the 30 days not from the execution but from the delivery of the deed.[24] Thus, in a typical house purchase there are 30 days after settlement of the transaction (which is when the disposition is delivered) for the disposition to be stamped. In practice, it is usually stamped immediately, so that it can then be registered in the Register of Sasines or Land Register. With fixed duty deeds, section 15(1) provides that the deed must be stamped before execution—in effect, that the deed must be written on prestamped paper. This provision is not strictly enforced.

In almost every case a deed can be stamped late, but subject to penalties. For most *ad valorem* deeds there is a penalty of £10 plus the full amount of the duty, so that in effect double duty must be paid.[25] For other deeds the penalty is £10.[26]

Effect of non-payment

Uniquely in revenue law, stamp duty is the tax that need not be paid. If payment is not made, there is nothing that the Inland Revenue can do about it. They cannot sue for payment. However, it is a criminal offence for the Keeper of the Registers to record or register a deed improperly stamped,[27] so that in effect the Keeper polices the system by insisting on proper stamping. Furthermore, an improperly stamped deed is inadmissible as evidence in civil proceedings.[28]

[24] For discussion see A.R. Barr at 1992 J.L.S. 280.

[25] Stamp Act 1891, s. 15(2)(*c*).

[26] Stamp Act 1891, s. 15.

[27] Stamp Act 1891, s. 17. The fine is only £10, and in any case one could hardly imagine a prosecution. The idea of criminal sanctions against the Keeper is preposterous. The practical point is that the Keeper will not accept a deed which appears not to be properly stamped.

[28] Stamp Act 1891, s. 14(1) and (4).

In practice, dispositions and other deeds requiring registration are always stamped. The same is not always true of other deeds—whether by accident or by design. It should be remembered that a deed which has not been stamped when initially drawn up can always be stamped later on, subject to penalties.

Impressed stamp

There are various types of stamp. The main type is the impressed stamp. This is a sort of seal put on the deed by the Inland Revenue. Each seal is marked by a value, and several such seals may appear so as to make up the right amount. Thus, it is possible to tell at a glance from a deed what duty has been paid on it.

Denoting stamp

Where a deed does not bear any duty, or not full duty, either because it is a duplicate or because it is not the principal deed effecting the transaction,[29] it must usually be marked with a stamp denoting that stamp duty has been paid on the other deed. Thus, the duplicate denoting stamp reads "Duplicate or counterpart—original fully and properly stamped." Duplicate deeds also bear a fixed duty of 50 pence and should carry an impressed stamp for this amount.

Adjudication stamp

If for any reason the amount of duty payable is uncertain, one may, and in certain circumstances must, submit the deed to the Inland Revenue for adjudication. The deed then bears (1) an impressed stamp or stamps in respect of any duty paid and (2) an adjudication stamp. An adjudication stamp is conclusive evidence that the deed is properly stamped.[30] By far the commonest case of adjudication used to be *inter vivos* gifts where the Inland Revenue had to decide the value of the property for the purposes of *ad valorem* duty. Now that *ad valorem* duty on donations has been abolished, adjudication is rare.

[29] *e.g.* a lease following an agreement to let.
[30] Stamp Act 1891, s. 12(5).

Produced stamp

Section 28 of the Finance Act 1931 requires that all conveyances on sale, leases for seven or more years, and assignations of such leases be produced to the Stamp Office within 30 days, accompanied by a detailed form giving certain specified information. The purpose of section 28 is essentially to gather information to assist the Inland Revenue, *e.g.* in the valuation of property. A deed produced to the Stamp Office in terms of section 28 is stamped with a produced stamp (*i.e.* a stamp saying "produced"). It will also bear an impressed stamp or stamps in respect of the duty actually paid. Failure to produce the deed carries a penalty of £400. The requirement to complete the section 28 form is inconvenient. Fortunately, there is a major exemption: by section 35(*x*) of the Act,[31] section 28 does not apply to deeds registered in the Register of Sasines or Land Register. This reduces the deeds falling within section 28 to those which either cannot be registered (*i.e.* short leases or assignations thereof[32]) or those which it is not intended to register.

[31] Which applies only in Scotland.

[32] Leases of 20 years or less: Registration of Leases (Scotland) Act 1857, s. 1, as amended; Land Registration (Scotland) Act 1979, ss. 2 and 28.

CHAPTER 17

SASINE REGISTRATION

The Register of Sasines and the Land Register are often referred to as the property registers to distinguish them from the personal register (the Register of Inhibitions and Adjudications).[1] Both are public registers, and so any person can inspect them, on payment of an administrative fee. The property registers are subdivided into 33 registration counties, which are based on the traditional counties. The counties are grouped into certain "districts" but this is an administrative matter, and these districts (which are reorganised from time to time) have no legal status. The districts are somewhat heterogeneous: for instance, the "central" district includes at present areas as disparate as East Lothian and Orkney and Shetland.

The 33 counties are: Aberdeen, Angus, Argyll, Ayr, Banff, Berwick, Bute, Caithness, Clackmannan, Dumfries, Dunbarton, East Lothian, Fife, Glasgow (Barony and Regality of), Inverness, Kincardine, Kinross, Kirkcudbright (Stewartry of), Lanark, Midlothian, Moray, Nairn, Orkney and Shetland,[2] Peebles, Perth, Renfrew, Roxburgh, Ross and Cromarty,[3] Selkirk, Stirling, Sutherland, West Lothian and Wigtown.[4]

Registration dues

The idea is that the registers should be self-financing. So registration costs money, and has become more expensive since the intro-

[1] These registers are based at Meadowbank House, 153 London Road, Edinburgh, tel. 031–659 6111. Most of the volumes of the Sasine Register are kept at the Scottish Record Office (Old Register House) in Princes Street, Edinburgh. Part of the operation of the Land Register is scheduled to be devolved to Cowglen in Glasgow during 1993.

[2] Orkney and Shetland form a single area.

[3] Ross and Cromarty form a single area.

[4] The conveyancing practice is to refer to these counties without the final "-shire".

duction of registration of title. The cost of registering in the two property registers is the same; but since first registration in the Land Register involves a great deal of administrative time, there is, in effect, cross-subsidisation of the Land Register by the Sasine Register. The current registration dues are to be found in S.I. 1990 No. 1256. For conveyances the dues are based on the consideration, or, where there is no consideration, on the value of the property. For standard securities, and discharges thereof, the dues are based on the amount of the loan. The dues are as follows: (1) conveyances—£11 per £5,000 or part thereof subject to a maximum fee of £550; (2) securities—£11 per £10,000 or part thereof subject to a maximum fee of £275. However, a standard security recorded at the same time as a conveyance is charged a flat fee of £22. Hence, the practice is to register[5] both deeds together wherever possible. Most standard securities are granted when a house is bought, so there will be a disposition to be registered at the same time. Thus, a disposition of a £100,000 house plus a standard security for £50,000 would cost either £275 (£220 + £55) or £242 (£220 + £22). Payment is not due until the deeds are returned from the registers, which is usually not for some months. But to save the embarrassment—and possibly difficulty—of asking the client for money at this stage, this is usually requested at the same time as the purchase price and stamp duty.

Register of Sasines

The Register of Sasines was established by the Registration Act 1617[6] and is now regulated chiefly by the Land Registers (Scotland) Act 1868.[7] Its full title is the General Register of Sasines,[8] a title which distinguished it, historically, from the Particular Registers of Sasines and the Burgh Registers of Sasines, both now defunct.

[5] By tradition the verb "record" is used for the Sasine Register and "register" for the Books of Council and Session and other registers. But the terms are interchangeable, and in fact "register" is used for warrants of registration in the Sasine Register.

[6] Still in force. For the history, see L. Ockrent, *Land Rights: An Enquiry into the History of Registration for Publication in Scotland* (1942).

[7] See also the Register of Sasines (Scotland) Act 1987 which authorises the keeping of the register in microfiche form. See, further, a note from the Keeper at 1989 J.L.S. 235.

[8] Often called the GRS or the Sasine Register.

The Particular Registers were local registers. Until 1868[9] parties could elect to record in the local register rather than in the General Register in Edinburgh. Now all Sasine registration must be in the General Register.[10] Older deeds encountered in an examination of title, such as burdens writs, often turn out to have been registered in the Particular Registers. The Burgh Registers of Sasines were the local registers for land within burghs held on burgage tenure. Latterly, a grantee had the option to record either in the Burgh Register or in the General Register. Although burgage tenure itself was abolished in 1874, the Burgh Registers lived on for many years thereafter. Eventually a programme for phasing them out was introduced by the Burgh Registers (Scotland) Act 1926.[11]

Indexes and search sheets

The General Register of Sasines is indexed both by person and by property.[12] Most important of all are the search sheets.[13] For any given area of land[14] a separate sheet is maintained for all the primary interests therein, that is to say for (1) the *dominium utile* ("the property interest"), (2) superiorities, (3) any registered leases, and (4) any registered subleases. Whenever a deed is registered, a brief printed summary is prepared and pasted into the appropriate search sheet. The summary also states the place in the register itself where the deed can be found. So if A dispones to B the *dominium utile* of Whitemains, the disposition is entered into the *dominium utile* search sheet. If B then grants a standard security, the same is true. But if B subfeus to C, B's interest is reduced to a superiority

[9] These registers were phased out by 1871 under the Land Registers (Scotland) Act 1868.

[10] A list of these registers and the dates when they were discontinued can be found in the *Parliament House Book* (conveyancing section, Division J).

[11] For a list, and the dates of discontinuance, see the *Parliament House Book* (conveyancing section, Division J). The process of phasing out was much slower than for the Particular Registers, the last to be closed being Dingwall in 1963.

[12] For examples of the persons index and property index see G.L. Gretton, *Guide to Searches* (1991), pp. 6 and 8.

[13] For an example of a search sheet, see G.L. Gretton, *Guide to Searches*, p. 12. Search sheets have no statutory basis, though without them modern conveyancing would be impossible. They were introduced in 1871. Hence it can be difficult to trace pre-1871 deeds in the register unless one knows the date of registration.

[14] "Area" meaning a plot separately owned.

interest, and a new search sheet will be opened for C's interest, which is now the *dominium utile*. The search sheet system is powerful and efficient. It enables the state of the title to virtually any plot of land to be investigated quickly and easily.

Warrants of registration

All deeds presented for registration must contain a warrant of registration.[15] Broadly speaking, the warrant replaces the instrument of sasine, which was mandatory until 1858. The warrant is a request by the grantee (or rather his agent) to register the deed. There is a statutory form.[16] The warrant can appear anywhere on the deed but in practice is usually placed at the foot of the last page. A typical style of warrant is:

> REGISTER on behalf of the within named Alan Dewar Johnston and Clare Janet Macleod or Johnston in the Register of the County of Midlothian.
>
> *Dunlop & Fairbairn* [signature]
> W.S. Edinburgh
> Agents

In terms of 1868 Act[17] the warrant must contain three things. First, it must have the name and designation of the person on whose behalf the deed is presented for registration. This person will normally already have been designed in the deed, so that it is sufficient to say "within named." With dispositions it is obvious who this person should be, namely the disponee, but with some other deeds, such as discharges of standard securities or deeds of conditions, things are not so clear, for in such deeds there is in fact no true grantee.[18] A discharge is registered on behalf the debtor, and a deed of conditions on behalf of the grantor of the deed, there being no other party involved. The second requirement is that the registration county must be stated. The third requirement is the signature of the person on whose behalf the deed is presented or

[15] 1868 Act, ss. 15 and 141.

[16] 1924 Act, s. 10(1) and (3) and Sched. F.

[17] s. 141.

[18] In the case of a discharge of a standard security, what is happening is that a right ceases to exist. There is thus no recipient.

of his agent.[19] By section 2(7) of the 1924 Act, "agent" means law agent or notary public, and "law agent" is itself defined[20] to mean, in effect, solicitor. The signature may be either the solicitor's own name or that of his firm, and the latter is almost universal modern practice.[21] Failure to sign the warrant is a regular reason for writs being sent back ("bounced") by Meadowbank House.

If a grantee wishes to register part only of a deed—if, for example, a disposition is drafted as part of a larger deed—the deed must contain a "clause of direction" immediately before the testing clause which specifies which part is to be registered.[22] In such a case the warrant of registration takes a different form.[23] Clauses of direction are almost unknown in modern practice.

The registration process

After settlement of the transaction dispositions are sent to the Stamp Office for stamping. Then they are ready for recording. The deed is sent to Meadowbank House accompanied by the "letter to the Keeper," which is in fact a *pro forma*.[24] There is no timelimit for recording other than that the grantee must be alive,[25] but in practice recording should always be as soon as possible. One reason is to protect the purchaser against the possible insolvency of the grantor. Delay in registration is regarded as professional misconduct. Unless the deed is later rejected or withdrawn, the date of receipt at Meadowbank House is the date of recording. Two deeds arriving on the same day rank equally.[26]

The extent of the Keeper's power to reject deeds is uncertain.

[19] In practice, it is almost unknown for the warrant to be signed by the grantee personally.

[20] 1924 Act, s. 2(6).

[21] It is even sometimes supposed that the signature must be that of the firm, but this is not correct.

[22] 1868 Act, s. 12.

[23] 1924 Act, Sched. F, Note 1.

[24] The form was redesigned in 1992 to be read by computer, so that the Presentment Book can be kept on database. See a note by the Keeper at 1992 J.L.S. 98. Within a few days of receipt the Keeper sends an acknowledgement, showing the date of recording.

[25] 1868 Act, s. 142.

[26] 1868 Act, s. 142 as amended by the 1979 Act. Before the 1979 Act, deeds ranked not only by date but by hour of registration.

Probably it is not very extensive, although there are remarks in *Macdonald* v. *Keeper of the Registers*[27] which might suggest otherwise. In practice, deeds are rejected mainly for the following reasons: (1) not properly stamped; (2) subjects not properly identified (the situation in *Macdonald*); (3) the warrant of registration not signed; (4) deed not properly executed. Much more common than unilateral rejection is an invitation by Meadowbank House, usually by telephone, to withdraw a deed. All deeds are examined by the Keeper's staff and this may throw up errors. On being invited to withdraw a deed, it is necessary to weigh up the seriousness, or otherwise, of the error in question. It may be so minor that withdrawal is unnecessary. And occasionally it happens that what Meadowbank House thinks is an error is not an error.

Once a deed has been accepted for recording it goes through various registration processes.[28] The Presentment Book,[29] which is used as a receipt book for all writs, and which gives the date of presentment, the name of the writ, and the parties, has been computerised since April 1, 1992.[30]

As part of the recording process, the keeper takes a copy of the deed. The original deed is then returned to the ingiver. Originally, this was done manually by copying clerks. Nowadays it is by photocopy, or, most recently,[31] by microfiche. (Full sized copies were bound up into large and heavy record volumes.) A certificate of registration is stamped on the original of the deed and gives details of (1) the date of recording and (2) the fiche and frame number (or previously book and folio[32] number) of the copy preserved in the register. The full recording process takes around five months.[33]

Since all recorded deeds are preserved, in copy, anyone can obtain a copy of such copies. Copies come in two varieties. First there is the so-called quick copy, which is a simple photocopy.

[27] 1914 S.C. 854.

[28] See the *Stair Memorial Encyclopaedia*, vol. 6, para. 452 *et seq.*

[29] For an example of the Presentment Book in its traditional (precomputerisation) form, see G.L. Gretton, *Guide to Searches*, p. 2.

[30] See chap. 7.

[31] Under the Register of Sasines (Scotland) Act 1987.

[32] *i.e.* page.

[33] The period varies from county to county and from time to time. At the time of writing the average delay is being reduced.

Then there is an extract,[34] which is also a photocopy, but comes complete with a backing and a certificate that it is a true copy. By section 45 of the 1970 Act an extract copy is as good as the original deed.[35]

The record volumes, containing the copy deeds, are kept at the Scottish Record Office (Old Register House) at the east end of Princes Street, Edinburgh (behind the statue of the Duke of Wellington). This superb building, designed by Robert Adam, was erected with money obtained from the sale of the confiscated lands of those who rose in support of Bonnie Prince Charlie. The record volumes can be inspected, in the Dome Room, for a fee, but unless the book and folio number of the deed is known, it is necessary to go first to the search sheets to discover these details, and the search sheets are kept, inconveniently for solicitors, at Meadowbank House. Search firms can be instructed to trace deeds and to obtain a quick copy or extract as required.

[34] An "extract" of a document is not a short version of it but a full official copy.

[35] Quick copies and extracts can be obtained direct from Register House, or can be obtained through firms of searchers.

Chapter 18

OTHER REGISTERS

Introduction

The Sasine Register and the Land Register are dealt with in another chapter.[1] There exist numerous other registers, most of which, however, are of no importance to the conveyancer. In this chapter we will mention the Books of Council and Session, the Sheriff Court Books, the Companies Register, the Register of Inhibitions and Adjudications, the Register of Insolvencies, the Registers of Contaminated Land, and the planning registers.

Books of Council and Session

The Books of Council and Session are the Register of the Court of Session, but they are now administered by the Department of the Registers of Scotland. The regulating statutes are the Registration Act 1698 and the Registration of Writs (Scotland) Act 1868. To be registered a deed must be probative. Deeds are sent to this register either for "preservation," or for "preservation and execution." Registration for preservation is for safe keeping. The idea is simply to ensure that the document can never be lost. It is also convenient if the document needs to be referred to by other, later documents, for in such case it can simply be referred to as having been registered on such-and-such a date.[2] Like the Sasine Register, the Books of Council and Session are open to the public, and so anyone can obtain a copy of any registered writ. The original is kept in the register,[3] and may be removed only with the permission of the Court of Session. What is issued to the ingiver is a formally authen-

[1] Chaps. 17 and 20.

[2] A common example is a financial institution's "schedule of variations" used to lay down standard terms in standard securities. Instead of these having to be incorporated at length in each and every security, the security can simply refer to the registered version.

[3] Unlike the Sasine Register, where a copy is kept and the original returned.

ticated copy called an extract. Extract copies are equivalent to originals.[4] Registration for preservation is never necessary in law. Typically it is used for deeds which cannot be registered elsewhere, for instance deeds of trust, or powers of attorney. It is competent to have dual registration, in both the Sasine Register and in the Books of Council and Session.[5] Traditionally, this was done to preserve the deed against loss, because there was some doubt as to the validity of extracts from the Sasine Register. Now, however, extracts from the Sasine Register have the same status as the original.[6] Another reason for dual registration is that before the introduction of photocopying at Register House, plans attached to deeds could not be registered in the Sasine Register, so such deeds would sometimes be registered in the Books of Council and Session as a safeguard against loss. Section 48 of the 1924 Act introduced a system for recording plans in the Sasine Register. But because of photocopying at the register, section 24 now only needs to be used for very large plans. The net result of all this is that dual registration is now apparently pointless.

It is also possible to register a deed in the Books of Council and Session[7] for preservation and execution.[8] This is competent only where the document is a probative document of debt, in which the debtor expressly consents to such registration, which is done by the use of the words, within the deed: "I consent to the registration of these presents for preservation and execution." The effect of these words is that when the document is registered the extract issued is deemed equivalent in law to a decree[9] against the debtor for the debt expressed in the document. Technically this is called a decree of registration. The term summary diligence is also used, though what is summary is not in fact the diligence which follows the decree, but the decree itself. Registration for execution thus avoids the need for a court action. It is thus a useful and powerful

[4] Writs Execution (Scotland) Act 1877, s. 5.

[5] Land Registers Act 1868, s. 12.

[6] 1970 Act, s. 45.

[7] Or in the Sheriff Court Books.

[8] See G. Maher and D.J. Cusine, *Law and Practice of Diligence* (Butterworth, 1990), chap. 2; J. Graham Stewart, *Diligence* (1898), and standard texts on civil procedure.

[9] Of the Court of Session, if the registration is in the Books of Council and Session, or of the sheriff court in the case of the Sheriff Court Books.

weapon for a creditor. In conveyancing practice, clauses of consent to registration for execution are found most commonly in standard securities[10] and leases. Such clauses are pointless unless the deed imposes an identifiable pecuniary obligation on one of the parties. If the debtor disputes the debt, it is up to him to challenge the decree of registration, which is done by an action of suspension. Registration for execution is also competent in the case of notarial instruments of protest on dishonoured negotiable instruments.

The Sheriff Court Books

Sheriff courts also maintain their own registers, the Sheriff Court Books, although here only a photocopy is retained and the original deed is returned. In practice, the Sheriff Court Books are little used for registration for preservation. However, wills are automatically registered here, as part of the process of confirmation of executors.

The Companies Register

All Scottish companies are registered at Edinburgh.[11] Companies incorporated in England and Wales are registered in Cardiff. Each company has its own file, which is divided into three parts, or fiches, called the G fiche, the A fiche and the M and MR fiche. The G fiche contains general items, such as the company's memorandum and articles and amendments thereof, and also notices of liquidation or administration. The A fiche contains the accounts and annual return. The M and MR fiche contains company charges, and notice of receivership. The M and MR fiche is what is commonly called the register of charges.

The main significance of the Companies Register to the conveyancer is in connection with searches, which aspect is dealt with elsewhere in this book.[12] The importance must be stressed, whenever acting for a company, of being certain that it is in legal existence. This can be ascertained from the register. Cases occur from

[10] Indeed, the official style in the 1970 Act contains such a clause, though just why it seeks to give such rights is unclear. One would have expected the style to omit it, allowing its inclusion if the parties so wished.

[11] 100–102 George Street.

[12] Chap. 7.

time to time where a solicitor acts in good faith for a company which has never been validly incorporated, or which has been dissolved under section 652 of the Companies Act 1985. In such cases there may be personal liability on the solicitor, under the common law rule that an agent who acts for a non-existent principal can be personally liable to the third party who has relied on the agency.

Any floating charge or standard security granted by a company must be duly registered in the Companies Register within 21 days. For a floating charge the 21–day period runs from the date of execution, and for standard securities from the date of registration in the Sasine Register or Land Register.[13] In the case of standard securities this necessity for double registration is all too easy to overlook, but the consequence can be fatal. Thus, a standard security duly registered in the Sasine Register or Land Register may be effectively void if it has not also been timeously registered in the Companies Register.[14] If non-registration comes to light, the best response is usually a petition for permission to register late.[15] The Companies Act 1989 makes substantial changes in the detailed rules in relation to the registration of company charges. But these provisions of the 1989 Act have not yet been brought into force and there is no sign that they will be brought into force in the near future.

The Register of Inhibitions and Adjudications

The Register of Inhibitions and Adjudications[16] is usually referred to as the personal register or the diligence register. It is the home of entries concerning inhibitions, sequestrations, trust deeds for creditors, and company administrations, though the latter also appear in the Companies Register. Sequestrations and trust deeds are also registered in the Register of Insolvencies,[17] but in practice conveyancers seldom have recourse to that register. The personal register is more fully dealt with in chapter 7.

[13] Companies Act 1985, s. 410(5).

[14] Companies Act 1985, s. 410(2).

[15] Companies Act 1985, s. 420. See the standard texts on company law for details.

[16] Kept at Meadowbank House in Edinburgh.

[17] Bankruptcy (Scotland) Act 1985, s. 1A (as substituted by the Bankruptcy (Scotland) Act 1993).

Registers of contaminated land[18]

Under section 143 of the Environmental Protection Act 1990, local authorities are obliged to keep registers of property which is subject to contamination. The system has been criticised because uncontaminated land can enter this register, while contaminated land may not appear on it, and, moreover, there seems to be no process whereby land which has been decontaminated can be taken out of the register. These registers are potentially important to conveyancers, who will probably be expected to search these registers on property transfers and on the creation of securities. However, shortly before going to press the Government announced that it did not intend to bring these registers into operation, at least in their present form.

Planning registers

Local authorities keep public registers of planning applications[19] and of established use certificates.[20]

[18] See *Scots Law and the Environment: Liability for Contaminated Land* by Messrs. Brodies, W.S. (1992).

[19] Town and Country Planning (Scotland) Act 1972, s. 31.

[20] Town and Country Planning (Scotland) Act 1972, Sched. 12, para. 6.

CHAPTER 19

POST-SETTLEMENT CLAIMS

Introduction

This chapter deals with claims which may arise after settlement of a transaction has taken place. The subject has two aspects. The first is whether, after settlement, the missives can to any extent still be founded on as a basis for a claim. The second aspect, which relates only to defects and limitations in the title, is whether a claim can be made under the warrandice clause in the disposition.

1. Missives and the Prior Communings Rule

The rule against prior communings is a rule of the law of evidence.[1] What it says is that where parties reduce an agreement to writing, it is incompetent to refer to extrinsic matters (telephone conversations, other writings and so on) to alter the final written agreement. Such extrinsic matters are "prior communings" which, so the parties are deemed to have intended, are superseded by the written agreement. That doctrine in itself is fairly sensible and fairly straightforward. The difficulty lies in applying this rule to conveyancing, where there is not one written agreement but two, *i.e.* the missives of sale and the disposition.

So far as missives themselves are concerned there is no particular problem: the rule is that negotiations prior to the missives are disregarded. But what about the disposition? For a long time the law here was unclear, but in the last third of the nineteenth century the rule was laid down, in a series of decisions of the House of Lords, that missives and disposition stand together in the relationship of prior communing and final document. Accordingly, when the disposition is delivered, the missives themselves are superseded *in toto*. As Lord Meadowbank put it[2]: "When communings and

[1] For a full account see an article by K.G.C. Reid at 1981 J.L.S. 414.

[2] *Hughes and Hamilton* v. *Gordon*, 15 June 1815, Fac. Coll.

correspondence result in regular title deeds, you are to consider everything previous to the actual title as burnt." That, generally speaking, remains the law today.

Two points may be made about this application of the prior communings rule. First, it presupposes that which is not true, namely, that in a conveyancing transaction missives and disposition perform substantially the same function. For only if the disposition is treated as a later and final form of the missives can, logically, the prior communings rule operate as between them. Secondly, the application takes the rule a great deal further than seems warranted by a mere rule of the law of evidence. It provides not merely that the missives shall not govern the parties' relations after delivery of the disposition (which might be thought to be fair enough) but also that it will, retrospectively, cease to govern their relations even prior to delivery. This is so even for obligations which arose and were enforceable prior to settlement. What is happening here is much more than a rule of the law of evidence. Instead it is novation of the earlier contract by the acceptance of the later one. To say, with Lord Meadowbank, that the missives are "burnt" is to say that, on delivery of the disposition, the parties discharge all rights and obligations previously arising. It is as if the missives had never existed. (Interestingly, novation appears not to occur in the application of the prior communings rule to leases: see, e.g., *Korner* v. *Shennan*.[3])

It is, of course, far too late to challenge the way in which the prior communings rule has been applied to conveyancing transactions. But there can be no doubt that the rule in its present form is highly unsatisfactory. For, whatever the position may have been in the 1880s (when missives were very short), modern missives are detailed and contain a large number of provisions which have no counterpart in the disposition. It is true that some of these provisions merely regulate the period between conclusion of missives and settlement, so that it is no hardship if they are superseded at settlement. But many others are of continuing applicability—or at least are not shown to have been satisfied until after settlement has taken place and the buyer has taken entry. For these it is important that the missives survive, at least for a time.

Is it possible to get round the prior communings rule? In prin-

[3] 1950 S.C. 285.

ciple the answer is yes, but in practice the law here is extremely complex, and appears to be in a state of constant flux. For most of this century, down to 1981, it was thought that the rule could be avoided by virtue of the "collateral exception."[4] The argument was, and is, a simple one. The basis (however dubious) of the prior communings rule is that missives are, so to speak, an earlier version of the disposition itself. The disposition prevails precisely because it represents the later version of the parties' intentions. The real content of the rule is that it applies only to those matters which are common to both deeds—date of entry, description of the subjects and the like. In relation to the various other points covered in the missives, the disposition is silent, *so that there is no later version*. These other points are therefore collateral to the main thrust of the contract of sale. Accordingly, they are not superseded by delivery of the disposition. Of course, this view of the law deprived, and deprives, the prior communings rule of much of its content. Most of the provisions of missives would live on after settlement. Although severely damaged by the decision of the Second Division in *Winston* v. *Patrick* in 1981,[5] this view has recently enjoyed something of a revival.

Winston v. *Patrick*

No case this century has caused more surprise and worry to the conveyancing profession than *Winston* v. *Patrick*. The facts were simple. The pursuers bought a house from the defenders. Settlement took place and the pursuers moved in. Three years later structural problems developed with a kitchen extension which had been built by the defenders. It appears that, although a building warrant had been applied for and obtained, the construction of the extension had departed from the terms of the warrant. The pursuers sued for damages, founding on clause 9 of missives: "The seller warrants that all statutory and Local Authority requirements in connection with the erection of the subjects of sale and any additions, extensions and alterations thereto have been fulfilled."

On the law as it was generally understood in 1981, this clause

[4] Strictly, this is not so much an exception as a case which is outwith the scope of the rule.

[5] 1981 S.L.T. 41.

was a collateral provision of missives and so would survive the disposition. Nonetheless the defenders pled the prior communings rule and the Second Division upheld the defence. According to the court, the clause did not contain a collateral obligation. Hence it did not survive missives. The pursuers could not found on it after settlement.

This decision caused general consternation in the solicitors' profession. As a practical matter, some method had to be found of keeping missives alive. But how, after *Winston*, was this to be achieved? *Winston* itself seemed to provide the answer. According to Lord Justice-Clerk Wheatley[6]:

> "It was . . . accepted[7] that there were exceptions to that general rule.[8] Examples of these were: (a) where the missives incorporated obligations in relation to moveables which would not be appropriate to be included in a disposition of heritage, (b) where in the missives there was a collateral obligation distinct from the obligation to convey the heritage, and (c) where there was an agreement in writing either in the missives or in a separate document or in the disposition itself that a personal obligation included in the missives would subsist and remain in force even if it was not included in terms in the disposition."

Although these exceptions are described as "examples" it has since been said that they are exhaustive.[9] The passage just quoted from *Winston* has been enormously influential in the subsequent development of the law and it will be referred to again below. But it should be noted at this stage that, not only are the remarks *obiter*, but they purport to represent not the views of the judge, Lord Wheatley (though, of course, they may have done), but of counsel. Important as they are, it must therefore be doubted whether these remarks can be treated as a final and considered statement of the law.

Lord Wheatley lists three exceptions, but in fact, since (a) is really just an example of (b), they collapse into two. In the immediate aftermath of *Winston*, the collateral exception seemed utterly

[6] At p. 49.
[7] By senior counsel for the pursuers.
[8] *i.e.* the prior communings rule.
[9] *Taylor* v. *McLeod*, 1990 S.L.T. 194, *per* Lord Milligan.

hopeless and conveyancers sought to use exception (c), the express agreement route. At first this seemed the path to eternal happiness. But over the last few years a number of difficulties have arisen with the express agreement route, culminating in the suggestion in an important recent case that it is wholly ineffectual.[10] At the same time there has been a corresponding, and unexpected, revival in the fortunes of the collateral exception. The two exceptions will now be considered in turn.

The express agreement exception

It is nowadays standard practice for parties to agree in writing that missives shall remain in force notwithstanding the delivery of the disposition. A provision of this kind is known as a non-supersession clause. A typical one would run:

> "This offer and the missives following hereon will form a continuing and enforceable contract notwithstanding delivery of the disposition, except in so far as fully implemented thereby. But the missives shall cease to be enforceable after a period of two years from the date of settlement[11] except in so far as they are founded on in any court proceedings which have been commenced within the said period. A clause to this effect shall be included in the disposition."

Under such a clause, the missives are to continue in force for two years only.[11a] This is a compromise. The seller would like to be free of the contract immediately, while the buyer requires time to find out whether the seller's obligations have been properly implemented.[12] Sometimes sellers attempt to reduce the period to below two years but this should be resisted. It should also be borne in mind that for some contracts, two years may not be enough. A standard example is the sale of a tenement flat where the seller has agreed to meet the costs incurred on a common repair scheme

[10] *Porch* v. *Macleod*, 1992 S.L.T. 661, discussed below.

[11] Sometimes "date of entry" is used, but this can be ambiguous where contractual entry and actual entry differ.

[11a] See *Pera* v. *Ray* 1987 S.L.T. and *Ferguson* v. *McIntyre* 1993 G.W.D. 10–711.

[12] Since most obligations in missives are on the seller, non-supersession clauses are chiefly for the benefit of the purchaser. But in some cases they can be for the benefit of the seller, though more often in commercial sales than domestic ones.

whose completion takes longer than two years. Special provision is made in the clause about litigation, to avoid the argument (on which there are conflicting *dicta*) that any court action must be completed within the two-year period. Provision is also made for the non-supersession clause to be repeated in the disposition. Whether such repetition is actually necessary is difficult to say, for the case law is divided.[13] The argument in favour of repetition in the disposition is that, if it is really true that missives are superseded *in toto* on delivery of the disposition, then it is incompetent to look at the missives even to see whether there is a clause keeping the missives in force. So the non-supersession clause must appear in the disposition, as the later document. An alternative method of achieving the same thing is to have an exchange of letters at settlement between buyer and seller declaring that the missives remain in force. But this is not much used in practice.

The story so far is that *Winston* changed, and expanded, what had been believed to be the scope of the supersession doctrine. Conveyancers responded by adding non-supersession clauses to missives. There was then doubt as to whether even that was sufficient, so conveyancers started to add the clause to the disposition as well as to the missives. But now we come to another twist in the tale. Non-supersession clauses may not work at all. That, at least, seems to be the message from the recent case of *Porch* v. *Macleod*.[14] Briefly, the argument which prevailed in that case is the following. It starts with the literal words used by Lord Wheatley in *Winston*, quoted above. The express agreement exception[15] is said to be available only for "personal obligations."[16] What are "personal obligations"? The answer seems to be that they are obligations relating to the parties personally as opposed to obligations relating directly to the subjects of sale. They are similar to, or perhaps even identical with, "collateral obligations." Indeed, "collateral" and "personal" are bracketed together throughout Lord Wheatley's opinion. But here lies the rub. For if non-

[13] See *Finlayson* v. *McRobb*, 1987 S.L.T. (Sh. Ct.) 150; *Wood* v. *Edwards*, 1988 S.L.T. (Sh. Ct.) 17; *Fetherston* v. *McDonald*, 1988 S.L.T. (Sh. Ct.) 39; *Jamieson* v. *Stewart*, 1989 S.L.T. (Sh. Ct.) 13.

[14] 1992 S.L.T. 661. See, also, *Grieves* v. *Abercromby*, 1989 S.C.L.R. 11, and *Parker* v. *O'Brien*, 1992 S.L.T. (Sh. Ct.) 31.

[15] *i.e.* exception (c) in the passage quoted.

[16] Why it should be restricted in this way would be hard to explain.

supersession clauses are available only for collateral obligations there is no point in having them at all. A collateral obligation will survive anyway, by virtue of the collateral exception. There is no point in having a non-supersession clause as well.

It might be thought that the conclusion is all but fatal to the argument. In effect, the argument requires Lord Wheatley to be giving as his final exception (the express agreement exception) something which has no substance at all. And that seems improbable, to say the least. This difficulty was anticipated by Lord Milligan himself[17] in the earlier case of *Taylor* v. *McLeod*[18]:

> "For this exception to add materially to the second exception specified,[19] what must be envisaged is a non-collateral but personal obligation in the missives coupled with the agreement in writing referred to.[20] The circumstances in which a condition will fall within the third exception but not within the second exception appear unexplored. Pending such exploration, it does not appear clear in what circumstances such agreements in writing will be of critical importance."

No exploration of the distinction between "collateral" and "personal" was offered in *Taylor* and none is offered in *Porch* v. *Macleod*. In *Porch* the clause founded on was said by the court to be non-collateral and therefore, without further discussion, non-personal within the meaning of exception (c). Accordingly, it could not be rescued by a non-supersession clause. Thus, if there is such a thing as an obligation which is non-collateral but at the same time personal, there is nothing in *Porch* to indicate its nature.

It is, however, too early to abandon non-supersession clauses. At worst they do no harm and at best *Porch* v. *Macleod* may be overruled, or distinguished, by a higher court. One must wait and see. But what is now clear is that conveyancers can no longer afford to rely on non-supersession clauses alone. Some further step should also be taken if missives are to be kept in force. There are various possibilities here. One would be to repeat particular clauses from missives on which it is proposed to rely in the future in the disposition itself. But this would be tiresome. A second possibility would

[17] The judge in *Porch* v. *Macleod*
[18] 1990 S.L.T. 194 at 199.
[19] *i.e.* the collateral exception.
[20] *i.e.* a non-supersession clause.

be to draw up a formal post-settlement contract repeating such terms of the original missives as the parties wish to keep in force. But this method, although effective, would be rather too elaborate for an ordinary conveyancing transaction. In the normal case, therefore, a third possibility is perhaps to be recommended, which is for buyers to draft their offers in such a way that the collateral exception becomes available, and to this exception we now turn.

The collateral exception

The leading case on the collateral exception is of course *Winston* v. *Patrick* itself, where the following clause was held not to be collateral: "The seller warrants that all statutory and Local Authority requirements in connection with the erection of the subjects of sale and any additions, extensions and alterations thereto have been fulfilled."

Unfortunately, the grounds on which the decision was arrived at are opaque, so that in recent years two different views have developed as to the proper meaning of "collateral." The first view is that "collateral" means "future." So if a term of the missives is capable of giving rise to rights in the future, then it is collateral and will survive delivery of the disposition. Conversely, a clause which, as was said by Lord Wheatley in *Winston*, "did not incorporate any personal or collateral obligation to do anything in the future but was simply a statement of the state of affairs or condition of the property as at the date of the missives" would not be treated as collateral. So on this view a positive obligation on the seller to do something in the future, such as an obligation to deliver a clear search, will always be collateral.[21] Further, a simple warranty, for example that the central heating system is in good working order or that there are no statutory notices, will also be collateral provided that the warranty relates to some date in the future such as the date of entry.[22] On this view, what was wrong

[21] *Taylor* v. *McLeod*, 1990 S.L.T. 194; *Bourton* v. *Claydon*, 1990 S.L.T. (Sh. Ct.) 7.

[22] *Jones* v. *Heenan*, 1988 S.L.T. (Sh. Ct.) 53. A warranty which does not relate to a future date is not rescued by an ancillary positive obligation which does. So in *Porch* v. *Macleod*, 1992 S.L.T. 661 the following clause was held not to be collateral: "All necessary consents . . . have been obtained and complied with for any work undertaken on the subjects or for any use thereof and satisfactory evidence

with the clause in *Winston* was not that it was a warranty, but that the warranty related to the date of conclusion of missives and not to some future date.[23]

The other view of "collateral" is much stricter. It is that a clause is collateral only if distinct in subject matter from the normal terms and conditions involved in selling a property. In *Winston* v. *Patrick* this view appears most clearly from the judgment of the Sheriff Principal (Reid, Q.C.):

> "A collateral agreement, as I understand the term, is a separate agreement between the same parties but running alongside and distinct from the agreement to which it is collateral. Missives may well contain a multiple contract which provides not merely for the sale of heritage but also for the sale of moveables by way of fittings or buildings to be built or completed on heritage which is being sold to the purchaser . . . Where there is a multiple contract in the missives the disposition in my opinion is final in regard to the intention of the parties about the heritage existing and transferred, but in regard to other matters which are distinguishable from the heritage the intention of the parties thereanent continues after the granting of the disposition."[24]

As the Sheriff Principal indicates, the two main examples of a collateral obligation on this interpretation of the term are (1) obligations in relation to moveables[25] and (2) obligations concerned, not with the sale of a house, but with its construction.[26] But

to substantiate this will be exhibited to us before and delivered at the date of entry." On the same point, see also, *Grieves* v. *Abercromby*, 1989 S.C.L.R. 11.

[23] Thus, Lord Milligan in *Taylor* v. *McLeod*, 1990 S.L.T. 194 at 198: in *Winston* "the court accepted the contention for the defenders that the condition was simply a statement of the state of affairs or condition of the property as at the date of the missives. The decision accordingly applies only to a condition of which the same can be said."

[24] 1981 S.L.T. 41 at 46.

[25] *Jamieson* v. *Welsh* (1900) 3 F. 176. See also *Meek* v. *Bell*, 1993 G.W.D. 20–1238.

[26] *McKillop* v. *Mutual Securities Ltd.*, 1945 S.C. 166; *Hoey* v. *Butler*, 1975 S.C. 87; *Hardwick* v. *Gebbie*, 1991 S.L.T. 258; *Black* v. *Gibson*, 1991 G.W.D. 15–938; *King* v. *Gebbie*, 1993 S.L.T. 512.

standard terms of missives are not collateral, whether expressed in the form of a positive obligation[27] or of a warranty.[28]

These two views of the meaning of "collateral" are not reconcilable. Thus, the standard clause: "the central heating system will be in good working order at the date of entry" has on separate occasions been held both to be collateral[29] and also not to be collateral.[30] Both views of the law are represented in the cases decided since *Winston* v. *Patrick* although the first view (collateral as meaning future) appears currently to be the dominant one.

What is to be done?

The best advice which can be given at present is twofold. In the first place, to persevere with non-supersession clauses in the disposition, on the basis that they do no harm and may perhaps do some good. Secondly, to ensure that all obligations in missives which are intended to survive settlement are drafted in such a way that they appear to confer future rights on the buyer. They will then, it is to be hoped, be "collateral," at least on one view of the meaning of that term. Unfortunately, however, the law in this area does not stand still and, as with the missives themselves, it is all too likely that this advice will soon be superseded.

So much for missives, and for the difficulties of keeping them in force. The disposition itself contains a number of undertakings by the seller which may be of assistance for post-settlement claims. The most important of these is the clause of warrandice.

2. Warrandice[31]

Warrandice is a guarantee, expressed or implied in a disposition, of good and unencumbered title. There are three degrees of warran-

[27] *King* v. *Gebbie*, above, *per* Lord Caplan at p. 517.

[28] *Jamieson* v. *Stewart*, 1989 S.L.T. (Sh. Ct.) 13.

[29] *Jones* v. *Heenan*, 1988 S.L.T. (Sh. Ct.) 53; *Taylor* v. *McLeod*, 1990 S.L.T. 194.

[30] *Jamieson* v. *Stewart*, 1989 S.L.T. (Sh. Ct.) 13; *Parker* v. *O'Brien*, 1992 S.L.T. (Sh. Ct.) 31.

[31] The fullest account is K.G.C. Reid, "Warrandice in the Sale of Land" in D.J. Cusine (ed.), *Scots Conveyancing Miscellany: Essays in Honour of Professor J.M. Halliday*. See also the *Stair Memorial Encyclopaedia*, vol. 18, paras. 701–719.

dice,[32] which are, in ascending order, simple, fact and deed, and absolute. The higher includes the lower, so that if a claim could be made under simple warrandice, it could also be made under fact and deed warrandice, and if a claim could be made under fact and deed warrandice, it could also be made under absolute warrandice.

Simple warrandice

Simple warrandice is a guarantee that the grantor will do nothing subsequently to prejudice the title of the grantee. The content of this guarantee is minimal, for in most cases there is nothing that a grantor could do to incur liability. If A dispones to B with simple warrandice, A can thereafter do nothing to affect the title, because A is no longer owner. Simple warrandice would however cover the following case. A dispones to B on day 1, and fraudulently dispones to C on day 2. C records his disposition in the Sasine Register on day 3 and B records on day 4. C is now owner. B has nothing because by the time he recorded his disposition it had become *a non domino*—from a non-owner. B can sue A on the footing of simple warrandice.

Fact and deed warrandice

Fact and deed warrandice is a guarantee that the grantor will do and has done nothing which could prejudice the title of the grantee. It thus covers what simple warrandice covers, but also covers past acts by the grantor as well. Take the previous example and suppose that B had recorded first. Would C then have a claim against A? Not under simple warrandice, because the disposition by A to B was, at the time when A granted warrandice to C, not a future act but a past one. But if the warrandice by A to C was fact and deed warrandice, C would have a claim.

Absolute warrandice

Absolute warrandice guarantees the grantee against defects and limitations in the title whether caused by the grantor or not. Thus,

[32] In addition there is warrandice *debitum subesse* which is implied in onerous assignations of debt. This is a guarantee that at the date of the assignation the debt is payable to the cedent.

suppose that A dispones to B a 70 hectare farm, with absolute warrandice. It later turns out that title to one hectare is bad, this hectare being part of the title of the neighbouring farm. The reason is that the previous owner of the farm had sold 21 hectares to the neighbour, of which this one hectare was part. A is liable to B. He would not have been liable if he had granted to B only simple or fact and deed warrandice, because the defect did not arise from his own act.

Wording of warrandice clause

In practice, the warrandice is always expressed in the conveyance, usually as the final clause before the testing clause. The forms are: "I grant simple warrandice"; "I grant warrandice from my own facts and deeds"; "I grant warrandice." The last of these means absolute warrandice.[33]

Which type of warrandice?

If there is no warrandice clause, the law will imply one. In outline, the rule is that simple warrandice is implied in conveyances by way of gift, and absolute warrandice is implied in sales.[34]

In sales by trustees or executors the practice is for the trustees to grant fact and deed warrandice personally and to bind the trust estate in absolute warrandice. The practice in sales by heritable creditors is similar. The seller grants fact and deed warrandice personally and binds the debtor (the former owner) in absolute warrandice.[35]

Missives do not usually make provision about warrandice. The grantee is in that case entitled to the type of warrandice which is implied or is normally granted in transactions of that type. If, however, there is anything dubious about the title, or part of it,[36] the missives should have an express provision about the warrandice to be granted.

[33] 1868 Act, s. 8.

[34] Implied warrandice is overridden by express warrandice. Thus, if a disposition by way of sale grants simple warrandice, the implication of absolute warrandice is excluded.

[35] As has been suggested in chap. 12, it is arguable that a purchaser should ask for absolute warrandice from the selling creditor.

[36] For it is perfectly competent to grant absolute warrandice for part of the subjects disponed and lesser warrandice for some other part.

Remedies under warrandice

Warrandice is enforced by a claim for damages. If the defect in title is such that the disponee loses the property entirely, the *quantum* of damages is the market value of the property. If the defect is a lesser one, the *quantum* is the diminution in market value. Thus, suppose that A dispones a house to B and it then emerges that the garden ground is burdened by a servitude of way in favour of a neighbour. In a warrandice claim, the court will hear evidence as to what the market value would have been if the servitude had not existed, and as to the actual market value subject to the servitude. The difference is then the measure of B's loss and of A's liability to B.[37] Probably no claim can be entertained for *solatium*.[37a]

What does warrandice cover?

Warrandice is generally stated as being a guarantee that the title is (1) good and (2) unencumbered, and this is correct as far as it goes. But no liability under warrandice arises in respect of the first of these guarantees unless and until there has been "judicial eviction," that is to say a decree declaring the existence of a better right in some third party.[38] Thus, suppose that A dispones to B a farm of 70 hectares and it later turns out that one of these hectares, though possessed by A, and now by B, is in fact owned by C, a neighbouring farmer. It may be that A and B and C all assumed that this hectare was part of the title of the 70 hectare (or rather 69 hectare) farm. While matters stand thus, B has no claim under warrandice against A. For C, being unaware of the position, is making no claim, and B remains in possession, and annually ploughs and reaps the hectare. In the eyes of the law, unless and until C reclaims this hectare, B has suffered no loss and thus A is not liable. This is on the whole a sensible rule, but sometimes can be slightly unsatisfactory. Thus, suppose that five years later B

[37] The leading case is *Welsh* v. *Russell* (1894) 21 R. 769.

[37a] *Palmer* v. *Beck*, 1993 S.L.T. 485, *per* Lord Kirkwood at p. 492.

[38] See, *e.g. Palmer* v. *Beck*, 1993 S.L.T. 485. If the action is settled without decree, there is still eviction provided that there was no good defence. See *Watson* v. *Swift's J.F.*, 1986 S.L.T. 217.

wishes to sell the farm to D.[39] D's solicitor checks the title more carefully than B's solicitor did. He picks up the fact that B has a good title only to 69 hectares. As a result, D insists on a small reduction in the price. B has now lost money, but has no claim in warrandice against A, because there has been no eviction by the true owner. In practice, B's solicitor must pick up the bill. He should have noticed the defect at the time of the original purchase, and, had he done so, B would have had a claim against A under the good and marketable title provisions of the missives.

The guarantee as to unencumbered title is somewhat different. No eviction is required to trigger liability, and a claim can be made in respect of any encumbrance (such as a standard security or a real burden[40]) which was unknown to the purchaser at the time when warrandice was granted. The second point requires emphasis. Thus, if land is subject to a servitude in favour of a neighbour, and the grantee was aware of this, he cannot subsequently turn round and sue the grantor under warrandice. This is simple equity. If there was some third party right which he objected to and knew about, he should have raised the point before settlement. This is one of the reasons why a disposition narrates all the burdens which affect the land, so as to make absolutely clear what the grantee is acquiring.

Leases are treated differently from other encumbrances, and appear not to give rise to a warrandice claim.[41] However, where it is intended to convey property with vacant possession, it is nowadays standard practice to state this fact expressly in the deed,[42] so that in such a case the existence of a lease would give rise to a claim. Usually, of course, the existence of a lease will be obvious, in which case the grantee may be barred from a claim by his knowledge of the lease.

Transmission of warrandice

Suppose that A sells land to B, and B later sells to C. A defect in title then emerges. C can sue B under the warrandice which B

[39] If 10 years had passed, B's title would, in the normal case, be good by prescription.

[40] Though only if the burden is of an "unusual" type.

[41] *Lothian and Border Farmers Ltd.* v. *McCutchion*, 1952 S.L.T. 450. The correctness of this decision is, however, not wholly free from doubt.

[42] "With entry and vacant possession as at."

granted to him. But he may not wish to do this. Perhaps B is bankrupt, or has disappeared. Can C sue A? The answer is that he can do so, because the clause of assignation of writs which will normally have been part of the disposition by B to C[43] operates as an assignation to C of B's warrandice rights against A.[44]

This, however, is subject to certain qualifications. A can be liable to C only to the extent that he would have been liable to B if B had not sold to C: *assignatus utitur jure auctoris*. Thus, if A had granted only simple warrandice to B, he would be unlikely to be liable to C. Or if the defect was caused by B's act, or by diligence by B's creditors, A cannot be liable to C. Moreover, A's liability may be barred by negative prescription.

[43] This clause is now implied, unless expressly excluded: 1979 Act, s. 16.

[44] Stair, II, iii, 46. If, however, C sues B, then it appears than B can sue A. See *Christie* v. *Cameron* (1898) 25 R. 824; *Cobham* v. *Minter*, 1986 S.L.T. 336.

CHAPTER 20

REGISTRATION OF TITLE

Introduction[1]

The Register of Sasines is a register of deeds. It consists of huge numbers of deeds stretching back to the establishment of the register in 1617. These are divided by registration area, but apart from that there is no arrangement, except chronological. The deeds affecting a given plot are thus scattered in an unconnected way over countless record volumes. They are traceable by the indexes and by the search sheets. The register is not a register of title, as such. Nowhere in the register is there anything which gathers together the real rights in a plot of land and states what those rights are in a definitive way. Moreover, although, subject to minor qualifications, registration in the Sasine Register is a necessary condition of obtaining a real right, it is not a sufficient condition, for a deed in the Sasine Register may be void. Edinburgh Castle belongs to the Crown. Yet the reader could grant a disposition of it to a friend, and, provided that the disposition was properly executed, properly stamped, and properly described the castle, the Keeper would have to accept the deed for recording. That, however, would not pass ownership. *Nemo dat quod non habet.*[2] The disposition would be ineffectual and the Crown would still be the owner. Thus, the fact that there exists in the Sasine Register a deed ostensibly passing ownership to X does not necessarily mean that X thereby became the owner. Hence, the task of ascertaining from the Sasine Register what are the real rights in a plot of land or a house, and in whom such rights are vested, is not a straightforward one. It is a task for a trained conveyancer.

[1] The ROTPB is the standard guide, and is almost exhaustive on the practicalities. A.J. McDonald, *Registration of Title Manual* (1986) is also of assistance.

[2] Or, to put the maxim in its other form, *nemo plus juris ad alium transferre potest quam ipse habet.*

The 1979 Act,[3] therefore, adopted the alternative system, widely, though not universally, employed in other countries, of registration of title.[4] In registration of title there is a single, self-contained document[5] which sets out the rights for each plot or house, and the persons in whom those rights are vested. To change those rights the same deeds are used as in the Sasine system—dispositions, standard securities, and so forth—but such deeds, instead of being recorded,[6] are used by the Keeper as the basis for amending the title sheet. Registration (*i.e.* amendment of the title sheet) is necessary, as in the Sasine Register, in the sense that, subject to minor qualifications, there can be no real right without registration. But the system goes further than this. In registration of title, there is, again subject to minor qualifications, no such thing as a void registration. Registration is, thus, not only necessary to obtain a real right, but it is also sufficient.

The phasing in of the new register

The Land Register is based on exactly the same 33 registration areas as exist for the Sasine Register. It is being brought into operation area by area, the areas where it has been introduced being called operational areas. So far there are six such areas: Renfrew (from April 6, 1981); Dunbarton (from October 4, 1982); Lanark (from January 3, 1984); Glasgow (from September 30, 1985); Clackmannan (from October 1, 1992); and Stirling (from April 1, 1993). This progress has been far slower than the original intention, which was to have phased in all 33 counties by about 1990.[7] The current plan[8] is that one further county should become operational in 1993, namely West Lothian, and that the process should be fully completed by 2003. Whether this timetable will be kept to remains to be seen.

[3] This chapter cannot give a full account of the law relating to registration of title, some knowledge of which is assumed.

[4] Our system was largely copied from the English one, a fact which doubtless explains a great deal.

[5] The title sheet. In fact, it is kept in the form of computer data.

[6] Though the Keeper does retain a copy of all such deeds.

[7] ROTPB, para. A 1.02. In England and Wales registration of title began with the Land Registry Act 1862, but the process is still uncompleted.

[8] See 1992 S.L.T. (News) 230.

Non-operational areas remain wholly subject to the old system. The Keeper can at his discretion authorise registration of title for particular properties in non-operational areas, but this almost never happens in practice.

When a county becomes operational, that does not mean that all the properties in that county promptly switch into the new register. Properties remain in the Sasine Register until they are individually transferred to the new register.[9] This happens when the property is sold: sale triggers a compulsory switch. There are also certain other cases where the switch happens, but they are of little importance in practice.[10] Gratuitous transfers, such as gifts or conveyances to a beneficiary, do not trigger the switch.

Primary and secondary interests

The 1979 Act effectively divides real rights in heritage[10a] into two classes, primary and secondary interests, though the Act does not expressly use these terms. Primary interests are *dominium utile*, *dominium directum*, and long lease.[11] Other interests are secondary. Examples are standard securities, short leases, real burdens, and servitudes. Primary interests have their own title sheet, whereas secondary interests exist by being noted on the title sheet of a primary interest, unless they are "overriding interests" in which case they can exist as real rights without being registered at all. If a primary interest is still in the Sasine Register, and another primary interest is carved out of it, usually the new primary interest goes into the new register while the balance of the existing primary interest remains for the time being in the old register. There are two examples of this. One is where land is feued. The new feu will be entered in the new register, while the retained superiority continues, for the time being, in the old register. (If, a year later, the superiority were sold, it would then switch to the new register also.) The other example is where a long lease is granted. The ownership retained by the landlord remains for the time being in

[9] The switch can only be one way. A property cannot switch from the new register back to the old one.

[10] 1979 Act, s.2.

[10a] Or, in the coy phraseology of the Act, "interests in land."

[11] *i.e.* a lease for over 20 years.

the old register, while the newly created long lease enters the new register.

The creation of a new secondary interest is entered in the same register as the primary interest to which is relates. Thus, if a standard security is granted over land which is still in the old register, the security is also entered in the old register. But a standard security over land which is in the new register will itself enter the new register.

The title sheet and the land certificate

The title sheet is divided into four parts.[12] The first is the property section, which defines the property. There is a general description, typically no more than the postal address, and the property is then defined by a detailed plan, based on the Ordnance Survey map. The scale depends on the circumstances, but for a dwelling-house the scale of 1:1250 is standard. The second section is the proprietorship section. This simply names the person who owns the property. Section 3(1) of the 1979 Act makes it clear that a person so registered has the real right of ownership: the right may in some cases be voidable but it cannot be void. The third section is the charges section, which states any heritable securities which exist. The fourth section is the burdens section, which lists the real burdens affecting the property. Servitudes may also be entered here. Only those limitations (burdens, securities, etc.) as are listed in the title sheet, affect a proprietor, except for overriding interests.[13] The title sheet thus gives an almost complete picture of the state of the title. Any educated person can understand it.

The title sheet exists at Register House and never leaves it. The land certificate is simply a certified copy of the title sheet.[14] This is what the owner will receive. There is only one land certificate for each title sheet, but additional copies, called office copies, can also be obtained.[15]

[12] Land Registration (Scotland) Rules 1980, Pt.II.

[13] 1979 Act, s. 3(1)(*a*). For overriding interests, see below.

[14] For an example of a land certificate, see the ROTPB, Pt.D. App. 1.

[15] 1979 Act, s. 6(5).

The charge certificate

A standard security is not a primary interest and so does not attract its own title sheet or land certificate. Instead, it is simply noted in the charges section of the title sheet to which it relates. However, the Keeper issues to the creditor a document called a charge certificate which contains the security deed itself with certification that it has been entered on the title sheet.[16] As with a land certificate, the role of this type of certificate is purely evidential. The security exists as a real right by virtue of its entry in the title sheet.

Overriding interests

The principle of registration of title is that all rights affecting a property are entered in the title sheet, and that, consequently, any right not so entered is of no effect. But this ideal is not fully realizable in practice. Hence, there exists a category of rights called overriding interests[17] whose validity is unaffected by their omission from the title sheet. Servitudes are one example, the reason for this being that a servitude can be created by unregistered deed, or by implication, or by prescription, so that the Keeper can never be certain that he knows of all servitudes. Even here the ideal is for servitudes and other overriding interests to be noted in the title sheet, and the Keeper will so note them if he knows of their existence.[18] One exception to this latter rule is that of short leases, which are overriding interests but cannot be noted in the title sheet. The reason is that as short-term rights they should not be allowed to clutter up the register.[19] Other important examples of overriding interests include floating charges, and occupancy rights of non-entitled spouses under the 1981 Act.

[16] 1979 Act, s. 5(3); Land Registration (Scotland) Rules, r. 15 and Form 7. For an example of a charge certificate, see ROTPB, Pt. D, App. 2.

[17] Defined in the 1979 Act, s. 28.

[18] 1979 Act, s. 6(4).

[19] 1979 Act, s. 6(4). Long leases are not overriding interests and accordingly must be registered, which failing they are not real rights. See s. 3(3). Thus, in operational areas, long leases become real by virtue of registration, while short leases become real, as before, by possession in terms of the Leases Act 1449.

Rectification

The general principle is that the title sheet is conclusive, but there are certain qualifications to this principle. The Keeper can amend (rectify[20]) the title sheet where there is an "inaccuracy."[21] However, his power to do this is very limited. In outline, he can do so only where (1) all parties having an interest so agree, or (2) where the point is one about which he had previously excluded indemnity, or (3) where the inaccuracy has been caused by the "fraud or carelessness" of the proprietor,[22] or (4) where the proprietor is not in possession. The Keeper contrues "possession" widely to include civil as well as natural possession. Thus, the owner of leased property is considered as being in possession. In practice, rectification is rare.

Indemnity

Unless the Keeper has excluded indemnity, he will pay compensation in the event that he prejudices the rights of a person (1) by rectifying the title sheet or (2) by refusing to rectify it,[23] the latter being relevant where there is an "inaccuracy" which prejudices the claimant. Indemnity may be expressly excluded by the Keeper.[24] It is also excluded in certain other cases.[25] For example, the Keeper does not guarantee the validity of any real burden or the amount due under any standard security.

First registration and subsequent dealings

"First registration" means the conveyancing procedures appropriate where an interest enters the Land Register for the first time. A "dealing" means the conveyancing procedures applicable to an interest which is already in the new register. These procedures are

[20] Application for rectification is made on Form 8.
[21] 1979 Act, s. 9. The meaning of "inaccuracy" is not wholly clear.
[22] The scope of these words is uncertain.
[23] 1979 Act, s. 12.
[24] 1979 Act, s. 12(2).
[25] 1979 Act, s. 12(3).

by no means the same, and accordingly are considered separately below. Both are treated in exhaustive detail in the ROTPB.

First registration: pre-missives

The official recommendation is that the seller's solicitor, before missives, should instruct a Form 10 report.[26] This is simply a search of the Sasine Register, setting forth a prescriptive progress, and is also a personal search against anyone (typically the seller) as requested. The idea is that after missives but shortly before settlement this report is then updated by a Form 11 report.[27] However, it is common in practice to instruct the Form 10 shortly before settlement, and not to bother, therefore, with the Form 11. The Form 10 report does not constitute a guarantee that the Keeper will issue a land certificate without exclusion of indemnity, and indeed there is no way that a seller can obtain any guarantee about this, apart from the theoretical possibility of first making a voluntary registration. At the same time the solicitor will normally instruct a P16 report, which is a report stating whether the boundaries as defined in the existing title correspond with the physical boundaries of the property as disclosed in the Ordnance Survey map. The P16 report is not essential, but is commonly obtained, except for flats.

First registration: missives

Nowadays it is usual for missives to be drafted to cover three cases as alternatives: Sasine cases, first registrations, and dealings. For first registration the standard clause[28] calls for: (1) good and marketable title; (2) "a Form 10 report brought down to a date as near as practicable to the date of settlement showing no entries adverse to the seller's interest"; (3) "such documents and evidence including a plan as the Keeper may require to enable the Keeper to issue

[26] The request for the report is made on Form 10, while the report itself is headed 10A. A similar pattern exists for other reports. The forms are as laid down in the Land Registration (Scotland) Rules 1980, as amended from time to time. As with everything else in connection with registration of title, see the ROTPB.

[27] Form 10 and 11 reports can be obtained either from the Keeper or from independent search firms. See 1992 J.L.S. 500.

[28] See ROTPB, para. G 2.08.

a land certificate . . . containing no exclusion of indemnity." It is also advisable to add a further provision that the land certificate shall contain a statement that there are no subsisting occupancy rights[29] in respect of former owners.

First registration: after missives

After missives the seller's agent sends to the purchaser's agent the Form 16 report, the Form 10 report (with P11 extension if available), the title deeds, the draft discharge of the existing standard security, and the draft letter of obligation. The latter is in a style somewhat different from that used in Sasine transactions.[30] Its main thrust is that the land certificate when issued will include no exclusion of indemnity. It may also be wise to guarantee that the certificate will contain a note that there are no outstanding matrimonial occupancy rights.

First registration: examination of title

In a first registration, the purchaser's solicitor examines the title in essentially the same way as for an ordinary Sasine transaction, the reason being, of course, that at this stage the subjects are not yet in the new register and so there is no land certificate. However, the purchaser's agent may in some respects be more stringent and in other respects less stringent than in an ordinary Sasine transaction. He may need to be more stringent because he needs to ensure that the evidence produced is enough to satisfy not only him but the Keeper. He may be less stringent because there are cases where a technical defect is of a type to which the Keeper would be prepared to turn a blind eye. The answers to the questions in Form 1 (see below) should be mutually agreed between the agents. The Form is drafted by the purchaser's solicitor.

One crucial point is to ensure that the Keeper will be able to map the subjects. The existing titles may contain an adequate plan. If not, the seller must[31] produce one, an obligation which is provided for in the missives. This can then be made part of the current disposition.

[29] Under the 1981 Act. See chap. 8.
[30] For a style, see ROTPB, para. G2.20.
[31] In most cases at least.

First registration: drafting the deeds

On a first registration, the form of the disposition is the same as in a Sasine transaction, except that no warrant of registration is necessary. The title number is not, and cannot, be included because at this stage it will not yet have been allocated. If the grantor is an uninfeft proprietor, there must be the usual clause of deduction of title.

The standard security to be granted by the purchaser will also take the same form as in a Sasine transaction (minus the warrant of registration) provided that it is to be submitted along with the disposition. The same remarks apply equally to the discharge of the existing standard security.

Applying for first registration

After settlement, the purchaser's solicitor must immediately apply for registration, just as in a Sasine transaction he would record the deeds. He sends to the Keeper (1) the disposition or feu disposition; (2) the new standard security; (3) the discharge of the old standard security[32]; (4) a prescriptive progress of title, and any other necessary documents such as affidavits, feuduty redemption receipts and death certificates; (5) Form 4 in duplicate listing the writs being submitted; (6) a Form 1 (which is the application for first registration); (7) Form 2. Form 2 is the form for registration of a dealing. The "dealing" is the new standard security, for first the disposition will trigger registration, and thereafter the security will be in respect of an interest which has already (by a single moment) become a registered interest. However, the title number cannot be inserted because at this stage it has not been allocated. If the standard security is submitted later, the title number, which by this stage will be known, can simply be written in at the top of the first page: a new deed is not required.

Form 1 (the "pink form"), read with the notes thereto,[33] is fairly self-explanatory. The section headed "schedule of heritable securities, etc." is for existing, undischarged securities, including those to

[32] This does not require a separate application for the Keeper to give effect to it.

[33] The notes are not on the forms themselves, but are in a schedule to the Land Registration (Scotland) Rules 1980.

be discharged as part of the application, but not including the new security being granted by the purchaser. The section headed "schedule of burdens" should simply list the burdens writs by reference to the Form 4. The "FAS" number is the Keeper's account number for the law firm submitting the application. Where a question is inapplicable, instead of answering yes or no, one simply writes "N/A." For instance, where the disposition is from one individual to another, "N/A" will be the response to questions 4, 5, 6 and 7, which are concerned only with bodies corporate. All the forms must be signed by the grantee's agent.

Only the relevant title deeds need to accompany the application, *i.e.* chiefly the foundation writ, writs since then, burdens writs, and writs referred to for descriptions. A specimen list is given in paragraph D 2.09 of the ROTPB. Thus, many of the deeds handed over at settlement need not and should not be forwarded to the Keeper.

Issue of the land certificate

In due course the Keeper will issue the new land certificate, together with the charge certificate in relation to the standard security. These must be carefully checked. If everything is in order, the letter of obligation should be returned to the seller's agent marked as implemented, and the certificates sent to the lender for custody. One photocopy should be sent to the purchaser, and another retained on the file. In general, a solicitor should not part with a land certificate without taking a copy. Once the land certificate has been issued with no exclusion of indemnity, the existing Sasine writs cease to be relevant. Some agents keep them, others throw them out, others send them to the client, to do with what they will.

Dealings: Form 12

In general, a dealing is simpler than a first registration. Before missives, the seller's agent will obtain the land certificate, which in most cases will have been held by the lender. He will also request a Form 12 report which will disclose whether there have been any entries in the Land Register or personal register which could affect the proposed sale. (A land certificate can be updated at any time by the use of Form 8, but this is not common.) In the normal case the report will be a Form 12A but there are other possibilities, notably the Form 12B, which is issued where the previous transaction was a first registration and due to a quick resale the land certificate has still not been issued.

Dealings: missives

The missives are similar to a first registration,[34] the main thrust being that a land certificate will be issued to the purchaser with no exclusion of indemnity. The seller is also taken bound to deliver the existing land certificate.

Dealings: post-missives

The purchaser's agent will not examine the Sasine writs, but only the land certificate, the Form 12 report, and any other relevant documents such as death certificates, confirmations and affidavits. Examining title in a dealing is simpler than in Sasine transactions or first registration, because of the conclusive nature of the land certificate. If the Keeper says that X owns Y, then indeed X owns Y. The terms of a land certificate are conclusive. The certificate must of course be checked carefully, and in particular the plan should be checked with the purchasing client to ensure that it corresponds with what he thinks he is buying. The certificate should also be checked to see that it contains a statement that there are no matrimonial occupancy rights in respect of previous parties. The real burdens will appear from the burdens section, and while it is the case that property is not affected by burdens which do not appear on the title sheet, it does not follow from this that all the burdens which do so appear are actually enforceable.[35] In this respect, at least, there is little difference between burdens in the new register and the old.

[34] See ROTPB, para. G 3.05.

[35] Section 6(1)(*a*) enjoins the Keeper to enter in the register only "subsisting" real burdens, but in practice he naturally errs on the side of caution. See *Brookfield Developments Ltd.* v. *Keeper of the Registers of Scotland*, 1989 S.L.T. (Lands Tr.) 105.

Dealings: forms of deeds

Dispositions and other deeds affecting subjects in the new register are simplified.[36] The description of the property is simply by reference to the title number,[37] though it is normal to add also the postal address. There is no parts and pertinents clause.[38] Reference to burdens is unnecessary.[39] Where the grantor is uninfeft, no clause of deduction of title is required,[40] though the midcouples must exist and be produced to the Keeper. If an uninfeft proprietor wishes to complete title in his own name, he does so simply by application, producing the midcouples, and it is not necessary to have a notice of title.[41]

Registration of dealings

The disponee's agent completes the "blue form," Form 2 (whose terms will have been adjusted with the seller's agent), Form 2 being an application for registration of a dealing. This is sent to the Keeper together with the disposition, the existing land certificate, the existing charge certificate, the discharge of the existing standard security, any other relevant documents, such as midcouples, plus a Form 4 inventory of writs. The Keeper does not require a Form 2 to give effect to the discharge provided that this is being done at the same time as a disposition.[42] If a new standard security is being granted at the same time, a separate Form 2 is needed.

Split-offs

Where there is to be a split-off from a registered property, the disposition (or feu disposition) should contain a plan-based

[36] Styles of deeds are given in the ROTPB, para. G 3.22. These incorporate some modifications of the traditional styles which are not, in fact, connected with registration of title.

[37] 1979 Act, s. 15(1). "The subjects registered under title number" is the official style: Land Registration (Scotland) Rules 1980, Sched. B.

[38] *Cf.* 1979 Act, s. 3(1)(*a*).

[39] 1979 Act, s. 15(2).

[40] 1979 Act, s. 15(3).

[41] 1979 Act, s. 3(6).

[42] ROTPB, para. G 3.30.

description, followed by a "part and portion" clause referring to the title number of the whole subjects.[43] The plan can be simply a copy of the existing land certificate plan with the part disponed clearly marked, with boundary measurements. A detailed verbal description is not necessary.[44] If new real burdens are to be imposed, they should be stated in the disposition in the ordinary way. The disponee applies for registration by Form 3. The existing land certificate is submitted. The Keeper will then amend the existing title by removing from it the split-off area, though the title number will not be changed, and he will issue a new land certificate accordingly.[45] He will also issue a new land certificate for the split-off area, with its own, previously unallocated, title number. This will contain, among the other burdens, any new burdens imposed in the break-off deed.

Typically, a standard security will be granted at the same time over the split-off area. This cannot describe the subjects by reference to the new title number, since at this stage that new number will not yet have been allocated. The description in the break-off deed should be repeated.

Prescription

The role of positive prescription in the Land Register is a very limited one, for once a person has been registered as owner, he is owner, and the running of time in his favour can usually have no application. Hence, when examining title to a registered interest there is no question of checking for a prescriptive progress. Only where title has been registered with an exclusion of indemnity, does positive prescription have a role to play. In practice, such titles are usually vulnerable to rectification and hence are voidable, in whole or in part, and the effect of 10–years' possession is that they become exempt from challenge.[46] The exclusion of indemnity then falls to be deleted. There is, however, a minor defect in the legislation at this point, for there is no provision for prescription to pro-

[43] Land Registration (Scotland) Rules, Sched B, Note (a).

[44] ROTPB, para. E 42.

[45] Subsequent conveyances of the retained area will therefore not need to make any reference to the fact of split-off.

[46] 1973 Act, s. 1 as amended by the 1979 Act.

tect a person against rectification in other types of case. Fortunately such cases are rare.

A non domino conveyances

If there is a conveyance from A to B and B applies for registration and the Keeper considers that A was not the owner and had no power to grant the deed, then the Keeper has two choices. The first is to reject the application.[47] The second is to accept it, but with exclusion of indemnity.[48] Usually, he adopts the second course, which means that B is now the owner, but the effect of exclusion of indemnity is that if the rightful owner[49] turns up within 10 years and objects, B can be deleted and will have no claim for compensation.

In certain cases it is the Keeper's practice to enter both names on the title sheet, *i.e.* both B and the rightful owner. If the latter applies for rectification, B's name is deleted. Otherwise, after 10 years B can apply for the rightful owner's name to be deleted. It is, however, open to question whether this double entry is a competent procedure.[50]

[47] As he is entitled to do under s. 4(1) of the 1979 Act.

[48] In certain exceptional cases, the Keeper may choose not to exclude indemnity.

[49] He will not be the actual owner, who at this stage is B. Rather, he is the person entitled to ownership.

[50] See K.G.C. Reid at 1991 J.R. 79.

Chapter 21

FEUDAL CONVEYANCING

Once upon a time all conveyancing was feudal conveyancing. Even an ordinary disposition necessitated the involvement of the superior in order for the purchaser to complete his title. But feudal law has now been largely abolished,[1] and those aspects of conveyancing which still bring in the relation of superior and vassal are thus now fairly uncommon. Hence this chapter will be brief. Note that of the original types of feudal tenure, wardholding was abolished after the rebellion of Bonnie Prince Charlie,[2] and burgage was converted into feufarm by the 1874 Act.[3] That leaves feufarm and blench, which, however, are effectively identical in the modern law.

Feu dispositions

The basic deed for creating new feudal estate is the feu disposition (or the feu charter, a deed which is now identical, except in name, to the feu disposition). At one time feu contracts were also used widely, though today they are almost unknown. These ran in the third person and were bilateral in form (*i.e.* they were expressed as bilateral contracts). The grantor of a feu disposition has, immediately before the grant, the *dominium utile*, and after the grant will have only a superiority. He must at the time be infeft in the *dominium utile*, for there is no facility for deduction of title in feu dispositions.

If nowadays a feu disposition is used, which is unusual,[4] it is

[1] For feudal law see vol. 18, paras. 41–113 of the *Stair Memorial Encyclopaedia*. The final abolition of what remains of the feudal system has been proposed by the Scottish Law Commission in their Discussion Paper No. 93 (1991).

[2] Tenures Abolition Act 1747. This was one of the measures adopted to break the powers of the Highland chiefs.

[3] s.25.

[4] A seller who wishes to feu rather than dispone must ensure that this is expressly stated in the missives. Otherwise the purchaser can demand a disposition.

generally because the seller wishes to impose real burdens. In practice, this will almost always be where the sale is a split-off. Although real burdens can also be imposed in a disposition, the dominant tenement in such burdens can then only be the neighbouring properties, whereas if a feu disposition is used, the seller can enforce the burdens in his capacity as superior. Some sellers like this idea. It then depends on the terms of the deed whether neighbours will also have a right to enforce the burdens. Another possible motive is that a real burden can be enforced by the superior by irritancy, whereas a neighbour, as such, cannot irritate. Situations in which feu dispositions continue to be used include the following:

(1) New housing estates. The right to enforce is attached to the superiority which is retained by the developer, though the right will typically also be conferred on the neighbouring owners. If ordinary dispositions are used, nothing is reserved to the developers as a dominant tenement, and therefore they cannot enforce the burdens. Until a few years ago most of the volume housebuilders sold by way of feu disposition, but recently the trend has been strongly towards the use of ordinary dispositions.

(2) Large rural estates. These may extend to thousands of hectares, and for one reason or another the owner will over the years sell off parts, larger or smaller. The sales may be to farmers (who previously were tenants) or to cottagers, or for holiday homes, and so on. In the crofting counties, where the crofter buys his croft house or the whole croft, it is usually a feu disposition that is granted. Many landowners find a strong attraction in the idea that their neighbours are their vassals. It should be noted that such estates thereby become mixed estates, which is to say partly *dominium utile* and partly *dominium directum*. When the estate comes to be transferred as a whole, the various areas sold off over the decades will be listed in the disposition to show that for these areas the superiority only is being conveyed.

(3) Sales of council houses by local authorities. There is no legal necessity for the use of feu dispositions here, but housing departments like to retain as much legal title as they can. The real burdens imposed can be used by the local authority as a sort of supplement to planning controls.[5]

[5] In practice, local authorities often use archaic styles of feu writ.

The form of a feu disposition is almost identical to that of an ordinary disposition. The main differences are these:

(1) The words of transfer are: "Hereby *in feufarm* dispone."

(2) The pertinents clause reads: "Together with . . . my whole right, title and interest, present and future, *in and to the dominium utile hereinbefore disponed*." (This is to exclude the argument that the superiority is also being conveyed.)

(3) There is an additional clause, the *tenendas* clause, immediately after the entry clause: "To be holden of and under me and my successors as immediate lawful superior thereof in feufarm, fee and heritage forever."

(4) Until the 1974 Act there was also a clause imposing feuduty, but such clauses have been incompetent since that Act.

(5) Two of the clauses implied by section 16 of the 1979 Act have slightly different meanings where the conveyance is a feu disposition. These are the clause of assignation of writs[6] and the clause of obligation of relief.[7]

(6) There will usually be an irritancy clause attached to the real burdens. This is probably incompetent in a disposition imposing real burdens.[8]

If the grantor of the feu disposition owns the minerals, he will in most cases reserve ownership of them to himself.[9] But in that case he does not hold the minerals in his capacity as superior, for his right to the minerals is one of *dominium utile*. The result is that the superior finishes up holding a type of mixed estate, *i.e.* part superiority (the lands themselves) and part *dominium utile* (the minerals).

Disposition of superiority

Like the *dominium utile*, the superiority of land is transferred by disposition.[9a] Financially speaking, the benefits of holding a superiority are first, feuduty, which, of course, is of rapidly diminishing importance, and secondly the hope of charging for waivers of real

[6] s.16(2).

[7] s.16(3)(*b*)

[8] Though occasionally this will be encountered.

[9] Of course, if he intends to do this, he must so provide in the missives. See *Campbell* v. *McCutcheon*, 1963 S.C. 505.

[9a] A superiority is classified as corporeal heritable property.

burdens. Superiority titles often cover very extensive areas, so that the same party is superior for a number of streets or for a large country estate. There can also be a third benefit. When a superiority of large extent is held, it sometimes turns out that some plots of ground were never in fact feued out at all.[10] These may be waste pieces of ground, or, very occasionally, buildings or other land which are occupied by people who think they own them but do not.[11] In such cases the superior is not the superior of such areas, but something much better, namely the proprietor of the *dominium utile*, and can then demand a full price for granting a title. A possible fourth benefit is that, very rarely, a superior may be able to irritate a feu, which will mean that he will acquire ownership of it without having to pay compensation.[12] Lastly, some people like to buy a superiority because it makes them feel superior.[13]

Dispositions of pure superiorities are not encountered very frequently. Thus, transfers on death are rare because pure superiorities usually belong either to juristic persons (who do not die) or to trustees (who are regularly replaced), or the superiorities are so small and valueless that the executor of a deceased superior does not bother to deal with the title. Transfers of mixed estates, however, are common. A typical case is Colonel Y, the local landowner, selling out. The Colonel will own the *dominium utile* of some parts of the estate and the *dominium directum* of others.

The form of the disposition depends on whether the land is held on the Sasine or on the Land Register. In the case of sasine titles, the disposition is almost identical to the disposition of a *dominium utile*. In feudal theory superiors—like their vassals—are owners of the land, and so in both cases what is conveyed is the land itself and not merely the superiority or the *dominium utile*. It is incorrect[14] to

[10] If superiority titles were all well kept with proper plans, such unfeued areas would be obvious. However, in practice superiority titles are often obscure, and much spade work is needed to find out exactly what has, in plan-based terms, been feued out over the past century or whatever.

[11] This can happen only where the conveyancing has been bungled.

[12] This is rare, especially because the feuar, if threatened by an action of irritancy, can normally "purge the irritancy" by ceasing to breach the terms of his title. See further *Precision Relays Ltd.* v. *Beaton*, 1980 S.C. 220. Occasionally, the feuar has vanished, so that the superior can irritate unopposed.

[13] This is not intended as a joke, but as a curious fact of human psychology.

[14] But probably not invalid.

restrict the conveyance to the superiority although, as Stair[15] observed, "sometimes, through the ignorance of writers [*i.e.* solicitors], infeftments bear expressly to be 'of superiority'." A practical advantage of the approved method is that in conveyances of mixed estates there is no need to distinguish between those parts which are *dominium directum* and those which are *dominium utile*. Another advantage is that it facilitates feudal consolidation by prescription. The only difference from a disposition of the *dominium utile* is that feu rights are excluded from the grant of warrandice. In other words, the grantor declines to warrant that the land being conveyed has not been subfeued. If a substantial estate is being transferred, the usual practice is for the warrandice clause to list the properties which have been feued.[16]

In the case of Land Register titles, the approved style is given at paragraph G.3.22(b) of the ROTPB. In fact, it is absolutely identical to a (Land Register) disposition of the *dominium utile*. This is because in registration of title conveyancing, what is transferred is the property as disclosed on the title sheet; and in this case the title sheet will disclose the fact of superiority or of mixed estate.

Consolidation

Consolidation is where both superiority and property[17] are held by the same person, who decides to merge them.[18] This is generally done by a recorded minute of consolidation. Where the person already holds the superiority, and the property is disponed to him by his vassal, consolidation can be, and normally is, effected simply by adding the words "and I resign the subjects hereby disponed *ad perpetuam remanentiam*." This is, in practice, called a disposition *ad rem*. Consolidation is a tidying-up operation, but beyond that it is difficult to see that it has any particular value. Consolidation does not normally affect the rights of third parties, for instance the rights, if any, of neighbours to enforce real burdens.

[15] II, iv, 1.

[16] Sometimes the list, if it is long, is put into a schedule.

[17] In practice, the *dominium utile* is often called the "property."

[18] The main statutory provisions are the 1874 Act, s.6 and Sched.C and the 1924 Act, s.11 and Sched. G. See, generally, Halliday, paras. 17–109 to 17–121.

Charters of *novodamus*

A charter of *novodamus*[19] is granted by the superior to the vassal for the purpose of varying the terms of the feudal relationship. Of course, the vassal must agree to any such variation. Nowadays they are fairly rare, and are used only to change the real burdens. It is sometimes thought that if the vassal's title is defective, this can often be cured by a *novodamus* from the superior. But this is true only in one case, which is where the person entitled to challenge that title is the superior himself. In other cases, *novodamus* has no effect and cannot improve a defective title. Whatever party is entitled to make the challenge remains free to do so.

Minutes of waiver

If a real burden is to be waived by the superior, this can be done by *novodamus*, but nowadays is more usually done by a minute of waiver. If the real burden can be enforced not only by the superior but also by one or more neighbours, which is often the case, then obviously the latter should also grant the minute.[20] Minutes of waiver are also used to waive non-feudal real burdens, *i.e.* burdens originally created in dispositions. A formal minute is not always necessary, for where the form of the real burden is to prohibit a particular act without the consent of the superior, all that is required is that he gives that consent. A letter from the superior's solicitors will suffice.

Naturally, a superior will generally refuse to grant a minute of waiver unless his palm is crossed with silver. This, indeed, is one of the sources of income from a large superiority estate. The price is a matter for negotiation. If the superior asks for too much, the vassal may decide it is not worth it. There is also the possibility that the vassal will apply to the Lands Tribunal[21] for a variation

[19] See Halliday, paras. 17–96 to 17–105.

[20] Though obvious, this is sometimes overlooked in practice. If they do not grant the minute, they still have the right to enforce. If there are numerous parties with enforcement rights, obtaining a minute of waiver may not be practicable.

[21] Under the 1970 Act, s. 1. The Tribunal's jurisdiction is largely discretionary, and so the outcome of an application is necessarily somewhat speculative.

or discharge of the burdens. If the application is successful, the Tribunal will not normally award compensation to the superior.[22] Thus, if the burden is one which the Tribunal would very likely waive, the superior must ask a price which is low, *i.e.* cheaper to the vassal than the expense of applying to the Tribunal. But if the burden is such that the Tribunal would probably not waive it, the superior can ask a higher price. If the vassal needs the waiver for a commercial development, the price of a waiver can be very high indeed. Similar remarks apply to waivers granted by neighbours.

There is no statutory form of minute of waiver.[23] But a minute of waiver has a statutory effect: by section 18 of the 1979 Act the deed, once registered, binds successors of both parties.

Instead of discharging a burden outright, minutes of waiver often vary it, to the effect simply of permitting the use intended by the servient proprietor, and this is authorised by section 18. But a minute of waiver cannot be used for the imposition of a new burden. This requires a re-grant of the feu by means of a charter of *novodamus*, or a deed of conditions.

Feuduty

The 1974 Act provided that no feu disposition after the Act could impose feuduty.[24] It also provided machinery for the redemption of existing feuduties. This subject is dealt with elsewhere.[25] Of course, redemption of the feuduty does not extinguish the superiority, a distinction which clients sometimes fail to understand.

Old feudal conveyancing

We cannot here discuss the vast subject of the old system of feudal conveyancing. But one point is worth mentioning. Conveyancers will often come across Instruments of Sasine. Before 1858,[26] a disposition or feu disposition could not be recorded directly in the Sasine Register. Instead, a subsequent document, the Instrument of

[22] Though it can do so: 1970 Act, s.1(4).
[23] See Halliday, para.17–106 for a style.
[24] 1974 Act, s.1.
[25] Chap. 6.
[26] Titles to Land (Scotland) Act 1858.

Sasine, was recorded, which explains the name of the register. Thus, pre-1858 real burdens will be found contained in Instruments of Sasine. The instrument copied out all the material terms of the disposition or feu disposition on which it proceeded.

Chapter 22

DEEDS BY UNINFEFT PARTIES

Introduction

This chapter deals with "uninfeft proprietors," with the manner in which they can complete title (obtain infeftment), and with the manner in which they can dispone even without having first completed title. The chapter is based on Sasine conveyancing. The situation for registered conveyancing is fundamentally similar, but simpler, and will be considered near the end of the chapter.

Notices of title

How does a person become infeft? How does he complete title? In other words, how does he become owner of land? In general, the answer is that he simply records or registers the disposition in his favour. This has been the case since section 1 of the Titles to Land (Scotland) Act 1858, later replaced by section 15 of the 1868 Act. Before that, the grantee could not record his disposition.[1] Instead, after (1) obtaining the disposition he had (2) to take Sasine on the land, then (3) obtain a notarial Instrument of Sasine evidencing the Sasine, then (4) record that instrument, and then (5) get a charter of confirmation[2] from the superior. Of the three deeds (disposition, Instrument of Sasine, charter of confirmation) only one, the Instrument of Sasine, found its way into the Sasine Register.[3] Things were rather simpler for feu dispositions, where only two deeds were required, the feu disposition and the Instrument of Sasine, the latter being the one recorded. After 1858 the disposition or feu disposition could be recorded direct, though it was not till the 1874 Act that the need for the charter of confirmation was dispensed with.

But while these reforms allowed the grantee to record his deed,

[1] Subject to some minor qualifications.

[2] Alternatively, he could take entry by the resignation system, but this was less usual.

[3] Hence the name of the register.

they did not require him to do so. He could still record instead a notarial instrument, which would narrate the substance of the disposition or feu disposition. In that case, only the notarial instrument was recorded.[4] The 1924 Act[5] introduced a new deed called the notice of title, which must be signed by a solicitor, which is functionally the same as the old notarial instrument, and which has, in practice, replaced it. Thus, even today a disponee could complete title without ever recording the disposition, by obtaining and recording a notice of title (or notarial instrument).[6] The latter process does not dispense with the disposition: it would simply be an extra deed. Observe that the notice of title is in a sense a descendant of the old notarial Instrument of Sasine.

Normally, of course, one would register the disposition direct, for there is no point in using two deeds when one would suffice. But nevertheless there are certain situations where notices of title are used, and in one of them it is actually the only way to complete title. That is where the conveyance is a general conveyance as opposed to a special conveyance. A special conveyance is the usual deed. Its mark is that it gives a conveyancing description of the land in question. A general conveyance differs in that it contains no description (or an insufficient description) of the land. It may seem surprising that a conveyance of land should lack a description, but it does happen in certain types of case. One example would be a will which conveys to X all the testator's heritable property, without specifying what that property is. Another example happens in sequestration. In a sequestration the court issues an order called an act and warrant declaring that all the bankrupt's property is vested in the trustee. (At that stage, neither the court nor the trustee may have any clear idea of what the bankrupt owns.) This of itself does not make the trustee owner of the bankrupt's heritage, for he still has to complete title.

Where there is a general conveyance, it cannot itself be recorded in the Sasine Register.[7] The only way to complete title is, therefore, to use a notice of title (or notarial instrument). A notice of title is a statutory deed with a statutory form which must be followed.

[4] 1868 Act, s.17.

[5] s.4 and Sched. B.

[6] We are here dealing with Sasine conveyancing.

[7] The question of what is a sufficient description for the purposes of recording is discussed in chap. 9.

The appropriate form is almost always Form 1 of Schedule B[8] to the 1924 Act. It will be seen from Schedule B that the notice of title contains a proper conveyancing description.

Deduction of title

The notice of title contains a clause called a deduction of title. This begins by detailing the last recorded title, *i.e.* the last infeftment, and then explains how the present person has acquired right to the property. Thus, suppose that a Mr Boyle buys property in 1982 and is sequestrated in 1993. The notice of title in favour of the trustee will have a clause of deduction on the following lines:

> "which subjects were last vested in the said Lee Craig Boyle[9] whose title thereto was recorded in the said Division of the General Register of Sasines on the fourth day of September in the year nineteen hundred and eighty-two[10] and from whom the said Mary Helen Menzies as trustee in sequestration aforesaid acquired right by said act and warrant in her favour.[11]"

The deed will, of course, have already narrated the sequestration and the act and warrant and will also have given a proper conveyancing description of the property. Once this deed is recorded, Ms Menzies will be the owner, in trust for the creditors. Note that the statutory style of deduction has three parts: (1) identification of person last infeft; (2) date of that infeftment; and (3) reasons why the present party (Ms Menzies) is now entitled to infeftment.

Midcouples

To be able to deduce title in this way it is essential that the present party is able to connect himself by one (or, sometimes, more than one) conveyance with the party last infeft. These conveyances, which in the normal case will not have been recorded, though they

[8] The notes to which are important.

[9] The person last infeft must be designed, but he may have been designed earlier in the deed, in which case a simple reference is sufficient.

[10] Or simply "which subjects were last vested in the said Lee Craig Boyle as aforesaid" if the infeftment has been specified in an earlier part of the same deed.

[11] The midcouple must be specified fully, but here this has been done earlier in the same deed.

may have been registered in the Books of Council and Session, are called midcouples or links in title. In the example, there was just one midcouple, namely the act and warrant. But it is possible to have more than one, and this sometimes happens, as will be seen.

Note that a midcouple must be a conveyance. Thus, suppose A concludes missives to sell to B. B could not complete title by recording a notice of title deducing title through the missives. Missives are not a conveyance. The following are the main examples of midcouples[12]:

(1) Disposition or feu disposition.
(2) Confirmation of executor.
(3) English probate or letters of administration as affecting land in Scotland.[13]
(4) Trust deed for behoof of creditors.
(5) Act and warrant in a sequestration.
(6) Deed appointing a liquidator.[14]
(7) Will.[15]
(8) Deed of assumption and conveyance in favour of new trustees.
(9) Decree appointing a trustee or judicial factor.[16]
(10) Legislation transferring land to a public body. For instance, when local government reorganisation took place in the 1970s, land was transferred from the old county councils and burghs to the new authorities.[17] The latter did not become infeft until they had recorded notices of title to the various areas of land thus acquired. Thus, in a council house purchase, one will typically find that the land was acquired by an old burgh in, say, 1951, and that there has been a notice of title in favour of the present district council.

If the midcouple is a private deed, it is important from a practical point of view that it be registered in the Books of Council and Session, which fact will be stated in the deduction. The reason is

[12] See 1924 Act, s.5.
[13] Administration of Estates Act 1971, s.3.
[14] 1868 Act, s.25.
[15] The rules for wills are complex. In brief, a will can be used as a midcouple in favour of the executor but not directly in favour of a beneficiary. See chap. 23.
[16] Conveyancing Amendment (Scotland) Act 1938, s.1.
[17] Local Government (Scotland) Act 1973, s.222; S.I. 1975 No. 659.

simply that the deed can then never be lost, since it is publicly registered. There is no legal requirement for this, but it should always be done in practice. If, however, the midcouple is not a private deed, but (for instance) a confirmation or other judicial decree, such registration is not necessary. If the midcouple is a will, it will usually be the case that the will has been registered in the court books of the sheriffdom where confirmation was issued, in which case registration in the Books of Council and Session is not necessary. However, if there has been confirmation, it is unlikely that the will will be used as a midcouple, for in such cases the confirmation will be so used. In other words, where wills are used as midcouples, they will not normally have been registered in the Sheriff Court Books. Hence, in such cases registration in the Books of Council and Session is important.

A midcouple must be a conveyance

One of the basic rules of the law of deduction of title is that there can be no deduction of title through a mere beneficial interest. This is because a beneficial interest, such as a right under missives, or the right of a beneficiary under a will or a trust, is not a conveyance. Take a simple example. Mr Smith owns a house and dies, leaving the house to his widow. Mr Smith's executor is confirmed. Who can now complete title by notice of title? The widow has the beneficial interest, but that is not valid as a midcouple. Only Mr Smith's executor can complete title, deducing title through the confirmation in his favour. (In practice, however, he would very likely not record a notice of title, but convey direct to Mrs Smith either by disposition or by docket.[18]) The same principles apply even if the executor is the widow herself, as is likely to be the case. For then she has two capacities, as executrix and as individual beneficiary.

Deducing title in a disposition

Where a person has right to land by means of an unrecorded conveyance he can complete title by notice of title. But it is also possible for him to dispone such land without having first completed title. He does this by incorporating the deduction of title into the

[18] See below, and also the following chapter.

disposition itself.[19] Thus, consider again the example of the trustee in sequestration. She can, as has been seen, complete title by notice of title, deducing title through the act and warrant in her favour. But alternatively[20] she could convey to a purchaser direct without having first completed title. Such a disposition is in the ordinary form, except that immediately after the entry clause there is the clause of deduction. In the case of the trustee in sequestration this would run almost exactly as the clause in the notice of title. This facility never has to be relied upon, because a person who could deduce title in a disposition could always, if he chose, complete title first by notice of title and then grant a disposition in ordinary form. If a person intends to hold property for any length of time, he should complete title, but if he intends an early conveyance, it usually makes sense not to bother, and simply to deduce title in the disposition. The principle is that anyone who can record a notice of title can also dispone with a deduction of title, and vice versa.

A disposition by an uninfeft grantor is in theory a disposition *a non domino*, and thus anomalous. The best way to look at it is that it is a conveyance of the personal right to obtain infeftment under the previous midcouple. Even at common law it was also possible for an uninfeft party to convey. He did this by an assignation of his rights, in particular of his right to the unexhausted precept of Sasine. The assignee could then take infeftment. Nineteenth century legislation retained this system with various changes of detail, and the 1924 Act did the same, with further changes of detail. But because the 1924 Act also introduced deduction of title in a disposition, the system of assignation was given up in practice, and the 1970 Act finally repealed the statutory rules about assignation. But a disposition deducing title, and the old common law form of assignation, are in substance the same thing.

In what deeds can title be deduced?

It is competent to deduce title only in certain types of deed. The main ones are the notice of title itself and the disposition. It is also competent to deduce title in a standard security,[21] though this is

[19] 1924 Act, s.3 and Sched. A.
[20] And in practice this is more common.
[21] 1970 Act, s.12.

never done in practice. It is not competent to deduce title in a feu disposition, or a long lease, or a grant of servitude. Note also that it is not only a *dominium utile* to which title may be deduced. The provisions of the 1924 Act are wide, so that for instance title can be deduced to a superiority or to the creditor's interest in a standard security.[22]

Errors in deductions

It is not uncommon to find an error in a clause of deduction of title. In general, such an error will be fatal, in the sense that the deed will fail to give infeftment. However, it is usually easy to put right. Suppose that in our bankruptcy example Ms Menzies (the trustee in sequestration) granted a disposition to a purchaser (Mr Scott) direct without having first completed title herself. And suppose that in this disposition the deduction was faulty in that it gave the wrong date for Mr Boyle's infeftment. The effect would be that ownership could not pass to Mr Scott because of the error. Mr Boyle would still be legal owner in the sense that his is still the only effective infeftment.[23] But Mr Scott could put things right by recording a notice of title, deducing title through (1) the act and warrant and (2) the faulty disposition. Upon recording this, he would become owner. The reason is that although the disposition was invalid as a warrant for infeftment, it was still a conveyance, and therefore perfectly good as a midcouple.

Or suppose that Mr Scott discovered the error only when about to grant a disposition to another person, Ms Macdonald. (This is what typically happens—the solicitor for Ms Macdonald notices the error on examining the title.) It is not necessary to go back to square one and obtain a new conveyance from the trustee. It is not even necessary for Mr Scott to record a notice of title in favour of himself, as just described. He can grant a disposition to Ms Macdonald deducing title through (1) act and warrant (2) the (ineffectually recorded) disposition by Ms Menzies. When this is recorded, Ms Macdonald will become owner. Ms Menzies and Mr

[22] Including assignations, restrictions and discharges of standard securities.

[23] His sequestration divested him, and invested Ms Menzies. But at this stage she still has no real right, so that even after sequestration Boyle remained legal owner. His position was comparable to that of an ordinary owner who grants a disposition, during the short interval before the disponee has recorded it.

Scott were never owners since they were never infeft. They were uninfeft proprietors.[24]

Some terminological points

The word "vest" is ambiguous. In the 1924 Act it is used to mean "infeft." Thus, when a deduction of title clause says that the subjects were "last vested in" someone it means that the last infeftment (and therefore the current infeftment) was in that person. It should, however, be noted that the word is sometimes also used in a broader sense. Thus, in the law of succession, "vesting" is used to mean the acquisition of an indefeasible beneficial right.[25] Again, sequestration "vests" the estate of the bankrupt in the trustee, but this of itself gives the trustee a real right only for certain types of property, not including heritage.[26] Another example is the local government reorganisation in the 1970s, whereby land held by the old authorities "vested" in the new ones.[27] This was not infeftment. The legislation operated as a midcouple enabling the new authorities to obtain infeftment.

A person who could complete title in his own name but who has not done so is called an "uninfeft proprietor." This expression is somewhat illogical since by definition ownership is a real right and the only way to have the real right of ownership in land is to be infeft. But, all the same, it has long been the established term and no one would wish to change it now. The term is often found in deeds. Thus, if Ms Menzies has not completed title, and dispones to Mr Scott, the narrative clause will design her as "uninfeft proprietrix." The contrast here is with the expression "heritable proprietor," which means that the grantor is infeft.

Land registration

Deduction of title is not necessary in land registration.[28] But this is a change in form rather than substance. The midcouples are still

[24] See, generally, Halliday, para. 21–40.

[25] For discussion of this tricky subject, see articles at 1986 J.L.S. 148 (Gretton); 1986 J.L.S. (Maher); 1987 J.L.S. (Gordon); 1988 J.L.S. 98 (Patrick); and 1989 J.L.S. 338 (Styles).

[26] Bankruptcy (Scotland) Act 1985, s.31.

[27] Local Government (Scotland) Act 1973, s.222, and S.I. 1975 No. 659.

[28] 1979 Act, s.3(6) and s.15(3).

necessary. A person who is not in a position to deduce title in the Sasine system is no better off in land registration. The relevant midcouples are submitted to the Keeper as part of the application for registration. Thus, suppose Ms Menzies wishes to complete title for property in the Land Register. She will simply attach to her application the act and warrant in her favour. The Keeper will then register her as owner. No notice of title is necessary. Or if she wished to dispone to Mr Scott without having first completed title, Mr Scott would present the disposition to the Keeper together with the act and warrant, and would be registered as owner, and the disposition would not have to contain a clause of deduction. So in land registration practice midcouples are still needed in exactly the same way as for Sasine conveyancing. It should, however, be noted that deduction of title is dispensed with only in dealings with registered interests. It continues to be required in a deed which induces a first registration.

Some cases where deduction is not required

In the first place, there is no place for deduction where the disponer is infeft. Thus, suppose that A and B buy a house with a survivorship clause in the title, and A then dies. Under the law of survivorship destinations, B is deemed automatically infeft in A's half share the moment that A breathes his last. Hence when B comes to dispone, it is not necessary for her to deduce title. The disposition should simply mention the survivorship clause and mention A's death.

Next, a trustee in sequestration did not have to deduce title under the old law.[29] But the rule is different for post-1985 sequestrations.[30] Liquidators and receivers do not need to deduce title since dispositions by them are considered as being dispositions by the company itself.

Thirdly, where a standard security holder sells, no deduction is required. It might be argued that this rule is anomalous. But the

[29] Bankruptcy (Scotland) Act 1913.

[30] Bankruptcy (Scotland) Act 1985. The reason is that s.100 of the Bankruptcy (Scotland) Act 1913 provided that a disposition by the trustee in sequestration took effect as if it had been granted by the bankrupt with the consent of the trustee. The notional grantor was thus infeft, and so deduction was not required. The 1985 Act seems to contain no equivalent provision.

idea is that the standard security operates as an authorisation to the creditor to convey on behalf of the owner (in the event of default), so the position is comparable to a sale by an agent, where of course no deduction is needed.

Some worked examples of deduction of title

We give here, at the risk of repetition, some typical examples of deduction of title.

(1) A dies infeft. B is confirmed as executor. C is the beneficiary. B can dispone to C deducing title through the confirmation

> "Which subjects were last vested in the said A whose title thereto is recorded in . . . on . . . and from whom I acquired right as executor foresaid by said confirmation in my favour."[31]

(2) The same, but instead of disponing to C, B grants to C a docket.[32] The result of this is that C is uninfeft proprietor.[33] C could complete title by recording a notice of title deducing title through (1) the confirmation in favour of B and (2) the docket in favour of C. Or C could, without completing title himself, dispone to someone else, deducing title in the same way.

(3) A dies infeft. B is confirmed as executor. B grants a docket to C. C does not complete title. C dies. D is confirmed as C's executor.[34] D could record a notice of title, or dispone, deducing through (1) B's confirmation to A; (2) the docket to C; (3) D's confirmation to C.

> "Which subjects were last vested in A [design] whose title thereto was recorded in . . . on . . . and from whom I acquired right as executor foresaid by (primo) confirmation in favour of B [design] as executor of the said A issued by the Commissariot of . . . at . . . on . . . (secundo) docket endorsed on a certificate of the last-mentioned confirmation by the said B in

[31] In such a case the narrative clause will already have designed A and specified the confirmation.

[32] Succession (Scotland) Act 1964, s.15(2).

[33] Because the docket will not be recorded.

[34] This may seem a complex case, but is quite common in practice.

favour of the said C dated . . . and (tertio) said confirmation in my favour as executor of the said C dated as aforesaid."

(4) A, B and C are infeft trustees. A resigns and B dies. C executes a deed of assumption and conveyance appointing D and E as new trustees.[35] This deed could be recorded in the Sasine Register,[36] but let us suppose that it is not recorded. The three trustees (C, D and E) can complete title by notice of title deducing through the deed of assumption and conveyance. The clause would run thus:

> "Which subjects were last vested in the said A and B and C as trustees foresaid whose title thereto was recorded in . . . on . . . and from whom, following the resignation of the said A by minute of resignation dated . . . and registered in the Books of Council and Session on . . . and also following the death of the said B on . . . , we the said C and D and E acquired right as trustees foresaid by deed of assumption and conveyance by the said C as trustee foresaid in favour of the said C and D and E as trustees foresaid dated . . . and registered in the Books of Council and Session on. . . . "

As this example shows, the practice is that in a deed of assumption and conveyance, the grantor is himself to be one of the grantees.

(5) A, infeft, is sequestrated, and B is the trustee in sequestration. B dispones to C, deducing title through the act and warrant, but the deduction is defective because it misstates the date of A's infeftment. The result is that C is not owner, despite having recorded the disposition. But C is an uninfeft proprietor and could complete title by notice of title deducing through (1) the act and warrant and (2) the disposition by B to C. Or instead C could dispone to D deducing title in the same way. The disposition by B to C failed to confer infeftment but was otherwise valid as a conveyance, and this is the reason that it itself is a valid midcouple.

(6) A and B are infeft in common, with no survivorship clause. A dies and B confirms as A's executor. B is also the legatee of A's half share. B as executor dockets that half share to herself as an individual. B then sells the whole property. The deduction would run:

[35] See next chapter.

[36] If it has a proper conveyancing description of the heritable subjects in the trust.

> "Which subjects were last vested to the extent of a one half *pro indiviso* share in the late A [design[37]] whose title thereto is recorded in . . . on . . . and from whom I acquired right by (primo) confirmation in my favour as executor of the said A issued by the Commissariot of . . . at . . . on . . . [38] and (secundo) docket endorsed on a certificate of said confirmation by me as executor foresaid in favour of myself as an individual dated. . . . "

(7) Suppose in the last example that B was sequestrated after she had granted the docket to herself, and that X, her trustee in sequestration, dispones to Y. Here the two halves of the property will need separate deductions.

> "Which subjects were last vested to the extent of a one half *pro indiviso* share in the late A [design] whose title thereto is recorded in . . . on . . . and from whom I as trustee in sequestration foresaid acquired right by (primo) confirmation by the said B as executor of the said A issued by the Commissariot of . . . at . . . on . . . and (secundo) docket endorsed on a certificate of said confirmation by the said B as executor in favour of herself as an individual dated . . . and (tertio) the said act and warrant in favour of myself as trustee in sequestration foresaid, and which subjects were last vested to the extent of the other one half *pro indiviso* share in the said B whose title thereto is recorded in . . . on . . . and from whom I as trustee in sequestration foresaid acquired right by said act and warrant aforesaid."

[37] No designation is needed if A has been designed earlier in the deed, in which case the wording is "in the said A."

[38] Or "said confirmation" if it has already been specified earlier in the deed.

CHAPTER 23

TRUSTS AND EXECUTRIES

Introduction

When someone dies, body soul and estate pass on. The body is buried or cremated. The fate of the soul is a question for philosophers and theologians. For the estate, two questions arise. The main one is: who gets what? This is the province of the law of succession, and of inheritance tax. But there is also the question of how who gets what, or in other words how the successors are to obtain title. Every death thus involves a conveyancing problem of getting title from the deceased to the living.

The law before 1964

Prior to the 1964 Act there were two separate systems, according to whether moveable or heritable property was involved. For moveables, the process was (subject to minor qualifications) that the executor obtained confirmation from the sheriff. Confirmation is a type of decree. This procedure was used in both testate and intestate cases. This is still the law. But the executor had, as such, no right to administer the heritage. The administration of the heritage itself could happen in two ways. In the first place, if the deceased was intestate, he was succeeded by his heir.[1] If he had children, the heir was the eldest son. If there were only daughters, the daughters were co-heirs, under the name heir-portioners. In the absence of issue, the heir[2] would be a collateral heir, such as a brother, for always males were preferred to females. The procedure was that the heir petitioned the sheriff for a decree of service.[3] This decree then operated as a conveyance in his favour. Alternatively,

[1] The heir's right could, however, be subject to a liferent in favour of the relict, under the doctrine of terce (in favour of a widow) and courtesy (in favour of a widower).

[2] The full title was heir-at-law or heir-of-line, the two terms being synonymous.

[3] There were two types of service, special and general.

he could complete title by the *clare constat* procedure, which involved application to the superior. Both these procedures were abolished by the 1964 Act.

In the second place, if the deceased was testate, the heritable property would pass to whoever was entitled to it under the will. There are, in theory, two types of will, namely the will strictly so called, and the trust disposition and settlement. In the former, the legacies are made direct to the legatees, while in the latter everything is conveyed to trustees (who in practice would be the same as the executors for the moveables), with the legatees having the status simply of beneficiaries under a trust.[4] After the nineteenth century reforms, if there was a will (in the narrow sense) then either the legatee or the executor could deduce title through the will. (If the executor did so, he would, of course, then convey to the legatee.) But if there was a trust disposition and settlement only the trustee could complete title.[5]

The pre-1964 law, which has just been stated in only the briefest fashion, is important not only by way of background to the modern law, but also because knowledge of it can still be necessary in current practice. The pre-1964 law still applies to pre-1964 deaths. Consequently, if the last recorded title to land is in the name of someone who died before the 1964 Act, it is necessary to employ the pre-1964 law to make up title. It might be thought that this never happens nowadays, but in fact such cases still crop up surprisingly often. Thus, Mr Campbell buys a small farm in 1938, and his title is recorded. He dies intestate in 1959, and his son, Mr Campbell the second, takes over the farm, but no legal steps are taken to transfer title. The son dies intestate in 1986 and his son, Mr Campbell the third, takes over, again with no legal steps being

[4] In a trust disposition and settlement typical wording would be: "I . . . assign dispone and convey to my said trustees my whole means and estate heritable and moveable real and personal wherever situated which shall belong to me at the time of my death . . . but these presents are granted in trust only for the following purposes . . . (Tertio) to convey and make over to . . . my house at 17 Carey Gilson Street Kirkcudbright." A will in the narrow sense simply says: "I bequeath to . . . my house at 17 Carey Gilson Street Kirkcudbright . . . and I appoint . . . as my executor."

[5] See, generally, ss. 19 and 20 of the 1868 Act and s. 46 of the 1874 Act. For full discussion see John Burns, *Conveyancing Practice* and *Handbook of Conveyancing*. These nineteenth century reforms thus extended the role of the executor to heritage in testate cases.

taken. Mr Campbell the third now wants to sell, but the Sasine Register shows his grandfather as the person infeft. It will be necessary to establish whether the beneficial right to the farm did indeed pass in 1959 to Mr Campbell the second (which is a question for pre-1964 law) and then whether it further passed in 1986 to Mr Campbell the third (which is a question for post-1964 law). Assuming that the present Mr Campbell is the person beneficially entitled, there remains the technical problem of enabling him to grant a valid title to a purchaser. This in turn means finding midcouples to link the present Mr Campbell with the 1938 infeftment.[6]

The law since 1964

The 1964 Act made radical changes, both as to who gets what and as to the mechanics of transfer. On the latter point, it extended the confirmation procedure to cover heritage as well as moveables. That made the service procedure redundant and accordingly it was abolished, though it remains competent in relation to the estate of anyone who died intestate before 1964. Hence, in intestate cases, title to land is now obtained through confirmation. For testate cases the situation is rather more complex, for there is a choice. Title can be deduced in such cases either through confirmation or through the will.

Deducing title through the will

After the 1964 Act was passed, there was some uncertainty as to whether it was compulsory for title to be deduced through the confirmation, or whether deduction through the will remained competent as an alternative. To resolve the doubts, the Law Society of Scotland submitted a memorial to the Professors of Conveyancing, and the views which they expressed have been universally accepted.[7] They held that an executor can deduce title through a will,[8] but they were divided as to the position of a legatee. Because

[6] For discussion of this particular type of case, see an article by D.M. Allan at 1978 J.L.S. 438.

[7] See 1965 J.L.S. 153 and 1966 J.L.S. 84.

[8] And so *a fortiori* title can be deduced by a trustee through a trust disposition and settlement. The Professors added that "we strongly recommend that the confirmation should be used in preference to the will as a link in title."

the law on the latter point is uncertain, deduction through a will by a legatee is never attempted in practice, and a title which depended on such a deduction would certainly not be regarded as a good and marketable title. There is no case law on the subject.

One drawback which can arise where an executor deduces title through the will is that the protections afforded by section 17 of the 1964 Act[9] do not apply. However, the general view is that this drawback is not so serious as to justify an objection to a title which involves deduction through the will. In most cases there is no point in deducing through the will since confirmation will have been obtained in any case. Its utility is therefore restricted to the situation where there is no other estate of the deceased which would require confirmation.

Confirmation[10]

The general law and practice of confirmation falls outwith the scope of this book. But because of the importance of confirmation as a conveyancing document something needs to be said about it here. Four general points should be noted.

In the first place, confirmation is a conveyance, from the deceased to his executor. It is of course a judicial conveyance,[11] and may be compared in this respect with the act and warrant in a sequestration. However, unlike an act and warrant, it is a special conveyance, in that it lists the various items of the estate of the deceased. Logically, therefore, it should be possible for a confirmation to be recorded directly in the Sasine Register.[12] This, however, is never done in practice, and since in conveyancing settled practice tends to mature into settled law, it may be that a confirmation could not be so recorded. At all events, the attempt is never made.

Secondly, an executor is a species of trustee both at common

[9] See below.

[10] The standard text is *Currie on Confirmation of Executors* (7th ed., W. Green, 1972), A.E. McRae, editor.

[11] A confirmation is a decree.

[12] As was observed by Professor A.J. McDonald at 1965 J.L.S. 71 at 72. Confirmation will, however, serve for a registration in the Land Register: 1979 Act, s. 3(6).

law,[13] and also under the Trusts (Scotland) Act 1921.[14] This is of considerable importance, because it means that the general body of trust law applies to executors. For example, where an executor dies without having completed the administration of the estate, the rules of lapsed trusts can be applied. Or again, a purchaser from an executor has the protection afforded to any purchaser from a trustee under section 2 of the Trusts (Scotland) Act 1961. Again, the persons beneficially entitled to succeed, whether as legatees, or by legal rights, or prior rights, or as heirs *ab intestato*, are in the position of beneficiaries of a trust, the executor being the trustee. It is common for wills to declare that the executor is to be a trustee, but this would seem to be superfluous, at least under modern law.

The third point about confirmation is that it is not necessary to put in a full conveyancing description of the heritage, but merely "such a description as will be sufficient to identify the property or interest therein."[15] However, it is quite common to see a full conveyancing description used, and indeed when in doubt it should be used. Occasionally, dreadful descriptions are found in confirmations, from which it is impossible to know what land is in question. If the property concerned is simply a house, a postal address will usually be satisfactory. But in other types of property something fuller may be necessary. If the property is in the Land Register, a full conveyancing description is particularly easy, for all that is needed is a reference number, such as REN 4701.

Fourthly, once confirmation has been issued the sheriff clerk will issue, if asked, not only the confirmation itself but also one or more certificates of confirmation.[16] A certificate is a briefer document which refers to a single item of estate, and states that that item has been included in the confirmation. The point is that the executor will want to keep the confirmation itself, while the person taking the land—either a beneficiary or a purchaser—will also want it as a

[13] This statement is, in fact, an over-simplification, for the authorities on the question are inconsistent with each other. The subject is too complex to discuss here. A fair summary would be that at common law an executor is a trustee, but subject to certain qualifications. The issue, however, is of limited importance in modern law since an executor is a trustee under the Trusts Acts.

[14] s. 2. Originally this was true only of executors nominate, but s. 20 of the 1964 Act extended the 1921 Act to executors dative.

[15] Act of Sederunt (S.I. 1966 No. 593).

[16] These are regulated by Act of Sederunt: S.I. 1971 No. 1164.

midcouple. The problem is solved by the certificate of confirmation, which is delivered to the grantee. Sometimes title is actually deduced by reference, not to the confirmation, but to the certificate of confirmation. This is not strictly correct, for the link in title is the decree of the court and not a piece of paper evidencing that decree. Nevertheless, a deduction in such terms is not generally considered invalid.

The confirmation as a link in title

A confirmation does not of itself transfer title to the executor. For it is a conveyance and, like any conveyance of land, it can give no real right of itself: infeftment is necessary for a real right to be obtained, and infeftment can be obtained only by recording in the Sasine Register or registration in the Land Register.

Completion of title as executor

If the executor wishes to become infeft as executor, he records in the Sasine Register a notice of title deducing title through the confirmation. In land registration cases, no notice of title is necessary. The executor simply applies for registration, producing the confirmation as the midcouple. He can then dispone to a buyer or beneficiary. In such conveyance he would, of course, be designed as heritable proprietor since he is now infeft. However, it is not common for the executor to do this. More usually he conveys to the buyer or beneficiary without having first completed title. In practice, the executor only completes title as executor if the administration of the estate is likely to be prolonged, as where there is an ongoing trust.

Disposition to beneficiary without prior completion of title

In most cases the executor will wish simply to convey the property to the beneficiary without first having completed title in his own name as executor. He can do this in two ways. The simplest is just to grant a disposition deducing title through the confirmation. The alternative is the docket procedure laid down in section 15 of the 1964 Act.[17] What happens is that the executor endorses on the

[17] The style is given in Sched. 1 to the Act. Because of the wording of the style, it is uncertain whether it could be used where property is to be conveyed in imple-

confirmation[18] a docket nominating the beneficiary as the person entitled to the property in question. This of itself, of course, does not give the beneficiary a real right, because infeftment requires recording or registration. As with the confirmation itself, direct registration in the Land Register is competent, but probably not direct recording in the Sasine Register. So the beneficiary must complete title by a notice of title, the midcouples being (1) the confirmation and (2) the docket. Alternatively, the beneficiary could dispone to a third party with a deduction of title clause without having first completed title himself. Note that a docket can be in favour of the executor himself as an individual, and this is quite common, for it is common for the executor to be a beneficiary and, indeed, sometimes the sole beneficiary. In that case, the wording is simply that the executor does hereby nominate himself, and so forth.

The docket procedure is in a sense puzzling. For it means that two deeds[19] instead of one are needed for the beneficiary to complete title,[20] whereas the thing could be done by a single deed, namely a disposition. Possibly the draftsman of the 1964 Act did not appreciate that a docket would not give a real right. It is thought that a disposition is preferable to a docket, especially for Sasine titles. If a docket is used, all too often title is not completed, and the beneficiary then holds the property merely as uninfeft proprietor, which can in some cases cause subsequent problems.

Conveyance to a purchaser without prior completion of title

The docket procedure is available only where the grantee is a beneficiary, either as legatee or otherwise. Where the grantee is a purchaser from the executry estate an ordinary disposition must be used.

In most cases the grantee will be a beneficiary. However, sale by an executor may happen in three main types of case. In the first

ment of a deed of family arrangement. In such cases a simple disposition should be used.

[18] In practice, the docket is endorsed not on the confirmation itself but on a certificate of confirmation.

[19] The docket and the notice of title.

[20] This point, however, does not apply to land registration cases, where no notice of title is necessary.

place, the will may direct that the property be sold, and then make provision as to distribution of the proceeds. Secondly, it may prove necessary to sell in order to pay the creditors, who, of course, must be paid in full before any beneficial interests can emerge. A variant of this is where sale is necessary to meet tax liabilities. Thirdly, a beneficiary may not wish to take the property itself. In that case, he may take it and then sell it, or, more simply, he may ask the executor to sell and pay him the net proceeds.

Where deceased was uninfeft

Complexities sometimes arise where the defunct himself was not infeft. Take the following case. Mr Matheson is infeft in a house in Ayr and dies intestate. Mrs Matheson, his widow, is entitled to the house under prior rights. She is also the executrix dative. She confirms to her late husband's estate, and executes a docket transfer in her own favour, but does not complete title. Some years later she dies. Her will leaves the house to her niece Ms Christie, whom she also nominates as her executrix. Ms Christie confirms to her aunt's estate. The person last infeft was Mr Matheson. Ms Christie can validly dispone (to herself as beneficiary, or to a purchaser) by deducing title through three midcouples: (1) Mrs Matheson's confirmation to Mr Matheson's estate; (2) the docket transfer in favour of Mrs Matheson; (3) Ms Christie's confirmation to Mrs Matheson. In land registration cases Ms Christie could apply for registration in her own name, producing these three midcouples to the Keeper.

Lapsed trusts

Now consider a variation on the above case. Suppose that although Mrs Matheson confirmed to her late husband's estate, and although she was beneficially entitled to the house by virtue of prior rights, she did not grant a docket to herself, or otherwise transfer the property to herself as an individual. Here there is a problem. Mrs Matheson had the beneficial interest. Ms Christie can confirm to that beneficial interest, *i.e.* to Mrs Matheson's beneficial interest in the estate of Mr Matheson. But the title is still stuck in Mr Matheson's executry, for there has been no transfer out of his executry. In other words, there is a "lapsed trust".

A trust lapses where (1) there is still trust property undistributed but (2) there are no acting trustees, usually because all the trustees are dead. That is what has happened here. There are various ways of unscrambling a lapsed trust.[21] The first two mentioned below are applicable to all types of trust, including executries. The second two are applicable only to executries.

In the first place, where the beneficial interest is absolutely vested and no further trust administration is required with respect to that property, the beneficiary can apply to the court for an order authorising him to complete title.[22] This procedure is, however, almost never adopted in practice.

In the second place, anyone with an interest can petition the court for the appointment of a new trustee.[23] The petition will itself suggest to the court a suitable person to act. The decree then operates as a midcouple in favour of the person appointed. Such petitions are quite common.

In the third place, where the executor has died, a new executor can be appointed to the estate. In the example, this would mean someone else becoming executor to Mr Matheson. That person could then dispone to the ultimate beneficiary of Mrs Matheson's estate, the disposition incorporating the consent of Mrs Matheson's executor.[24] A new executor appointed in this way is called an executor *ad non executa*, *i.e.* an executor appointed to estate which had not been "executed" by the original executor.[25]

The fourth method, frequently used in practice, is the procedure set out in section 6 of the Executors (Scotland) Act 1900. Under

[21] The following is a list of the main ones. There are some others, such as the appointment of a judicial factor.

[22] Trusts (Scotland) Act 1921, s. 24. The decree is then a midcouple.

[23] Trusts (Scotland) Act 1921, s. 22. Curiously, this section does not in fact mention the death of the sole trustee (or all trustees) as a ground of petition. But the section has always been construed as covering such cases, and indeed is seldom used for any other purpose. See W.A. Wilson and A.G.M. Duncan, *Trusts, Trustees and Executors* (W. Green, 1975), pp. 270–271.

[24] In such a case, of course, it would be for Mrs Matheson's executor to determine the person to whom the property should be conveyed. Mr Matheson's new executor would then simply follow that request. Alternatively Mrs Matheson's executor could request Mr Matheson's new executor to convey to her, in her capacity as Mrs Matheson's executor. The position would be the same if a new trustee to Mr Matheson's estate had been appointed under s. 22 of the 1921 Act.

[25] The process is a common law one, subject to the Executors (Scotland) Act 1900, s. 7.

this procedure, the executor (Ms Christie) of the executor (Mrs Matheson) can confirm to the unexecuted estate. This will involve confirming to the house twice in the same inventory. In the main body of the inventory, Ms Christie would confirm to Mrs Matheson's beneficial interest in the estate of Mr Matheson. Then, in an appendix to the inventory, Ms Christie would enter the house itself. Confirmation issued in such terms operates as a midcouple in favour of Ms Christie. She can then dispone (to herself, if she inherits from her aunt) deducing title through (1) Mrs Matheson's confirmation to Mr Matheson's estate and (2) her own confirmation to her aunt's estate. One qualification to be noted is that this procedure is competent only where no further acts of administration are required in the trust or executry which has lapsed. In other words, it is available only where the only thing needed is to convey the property to the person beneficially entitled. This, however, is usually the case.

Lapsed trusts are a nuisance. So where it is anticipated that a trust will continue for some time, it is wise to have more than one trustee. In ongoing trusts there may, of course, be additional reasons for having more than one trustee, for difficult decisions may need to be taken, and two or three heads will be wiser than one.

In the example, it would not have been sufficient for Ms Christie merely to confirm to her aunt's beneficial interest in Mr Matheson's estate. Of course, such confirmation is necessary, for what may be called the internal purposes of Mrs Matheson's executry, or in other words such aspects as beneficial succession to Mrs Matheson, and tax liabilities for Mrs Matheson's estate. But such confirmation would be ineffectual for conveyancing purposes. The reason is that the entry in Ms Christie's confirmation to Mrs Matheson's estate concerns only Mrs Matheson's beneficial interest in the house, and title cannot be deduced through a mere beneficial interest.[26] Hence the necessity of confirming to the title itself in an appendix under section 6 of the Executors (Scotland) Act 1900, or adopting some other means of rescuing title from the lapsed trust.

[26] The same point applies equally in land registration practice, even though no deduction is required. For in land registration the same midcouples are required as in Sasine conveyancing.

Destinations

Destinations are dealt with in chapter 24, but a few words will be appropriate here. If there is a survivorship destination in the title there is no need for confirmation in respect of that property, on the first death, because the survivor is deemed automatically infeft. Of course, on the second death there will have to be confirmation to the property. More strictly, there will have to be confirmation on the *last* death, for one can have a survivorship destination among three or more people, such as three sisters.) Where, after the first death, the survivor dispones, no deduction of title is necessary because deduction of title is required only where the grantor is uninfeft. The fact of the earlier death is stated in the narrative clause.

A quite separate issue under the same heading of destinations is whether, in an *inter vivos* disposition in favour of trustees, it is necessary to add a survivorship destination. Though this is quite common, it is unnecessary and indeed in principle inappropriate. For trust ownership is joint ownership. Each trustee does not have a "share" of the property. There is thus no question of such non-existent "share" passing, on the death of one trustee, to the other trustees. When one trustee dies, he simply drops out of the picture. His death does not enlarge the rights of the others. The title is a single one, under joint administration.

Purchasing from an executor or trustee

In a purchase from an executor or trustee, it is not necessary to verify that there is a power of sale, because in such cases section 2 of the Trusts (Scotland) Act 1961 gives absolute protection to the purchaser. Good faith is not required. In other words, if an executor or trustee sells in breach of trust, the beneficiaries must pursue their remedy against the delinquent trustee, not against the purchaser. Such cases are, however, rare, partly because breach of trust is rare and partly because in most cases trustees have an implied power of sale.[27]

However, in such cases it may be necessary for the purchaser to

[27] 1921 Act, s. 4.

examine the will or other deed of trust for a quite separate reason. A spouse of the beneficiary of the property may have had occupancy rights.[28] Hence a consent or an affidavit may be required. Examination of the will or other trust deed may then be required to determine who should grant the consent or affidavit.

Lastly, a purchaser from a confirmed executor is protected, if in good faith, against the unlikely event of the subsequent reduction of the confirmation.[29]

Purchasing from a beneficiary

Suppose that an executor or trustee has conveyed to a beneficiary, and the beneficiary comes to sell within the period of positive prescription. Is it necessary for the purchaser to check that the executor or trustee conveyed to the right person? In other words, does the purchaser need to check the terms of the will or other deed of trust? In the case of a beneficiary who has taken title from a confirmed executor, section 17 of the 1964 Act provides that a purchaser from that beneficiary is protected,[30] provided that he is in good faith. No one is sure what good faith amounts to in this context. Some conveyancers think that the will must be checked in order to be in good faith, while others think not. The issue is unresolved.

Section 17 applies only where the beneficiary took title from a confirmed executor. In other cases where a purchase is from a beneficiary, the purchaser has no statutory protection. Thus, suppose that there is an *inter vivos* trust, and the trustees convey part of the estate, a house, to X. X then concludes missives to sell to Y. If the trustees should not have conveyed to X, X's title will be voidable. However, if Y is in good faith, he will be protected at common law.[31] Hence the position is in fact effectively the same as under section 17 of the 1964 Act.[32]

[28] See chap. 8.

[29] 1964 Act, s. 17.

[30] *i.e.* protected against the possibility that the beneficiary's title was reducible because the executor should have conveyed to someone else, or because the confirmation itself was reducible.

[31] At common law, voidability does not transmit against a disponee who gives value and is in good faith.

[32] Indeed, s. 17 is to that extent merely declaratory of the common law.

Joint property

Where there is more than one trustee, or executor, they hold as joint owners, not owners in common.[33] Indeed, trust ownership appears to be the only case where joint ownership is possible for heritable property. Joint owners, unlike owners in common, do not have identifiable shares. If there are two owners in common, each has a half share, if three, a third, and so on.[34] But nothing like that is the case for trustees. If there are two trustees and they assume a third, it would be quite wrong to suppose that the "share" of the first two fell from a half to a third. It is because the title is joint that, when one trustee dies, there is no "share" to pass to his estate. Instead, the surviving trustees carry on as before, infeft in the whole. The same is true if one trustee resigns. One way of expressing it is to say that each infeft trustee is infeft in the whole.

Assumption

Trustees, including executors nominate (but not executors dative[35]), can normally assume new trustees.[36] This is rare in executries, but common in long-running trusts. It is done by a deed of assumption and conveyance.[37] This can take the form of a special conveyance, but is more usually done as a general conveyance, *i.e.* as a conveyance of the whole trust estate without specification of any particular property. If some of the existing trustees are to continue, the practice is to convey to themselves and to the new trustee or trustees, so that the grantors will also be among the grantees. The new trustee or trustees adds a docket at the foot accepting office. The deed is, as a matter of good practice, registered in the Books of Council and Session. It is wise to complete title in the name of the new body of trustees by notice of title, but this is not always done. Naturally, the deed of assumption is a midcouple, and title can be deduced through it.

[33] The term *pro indiviso* ownership applies to both cases. For the differences between common and joint property, see the *Stair Memorial Encyclopaedia*, vol. 18, paras. 17 *et seq*.

[34] Unless some other, unequal, division, has been expressly provided for.

[35] 1964 Act, s. 20, proviso.

[36] 1921 Act, s. 3.

[37] See s. 21 and Sched. B to the 1921 Act for the statutory style.

Resignation

A trustee can normally resign, unless he is the sole trustee.[38] If a sole trustee wants to resign he will have to assume a new trustee first. A minute of resignation[39] by a trustee should be registered in the Books of Council and Session, even though this is not strictly a legal requirement. The resignation must be intimated to the other trustees. The effect of resignation[40] is to divest the resigning trustee. That he can be so divested without conveying is due to the fact that the co-ownership of trustees is not ownership in common but joint ownership.

Execution of deeds by trustees

The practice is to ensure that conveyancing deeds are signed by all the trustees, including any who are uninfeft. But it is unclear whether this is legally necessary or whether majority execution is sufficient: some solicitors will accept the latter. Section 7 of the 1921 Act may perhaps mean that a majority is sufficient, but its terms are obscure.[41]

Warrandice by trustees

In a disposition to a beneficiary the practice is for the trustees/executors to grant fact and deed warrandice only. If the disposition is to a purchaser the practice is to grant fact and deed warrandice and to bind the trust estate in absolute warrandice.

[38] 1921 Act, s. 3. There are various exceptions, stated in the section. Note also that an executor dative cannot resign: 1964 Act, s. 20.

[39] 1921 Act, s. 19 and Sched. A.

[40] 1921 Act, s. 20.

[41] The proper construction of s. 7 is a matter of immense complexity, which cannot be gone into here. One of the many problems about it is what is meant by good faith. Another is whether its references to trustees include uninfeft trustees. See *Harland Engineering Co.* v. *Stark's Trs.*, 1913 2 S.L.T. 448; 1914 2 S.L.T. 292 for background.

Charitable and religious trusts

Special conveyancing rules apply to religious and educational trusts.[42] The general rule here is that of "automatic infeftment." In other words, as, over the years, the trustees change, each new set of trustees is deemed to be infeft, the original infeftment of the original trustees continuing, by a fiction, in favour of their successors. Hence as and when the present trustees require to grant a deed, they do not deduce title, for deduction of title is not required by an infeft grantor. These rules thus come close to giving corporate status to the body of trustees. Similar rules apply where there is an *ex officio* trustee, such as the minister of the parish.[42a]

In practice, the terms of the original trust will often impose restrictions on the trustees, limiting their power to sell the land. The zealous landowner who, in 1877, gave the land and money for the building of a chapel for the Congregation of the Auchnashuggle Free Reformed United Presbyterian New Covenant Church of Scotland wanted to make sure that the building would never be used for any other purpose. The present congregation (the last left in Scotland) has decided to merge with the Church of Scotland down the road, and wants to sell the chapel. Can this be done? That can be a very difficult question. There are no easy answers, and we cannot go into the subject here. But this is a problem for the sellers, not for the purchaser, who will be protected by section 2 of the Trusts (Scotland) Act 1961.

Liferents

Viewed from the perspective of property law, there are two quite different types of liferent. In the "proper" liferent, both liferenter and fiar have real rights. The fiar has the real right of ownership, burdened by the real right of liferent. The fiar can sell, but of course the purchaser will obtain the same right, burdened by the liferent. But proper liferents are very rare. In practice, they seldom exist

[42] 1868 Act, s. 26.

[42a] 1874 Act, s. 45. The term *ex officio* trustee probably means the holder of a public office.

except as a result of a home-made will.[43] Much more common is the "trust" liferent. Here there is just one real right, namely the real right of ownership of the trustees. The rights of the liferenter and the fiar are reduced to beneficial interests under the trust. When the liferenter dies, the trustees dispone to the fiar. Before this happens, the fiar can sell his interest. But as with the sale of any beneficial interest under a trust, the sale is given effect to not by disposition but by assignation, for what is being conveyed is an incorporeal right, a personal right against the trustees.

It sometimes happens that the liferenter no longer wishes to live in the liferented property. He may wish to move to a smaller house, or a house in a different place, or move in with relatives, or to a nursing home. A well-drafted will or other deed of trust will have anticipated this possibility by allowing the trustees to sell, and providing that the proceeds of sale (whether invested, or used to buy another house) will be subject to the same division of rights between liferenter and fiar. If the deed is silent the same thing can still happen provided that both liferenter and fiar so agree. But it may be that the fiar is awkward. Or it may be that the fee is unvested.[44] Or it may be that the liferenter has become *incapax*. In such cases it is doubtful whether the trustees have an implied power of sale.[45] If necessary, the consent of the court may be sought.[46] However, this problem is the concern only of the trustees, not of the purchaser.[47]

Some further examples

Jack died in 1970, infeft in his house in Oban. He left a trust disposition and settlement directing his trustees to hold for his widow Mary in liferent and his daughter Kate in fee. The trustees confirmed and completed title, by notice of title. Mary lived in the

[43] In such a case the executor would grant a disposition "to A in liferent and to B in fee" and the warrant of registration is in similar terms.

[44] In which case no consent is possible.

[45] Section 4 of the 1921 Act implies a power of sale in all trusts, but only where that power is "not at variance with the terms or purposes of the trust." It may be that where a trust sets up a liferent, and confers no power of sale, sale would be "at variance" with the purposes of the trust.

[46] *e.g.* under s. 5 of the 1921 Act or s. 1 of the Trusts (Scotland) Act 1961.

[47] Who is protected by the Trusts (Scotland) Act 1961, s. 2.

house until her death in 1973. Thereafter Kate lived in the house. But the trustees never got round to granting a disposition to Kate. Kate died in 1991. She left a trust disposition and settlement giving the house to her son Paul. Paul, however, does not wish to live in the house, because he has a job in Aberdeen. He concludes missives to sell the house to Tom. How should the disposition to Tom be drafted?

In the first place, Paul, the seller, cannot dispone. He is not infeft, nor can he deduce title. Nor can Kate's trustees dispone. Of course, where there is a trust it is generally true that the legal title is vested in the trustees, with the beneficiary having a personal right. But here the right vested in Kate's trustees is itself a personal right only. There are thus, so to speak, two levels of personal right. Kate's trustees cannot dispone because they are not infeft and cannot deduce title. The current infeftment is that of Jack's trustees, and only they can grant the disposition. They hold for Kate, and since her death, for her trustees. They must therefore dispone to the person selected by Kate's trustees. The latter in turn must obtain a conveyance either to Paul himself or to Paul's nominee, *i.e.* Tom. In other words, Paul tells Kate's trustees to convey to Tom, and Kate's trustees then tell Jack's trustees to convey to Tom. The disposition is thus granted by Jack's trustees, and bears the consent of Kate's trustees and of Paul. The real seller, Paul, is thus in conveyancing terms merely a consenter. No deduction of title is called for since the grantors are infeft. The narrative clause will refer to Jack's trust disposition and settlement and its terms, to Mary's death, to Kate's death, to Kate's trust disposition and settlement and its terms, to the confirmation in favour of Kate's trustees, and to the sale by Paul to Tom.

Would it have made any difference if Jack's trustees had never completed title? The answer is, very little. The last infeftment would in that case be Jack's. Neither Paul nor Kate's trustees would be in a position to deduce title, because they would have no midcouples linking them to that last infeftment. (Kate's trustees have confirmed to her beneficial interest in Jack's estate, and title cannot be deduced through a mere beneficial interest.) The disposition would be granted by Jack's trustees in the same terms as above. The only difference is that there would be a clause deducing title through the confirmation in favour of Jack's trustees.

Take another example. Hamish and Morag were infeft in common in a house in Kinross in 1959. There is no survivorship clause. Morag died in 1962. Her will (which was a will in the narrow sense) left her half share to Hamish, who was also appointed executor. Hamish confirmed, but not to the house.[48] Hamish did not complete title. Hamish continued to live in the house until his death in 1985. His will left the house to his son Fergus. Fergus confirmed to his father's estate and granted a docket transfer to himself, but did not complete title before his death in 1993. Fergus died intestate and the house passed by prior rights to his relict, Elspeth. Elspeth confirmed as Fergus's executor. Elspeth wishes to sell the house, which is now too large for her. How is title to be granted to the purchaser?

Morag's estate is governed by pre-1964 law. Hence Hamish could have recorded a notice of title to her half share, either to himself as executor or directly to himself as an individual, in both cases using Morag's will as the midcouple. He did not do this. But his right to use the midcouple as an individual passed to his executor, Fergus.[49] Fergus could thus have recorded a notice of title in favour of himself as his father's executor, deducing through (1) Morag's will and (2) his own confirmation to his father's estate. Or he could have disponed direct to himself as an individual, deducing in the same manner. However, in point of fact he did not take infeftment, but simply granted to himself a docket transfer. But this itself is a good midcouple. Once Fergus's executor has confirmed, she can dispone, deducing title through (1) Morag's will, (2) Fergus's confirmation to Hamish's estate, (3) the docket transfer by Fergus to himself and (4) Elspeth's confirmation to Fergus's estate. In other words, these facts do not create a lapsed trust. If, however, Fergus had not executed a docket transfer to himself, there would be a lapsed trust.

It will be observed that the above concerns Morag's half share only. Hamish's original half can also be disponed by Elspeth, however, deducing title through (1) Fergus's confirmation to Hamish's estate, (2) the docket transfer by Fergus to himself and (3) Elspeth's confirmation to Fergus's estate.

In the example, Elspeth is selling as executrix. This, of course,

[48] Of course. Prior to the 1964 Act confirmation to heritage was, subject to minor qualifications, incompetent.

[49] Note that a right to use a midcouple *as an individual* passes on death, but the right to use a midcouple *as a trustee* in general does not pass on death, but lapses.

is perfectly competent, even though the ultimate beneficial interest is vested in her as an individual. The example could be varied so that after confirming to Fergus's estate she granted a docket transfer in her own favour as an individual. In that case the disposition to the purchaser would be from her as an individual, not as executrix, and both halves of the deduction clause would have an additional midcouple, namely the docket in her favour.

Chapter 24

DESTINATIONS

Introduction

There are two sorts of destinations. The first is the destination-over, which is found in wills and deeds of trust of various sorts. For instance, a will might provide that the testator's house is to go to X whom failing Y. Thus, if X dies before the testator, Y takes the house.[1] The second sort of destination is the special destination, which is found in conveyances of heritable property.[2] The only common form in modern practice is the survivorship special destination. Thus, A and B (typically, but not necessarily, spouses) take title to a house in the form "to the said A and the said B equally between them and to the survivor of them." This means that each takes a one half *pro indiviso* share, but each half share is subject to a destination in favour of the other. If A dies first, his share passes to B, and *vice versa*.

Why do both these devices share the name "destination?" The answer is that in both cases a deed which gives right to property makes provision for what is to happen to that property in the event of the death of the grantee.

Conditional institutions

There are two main types of destination-over, the conditional institution and the substitution. In the first, the grantee of the property (A) is called the institute and the person (B) who is to take the property in the event of the institute's death is called the conditional institute. The rule for conditional institution is that the conditional

[1] If a legatee predeceases, the legacy lapses, *i.e.* becomes void. A destination-over thus prevents lapse. There are also certain rules of succession law which can prevent lapse, notably the *conditio si institutus sine liberis decesserit*.

[2] Special destinations in moveable property can, in theory, exist in certain types of case, but are almost unknown in practice. A destination-over can be of moveables just as much as of heritage.

institute can take the property only if the institute has died before the date of vesting. Thus, suppose that a will leaves a house to A whom failing B and that this is by way of conditional institution. A dies before the testator. B then takes the property as legatee. However, suppose that A dies one day after the testator. In that case the legacy was vested in A. On A's death the property does not pass to B but forms part of A's estate.[3] In that case, B's contingent right is said to "fly off."

Suppose, however, that A did not die. He would then receive a disposition from the testator's executor. The disposition would simply be to him, A, not to "A whom failing B," even though that was the wording of the will. For B's right has flown off by the fact of A's survival of the date of the vesting.[4]

Substitutions

In a substitution, A is again called the institute but B is called the substitute. Substitution includes the effects of conditional institution, but additional effects as well. Thus, suppose that there is a will leaving a house to A whom failing B and A predeceases the testator. Then the house goes to B, just as in conditional institution. Or again, if A survived but B predeceased, the effect is the same as in conditional institution, namely that the property passes to A.

The difference between the two types of destination-over emerges where both A and B survive the date of vesting. Suppose (to take the earlier example) that A dies the day after the testator. Since this is a substitution and not a conditional institution, the legacy, although it had vested in A, passes to B on A's death. The testator's executor must convey to B, not to A's executor. Suppose, however, that A does not so die. In that case he will receive a disposition from the testator's executor. The form of the disposition should be to "A whom failing B." In other words, where a destination-over in a will or deed of trust is a substitution, the conveyance which

[3] A will not have had time to take a conveyance. So the testator's executor will convey to A's executor, who will in turn convey to whoever is entitled to the property in A's succession. Or more simply the conveyance could be direct by the testator's executor to the latter person, the conveyance incorporating the consent of A's executor.

[4] In most wills the date of vesting is the date of the testator's death. But sometimes it is postponed, and the same applies to many *inter vivos* trusts.

gives effect to it should copy out the terms of the destination, thereby converting the destination-over into a special destination.[5] Again, suppose a will leaves a house to "A and B and the survivor." If this is a substitution, the executor must convey to "A and B and the survivor of them."[6] If, however, the destination-over in the will is a conditional institution, the executor simply conveys to A and B.[7]

Where a special destination has to be used in a conveyance to a beneficiary, it is preferable that this be done in a disposition rather than a docket.[8] But there can be little doubt that a special destination in a docket transfer would be valid.

Identifying which is which

In a will or deed of trust the property may be given simply to "A whom failing B" or to "A and B and the survivor." How is it possible to tell whether this is a conditional institution or a substitution? In the first place, the deed may make it clear which is intended, and a well-drafted deed will always do this. If conditional institution is intended (and this is the most common case) this is typically done by saying: "To A whom failing by his predecease to B." This makes it clear that B is to take if and only if A predeceases. If the will or deed of trust does not make the intention clear, the common law supplies certain rules as to presumed intention.[9] These are as follows. (1) If the property in question is moveable, conditional institution is to be presumed. (2) If the property in question is heritable, substitution is to be presumed. (3) If the property is a mix of moveables and heritage, conditional institution is to be presumed.[10]

[5] In our example, this will be true only where both A and B survive the date of vesting. If either predeceases, the conveyance will incorporate no special destination.

[6] Unless A and B otherwise request.

[7] Unless A and B actually request a survivorship destination to be inserted.

[8] Docket transfer under s. 15(2) of the 1964 Act.

[9] The case law is of enormous bulk, but the following three rules are a fairly accurate summary.

[10] One example of a mixed legacy would be a legacy of a house and its contents. Again, a legacy of residue will, in many cases, be mixed.

Special survivorship destinations to purchasers

Special destinations inserted in a conveyance to beneficiaries under wills or trusts are not common in practice. The vast majority of special destinations are contained in conveyances to purchasers, in which case they are inserted at the request of such purchasers. Such destinations can be of various types.[11] By far the commonest is the ordinary survivorship destination. Here, two persons buy a house in common, the title being granted, at their request, to them both and the survivor of them. The usual case is spouses, but sometimes cohabitants do this, and it can also be found in other cases, such as siblings who live together. It is possible to have more than two parties involved. For instance three sisters might buy a house with the disposition to "A and B and C equally between them and to the survivors and survivor of them." That would give each a one-third *pro indiviso* share in common ownership. If B then died, half of her share[12] would pass to A and the other half of her share to C, thus leaving A and C with a half of the whole. If C then died her half share of the whole would pass to A, who would thus then be the sole owner.

In a great majority of cases, where two or more people buy a property a survivorship destination is inserted.[13–14] However, such a destination should never be inserted without the express instructions of the clients. The reason is that the substantive effect of a survivorship destination is that of a legacy of the share of the property. Thus, if Mr and Mrs X buy a house with a survivorship destination, the substantive effect is that Mr X is making a legacy to Mrs X of his half share, and *vice versa*. Obviously this requires instructions from the clients. Indeed, the need for instructions is even stronger because, as will be explained below, in the majority of cases the effect of the destination cannot be defeated by will. Thus, suppose that Mr and Mrs X quarrel. Mrs X makes a will leaving her half share to her sister. Soon afterwards, Mrs X dies.

[11] The fullest account is probably to be found in John Craigie, *Scottish Law of Conveyancing: Heritable Rights* (commonly called *Heritable Rights*) (3rd ed., 1899).

[12] *i.e.* a sixth of the whole.

[13–14] For an excellent and detailed survey, see David Nichols, "Survivorship Destinations in Scotland," 1990 J.L.S. 189.

The legacy will normally be ineffective and the half share will pass to Mr X under the destination. Thus a special destination is not only in substance a legacy, it is a legacy which cannot normally be revoked. That is a serious matter, and the point must be clearly explained to the clients, and their informed wishes ascertained. It should be borne in mind, and explained to the clients, that if each party wishes his or her share to pass, on death, to the survivor, this can equally well be secured by each party making a will to that effect. This presents little practical difficulty since it is very common for people to make wills, or new wills, when buying a house.

The commonest argument in favour of the use of survivorship destinations is that on the first death the share passes to the survivor automatically, without need for confirmation or conveyance.[15] This can indeed be useful. However, in most deaths involving a person who owns heritage, confirmation will be needed anyway, in which case the fact of automatic infeftment confers little benefit. It should also be said that special destinations frequently bring up difficult issues of law and have often resulted in litigation,[16] which cannot be welcomed by clients. Judges and legal writers have tended to cast doubt on the utility of special destinations in ordinary cases, and the view of the authors of this work is that clients should not be advised to use them in ordinary cases, and that, if they are used, this should be done only after careful discussion with the clients and clear instructions[17] from them. However, it must be conceded that there can be cases where special destinations are undoubtedly useful.

Terminology

The distinction between conditional institution and substitution has already been explained. In a special destination, the second party can only be a substitute, not a conditional institute, for the institute cannot die before vesting. Thus, if property is disponed to A and B and the survivor, A is institute for one half share, and B is the substitute for that share, and, for the other half share, B is

[15] See below.
[16] See, *e.g.* Lord Cooper's remarks in *Hay's Tr.* v. *Hay's Trs.*, 1951 S.C. 329.
[17] Preferably confirmed in writing.

the institute and A is the substitute. Another term for a substitute is "heir of provision." This means a person who inherits (heir) not by the general law of succession but by a special provision in the title to some property. One other terminological point worth noting is the "clause of return." A clause of return is a special destination where the substitute (or heir of provision) is the grantor of the conveyance which creates the destination. Thus, if A dispones to B whom failing A, that is a clause of return. Or suppose a wife, owning a house, dispones it to herself and her husband equally and to the survivor. Then the destination attached to her resulting half share would be an ordinary special destination, but the destination attaching to her husband's half share would be a clause of return.

Where husband and wife (or siblings or whatever) take title, their title is said to be *pro indiviso* whether or not there is a survivorship destination and whether or not any survivorship destination that has been used is or is not capable of evacuation.[18] Further, the use of a survivorship destination, even one not capable of evacuation, does not convert the ownership from ownership in common to joint ownership.[19] The only case of joint ownership of heritage is ownership by trustees.[20]

Completion of title

When the institute in a special destination dies, the property passes to the substitute, unless the destination has been evacuated. But how does the substitute complete title? The answer depends on whether the special destination is a survivorship one, or of some other type.

If, as is nowadays almost always the case, the destination is a survivorship destination, the substitute is deemed to be infeft automatically by the death of the institute.[21] Thus, if Mr and Mrs X take title to their house to each and to the survivor, and Mr X dies, Mrs X is infeft at the very moment when Mr X's heart ceases to beat. This seems to be the only case in our law when infeftment in heritage can pass from one person to another without a recorded

[18] For evacuation, see below.

[19] *Munro* v. *Munro*, 1972 S.L.T. (Sh. Ct.) 6 held the contrary, but is incorrect. The law is quite settled.

[20] See, further, *Stair Memorial Encyclopaedia*, vol. 18, para. 34.

[21] Unless the destination has been evacuated, for which see below.

or registered conveyance. It is, thus, a somewhat anomalous doctrine. It was introduced by the case of *Bisset* v. *Walker*.[22] There are good grounds for arguing that that decision was incorrect. But, of course, false legal doctrines, once they become settled and accepted, become true doctrines, and the doctrine of automatic infeftment is now, and has long been, settled and accepted as good law.

In the rare cases of other types of special destination, the rule is different. Thus, suppose that property is disponed to "A whom failing B." A dies. B takes the property, of course, but he is not automatically infeft. A conveyance to him by A's executor is required, and A's executor has no choice but to grant it.[23]

Evacuation of special destinations *mortis causa*

A special destination may be "evacuated" either *inter vivos* or *mortis causa*. *Inter vivos* evacuation is discussed below. *Mortis causa* evacuation is effected by bequeathing the property to some person other than the substitute (heir of provision).

This subject has two aspects. First, there is the question of power to evacuate. If there is no power, a purported evacuation will be null, and the legatee will not take the property, which, notwithstanding the legacy, will pass to the substitute. Secondly, if power to evacuate does exist, there is the question of how it is competently exercised.

Power to evacuate *mortis causa*

In the first place, the conveyance creating the special destination may have a provision expressly stating whether or not it can be evacuated *mortis causa*, though such clauses are uncommon in modern practice. If there is such a clause and it forbids evacuation, the traditional practice was to ensure that the deed was executed by the grantee/s as well as by the grantor. But this is probably not strictly necessary, for by acceptance of the disposition a grantee is deemed to accept its terms. Such a clause is simple to draft. After

[22] 26 Nov. 1799, Fac. Coll.

[23] 1964 Act, s. 18(2). Note the words in that section: "if such conveyance is necessary." In most cases no such conveyance is necessary because in most cases there will be automatic infeftment. Before the 1964 Act, B completed title by a special process called service as heir of provision.

the destination follow some such words as the following: "But expressly declaring that the said grantees and each of them shall have full right and power" (or, "no right and power") "to evacuate the foregoing destination."

If the deed has no express clause, the law has certain presumptions. Power of evacuation is presumed to be excluded in cases of marriage contracts and clauses of return and in cases where there is an implied contract not to evacuate. In other cases power to evacuate is presumed.[24] It is the third of these which is much the most important in practice.

The leading case, which virtually invented the doctrine of the implied contract not to evacuate, is *Perrett's Trustees* v. *Perrett.*[25] This case, and later cases which elaborated the doctrine,[26] holds that where there is a survivorship destination, and both parties have contributed to the price,[27] there is a presumed contract that neither can evacuate. If, however, only one party paid the price, there is a presumed contract that that party can evacuate but that the other party cannot. In determining whether both parties have contributed to the price, it has been held that the narrative clause of the deed is conclusive.[28] This is a practical point to be watched. Some conveyancers tend, in cases of a purchase by husband and wife, to declare in the narrative clause that both have paid the price, and they do this as words of style without checking the true facts. If in truth it was, say, the wife who paid the whole price, the narrative clause will destroy the power of evacuation she would otherwise have had.

The modern practice of leaving the question of power to evacu-

[24] However, it is uncertain whether a special destination can be evacuated if it was inserted in a conveyance to a beneficiary. See *Massy Scott's Trs.* (1872) 11 M. 173; *Robertson* v. *Hay-Boyd*, 1928 S.C. (H.L.) 8, *per* Lord Dunedin; McLaren on *Wills and Succession* (3rd ed.), pp. 629–630 and Candlish Henderson, *Vesting* (2nd ed.), p. 328.

[25] 1909 S.C. 522. The case is unimpressive and arguably wrong. But it became settled law and so cannot now be questioned: see *Shand's Trs.* v. *Shand's Trs.*, 1966 S.C. 178.

[26] *Renouf's Trs.* v. *Haining*, 1919 S.C. 497; *Taylor's Exrs.* v. *Brunton*, 1939 S.C. 444; *Brown's Tr.* v. *Brown*, 1943 S.C. 488; *Hay's Tr.* v. *Hay's Trs.*, 1951 S.C. 329. For a review, see M. Morton at 1984 S.L.T. (News) 133.

[27] Equal contribution is not necessary.

[28] *Gordon-Rodgers* v. *Thomson's Exr.*, 1986 S.L.T. 618; *Smith* v. *MacIntosh*, 1989 S.L.T. 148.

ate to implication is unwise. The clients must have some definite intention about the matter, which the solicitor must ascertain, and it is surely sensible to declare that intention in the deed itself, thus avoiding all doubt.

Exercise of power to evacuate *mortis causa*

If there is no power to evacuate, a legacy will be null. But if there is power, the legacy will still be null unless it complies with a statutory form.[29] This is an important point to note when drafting a will.

Evacuation by death of substitute

A special destination becomes null where the substitute (heir of provision) dies before the institute. Thus, suppose that property is disponed to A whom failing B, and B then dies. The destination is evacuated by B's death, and if A were to die the next day the property would simply be part of his estate and B's representatives would have no rights. Or again, suppose that husband and wife own their house in common with a survivorship destination. The husband dies. His share passes to his widow. She then dies. The destination attached to her original half share of the house became void when her husband died. So the whole house becomes part of her estate. Her husband's representatives have no rights.

Waiving the bar to evacuation

The substitute may agree to authorise the institute to evacuate (assuming that power to evacuate did not already exist). This can be done by a probative deed, which does not have to be registered, though registration in the Books of Council and Session would be good practice. Even better would be a new conveyance which would have a clause expressly authorising evacuation. Thus, if Mr and Mrs X hold title in common with a survivorship destination which is not capable of evacuation, they could dispone to themselves with a clause authorising evacuation. The practical benefit

[29] 1964 Act, s. 30. For case law see *Stirling's Trs.*, 1977 S.L.T. 229 and *Marshall* v. *Marshall's Exr.*, 1987 S.L.T. 49.

of this method is that the waiver of the bar to evacuation could not be overlooked at a later stage.

Voluntary discharge of destination

More radically, the substitute may waive the destination in his favour altogether. This is done by a new conveyance of the property, omitting the existing destination. Thus, suppose that Mr and Mrs X have a house with a survivorship destination in the title. They wish to discharge it. The practice in such a case is for them to dispone the property to themselves, with no survivorship clause in the deed.

Could a survivorship destination be discharged by probative unregistered deed? Such a deed would certainly discharge the destination in one sense. But it might be that on the first death automatic infeftment would still operate, the position then being that the substitute would be under an obligation to convey to the executor. If this is the law (and it is uncertain), this would obviously be an inconvenient outcome. Hence the practical importance of ensuring that a discharge of a destination is embodied in a registered conveyance.[30]

Evacuation *inter vivos* by conveyance

Evacuation *inter vivos* means some act, other than a will, which defeats a special destination. Voluntary discharge (see above) is thus a sort of *inter vivos* evacuation. But a special destination can also be evacuated by a conveyance. Thus, suppose that property is disponed to A whom failing B. If A subsequently dispones the property to C, then B's contingent right is defeated. For a special destination can operate only where the institute still owns the property at the date of his death. Thus, a person who owns property, or a share of property, which is subject to a destination, can always defeat that destination by alienating the property, or share therein, *inter vivos*, and this is true even if there is no power of *mortis causa* evacuation.

[30] The potential problem would not exist in the case of destinations not of the survivorship type, for the doctrine of automatic infeftment does not extend to such destinations.

There is some older authority[31] indicating that evacuation can be effected only by onerous alienation (typically sale), and not by gratuitous alienation (donation or gift). But the trend of the modern authorities is that it does not matter whether the alienation is onerous or not.[32] Thus, if Mr and Mrs X hold their house subject to a survivorship destination, and if Mr X gratuitously dispones his half share to his brother, and then dies, a modern court would probably hold that Mrs X has no rights in that half share.

A trap

There exists a well-known trap into which the unwary solicitor may fall.[33] It happens typically as follows. Mr and Mrs X own a house in common with a survivorship destination. Mr X goes off on the razzle-dazzle leaving Mrs X to cope with the house and the children. She sees her lawyer, he sees his lawyer, and it is agreed that he will make over his half share of the house to her. The court department of the wife's law firm send down a note to the conveyancing department asking them to draw up a conveyance. A conveyance of the half share is accordingly prepared and Mr X signs it. It is registered. Mrs X is now owner of the whole house. A year or two later she dies. Her original half share is still subject to an unevacuated destination in favour of that scum-of-the-earth, Mr X. So it passes to him.[34] This is almost certainly not what had been intended when the settlement between the parties was reached. From a practical point of view, the problem arises because the deal has been put together in the respective court departments of the firms, who have passed the conveyancing to the conveyancing department for implementation, without proper discussions.

If the problem comes to light while Mrs X is still alive and still owns the property,[35] what can be done? Mr X could be approached to assist in putting matters right, by a deed renouncing the destina-

[31] See, *e.g.*, *Grahame* v. *Ewen's Trs.* (1824) 2 S. 612 (NE 522); *Gillon's Tr.* v. *Gillon* (1890) 17 R. 435; *Macdonald* v. *Hall* (1893) 20 R. (H.L.) 88.

[32] *Steele* v. *Caldwell*, 1979 S.L.T. 228; *Smith* v. *MacIntosh*, 1989 S.L.T. 148.

[33] First drawn to general attention by D.A. Johnstone at 1985 S.L.T. (News) 18.

[34] There has been no test case but this would seem to be the result.

[35] She can, of course, sell the property and if she does so Mr X's contingent rights will fly off.

tion.[36] Or she could dispone the property to a nominee, which would probably have the effect of washing out the undesired destination.[37]

The whole problem can and should be avoided. The correct practice is for the disposition to be a disposition of the whole property, not merely Mr X's half share. The disposition is granted by both Mr and Mrs X and Mrs X as the sole disponee. This, on being registered, will wash the destination out of the title.

Conveyance by the survivor

Suppose that title is taken by Mr and Mrs X with a survivorship destination, and Mr X dies, so that Mrs X is automatically infeft in his share. She is thus now infeft in the whole. She then sells. Are there any specialities about the disposition she will grant? Halliday[38] says that in such a case Mrs X should deduce title in respect of the half share formerly owned by her husband, the midcouple being the fact of Mr X's death. Although a conveyance in such terms would be perfectly valid, in fact no deduction of title is required. The reason is that title needs to be deduced only where the grantor is uninfeft, or partially uninfeft. Here Mrs X is infeft in the whole. Hence no deduction is needed. However, where Halliday's style is not used, it is wise, though not strictly necessary, to make reference in the disposition to Mr X's death, in order to show how it is that Mrs X is infeft in the whole. This can be done in the narrative clause. That clause will narrate that title was taken by such-and-such a disposition to Mr and Mrs X and the survivor, and that Mr X died on such-and-such a date without having evacuated the said destination, etc.

Verifying non-evacuation

The previous paragraph considers the form of the disposition by Mrs X. But how can the disponee be sure that Mr X's share did indeed pass to her? He can verify the existence of the survivorship destination, and he can verify the death of Mr X by asking for the

[36] See above.

[37] This may cause practical problems if there is a heritable security.

[38] Para. 22–54.

death certificate.[39] He can also verify, by a property search, that Mr X did not alienate his share *inter vivos*. But how can he be sure that Mr X did not evacuate the destination by will?

In most cases the destination will not have been capable of evacuation *mortis causa*, and this fact can normally be ascertained from the deed which created it. Even there, however, there is the theoretical possibility that Mrs X had by unregistered deed authorised Mr X to evacuate, and that he did so. This risk is, however, virtually negligible. The risk would be greater where the destination was capable of evacuation *ab initio*, though this is less common in practice.

It has been suggested by Burns[40] that "a purchaser has no duty of inquiry," which presumably means that in a case of latent evacuation a purchaser would be protected by good faith. Whether this is correct, however, must be speculative. The law is unclear and accordingly good practice is likewise unclear. In circumstances where there seems to be some risk of latent evacuation, it is wise to insert a declaration in the disposition that the destination had not been evacuated, for that amounts to an express representation by Mrs X of non-evacuation. Indeed, it is probably wise to go a little further than this. If Mr X left a will, the purchaser should ask to see a copy. Another possibility is to ask Mr X's executor to confirm non-evacuation. The chance of a problem existing becomes smaller the longer it is since Mr X's death.

Destinations and leases

A destination in a lease is subject to different rules from a destination in a disposition or feu disposition, the reason being that the landlord, as well as the substitute, is presumed to have an interest, by virtue of the doctrine of *delectus personae*. But destinations in assignations of leases are probably subject to the ordinary rules, though the point is uncertain.[41]

[39] This should always be done.

[40] John Burns, *Conveyancing Practice* (4th ed., 1957), p. 259.

[41] See an article by G.L. Gretton at 1982 S.L.T. (News) 213 for full discussion.

Destinations and insolvency

Suppose that when Mr X dies, he is insolvent, and that his estate is then sequestrated. Can his trustee in sequestration demand from Mrs X the return of the half share, or demand that she pay to him the value of the half share? *Barclays Bank* v. *McGreish*[42] held that the trustee had no such rights. This decision prompted a flurry of academic discussion, the majority view being that the decision was unsound.[43]

[42] 1983 S.L.T. 344.

[43] See articles by M. Morton at 1984 S.L.T. (News) 133; D.J. Cusine at 1984 J.L.S. 154; J.M. Halliday at 1984 S.L.T. (News) 180 and G.L. Gretton at 1984 S.L.T. (News) 299.

Chapter 25

PARTNERSHIPS

The firm itself has no title

A partnership has its own separate legal personality, distinct from its partners. But this personality is more limited than that of other juristic persons. In particular, a partnership, unlike a corporation, cannot be infeft.[1] Hence, when a partnership acquires heritage, this must be done by title being taken by trustees for behoof of the firm.[2] In theory it does not matter who the trustees are. They need have no beneficial connection with the firm. The practice, however, is to appoint as the trustees some or all of the partners. If the number of partners is large, it may be unwise to make all of them trustees, if only because this can cause inconvenience at a later stage, when a large number of people will have to execute a disposition or whatever. Being a trustee confers no real advantage on a partner. His beneficial interest rests on the fact of being a partner and not on the fact of being trustee.

The three levels of right

Where a partnership holds land, there are three levels of right. At the top level there is the infeftment of the partners, or some of them, as trustees for the firm. Heritable property held by a firm is thus simply part of the general law of trusts, and this is the master key for understanding the law. A trust must, of course, have a beneficiary, which in this case is the firm itself, as a separate juristic *persona*. The firm thus comes in at the second level. The partners themselves are not the beneficiaries of this trust. The partners come in at the third level. They hold rights, not in the firm's property itself, but in the firm, of which they are the owners. Their interests are rather like the interests of the members of a company. Share-

[1] See, further, S. Styles at 1989 J.L.S. 414 and G.L. Gretton at 1991 J.L.S. 232.
[2] Though a lease can be taken by a partnership in its own name.

holders hold shares in the company, not in the company's property.[3]

In general, a trust requires a deed of trust, which in the normal case will be the disposition to the partners as trustees, which will declare that the property is vested in the disponees in trust. The trust is a "bare trust," which is to say that the trust purposes are simply to hold for the benefit of a single beneficiary and to dispose of the property at the direction of that beneficiary.

A trust cannot exist without a beneficiary, and the question of whether the beneficiary of this trust is the firm or the partners of the firm is sometimes not properly focused.[4] Dispositions to firms sometimes state that the disponees are to hold in trust for the firm, and sometimes that they are to hold in trust both for the firm and for the partners present and future thereof. It seems open to question whether this latter style is correct. The general view, both traditional and modern, is that the beneficiary of the trust is the firm. To make both the firm and the partners the beneficiaries is to depart from this simple conception and may produce odd results. Thus, suppose that A and B take title in trust for the firm of Messrs. A & B and for the partners present and future thereof. Such a clause appears to say that there are, at least at this stage, three beneficiaries, namely Messrs. A & B, Mr A and Mr B. Does this mean that the beneficial interest is divided into thirds? That seems to be the ostensible meaning, but it cannot be the real intention. The point might seem merely theoretical, but it could become a live one in some cases of insolvency. In addition, is it really intended that, for example, a so-called salaried partner should have a beneficial interest which is ostensibly equal to that of the senior partner? On the contrary, it is the partnership deed, and variations to it made from time to time, which does and should determine the rights and interests of the several partners.[5] Thus, the better practice is therefore simply for the disposition to declare that the disponees hold in trust for the firm.

Of course, there is a sense in which partnership property is held for the benefit of the partners. But it is equally true to say that

[3] See G.L. Gretton at 1987 J.R. 163.

[4] For instance J. Bennett Miller, *Law of Partnership in Scotland* (W. Green, 1973), p. 387 seems to say both that the trust is for the firm and that it is for the partners. It is difficult to see how both could be true.

[5] See Halliday, para. 11–09.

company property is held for the benefit of the shareholders. But a company does not hold its property in trust for the shareholders in a legal sense (though of course there may be fiduciary duties involved) and so the shareholders are not legally speaking beneficiaries. Likewise partners, though functionally they may be the beneficial "owners" of the land of the firm, are not legally in the position of beneficiaries. The beneficiary is the firm. The role of the partners is to own the beneficiary.

Heritable property brought in by one partner

It sometimes happens that an incoming partner brings with him heritable property in which he is infeft and which he has hitherto held for his own benefit. This may happen either where a new partner joins an existing firm, or, more commonly, where a sole trader takes in partners, himself contributing the heritable property. A familiar example is where a farmer, owning his own land, takes his sons into partnership with him. In such a case the original disposition of the land to the infeft partner obviously cannot itself be the deed of trust. Ideally, in such cases the partnership deed should identify the land as partnership property, and in that event the partnership deed will be the deed of trust. Sometimes the partnership deed is silent on the point, and disputes can then arise as to whether the land is partnership property or not. (That is, a dispute as to whether the infeft partner holds for himself or holds as trustee for the firm.) An alternative approach would be for the incoming partner to dispone to himself and his fellow partners, with the disposition declaring the trust, but in the typical case this will hardly be worthwhile.

Deeds granted by a firm

A disposition or other deed by a firm should not be granted simply by the firm itself, because the firm itself is not the legal owner. The deed must be granted by its trustees. Need all the infeft trustees sign, or is a majority sufficient? This is a general problem in trustee conveyancing, and is considered in chapter 23. The prudent approach is to have all sign.

Need the firm itself be a party?

The infeft trustees may not make up the complete number of current partners. If not, is it necessary that the other partners be party to the deed? It is the practice for this to be done[6] but it is not strictly necessary.[7] The infeft partners hold as trustees for the firm, and section 2 of the Trusts (Scotland) Act 1961 enacts (in effect) that where trustees sell trust estate, the title of the purchaser shall not be challengeable on the ground that the sale was in breach of trust. Thus, even if the sale was without the consent of the firm, a purchaser will have a good title. This rule also applies to the grant of standard securities, though not to gratuitous deeds. Despite the modern rule, the pre-1961 practice of taking all current partners into the deed has continued, and this is sensible, if only to put the matter beyond dispute as between the partners themselves.

Occasionally in dispositions the firm itself, as well as all the partners, is a consenter, though this is hardly necessary. In standard securities, however, the lender will usually require the personal bond element to be entered into by the firm itself as well as by all the partners,[8] and it is often found that the lender will expect the firm itself to be a co-grantor of the security element of the deed, though as has been said this is not actually necessary.[9]

Outgoing partners

Suppose that the firm of X buys property, the title being taken in the name of A, B, C, D and E, the partners at the time, as trustees for the firm of X. Later A, B and C retire. If the firm then sells the property, can the disposition be granted by D and E on their own, or do the retired partners have to be brought in? The latter is the correct answer. A, B and C are no longer partners, but they are still infeft as trustees. There is no rule of law to the effect that the trustees for a firm and its partners must be the same. It is perfectly

[6] See Halliday, para. 22–47.

[7] See Halliday, para. 2–127.

[8] If the firm is personally bound, then the partners will be as well. But lenders nevertheless like all the partners to sign.

[9] If (see below) the standard security has to be signed by a former partner, the deed should be so drafted as to make it clear that that person incurs no personal liability.

possible to be a partner without being a trustee and conversely it is perfectly possible to be a trustee without being a partner. (Presumably indeed, title could be taken in the name of one of the office cleaners, however undesirable in practice this might be.) So the fact that these persons have retired as partners has no effect on their continuing status as infeft trustees. They should therefore sign the deed, or resign as trustees.

Resignation of trustees

It may be inconvenient to get hold of a retired partner. So the simplest way of avoiding the problem is to have an outgoing partner execute a minute of resignation. By this is not meant resignation as a partner, though that will be required as well, but resignation as a trustee. This can be signed at the time he resigns as a partner. The deed should be done in conformity with section 19 of the Trusts (Scotland) Act 1921. The Act prescribes a style in Schedule A, but this often requires a certain amount of modification in partnership cases. The deed of trust referred to in the style is usually the original disposition to the firm. The resignation extinguishes the infeftment of the resigning trustee.[10] The reason for this is that trust property is joint property not common property. A sole trustee cannot resign.

Assumption of trustees

Such resignations may excessively thin out the number of infeft trustees, and accordingly it may be wise from time to time to have additional partners assumed as trustees.[11] Since it is likely that the only trust estate is a single piece of heritable property, it may be appropriate to modify the statutory style of deed of assumption so as to convert it into a conveyance of the specified property, from the existing trustees to themselves (unless they are at the same time resigning) and the new trustees.[12] The advantage[13] is that the grantees may then complete title by recording of the deed direct, without need for a separate notice of title.

[10] Trusts (Scotland) Act 1921, s. 20.
[11] Trusts (Scotland) Act 1921, s. 21 and Sched. B.
[12] This is authorised by the statutory style.
[13] At least in counties still in the Sasine system.

Dissolution

If the partnership is dissolved, this has no direct effect on the title, which continues to be held by the trustees. Of course, the beneficial interest in the trust may pass to one partner or to a group of partners, but that is a separate issue. Thus, a disposition will generally be necessary, the identity of the grantee being determined by the circumstances of the dissolution. In a typical case there will be a minute of dissolution which will regulate the matter. However, if the minute of dissolution directs that the property is to pass to a successor partnership, the title could be left as it is. For in that case the minute of dissolution operates as an assignation of the beneficial interest to the new firm, and all that is needed is for that to be intimated to the trustees.

Does an outgoing partner need to dispone?

Generally speaking, an infeft outgoing partner should not grant a disposition of any particular share in the heritage to the remaining or incoming partners. He is infeft solely as trustee and therefore does not have any share with which he can deal on his own. This is because the infeftment of trustees is a joint infeftment and not an infeftment in common. An outgoing partner may be handing over to the continuing partners his share in the firm, but that has nothing to do with the state of title. Hence, the only thing an outgoing infeft partner should do is to resign as trustee at the same time as he resigns as partner.

In most cases, the only conveyance which is or may be rendered necessary by changes in the membership of the firm is a deed of assumption and conveyance of new trustees. Halliday[14] has an interesting paragraph on this subject. He takes the view that where the title was originally taken to "A, B and C the partners of the firm of A, B & C Co. and the survivor of them as trustees for the said firm of A, B and C Co. and the partners thereof present and future," a deed of assumption and conveyance is appropriate. But where the original infeftment does not refer to future partners, he takes the view that any change in the constitution of the firm may

[14] Para. 11–74.

amount to a change in the trust purposes, with the result that the existing trustees should grant a disposition to trustees for the firm as newly constituted. The same would be true where the firm is dissolved and replaced by a new firm carrying on the same business. With respect, we doubt this view of matters. If the firm is dissolved and reconstituted, then the trustees hold for whoever it is that succeeds to the firm's beneficial interest, for which see above. If, however, what has happened is merely a change in the membership of an existing firm, then the title can be left as it stands, for the identity of the beneficiary is unchanged. In either case it seems to make little difference in what form the original disposition was drafted.

Incoming partners

Just as an outgoing infeft partner does not cease to be infeft merely because he has ceased to be a partner, so likewise an incoming partner does not become a trustee merely because he has become a partner. To become a trustee he must be assumed as such. Thus, suppose that title is taken in the names of A, B and C, and at the time of sale the current partners are C, D and E, and that there has been no resignation (as trustees) by A or B and no assumption (as trustees) of D or E. The disposition falls to be granted by A, B and C. D and E should adhibit their consent, though (see above) even this is strictly speaking not required for the validity of the deed.

Incapacity, death, or sequestration of partners

Incapacity will normally entail ceasing to be a partner, but it does not terminate infeftment. Moreover, if a *curator bonis* has been appointed, the *curator* has no power to deal with trust estate. Since an *incapax* trustee cannot execute a deed of resignation as trustee, it may be necessary to have him removed.[15]

Death or sequestration of one partner may operate the dissolution of the firm[16] but in practice partnership deeds commonly provide that the firm shall continue notwithstanding these events. The

[15] Under s. 23 of the Trusts (Scotland) Act 1921.

[16] Partnership Act 1890, s. 33.

death of an infeft partner extinguishes his infeftment. This is because the infeftment of trustees is not an infeftment in common but a joint infeftment. So any infeft partner who has died can be left out of account entirely, though a copy of the death certificate should be put up with the titles, and the death should be narrated in the next deed. For the case where the death is of the sole, or sole surviving, infeft partner, see below.

The sequestration of a person who happens to be a trustee under some trust has no effect on the trust estate. This is true both at common law and by statute.[17] In addition, such sequestration generally has no effect on the bankrupt's status as trustee. There is no rule of law that a bankrupt cannot be a trustee. The bankrupt partner thus continues as trustee, even though his sequestration will normally entail that he ceases to be a partner. So unless he resigns as trustee he will have to be one of the grantors of any future deed affecting title. His trustee in sequestration has no right or title to the partnership property itself. His interest is solely a right to the bankrupt partner's share in the partnership. The same is true, *mutatis mutandis*, of the case where a partner grants a trust deed for behoof of creditors.

Lapsed trust

If the sole trustee, or sole surviving trustee, dies, the result is a lapsed trust. This can be sorted out in the ordinary way, such as a petition for new trustees under section 22 of the Trusts (Scotland) Act 1921 or (in most, though not all, cases) by procedure under section 6 of the Executors (Scotland) Act 1900.[18] It has been suggested[19] that section 24 of the 1921 Act could also be used, but this seems open to question. That section provides that where a trust is lapsed, a beneficiary can, by court process, complete title in his own name. The difficulty is that with partnerships the beneficiary in such a case is the firm itself, and a firm cannot complete title in its own name.

[17] Bankruptcy (Scotland) Act 1985, s. 33.
[18] See, further, Halliday, para. 22–28.
[19] Halliday, para. 22–28.

Contracting out

It has been said above that an outgoing partner does not cease to be a trustee, unless he resigns as such, and likewise that an incoming partner does not become a trustee, unless he is assumed as such. Could these rules be contracted out of? In other words, could it be provided that every resigning partner (or partner becoming insane) should automatically cease to be a trustee, and that every incoming partner automatically be deemed to be assumed as trustee? These are difficult questions. It is possible to have trustees *ex officio*, so that it might be thought that it could be provided that every partner for the time being would be a trustee *ex officio*. Indeed, if this could be done it would not even be necessary for future partners to complete title or deduce title, because of the provisions of section 45 of the Conveyancing (Scotland) Act 1874. But such a plan would depart considerably from the normal understanding of a trustee *ex officio*. The typical trustee *ex officio* is the holder of some public office, such as the parish minister. So the idea cannot be recommended.

Might there be a consensual provision that an outgoing partner would automatically cease to be a trustee? In principle this might seem unobjectionable, but again it cannot be recommended in practice. There seems to be no authority for such a device. Moreover, section 19 of the 1921 Act presupposes that any resignation by a trustee will be a resignation *de praesenti* whereas the suggested idea would involve a resignation *de futuro*. Although resignation *de futuro* is arguably competent, the prudent conveyancer should seek to avoid attempting it.

Bankruptcy of firm

A partnership may be sequestrated as such, either with or without the sequestration of its individual partners.[20] The firm's trustee in sequestration probably cannot grant a disposition of its heritable property. The problem here is that the title is held not by the firm itself but by trustees for the firm, so *prima facie*, while the trustee in sequestration has power of sale, the disposition must be granted

[20] Bankruptcy (Scotland) Act 1985, s. 6.

by the infeft trustees. This seems unsatisfactory in a practical sense, especially if the infeft partners are themselves bankrupt, as is likely to be the case. It might be argued, on the other side, that section 31 of the Bankruptcy (Scotland) Act 1985 vests the estate in the trustee. But what is vested? Vesting is *tantum et tale* and what the firm had was not title but only a beneficial interest.[21] Again, it might be argued that the sequestration of the firm dissolves it and so each partner is deemed to have a share. But this is probably not an accurate way of stating the position. (There is authority that a sequestrated firm still exists as a juristic *persona*, the effect of the sequestration being to dissolve the contract rather than the personality.) In addition, even if true it would take us no further because title would still be stuck inside a trust. All that would have changed would have been the identity of the beneficiary.

Where a firm is sequestrated, it often happens that the partners are also sequestrated, or grant trust deeds, and it commonly happens that the insolvency practitioner who is trustee of the firm is also trustee for the partners. Will this fact be of assistance? Probably not. For (see above) a bankruptcy trustee has no right to deal with property vested in the bankrupt not beneficially but in trust. The result may seem absurd: we have an insolvency practitioner who is trustee for the bankrupt firm and also for all the bankrupt partners, yet he cannot, on his own, grant a disposition of the firm's property, if this line of reasoning is correct.

What sometimes happens in practice is that the firm's trustee in sequestration does grant the disposition, deducing title through his act and warrant, without getting the infeft partners to sign. If the argument outline above is correct, this procedure is improper. The practical advice is that the disposition should be signed not only by the firm's trustee in sequestration but also by the infeft trustees, even if themselves bankrupt. This may be unsatisfactory from the practical point of view, but in the absence of any clear provision on the point in the legislation, and in the apparent absence of authority, it seems the wise approach. The infeft trustees would be under a legal obligation to co-operate.

[21] If X is a beneficiary under his aunt's trust, and is sequestrated, no one would suggest that the infeftment of the aunt's trustees could pass to X's trustee in sequestration.

CHAPTER 26

COMPANIES

Introduction

This is a brief chapter, for two reasons. The first is that this book does not attempt to cover commercial conveyancing in general, and the second is that some aspects of companies are dealt with elsewhere.[1]

Vires

The Companies Act 1989[2] has the general effect of abolishing the *ultra vires* doctrine as far as outsiders are concerned. The result is that in general a person dealing with a company need not concern himself with the question of whether the company is acting within its powers. Good or bad faith is irrelevant. However, these provisions apply only to companies incorporated under the Companies Acts, and other corporations are generally still subject to the common law rules concerning *ultra vires*.

Powers of directors

It can happen that while an act would be valid if properly authorised by the company, the directors of the company, when entering into it, were exceeding their powers as laid down in the company's memorandum and articles. Here again, however, the Companies Act 1989 will, in general, protect a third party,[3] and

[1] For execution of deeds by companies see chap. 15. For company searches see chap. 7. For company insolvency see chap. 27. For the Register of Charges see chap. 18.

[2] Section 35 as substituted by s. 108 of the Companies Act 1989. The protection, however, is not absolute if the company is a charitable one: Companies Act 1989, s. 112. That section also requires any conveyance by a charitable company to state its charitable status.

[3] Companies Act 1985, ss. 35A and 35B, as substituted by the Companies Act 1989, s. 108.

though the protection requires good faith on the part of the third party,[4] such a party is not in bad faith merely because he knows that the directors have exceeded their powers,[5] which comes close to saying that good faith is not necessary. The protection applies only where the transaction has been authorised by the "board of directors." Thus, for instance, missives entered into by a managing director in excess of his powers might not be binding on the company. In large transactions, or transactions of an unusual nature, a copy of the board resolution authorising the transaction should therefore be obtained. But this is not normally done when merely purchasing a dwelling-house.

Execution of deeds

Execution of deeds by companies is dealt with in chapter 15. But a point worth noting is that where a company has executed a conveyancing deed in the proper manner, it is a deed of the company itself. Thus, suppose that a managing director entered into missives of sale outwith his authority. The company would probably not be bound. But then suppose that the managing director and the company secretary signed the disposition. That would then be a valid deed by the company, which could therefore not challenge it. Obviously, it is necessary that the deed be executed by the proper persons. Good practice is for the purchaser to insist on a search at the Companies Office to verify that the signatories are indeed registered as directors, or secretary. However, if the execution is not by two directors, or a director plus the secretary, but by persons authorised to sign by the company, the validity of the deed depends on the validity of the authorisation.

Registration of charges

When a company grants a standard security it must be registered not only in the Sasine or Land Register but also in the Charges Register. The latter must happen with 21 days of its registration in the Sasine or Land Register.[6] Failure to register will cause the

[4] Companies Act 1985, s. 35A(1), as substituted.

[5] Companies Act 1985, s. 35A(2)(*b*), as substituted.

[6] The present rules are to be found in s. 410 *et seq.* of the Companies Act 1985. The Companies Act 1989 replaces these with new provisions inserted in s. 395 *et*

security to be null,[7] though the debt secured remains a valid debt. Registration out of time is possible but only with the sanction of the court.[8] If a solicitor realises that he has failed to make timeous registration he should, in the typical case, petition the court immediately. Failure to register is a common error, and amounts to negligence.

Buying from a company: some pitfalls

When taking a deed from a company it is necessary to make sure that the company is duly incorporated and is not in insolvency. The main dangers are: (1) striking off[9] (2) liquidation; (3) receivership; (4) administration. All these can be checked, and must be checked, by a search in the company file at the Companies Office.[10]

Certificate of non-crystallization

A floating charge is automatically discharged on a sale of property, provided that it has not attached (crystallized).[11] This is because a floating charge can affect only that which is in the ownership of the debtor company. The effect of attachment is to convert the floating charge into a "fixed" charge, which is a real right, with the result that the company can no longer alienate property free of the charge. So what the buyer should ask for[12] is a certificate from the charge holder certifying that the charge has not attached and that it will not be made to attach for a stated period, typically seven days from date of certificate. This is called a certificate of non-crystallization. Since it is common in a floating charge to have a clause forbidding sale of heritage without the consent of the charge holder, it is advisable for the certificate to contain such a consent as well.

seq. of the 1985 Act, the present sections bearing those numbers being repealed. However, these new provisions have not yet been brought into force and there is no sign of this happening in the foreseeable future.

[7] Companies Act 1989, s. 410.

[8] Companies Act 1985, s. 420.

[9] Companies Act 1985, s. 652.

[10] For searches, see chap. 7.

[11] The two terms mean the same. The first is Scottish, and the second English, but the English term is widely used here.

[12] And stipulate for in the missives.

Letter of obligation and certificate of solvency

The solicitors for a company will normally grant a standard letter of obligation for the personal and Sasine searches, but not, normally, for the company search. The final company search might have something nasty which did not show up on the interim report, such as liquidation. The practice is, therefore, to require some or all of the directors to grant what is sometimes called a certificate of solvency guaranteeing that the company is not insolvent and will not become so prior to the registration of the grantee's title. Both this and the certificate of non-crystallization should be stipulated for in the missives.

Some of the same considerations apply where a previous owner within the prescriptive period was a company, though in that case the certificates of non-crystallization and of solvency are not normally required because the situation can be fully checked from the company search, which should be with the title deeds. If it is not, then another search will be necessary. This also must be stipulated for in the missives.

Lending to a company on standard security

Although a floating charge will not, subject to some qualifications, concern a purchaser from a company, it will usually concern someone taking a standard security. This is because floating charges usually have a clause[13] forbidding future standard securities or postponing them to the floating charge. It is, therefore, particularly important for the lender to ascertain whether any prior floating charge has been granted, and if so, on what terms.

[13] Under the Companies Act 1985, s. 464(1).

CHAPTER 27

INSOLVENCY

Introduction

This chapter covers purchases from an insolvent estate, that is to say from a trustee in sequestration, or a trustee under a trust deed for creditors, a liquidator, a receiver or an administrator. Purchases from a heritable creditor are dealt with elsewhere.[1] The whole subject is a complex one and we will give only an outline.[2]

General points

One general point is that missives will usually be different from the standard case. On the one hand, the purchaser will wish to insert certain additional clauses in his offer, dealing with some of the specific issues discussed below. On the other hand, the seller will be reluctant to grant some of the warranties which would be the usual case in a normal sale. One example would be the warranty against unauthorised alterations. In general terms, the seller may decline to warrant the types of things which involve the personal knowledge of an owner, for the good reason that the insolvency practitioner who is selling will very likely not be in possession of such knowledge.

Another general point is that the narrative clause of the disposition should of course narrate the insolvency. For instance, a disposition by a trustee in sequestration would typically run: "I . . . permanent trustee in sequestration on the sequestrated estate of

[1] Chap. 12.

[2] For insolvency law generally, see W.W. McBryde, *Bankruptcy* (W. Green, 1989); J.B. St Clair and J.E. Drummond Young, *Law of Corporate Insolvency* (Butterworth, 2nd ed.) and J.H. Greene and I.M. Fletcher, *Law and Practice of Receivership in Scotland* (2nd ed.), though these works do not have extensive coverage of conveyancing questions. See G.L. Gretton at 1992 J.L.S. 346 for discussion of insolvency conveyancing.

. . . conform to act and warrant . . . and as such trustee uninfeft proprietor of. . . ."

A third general point is that the right of the trustee, or liquidator, or receiver, or administrator, to sell the property will, subject to minor qualifications, be no better than that originally held by the insolvent person or company. So if X buys land, but his title is bad, his trustee in sequestration will, generally speaking, have no better right to sell the land than X had. Thus, in addition to the specialities applicable to the insolvency itself, the purchaser's agent must make the usual examination of title.

Lastly, some of the recommendations below are requirements imposed by legislation on the seller, of an administrative nature, and sanctioned typically by fines. (For example, registration of a liquidation in the Companies Register.) Non-compliance thus generally affects the seller but not the purchaser. However, there is an increasing tendency nowadays for purchasers to require that these steps have been taken. Though arguably unnecessary, such requirements generally cause no difficulty since a competent seller will have ensured compliance. The positive argument for a purchaser making these requirements is that there might possibly be situations in which a purchaser might have to defend his title on the basis of good faith.

Buying from a trustee in sequestration

The key document in a sequestration is the act and warrant, which is the interlocutor vesting the estate in the trustee. Accordingly, the purchaser must see this and put a copy of it with the titles at settlement. The disposition will deduce title through it.[3] It is good practice, though perhaps not strictly necessary, for the purchaser to require evidence that the seller is a qualified insolvency practitioner.[4] It is likewise prudent to stipulate that there has been due registration in the personal register under section 14 of the Bankruptcy (Scotland) Act 1985.[5] Any outstanding heritable security

[3] Except in the unusual case where the trustee has already completed title in his own name.

[4] Insolvency Act 1986, s. 388.

[5] Registration under this section has the effect of an inhibition against the bankrupt. The obligation to register is placed on the clerks of court, who, however,

must be discharged. This can be done either by an ordinary discharge or by the consent of the heritable creditor embodied in the disposition by the trustee. However, inhibitions against the bankrupt need not be discharged.[6] If the subjects are a dwelling-house, the trustee should be asked for evidence that his power of sale is not prejudiced by the terms of section 40 of the Bankruptcy (Scotland) Act 1985.[7]

Buying from a trustee under a trust deed

The key document in a trust for behoof of creditors is the trust deed itself. This should have been registered in the Books of Council and Session,[8] and it must be exhibited, and a copy (preferably an extract) should be retained. Title will be deduced through it in the disposition, except in the unusual case where the trustee has already completed title in his own name. The remarks made in connection with sequestration (about section 40 of the Bankruptcy (Scotland) Act 1985) are probably equally applicable in this type of case. But, in addition, the "anti-dealings" provisions of the 1981 Act,[9] though they do not restrict the powers of sale of a trustee in sequestration, are capable of adversely affecting the powers of sale of a trustee under a trust deed. So the seller must satisfy the purchaser that there are no adverse occupancy rights. Lastly, a purchaser should normally stipulate that the trust deed be a protected one.[10] Provided that it is so protected, it is not necessary that any inhibitions against the bankrupt be discharged. However, any outstanding heritable security must be discharged. Evidence should be obtained that the seller is a qualified insolvency practitioner.

occasionally fail in this duty. One danger is that another party might, in the absence of this registration, take a deed in good faith from the bankrupt.

[6] Bankruptcy (Scotland) Act 1985, s. 31(2)

[7] This section restricts the trustee's power of sale in certain cases so as to protect the family of the bankrupt.

[8] This is not strictly a legal requirement.

[9] 1981 Act, s. 6(1). See chap. 8.

[10] See the Bankruptcy (Scotland) Act 1985, Sched. 5, as amended by the Bankruptcy (Scotland) Act 1993.

Buying from a liquidator

If the liquidation is a compulsory one, the key document is the interlocutor ordering winding up, and this must be exhibited, and a copy kept. If the liquidation is a voluntary one, the key document is the special resolution of the company, which again must be seen. The interlocutor or resolution should have been registered at the Companies Office,[11] as should the appointment of the liquidator.[12] Evidence should be required as to the liquidator's status as an insolvency practitioner, as for sequestrations. Outstanding heritable securities must be discharged. There is some uncertainty as to whether outstanding inhibitions need to be discharged, but the general view is that they need not be. If there is a floating charge, the charge holder should consent to the sale, and if a receiver has been appointed under the charge, the receiver must consent to the sale.[13]

Subject to some qualifications, there is no vesting of the company's property in a liquidator. Approximately speaking, the liquidator simply replaces the board of directors.[14] Hence, the disposition is from the company itself, though the practice is to make the liquidator a co-disponer with the company itself. The liquidator signs, with two witnesses. It is not necessary to affix the company's seal, though this is commonly done.

Buying from a receiver

In a receivership, there are two key documents, which must be seen and copies of which should be kept. The first is the floating charge itself. This must be checked carefully, to see that it was properly executed, and to see that it covers the property now being sold.[15]

[11] Insolvency Act 1986, ss. 84 and 130.

[12] See the Insolvency Act 1986, s. 109 and the Insolvency (Scotland) Rules 1986, rr. 4.18, and 4.19, while r. 4.20 deals with evidence of appointment.

[13] In that case, consent by the charge holder is not necessary. In cases where consent is required, it should be incorporated in the disposition.

[14] A company in liquidation still exists as a legal person. It continues to exist as such until dissolution. It is dissolution, not liquidation, which marks the end of the juristic personality. Much the same is true of receivership and administration.

[15] A floating charge describes the property it affects not specifically but generically. The standard phrase is "the whole property and undertaking" of the company,

It must also be verified that the charge was duly registered within the 21–day period.[16] The second key document is the instrument of appointment. This is the deed by which the charge holder appoints the receiver.[17] The purchaser should verify that it was validly executed, that the appointee accepted the appointment,[18] and that the receivership was duly registered.[19] He should also verify that the receiver is a qualified insolvency practitioner.

It sometimes happens that there is more than one receiver. In that case the purchaser should normally insist that both of them execute the disposition. However, if the company is simultaneously in receivership and in liquidation, it seems that there is no need to ask the liquidator also to consent.[20] A receiver executes the disposition in the same manner as a liquidator, and the practice is for the deed to run in the name of both the company and its receiver.

A floating charge granted within two years[21] prior to liquidation can, in certain cases, be subject to challenge of by the liquidator under section 245 of the Insolvency Act 1986.[22] But there would appear to be no danger to a purchaser where there has been no liquidation at the time of the sale. The potential danger arises only where (1) there is a concurrent liquidation and (2) the sale is by the receiver and not the liquidator and (3) the liquidator does not consent and (4) the charge was created within the period of challenge. Even in such cases the charge will usually be at least partly valid because of section 245(2).[23] There seems to be no generally

and this will cover all heritage, present and future. But occasionally a floating charge is restricted, *e.g.* to the moveables. Such a charge would obviously be no basis for selling the heritage.

[16] Companies Act 1985, s. 410; Companies Act 1989, s. 95.

[17] In theory, a receiver can be appointed by the court, but this never happens in practice.

[18] Insolvency Act 1986, s. 53(6).

[19] Insolvency Act 1986, s. 53(1).

[20] Subject to what is said below.

[21] In some cases the challenge period is one year.

[22] Under these provisions a floating charge may be challengeable if granted to secure a pre-existing debt.

[23] Whereby a floating charge is protected from challenge to the extent that it secures new money advanced after its creation. The rule in *Devaynes* v. *Noble* (1816) 1 Merivale 529 (called, with English logic, *Clayton's Case*), adopted into Scots law by *Royal Bank* v. *Christie* (1841) 2 Rob. 118, operates in favour of the charge holder in such cases.

accepted good practice, but we would suggest that where (1), (2) and (4) apply the receiver should be required to satisfy the purchaser, either by obtaining the liquidator's consent, or by giving an indemnity, or by providing a title insurance policy, or by producing evidence that section 245 is inapplicable.

Whether outstanding heritable securities need to be discharged is a complex question, but in general the purchaser should insist on this, or on a court order enabling the receiver to sell free of them.[24] There is a parallel problem for inhibitions against the company. An inhibition created before the creation[25] of the charge must certainly be discharged, or the receiver must obtain judicial sanction to sell free of it.[26] An inhibition created at a later stage seems not to affect a receiver's power of sale.[27]

Buying from an administrator

Administrations are not very common. The key document is the court interlocutor making the administration order,[28] which must, of course, be seen and checked, as should the administrator's status as an insolvency practitioner. The order should have been registered in both the Company Register[29] and the personal register.[30] The disposition typically runs in the name of both the company and its administrator, and is executed in the same way as by a liquidator. Though the point is uncertain, an administrator probably has no power to sell free of an inhibition, unless at the direction of the court. Outstanding heritable securities must be discharged, unless there is an order by the court made under section 15 of the Insolvency Act 1986.

[24] Insolvency Act 1986, s. 61.

[25] Not the attachment.

[26] Insolvency Act 1986, s. 61.

[27] But in such cases purchasers sometimes insist on a s. 61 order: see *Armour & Mycroft, Petrs.*, 1983 S.L.T. 453.

[28] Insolvency Act 1986, s. 11.

[29] Insolvency Act 1986, s. 21(2).

[30] Insolvency (Scotland) Rules 1986, r. 2.3.

CHAPTER 28

MISCELLANEOUS CASES

1. Flats[1]

In law, a "tenement" means not only a purpose-built block of flats, but also conversions. Even a Victorian detached house which has subsequently been divided into upper and lower "villa flats" will be subject to the law of the tenement. The law of the tenement applies except in so far as the provisions in the titles modify it. Traditionally, any such modifications were made in the split-off deed for each flat. The split-offs would usually be granted by the original builder as soon as the construction was complete. But sometimes a tenement would be built and the flats let out rather than sold. Many years later the flats would eventually be sold off one by one. Thus, one sometimes comes across a tenement built in, say, 1890 with the break-offs being granted in, say, the 1930s.

In more modern developments there is usually a deed of conditions,[2] to which each break-off refers. This is obviously more convenient. It is also generally true that the more modern the development the more complex the conditions are. A split-off of a flat in 1890 may just have a few words about the roof and the back green. A modern break-off deed for a flat may have pages of provisions. Where a deed of condition is used it is quite common to have provisions for decisions to be taken by majority vote,[3] and also for the appointment of a factor by the owners, *i.e.* a person who inspects the tenement regularly and organises repair work. Sometimes, especially in the Glasgow area, there is a single fire insurance

[1] For further detail see *Stair Memorial Encyclopaedia*, vol. 18, paras. 227–251.

[2] 1874 Act, s. 32, and 1979 Act, s. 17. Deeds of conditions for flats are commoner in the Glasgow area than elsewhere. For an example, see Halliday, para. 19–37.

[3] This is obviously useful. Obtaining unanimity can be very difficult. To what extent unanimity is necessary (if the titles do not provide for majority voting) is complex and obscure, and may depend on the type of question which is to be decided.

policy for the whole tenement, typically kept in the name of the factor on behalf of the owners. The factor pays the premiums and bills the owners. In other tenements there is no such policy and it is for each owner to insure as he sees fit.

Roof

The most important issue for flats concerns liability for upkeep of the roof. The common law position is that the owner of the roof is liable for its upkeep, and the common law further provides that the top flat owner is the owner of the roof above his flat.[4] When buying a top flat for a client it is therefore vital to check whether this common law position has been varied by the titles. In a majority of cases it will be found that this has been done, but in a significant minority the common law position prevails. In such cases the effect of the common law rule is to diminish the capital value of the top flat, to reflect the responsibility for future repairs.

The common law position may be altered in one of two ways. The first is that the roof may be the common property of all parties. That will do the trick, for liability for upkeep will then be mutual, on the common law principle that the owner or owners of the roof must maintain it. The other method is to have a real burden imposing a share of the liability for upkeep. Often both methods are used, and in that case the second method is the ruling one. Thus, suppose that there are eight flats, and the roof is owned in common, and that the real burdens provide for the two ground flats to have a 20 per cent. share each in the liability and the other six flats 10 per cent. each. The equal ownership would, in itself, give rise to an equal liability (12.5 per cent.), but this is overridden by the real burdens. Where a dormer window has been added since the titles dealt with liability, it seems that the maintenance of the dormer window is solely the responsibility of the person whose flat the dormer serves.

In order to determine whether, and to what extent, the common law position has been altered, what is important is not the title to the top flat in question, but the titles to the other flats. Thus, suppose that a client is purchasing a top flat, and the title says that

[4] The roof over the common passage and stair is, at common law, in common ownership of all the flats.

the owner is liable to 15 per cent. of the liability. That does not help. For the lower proprietors can be liable only to the extent that their titles make them liable, and what the top flat title says is, therefore, of very limited relevance. In other words, to the extent that a lower title does not impose liability, the "slack" must be taken by the top owner. Hence, when purchasing a top flat, the titles to the lower flats must be examined.[5] This must be provided for in the missives. In most cases what needs to be checked is the original split-off deed, which typically will have been granted immediately after the original construction of the tenement. Often photocopies of these deeds have been added to the title deeds of the top flat. In practice, a purchasing solicitor is sometimes content to examine a sample of the other titles. If the purchasing agent finds that the common law position has not been changed, that will generally amount to a breach of the missives. Sometimes the client will be prepared to go ahead on the basis of a reduction in the price to reflect future liability. For a purchasing solicitor not to check the roof position when purchasing a top flat is normally negligence. Hence, if a client does decide to buy a top flat with full roof liability, his solicitor should carefully inform him of the position and retain evidence of this in his file.

Roof void

The roof void (the space which typically exists between the ceiling of the top flat and the roof itself) does not usually present problems about upkeep. But sometimes a top owner wishes to build an upper floor in the roof void. At common law the roof void belongs to the owner of the top flat. Title deeds often vary this. But if they merely say that the "roof" is owned in common, without also specifiying the roof void, the latter is not included, and so remains subject to the common law rule. Sometimes a top proprietor has built a room in such a roof space without obtaining dispositions from the other parties. This obviously can cause major problems and when buying a top flat for a client it is wise to check whether there has been a roof void extension and if so whether the title to the extension is good.[6] If the airspace is to be encroached upon, for instance by the

[5] See, *e.g.*, 1990 J.L.S. 531 for a cautionary tale.
[6] For a cautionary tale see 1991 J.L.S. 77.

construction of a dormer window,[7] it should be noted that the airspace above a tenement belongs to whoever owns the *solum.*

Other parts

The other parts of the tenement are less important because repair costs are usually minor in comparison with the roof. Responsibility for upkeep coincides with ownership, except in so far as varied by the titles. Titles often have a vague provision about upkeep of "common and mutual parts," which may mean everything which is used in common.

Calculation of liability for repairs

Usually there is express provision in the titles for repair of the roof and a number of other parts. Sometimes titles will specify the share of liability in fractional terms (*e.g.* one-eighth) or percentage terms (*e.g.* 12.5 per cent.). That is obviously the simplest and most convenient. But very often it will be found that liability is divided either according to the ratio of the feuduty or according to the ratio of the rateable value. In such cases it is necessary to ascertain the feuduty, or rateable value, for all the flats, and then to make a calculation. Rateable values have now been abolished except in respect of non-domestic property, but the last valuations remain accessible.[8]

The *solum*

At common law the *solum*—the ground on which the tenement is built—belongs to the owners of the ground floor. The *solum* under the common passage and stair is thus at common law owned in common by everyone. Titles often vary the common law rule by making the whole *solum* common property. Some purchasers' agents will object to a title of a flat (other than a ground flat) which does not have a share in the *solum*. This is probably unnecessary.[9]

[7] See, *e.g.* K.G.C. Reid at 1990 J.L.S. 368.

[8] Abolition of Domestic Rates Etc. (Scotland) Act 1987, s. 5.

[9] See D. J. Cusine (ed.), *The Conveyancing Opinions of Professor J.M. Halliday*, p. 154; K.G.C. Reid, "The Law of the Tenement: Three Problems," 1990 J.L.S. 368.

The *solum* has little significance. If a tenement subject to the common law were to be burnt down or demolished, the owners of the (former) ground flats, or their successors, could not redevelop without the consent of the other parties, partly because the airspace above would still be owned by the latter and partly because of the common ownership of the *solum* of the (former) common passage and stair. Moreover, in the typical case there will be insurance cover for loss by fire. Where there is no share in the *solum*, some purchasing agents ask for a title indemnity policy. But this would seem to be an impossibility. It is difficult to see what "loss" the policy could cover, nor how prescription could "cure" the alleged "defect" in the title.[10]

Statutory notices

Where there is a statutory repairs notice and the work is done by the local authority, the latter can recover from the current owner, even though the current owner is a recent incomer.[11] It is important for missives to provide for this danger in the event that the property inquiry certificates disclose a statutory notice. One method is for the seller to be required to place the expected amount, plus a percentage for safety, on deposit receipt in the joint names of both law firms. This should be coupled with a provision keeping the missives in force for a sufficient time, such as five years, for the matter to be fully resolved, since it often takes more than the usual two years for the position to be clarified.

It is common practice for the council to serve a notice on all the flats even though not all are liable under the common law or the title deeds and even though the problem in question (*e.g.*, wood rot in joists) does not affect all the flats. This blanket-bombing is lawful,[12] and if the council does the work it will normally bill all

[10] A prescriptive title to the *solum* could be acquired only by possession. Although a right to the *solum* might be added to the title, it could presumably never take effect because it is not easy to see what distinctive acts of possession could be carried out.

[11] *Purves* v. *City of Edinburgh District Council*, 1987 S.C.L.R. 381; 1987 S.L.T. 366.

[12] *Court of the University of Edinburgh* v. *City of Edinburgh District Council*, 1987 S.L.T. (Sh. Ct.) 103; *City of Edinburgh District Council* v. *Gardner*, 1990 S.L.T. 600.

the owners.[12a] If that happens, readjustment in terms of the title deeds (or common law) can be insisted on by any party, but that readjustment is simply as between the parties, and does not affect the council.

2. New Houses[13]

For second-hand houses, the terms of missives are a matter for negotiation. But in the case of new houses the builder usually has a standard style, the terms of which are presented as being non-negotiable. Generally, it is in the form of an offer addressed to the builder to be signed personally by the prospective buyer. The builder promptly adds his acceptance. Often the buyer receives no legal advice, and simply arrives at a law office holding the concluded contract in his hands. Even if he sees his solicitor before signing anything, the builder may refuse to consider alterations of the terms. Because these contracts are drafted by the builder, they are often very one-sided documents. They often amount to this: that the seller will pay the price whenever the seller asks for it, whether or not the house has actually been built, whether or not it has any defects, and whether or not the support works (roads, sewers, etc.) have been constructed. Very often there is no proper description of the property being bought. The missives may absolve the seller of the need to show good and marketable title or clear searches or planning permission or building warrants or completion certificates or road bonds. The missives may also reserve to the seller the right unilaterally to alter the design of the house or the shape of the plot.[14] If the prospective purchaser seeks legal advice before signing, the solicitor must advise strongly that the terms of the missives be altered. The builder will resist, but if threatened with the loss of the sale will in practice often agree to be less unreasonable. At all events, if unfair missives are entered into, the buyer's solicitor must inform his client of the possible dangers, and do this in writing.

[12a] Though whether this is authorised by the legislation is arguable: see 1990 J.L.S. 368 at p. 371–372.

[13] For an excellent study see D.M. Allan, "Housebuilders Missives," 1980 J.L.S. 17. See also 1990 J.L.S. 77.

[14] Not all builders missives have such provisions.

Builders almost always use *pro forma* dispositions or feu dispositions, and sometimes a copy of this is attached to and is referred to by the missives. It will contain real burdens either directly or by reference to a deed of conditions, and of course the client must decide whether these burdens are acceptable. It is important to check the terms of the disposition carefully. There is a temptation to assume that the builder's solicitors have done a perfect job. Surprisingly often this is not so. For instance, there may be errors in the description of the property, or the common parts, or amenity areas, and so on. Sometimes the purchaser's solicitor points out some defect to be met with the reply that the *pro forma* has already been examined by 10 other firms without objection. He should not be intimidated by such a reply. If the defect is a real one, so much the worse for the other 10 firms, and their clients.

Public law consents[15]

New houses require various consents in public law. The main ones are planning permission, and building warrant with completion certificate. These should be stipulated for in the missives and exhibited at or before settlement. The missives ought also to stipulate for a road bond where road construction is necessary.

NHBC scheme[16]

In most cases the builder will be a member of the National House Builders Council (NHBC). This organisation inspects houses in the course of construction and offers to purchasers a 10–year limited guarantee against major faults. The guarantee is mainly useful where the builder has become insolvent and so unable to put defects right. The missives should stipulate for a NHBC guarantee. In the case of a non-NHBC builder the missives should stipulate for certification by an independent architect.

3. Council Houses: the Right-to-Buy Legislation

One of the slogans of Thatcherism was "a property-owning democracy." Soon after coming to power in 1979, the Conservatives

[15] See chap. 3.

[16] See D. Calder, "Buildmark", 1990 J.L.S. 151 for current NHBC developments.

introduced legislation to allow the tenants of council houses, and certain other public-sector tenants, compulsorily to purchase their houses or flats at below-market prices. The Scottish legislation was at first contained in the Tenants Rights Etc. (Scotland) Act 1980 and is now in the Housing (Scotland) Act 1987.[17] These provisions are commonly called the "right-to-buy" legislation.[18]

Those eligible to buy are tenants of at least two years standing, holding a secure tenancy[19] from a local authority, or a New Town Development Corporation, or a housing association, or Scottish Homes. The first step is to complete and submit the official "application to purchase" form. The landlord will then arrange for the property to be valued by the district valuer. The landlord should then make a formal offer to sell. If this is not done, or if the terms are considered unreasonable by the tenant, the latter can apply to the Lands Tribunal. The sale price is the valuation figure less a "discount" which is calculated on a sliding scale, depending on how long the buyer has been the tenant. The buyer's solicitor should carefully check the terms of the offer to sell. He should ensure that the discount has been calculated correctly. He should ideally inspect the property, because there may be problems about shared amenity areas, access routes and so on. Council properties were not originally constructed with individual ownership in mind. In addition, some are poorly built, though here the purchaser has some protection under the Housing (Scotland) Act 1987, Part XIV.[20]

Missives are concluded when the tenant sends to the landlord a "notice of acceptance" of the offer to sell. Once missives have been concluded, matters cease to be regulated by the legislation,[21] and so ordinary law and conveyancing practice apply. Thus, if the tenant dies after missives but before settlement, his rights pass to his executor.[22]

[17] At the time of writing, amending legislation is in Parliament.

[18] For an overview see Chris Himsworth, *Public Sector Housing Law in Scotland.*

[19] The standard form of public sector tenancy, regulated by the Housing (Scotland) Act 1987.

[20] This gives a right of compensation, or in some cases a right that the property be re-purchased at full value. The idea is that since the Government encourages public sector tenants to buy their houses, the public should be in some measure liable where there are latent defects.

[21] Apart from repayment of the discount.

[22] *Cooper's Exr.* v. *City of Edinburgh District Council*, 1991 S.L.T. 518; 1991 S.C.L.R. 664.

If the new owner resells within three years,[23] part of the discount is repayable according to a sliding scale which is based on the period between the original purchase and the proposed sale. This contingent debt is secured to the seller by a standard security, called in practice the discount standard security. The precise meaning of the provisions dealing with repayment of discount[24] has been the subject of some controversy and is by no means clear.[25]

It is quite common for an elderly tenant, who usually qualifies for maximum discount, to exercise the right to buy at the suggestion of, and with finance provided by, a grown-up child or other friend or relative. The arrangement is then commonly that when the tenant/purchaser dies, the property will pass to the relative or friend. This can be done simply by a will, but the obvious danger here is that a will is revocable. Sometimes some form of contract is entered into, or a trust created in favour of the relative or friend. The danger of such schemes is that they may well amount to a "disposal" thereby triggering liability to repay the discount. Moreover, if liability is triggered, the full 100 per cent. discount would be repayable because the "disposal" would be at the time of the purchase, and thus within the first 12 months after the exercise of the right to buy. It is difficult to be certain as to whether such schemes do trigger liability, because the legislation does not define "disposal." However, in practice repayment may not be demanded simply because the ex-landlord is unaware of the arrangement. It is difficult to give reliable advice as to how to arrange matters so as to avoid entirely the danger of triggering liability for discount. One safe method is simply to secure the finance by standard security, but that of itself does not achieve the object to ensuring that the property will pass on death. Moreover, if the value of the house rises, the amount secured will no longer reflect the value of the house. Another possibility is to confer on the relative an option to buy (on the death of the tenant/purchaser) at a fixed sum (representing the original finance), which option can then be secured by standard security. Such an option would probably not

[23] This period is calculated from the notice of acceptance: Housing (Scotland) Act 1987, s. 72.

[24] Housing (Scotland) Act 1987, ss. 72 and 73.

[25] See, *e.g.*, D.J. Cusine, "The Right to Buy Legislation: Sales by Executors," 1991 J.L.S. 292; letter by E. Paterson, 1992 J.L.S. 292; *Jack's Exrs.* v. *Falkirk District Council*, 1992 S.L.T. 5.

be a "disposal" in itself, though it would become one at the date of its exercise, which, however, with any luck would be outwith the three-year period.

We cannot here give detailed analysis of this complex subject, but will conclude with two words of warning. The first is that such arrangements can be complex to draft and set up, not only because of the need to steer round the "disposal" rules, but also because of the need to regulate matters properly between the parties, for instance in relation to insurance, upkeep, the possibility that the tenant/purchaser might wish to move house, and so on. The second warning is that in all such arrangements different solicitors must act for each party.

INDEX

a non domino conveyances, 376
disposition, 115, 273
registration of title, 362
acceptance, 29–31
qualified, 43
actio quanti minoris, incomplete performance of missives, 84
administrators, buying from, 435
advertising, sales by standard security holder, 272
affidavits
matrimonial homes, 152, 153
notarial execution, 306, 307
agency, 304, 305
solicitors, 6, 7
arrears, mortgage, 264–266
assignations, 289–296
implied, 185–188
in security, 291–296
enforcement clause, 294, 295
implications, 293, 294
life policies, 291, 292
mandates, 295, 296
personal bonds, 294
postponed securities, 293, 294
rents, 187, 188
writs, 185–187

bankruptcy, partnerships. *See* sequestration.
bargaining, 27
best advice, mortgage package, 220
bonds of corroboration and discharge, 252
Books of Council and Session, 329–331
boundaries
comparison, 6
dispositive clauses, 174–179
building consent, 19
building control, 62–68
minor works, 65–68
building societies, 222
building warrants, 63, 64
new houses, 442
buildings
dangerous, 60
disrepair, 61
tolerable standard, 60, 61
burdens. *See* real burdens.

claims. *See* post-settlement claims.
closing dates, 28
coal, 181
common ownership, matrimonial homes, 155–157
common property, dispositive clauses, 171
communications, solicitors with selling clients, 7–10
companies
dangers of purchase from, 428
directors
certificates of solvency, 429
powers, 426–427
execution of deeds, 427
foreign companies
execution of deeds, 309
searches, 143
good faith, 426
letters of obligation, 429
registration of charges, 427, 428
standard security loans, 429
ultra vires, 426
Companies Register, 331, 332
searches, 106
completion certificates, 64
new houses, 442
completion of title
destinations, 407, 408
executries, 388–392
computerisation, presentment book, 129, 130, 144
confirmation of executors, 386–388
consent, defects; missives, 34, 35
Consumer Credit Act, standard securities, 260
contaminated land, 333

conveyancers
  authorised, 1–2
  licensed, 1
conveyancing. *See a non domino* conveyances; feudal conveyancing.
council houses
  feu dispositions, 364
  right to buy, 442–445
Crown property, 181
curators, matrimonial homes, 158, 159

damages
  breach of missives, 79–82
  precontractual, 70–71
damp, 128
death
  partners, 422, 423
  standard securities, 259–260
deduction of title, 373–382
  dispositions, 375, 376
  errors, 377
  examples, 380–382
  land registration, 378, 379
  midcouples, 373–375
  requirement, 379, 380
  standard securities, 251
  types of deeds, 376, 377
  wills, 385, 386
deeds of conditions
  real burdens, 205–207
  tenement, 436, 437
delay
  settlement, 85–87
    interest, 86, 87
    mutality principle, 85, 86
deposits, 73
  settlement delay, 89, 90
descriptions
  dispositive clauses, 172–179
    description by reference, 179
    verbal descriptions, 175—179
designations
  dispositions, 168, 169
  witnesses; execution of deeds, 298
destinations, 393, 402–415
  completion of title, 407, 408
  conditional institutions, 401–404
  conveyance by survivor, 413
  evacuation
    death of substitute, 410
    inter vivos by conveyance, 411–413
destinations—*cont.*
  evacuation—*cont.*
    special destinations *mortis causa*, 408–410
    waiver, 410
  insolvency, 415
  leases, 414
  special survivorship destinations, 405
  substitutions, 403, 404
  terminology, 406, 407
  verifying non-evacuation, 413, 414
  voluntary discharge, 411
diligence, default of standard securities, 275, 276
directors
  certificates of solvency, 429
  powers, 426, 427
dispositions, 162–197
  a non domino, 115, 273
  alterations, 194
  contents, 73
  contractual obligations, 188–192
    entry, 188–190
    relief, 190–192
  deduction of title, 375, 376
  deeds of constitution, 162
  deeds of extinction, 162
  deeds of transfer, 162
  delivery, 196, 197
  dispositive clauses, 171–185
    boundaries, 174–179
    deeds of conditions, 183
    description, 172–179
    description by reference, 179
    discrepancies, 178
    measurements, 178
    part and portion clauses, 180, 181
    parts and pertinents, 181–184
    plans, 174, 175
    real burdens, 184, 185
    registration requirements, 179
    reservations, 185
    verbal descriptions, 175–179
  drafting, 193–195
  ex-facie absolute disposition, 246–248
  implied assignations, 185–188
  interpretation, 195, 196
  judicial rectification, 194, 195
  narrative clauses, 166–171
    cause of granting, 170
    consenters, 167, 168
    consideration, 170

dispositions—*cont.*
narrative clauses—*cont.*
designation, 168, 169
purchase from insolvent estate, 430
non-supersession clauses, 339
partnership, 419
pro forma; new houses, 442
structure, 163–166
superiority, 365–367
testing clauses, 192, 193
warrandice clause, 345
dispositive clauses, 171–185
drafting
dispositions, 193–195
missives, 39–44
postponed standard securities, 262
drains, 18

ECU mortgages, 237
electricity, 18, 58
endowment mortgages, 231–236
England
differences from Scotland
mortgage arrangements, 220
selling chain, 3
suspensive conditions, 37, 38
entry, 188–190
date, 29, 41, 42, 51, 52
environment law, 192
equity, negative equity, 266, 267
errors
deduction of title, 377
description of new property, 442
dispositions, 194, 195
missives, 34, 35, 42
title deeds, 116
excambions, 193
evacuation of destinations, 408–412
stamp duty, 316
execution of deeds, 297–310
affidavits, 306, 307
attestation, 297–299
by companies, 307–309, 427
by other juristic persons, 309
discharges, 309
holograph, 302, 303
law reform, 310
notarial execution, 305, 306
powers of attorney, 304, 305
probativity, 301, 302
s.39 deed, 303
signatures, 299, 300
standard securities, 280

execution of deeds—*cont.*
testing clauses, 300, 301
trustees, 396
vitiation, 303
executors
matrimonial homes, 159
searches, 137
executries, 383–401
assumption of new executors, 395
before 1964, 383–385
completion of title, 388–392
confirmation, 386–388
examples, 398–401
joint property, 395
purchase from beneficiary, 394
purchase from executors, 393, 394
since 1964, 385
expenses, 20
moving house, 282
sales, 8

fax, offer and acceptance, 33
feu dispositions, 363–365
council houses, 364
housing estates, 364
large rural estates, 364
feudal conveyancing, 363–370
charters of *novodamus*, 368
consolidation, 367
feu dispositions, 363–365
feuduty, 365, 369
instruments of sasine, 369, 370
minutes of waiver, 368, 369
superiority, 365–367
feuduty, 365, 369
redemption, 122–125
redemption receipt, 106
files, closing, 17
fixtures, 49, 50, 183
floating charges, 353
and standard security loans, 429
certificate of non-crystallization, 428
challenge, 434
company searches, 142
registration, 332
foreign companies
execution of deeds, 309
searches, 143
foreign currency mortgages, 237, 238
forgery, deed, 112
fraud, 23

gas, 18, 58
good faith
  companies, 426
  purchase from executors or trustees, 393
  voidable title deeds, 117
gratuitous alienations, 117, 118
guarantees. *See also* warrandice.
  mortgage indemnity guarantees, 244, 245

heritable securities, 92, 246–276. *See also* standard securities.
  discharge, 136, 137, 435
  ex facie absolute disposition, 246–248
  examination of deeds, 121, 122
  pre-1970, 246–248
holograph writing, 302, 303
homologation, contract, 33
houses
  dispositive clauses, 173
  new
    dispositions, 442
    missives, 441, 442
    public law consents, 442
housing estates
  dispositive clauses, 173
  feu dispositions, 364
  real burdens, 200

implied terms, reasonableness, 44
incapacity
  matrimonial homes, 158–160
  partners, 422, 423
indemnity
  mortgage indemnity guarantee, 244, 245
  registration of title, 354
  title indemnity policies, 100
infeftment, 371–383
  meaning, 378
inhibitions
  after conclusion of missives, 139
  discharge, 435
  searches, 132, 133
insolvency, 430–435
  destinations, 415
insurance, 70. *See also* life assurance.
  building, 12
  property, 262, 263
  sickness and unemployment, 263
  title indemnity policies, 100
interest
  delay in settlement, 86, 87
  mortgages, 223–226
  rate, 250
interim reports, 130
interpretation
  dispositions, 195, 196
  missives, 44, 45
  real burdens, 211–213
  servitudes, 213, 214
investment trusts, mortgages, 236
irritancy clauses, 365

joint property
  dispositive clauses, 171
  trustees and executors, 395

keys, 15

land certificates, 352, 358
land obligations. *See* real burdens; servitudes.
Land Register, 2
  certificates, 98
  occupancy rights, 160
  phasing in, 350, 351
  real burdens, 214, 215
  servitudes, 215
Lands Tribunal, land obligations, 216
law reform, execution of deeds, 310
Law Society, standard clauses, 31, 32
leaseholds, standard securities, 284, 285
leases
  destinations, 414
  short, 353
  stamp duty, 316, 317
  warrandice, 347
letters of obligation, 130, 131, 143–145
  companies, 429
  prescription, 145
LIBOR, 223
life assurance, 228–231
  policies; assignation, 291, 292
liferents, 397, 398
liquidation, buying from liquidators, 433

mandates, 295, 296
matrimonial homes, 72, 147–161
  common ownership, 155–157
  consent; dispensation, 158
  curators, 158, 159

matrimonial homes—*cont.*
- definition, 147, 148
- effect on conveyancing, 148–150
- executors, 159
- missives, 160, 161
- occupancy rights, 146, 147, 149–154
  - affidavits, 152, 153
  - consents, 152
  - meaning of "dealings", 153, 154
  - renunciation, 151, 152
- prescription, 157
- standard securities, 254
- trustees, 159

measurements, old Scots measures, 178
minerals, 50, 51, 181, 365
MIRAS, 240, 282–284
misrepresentation, 35
missives, 26–90. *See also* acceptance; offer.
- breach; prior to settlement, 74–90
- collateral exceptions, 341–343
- contents, 47–73
  - parts and pertinents, 49–51
  - subjects, 47–49
- defects of consent, 34–35
- drafting, 39–44
- errors, 34, 35, 42
- fax, 33
- formal writing, 27
- formation, 27
- interpretation, 44, 45
- Law Society standard clauses, 31, 32
- matrimonial homes, 160, 161
- new houses, 441, 442
- non-supersession clauses, 338–341
- *obligatio literis*, 2
- personal bar, 33
- prior communings, 334–343
  - *Winston* v. *Patrick*, 336–338, 341–343
- promises and options, 35, 36
- purchase from insolvent estate, 430
- registration of title
  - dealings, 359–362
  - first registration, 355, 356
- suspensive conditions, 36–39
- value of recent developments, 30
- variation and waiver, 45, 46
- warranties, 41
- work after conclusion, 8–10
  - missives to buy, 14–16

mortgages, 218–245. *See also* heritable securities; standard securities.

mortgages—*cont.*
- arranging, 277, 278
- arrears, 264–266
- capital repayment method, 227, 278
- choice of mortgage package, 220–222
- indemnity guarantee, 244, 245
- interest, 223–226
- life assurance, 228–231
- repayment; gross profile and constant-net, 284
- size of loan, 242, 244
- terms, 226, 227
- types, 222–242
  - builders' schemes, 238, 239
  - endowment mortgages, 231–236
  - equity release, 241, 242
  - equity share, 238
  - foreign currency mortgages, 237, 238
  - further advances, 240
  - indexed, 238
  - non-purchase, 239
  - pension mortgages, 236, 237
  - remortgages, 239, 240
  - second mortgages, 240
  - self-certified, 239
  - unit trust, investment trust, and PEP, 236
- types of lenders, 218–220

moveables, 70
moving, costs, 282

narrative clauses
- dispositions, 166–171
  - cause of granting, 170
  - consenters, 167, 168
  - consideration, 170

negligence, solicitors, 7, 17, 22, 23
NHBC, guarantees, 442
notarial execution, 305, 306
notes on title, 29, 108
- real burdens, 209

notices of title, 371–373
novodamus, 368
nuisances, 213

obligations
- collateral or personal, 339–340
- disposition
  - contractual, 188–192
  - relief, 186
  - warrandice, 186

occupancy rights, 96, 353, 359
  Land Register, 160
  matrimonial homes, 146–147, 149–154
    consent, 152
    renunciation, 151, 152
offers, 13, 14
  and acceptance, 32, 33
  closing dates, 28
  pro forma, 40
  successful, 8
  tactics, 27–31
options, sale of land, 35, 36
overriding interests, 353

partnerships, 416–425
  all partners party to deeds, 419
  bankruptcy, 424, 425
  deeds granted by the firm, 418
  dissolution, 421
  heritage brought in by one partner, 418
  incapacity, death, or sequestration of partners, 422, 423
  incoming partners, 422
  lapsed trusts, 423
  levels of right, 416–418
  no infeftment, 416
  outgoing partners, 419, 421, 422
  trustees
    assumption, 420
    contracting out, 424
    resignation, 420
parts and pertinents, 49–51, 181–184
PEPs, mortgages, 236
performance
  missives
    incomplete, 83–85
    late, 82, 83
personal bar, missives, 33
personal bonds, assignations, 294
planning
  and real burdens, 200, 201
  problems, 18
  registers, 333
planning permission, 61, 62
  new houses, 442
plans
  dispositive clauses, 174, 175
  registration of title, 356
plumbing, 18
possession, 98–99, 113, 114
  vacant
    meaning, 189–190

possession—*cont.*
  vacant—*cont.*
    right, 96
post-settlement claims, 334–348
  collateral exception, 341–343
  missives and prior communings, 334–343
  non-supersession clauses in missives, 338–341
  warrandice, 343–348
  Winston v. *Patrick*, 336–338, 341–343
powers of attorney
  execution of deeds, 304, 305
  execution of discharges, 309
prescription, 114, 115
  creation of servitudes, 208, 209
  letters of obligation, 145
  matrimonial homes, 157
  positive prescription, 110
  registration of title, 361
presentment book, computerisation, 129, 130, 144
prices, 51
  best price; sales in default of standard security, 272
  fixed, 4
  upset sales, 4
prior communings, 45, 334–343
  Winston v. *Patrick*, 336–338, 341–343
probative writing, 301, 302
  missives, 27
  promises of sale of land, 35
promises, sale of land, 35
property inquiry certificates, 5, 53, 54
property transfer orders, 72, 73
pulling out, 75, 77–79
purchases
  finance, 12
  instructions, 12

quick copies, 106
  Sasine registration, 327

ranking, standard securities, 260, 261
real burdens, 19, 43, 52, 53, 93, 94, 198–217
  and planning law, 200, 201
  creation, 204–207
    deeds of conditions, 205–207
  description in standard securities, 250, 251
  discharge, 215

real burdens—*cont.*
  dispositive clauses, 184, 185
  dominant and servient subjects, 202–204
  examination of deeds, 119–121
  feu dispositions, 364
  housing estates, 200
  interest to enforce, 214
  interpretation, 211–213
  Land Register, 214, 215
  new houses, 442
  pecuniary, 246
  reference, 209, 210
  registration of title, 359
  restrictions, 210
  tenement, 200
  transmission of liability, 217
  variation, 368
  waiver, 216, 365, 366
  writs, 105
receivers, buying from, 433–435
rectification, 98, 194–195, 354
redemption, standard securities, 274, 275
Register of Inhibitions and Adjudications, 332
Register of Insolvencies, 134
registration. *See also* Land Register; registration of title; Sasine registration.
  Books of Council and Session, 329–331
    extracts, 330
  charges; companies, 427, 428
  Companies Register, 331, 332
  contaminated land, 333
  planning, 333
  Register of Inhibitions and Adjudications, 332
  requirements; dispositive clauses, 180
  sheriff court books, 331
  standard securities, 280, 281
registration of title, 349–362. *See also* Land Register.
  a non domino conveyances, 362
  charge certificates, 353
  dealings
    form, 12, 358
    forms of deeds, 360
    missives, 359
    post-missives, 359
    split-offs, 360, 361
  first registration
registration of title—*cont.*
  first registration—*cont.*
    after-missives, 355, 356
    application, 357
    drafting deeds, 357
    examination of title, 356
    missives, 355, 356
    pre-missives, 355
  indemnity, 354
  land certificates, 352, 358
  overriding interests, 353
  plans, 356
  prescription, 361
  primary and secondary interests, 351, 352
  title sheets, 352
    rectification, 354
rei interventus, 33
relief, 186, 190–192
rents, assignation, 187, 188
repairs, tenement, 439
report on title, 279, 280
  pre-registration, 5
repudiation, missives, 76
rescission
  missives, 76
    warranties, 79
reservations, dispositive clauses, 185
right to buy, 442–445
rights of way, 55
risk, 68–71
roads, 54–56
roof, 18
  tenement, 437–439
    void, 438
rot, 72
roups, 8n
sales
  communications from solicitor to client, 7–10
  default by standard security holders, 268–275
    proceeds, 275
  first steps, 5
  parts and pertinents, 49–51
  subjects, 47–49
salmon fishings, 181, 183
Sasine registration, 2, 322–328
  extracts, 328
  fees, 332, 323
  indexes, 324
  instruments of sasine, 369, 370

Keeper's power to reject deeds, 326, 327
process, 326–328
quick copies, 327
Register of Sasines, 323, 324
search sheets, 324, 325
warrants, 325, 326
Scottish Record Office, 328
searches, 126–145
clear searches, 101–104
company searches, 98, 140–143
foreign companies, 143
length, 141, 142
nature, 142
interim reports, 130, 131
length, 128, 129
memorandum, 128
personal searches, 98, 106, 132–140
heritable creditors, 136, 137
identification, 135
instructions, 134
purchaser, 139
sales by special parties, 137–139
presentment book; computerisation, 129–130
professional firms, 127
sales by standard security holder, 273
Sasines, 97, 105–125, 127–131
nature of deeds, 105, 106
standard securities, 281, 282
start and closing dates, 131
timing, 129
section 19 agreements, 193
sequestration
buying from trustees in sequestration, 431, 432
partners, 422, 423
searches, 133, 134
trustees, 138
service of heir, 383, 384
servitudes, 198–217, 353
creation, 207–209
by implication and prescription, 208, 209
discharge, 215
dominant and servient subjects, 202–204
examination of deeds, 119–121
interest to enforce, 214
interpretation, 213, 214
Land Register, 215
reference, 209, 210
writs, 105
settlement, 10–11. *See also* post settlement claims.
dates, 42
delay, 85–87
special arrangements, 88–90
sewage, 57
signatures, execution of deeds, 299, 300
social security, mortgage payments, 265
solicitors
agency, 6, 7
clients' expectations, 17
negligence, 7, 17, 22, 23
role; preparation of standard security, 277
solum, 56, 439, 440
stamp duty, 311–321
adjudication stamp, 320
building plots, 315, 316
company exemptions, 316
conveyance, 311, 312
denoting stamp, 320
excambions, 316
fixed duties, 317, 318
impressed stamp, 320
leases, 316, 317
non-payment, 319
produced stamp, 321
rate of charge, 312, 313
sale of business, 314
sale of house with contents, 314
subsale, 315
time limits for payment, 319
VAT, 313, 314
standard securities, 4, 16, 248–276
acceleration, 263, 264
amount secured, 249, 250
and floating charges, 429
assignation, 255, 256
calling up, 268
Consumer Credit Act, 260
death, 259, 260
deduction of title, 251
default
diligence, 275, 276
disburdenment, 276
redemption, 274, 275
description and burdens, 250, 251
discharge, 11, 257–259
documentation, 277–288
checking, 279, 280
role of solicitor, 277
"double-glazing", 144

standard securities—*cont.*
- enforcement, 267–276
- execution, 280
- insurance
  - property, 262, 263
  - sickness and unemployment, 263
- interest rate, 250
- joint borrowers, 253, 254
- *jus in re aliena*, 274
- leaseholds, 284, 285
- matrimonial homes, 254
- notices of default, 269
- payment arrears, 264–266
- postponed securities, 262
  - assignation, 293, 294
- *pro forma*, 249
- ranking, 260, 261
- redemption, 285–288
- registration, 280, 281
  - by company, 332
- restrictions, 257
- s.24 applications, 269–271
- sales, 268–275
- searches, 281, 282
  - further advances, 281, 282
- security over, 256, 257
- standard conditions, 251, 252
- tenants, 285
- transfers subject to security, 252, 253
- variation, 254, 255

statutory notices, 58–60
- tenement, 440, 441

subjects
- dominant and servient, 202–204
- identification, 118, 119

subsidence, 18, 51

superiority, dispositions, 365–367

surveys
- building alterations, 19
- charges, 4

tax relief. *See* MIRAS.

teinds, 181

tenancies, and mortgage property, 285

tenement
- common parts, 439
- common passage and stair, 182
- deeds of conditions, 436, 437
- flats, 436, 437
  - dispositive clauses, 173
- real burdens, 200
- repairs, 439
- roof, 437–439

tenement—*cont.*
- *solum*, 439, 440
- statutory notices, 440, 441

testing clauses, 192, 193
- execution of deeds, 300, 301

timber, problems, 18

time limits
- payment of stamp duty, 319
- purification of suspensive conditions, 38
- real burdens, 212
- recording property transactions, 326
- registration of company charges, 332, 427, 428
- sending titles, 43

title. *See also* deduction of title.
- completion of title
  - destinations, 407, 408
  - executries, 388–396
- examination, 106–125, 356
- good and marketable, 91–104
  - implied conditions, 93, 94
  - obligation to demonstrate, 96–100
  - special express obligations, 95, 96
  - standard express obligations, 94, 95
- indemnity policies, 100
- notes on title, 29, 108
  - real burdens, 209
- notices of title, 371–373
- power to sell, 109, 110
- prior titles, 105
- report on title, 279, 280
  - pre-registration, 5
- sufficiency, 99, 100
- unusual conditions, 92

title deeds, 5, 281
- drafting; first registration of title, 357
- production, 98
- voidable, 117

transactions, non-standard, 21

trust deeds, searches, 133, 134

trusts, 383–401
- assumption of new trustees, 395
- charitable and religious trusts, 397
- examples, 398–401
- execution of deeds, 396
- joint property, 395
- lapsed trusts, 390–392
  - partnerships, 423
- liferents, 397, 398
- purchase from beneficiary, 394
- purchase from trustees, 393, 394

trusts—*cont.*
  trustees
    buying from trustees under trust deeds, 432
    matrimonial homes, 159
    resignation, 396
  trustees in sequestration
    buying from, 431, 432
    searches, 138
  warrandice, 396

ultra vires, companies, 426
unit trusts, mortgates, 236

VAT, stamp duty, 313, 314
vesting, 378

waiver
  minutes, 368, 369
  real burdens, 216, 365, 366
  suspensive conditions, 38
  terms of missives, 46
warrandice
  absolute, 344
  extent, 346
  fact and deed, 344
  leases, 347
warrandice—*cont.*
  obligations, 186
  post-settlement claims, 343–348
  remedies, 345, 346
  simple, 344
  transmission, 347, 348
  trustees, 396
  wording of clause, 345
warranties, 71
  missives, 41
  purchase from insolvent estate, 430
  rescission of missives, 79
warrants of registration, 325–326
water, 57
wills, deduction of title, 385, 386
witnesses
  execution of deeds, 297–299
    designation, 298
writs
  discharges of security, 105
  foundation, 97, 105, 110–112
  real burdens, 105
  schedules, 279
  security, 105
  subsequent to foundation writ, 115–117
  title; production, 97–100